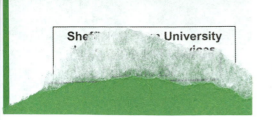

KESPEARE IN PRO1

ROMEO AND JULIET

Romeo and Juliet is not only one of the most popular of Shakespeare's plays, it is one of the most popular stories in the world. Yet while the play has rarely been off the stage, it has undergone radical transformations in performance. It has been abridged, rewritten, given a happy ending, reset in other times and places, and adapted into other media. While retaining its appeal as a definitive love story, *Romeo and Juliet* has been a dynamic and unstable performance text, endlessly reinvented to suit differing cultural needs.

This edition provides a detailed, thorough, and readable account of the play in production. The introduction examines shifts in interpretation, textual adaptations, and staging innovations over four centuries of perfor-mance. The commentary gives detailed examples of how different perform-ers, from Henry Irving and Ellen Terry to Leonardo DiCaprio and Claire Danes, have brought life and death to Shakespeare's star-crossed lovers.

SHAKESPEARE IN PRODUCTION

SERIES EDITORS: J. S. BRATTON AND JULIE HANKEY

This series offers students and researchers the fullest possible staging of individual Shakespearean texts. In each volume a substantial introduction presents a conceptual overview of the play, marking out the major stages of its representation and reception. The commentary, presented alongside the New Cambridge Shakespeare edition of the text itself, offers detailed, line-by-line evidence for the overview presented in the introduction, making the volume a flexible tool for further research. The editors have selected interesting and vivid evocations of settings, acting, and stage presentation, and range widely in time and space.

ALREADY PUBLISHED

A Midsummer Night's Dream, edited by Trevor R. Griffiths
Much Ado About Nothing, edited by John F. Cox
Antony and Cleopatra, edited by Richard Madelaine
Hamlet, edited by Robert Hapgood
The Tempest, edited by Christine Dymkowski

FORTHCOMING VOLUMES

Macbeth, edited by John Wilders
King Henry V, edited by Emma Smith
The Taming of the Shrew, edited by Elizabeth Schafer
The Merchant of Venice, edited by Charles Edelman
As You Like It, edited by Cynthia Marshall
Troilus and Cressida, edited by Frances Shirley

ROMEO AND JULIET

EDITED BY
JAMES N. LOEHLIN
Associate Professor of English,
University of Texas at Austin

CAMBRIDGE
UNIVERSITY PRESS

PUBLISHED BY THE PRESS SYNDICATE OF THE UNIVERSITY OF CAMBRIDGE
The Pitt Building, Trumpington Street, Cambridge, United Kingdom

CAMBRIDGE UNIVERSITY PRESS
The Edinburgh Building, Cambridge CB2 2RU, UK
40 West 20th Street, New York NY 10011-4211, USA
477 Williamstown Road, Port Melbourne, VIC 3207, Australia
Ruiz de Alarcón 13, 28014 Madrid, Spain
Dock House, The Waterfront, Cape Town 8001, South Africa

http://www.cambridge.org

First published 2002

Printed in the United Kingdom at the University Press, Cambridge

Typeface Ehrhardt 10/12½ pt.   *System* QuarkXPress [BTS]

A catalogue record for this book is available from the British Library

Library of Congress Cataloguing in Publication data

Romeo and Juliet / edited by James N. Loehlin.
p.   cm. – (Shakespeare in Production)
Includes bibliographical references (p.) and index.
ISBN 0 521 66115 3 – ISBN 0 521 66769 0 (pc.)
1. Shakespeare, William, 1564–1616. Romeo and Juliet.   2. Shakespeare, William,
1564–1616 – Dramatic production.   3. Shakespeare, William, 1564–1616 – Stage
history.   I. Loehlin, James N.   II. Series.
PR2831   .R63   2002
792.9'5 – dc21   2001037397

ISBN   0 521 66115 3   hardback
ISBN   0 521 66769 0   paperback

CONTENTS

ILLUSTRATIONS

SERIES EDITORS' PREFACE

It is no longer necessary to stress that the text of a play is only its starting-point, and that only in production is its potential realised and capable of being appreciated fully. Since the coming-of-age of Theatre Studies as an academic discipline, we now understand that even Shakespeare is only one collaborator in the creation and infinite recreation of his play upon the stage. And just as we now agree that no play is complete until it is produced, so we have become interested in the way in which plays often produced – and preeminently the plays of the national Bard, William Shakespeare – acquire a life history of their own, after they leave the hands of their first maker.

Since the eighteenth century Shakespeare has become a cultural construct: sometimes the guarantor of nationhood, heritage, and the status quo, sometimes seized and transformed to be its critic and antidote. This latter role has been particularly evident in countries where Shakespeare has to be translated. The irony is that while his status as national icon grows in the English-speaking world, his language is both lost and renewed, so that for good or ill, Shakespeare can be made to seem more urgently 'relevant' than in England or America, and may become the one dissenting voice that the censors mistake as harmless.

'Shakespeare in Production' gives the reader, the student, and the scholar a comprehensive dossier of materials – eye-witness accounts, contemporary criticism, promptbook marginalia, stage business, cuts, additions, and rewritings – from which to construct an understanding of the many meanings that the plays have carried down the ages and across the world. These materials are organised alongside the New Cambridge Shakespeare text of the play, line by line and scene by scene, while a substantial introduction in each volume offers a guide to their interpretation. One may trace an argument about, for example, the many ways of playing Queen Gertrude, or the political transmutations of the text of *Henry V*; or take a scene, an act, or a whole play, and work out how it has succeeded or failed in presentation over four hundred years.

For despite our insistence that the plays are endlessly made and remade by history, Shakespeare is not a blank, scribbled upon by the age. Theatre history charts changes, but also registers something in spite of those changes. Some productions work and others do not. Two interpretations may be entirely different, and yet both will bring the play to life. Why? Without setting out to give absolute answers, the history of a play in the theatre can often show where the energy and shape of it lie, what has made it tick, through many permutations. In this way theatre history can find common ground with literary criticism. Both will find suggestive directions in the introductions to these volumes, while the commentaries provide raw material for readers to recreate the living experience of theatre, and become their own eye-witnesses.

J. S. Bratton
Julie Hankey

This series was originated by Jeremy Treglown and published by Junction Books, and later by Bristol Classical Press, as 'Plays in Performance'. Four titles were published; all are now out of print.

EDITOR'S NOTE

Notes on cuts and textual alterations are based on the relevant promptbook or acting edition, and are not otherwise referenced. Unless otherwise specified, notes on productions since 1984 are based on my own observations of the production and/or an archival videotape; the same applies to all film versions. In the introduction, for reviews in modern newspapers and periodicals, I give the source information parenthetically. Promptbooks listed in Shattuck, *The Shakespeare Promptbooks*, are coded s, followed by Shattuck's catalogue number (see list in bibliography).

The text for this edition is that of the New Cambridge Shakespeare, edited by G. Blakemore Evans, to which I am heavily indebted. I have also made much use of Jill L. Levenson's excellent new edition for the Oxford Shakespeare. I have found several previous stage histories of *Romeo and Juliet* very valuable, especially those of Peter Holding, Jill L. Levenson, Felicia Harrison Londré, and Katherine Wright.

I am very grateful to the staffs of the Folger Shakespeare Library, the Shakespeare Centre Library in Stratford, the Theatre Museum, Covent Garden, the New York Public Library, and the Harry Ransom Humanities Research Center at the University of Texas at Austin.

I particularly wish to thank the series editors, Jacky Bratton and Julie Hankey, for their help and encouragement, and Sarah Stanton of Cambridge University Press for her diligence and patience.

I also wish to thank the students of the 2000 class of the University of Texas Shakespeare at Winedale programme, for exploring this play with me, and James B. Ayres, for leading the way.

My greatest debt is to my wife Laurel, whose bounty is as boundless as the sea.

ABBREVIATIONS

F	The First Folio, 1623
FSL	Folger Shakespeare Library
HTC	Harvard Theatre Collection
NY	New York
NYPL	New York Public Library
NYSF	New York Shakespeare Festival
Q1	*An Excellent Conceited Tragedy of Romeo and Juliet*, 1597 (the first quarto)
Q2	*The Most Excellent and Lamentable Tragedy of Romeo and Juliet*, 1599 (the second quarto)
RSC	Royal Shakespeare Company
RST	Royal Shakespeare Theatre
S	Shattuck, *The Shakespeare Promptbooks*, catalogue number
SCL	Shakespeare Centre Library
SD	stage direction
SMT	Shakespeare Memorial Theatre
SQ	*Shakespeare Quarterly*
SS	*Shakespeare Survey*
TM	Theatre Museum, Covent Garden

PRODUCTIONS

The following is a select chronology of English-language performances of *Romeo and Juliet*. The date is that of the first performance; 'Principal actors' are those who played the lovers. Under 'Venue', the city is London unless otherwise stated.

Date	Principal actors (Director)	Venue (Company)
1594–6?	Richard Burbage, Robert Goffe	The Theatre
1662	Henry Harris, Mary Saunderson	Lincoln's Inn Fields
1679 (Otway's *Caius Marius*)	William Smith, Elizabeth Barry	Dorset Garden
1730	Unknown (Joachimus Bertrand)	Revenge Meeting House, New York
1744 (Cibber version)	Theophilus Cibber, Jane Cibber	Haymarket
1746 (Sheridan version)	Thomas Sheridan, George Anne Bellamy	Smock Alley, Dublin
1748 (Garrick version, as in all subsequent productions to 1845)	Spranger Barry, Susanna Cibber (David Garrick)	Drury Lane
1750	David Garrick, George Anne Bellamy (David Garrick)	Drury Lane
1750	Spranger Barry, Susanna Cibber	Covent Garden
1752	William Rigby, Mrs Hallam	Williamsburg, Virginia
1753	Spranger Barry, Isabella Nossiter	Covent Garden
1789	John Philip Kemble, Sarah Siddons	Drury Lane
1814	Charles Kemble, Eliza O'Neill	Covent Garden
1815	Edmund Kean, Mrs Bartley	Drury Lane
1817	William Charles Macready, Eliza O'Neill	Covent Garden

Date	Principal actors (Director)	Venue (Company)
1829	William Abbott, Fanny Kemble	Covent Garden
1829	Ellen Tree, Fanny Kemble	Covent Garden
1832	Charles Kemble, Fanny Kemble	Park Theatre, NY
1836	George Bennett, Helena Faucit	Covent Garden
1837	James Anderson, Helena Faucit (William Charles Macready)	Covent Garden
1837	Charlotte Cushman as Romeo	Albany, NY
1841	Charles Kean, Ellen Tree	Haymarket
1845	Charlotte Cushman, Susan Cushman	Haymarket
1846	William Creswick, Laura Addison (Samuel Phelps)	Sadler's Wells
1851	J. William Wallack, Helena Faucit	Olympic
1855	Charlotte Cushman, Ada Swanborough	Haymarket
1863	Walter Montgomery, Stella Colas	Princess's Theatre
1864	John Nelson, Stella Colas	Stratford-upon-Avon
1866	John Nelson, Stella Colas	Princess's Theatre
1865	Adelaide Neilson	New Royalty Theatre
1869	Edwin Booth, Mary McVicker	Booth's Theatre, NY
1870	J. B. Howard, Adelaide Neilson	Drury Lane
1877	Joseph Haworth, Julia Marlowe	Star Theatre, NY
1881	Johnston Forbes-Robertson, Helena Modjeska	Court Theatre
1882	Henry Irving, Ellen Terry	Lyceum
1884	William Terriss, Mary Anderson (Mary Anderson)	Lyceum
1885	Frederick Paulding, Margaret Mather	Union Square Theatre, NY
1888	Kyrle Bellew, Cora Brown Potter	Grand Opera House, NY
1895	Johnston Forbes-Robertson, Mrs Patrick Campbell	Lyceum
1899	William Faversham, Maude Adams (Charles Frohman)	Empire Theatre, NY
1904	E. H. Sothern, Julia Marlowe	Illinois Theatre, Chicago
1905	Esmé Percy, Dorothy Minto (William Poel)	Royalty Theatre (Elizabethan Stage Society)

Date	Principal actors (Director)	Venue (Company)
1913	Phillip Merivale, Phyllis Neilson-Terry (Herbert Beerbohm Tree)	His Majesty's
1919	Basil Sydney, Doris Keane (Ellen Terry as Nurse)	Lyric, Shaftesbury Avenue
1923	Rollo Peters, Jane Cowl	Henry Miller, NY
1924	John Gielgud, Gwen Ffrangcon-Davies (Barry Jackson)	Regent Theatre
1930	Donald Cameron, Eva Le Gallienne (Eva Le Gallienne)	Civic Repertory Theatre, New York
1932	Christopher Hassall, Peggy Ashcroft (John Gielgud)	Oxford Playhouse (Oxford University Dramatic Society)
1934	Basil Rathbone, Katherine Cornell (Guthrie McClintic)	Martin Beck, NY
1935	Maurice Evans, Katherine Cornell (Guthrie McClintic)	Martin Beck, NY
1935	John Gielgud/Laurence Olivier, Peggy Ashcroft (John Gielgud)	New Theatre
1936	Leslie Howard, Norma Shearer (George Cukor)	Film
1940	Laurence Olivier, Vivien Leigh	51st St Theatre, NY
1947	Laurence Payne, Daphne Slater (Peter Brook)	SMT, Stratford
1951	Olivia de Havilland	Broadhurst, NY
1952	Alan Badel, Claire Bloom (Hugh Hunt)	Old Vic
1954	Laurence Harvey, Zena Walker (Glen Byam Shaw)	SMT, Stratford
1954	Laurence Harvey, Susan Shentall (Renato Castellani)	Film
1955	Tony Britton, Virginia McKenna	BBC-TV
1958	Richard Johnson, Dorothy Tutin (Glen Byam Shaw)	SMT, Stratford
1960	John Stride, Judi Dench (Franco Zeffirelli)	Old Vic
1960	Bruno Gerussi, Julie Harris (Michael Langham)	Stratford, Ontario

Date	Principal actors (Director)	Venue (Company)
1961	Brian Murray, Dorothy Tutin (Peter Hall)	RST, Stratford (RSC)
1968	Christopher Walken, Louise Marleau (Douglas Campbell)	Stratford, Ontario
1968	Leonard Whiting, Olivia Hussey (Franco Zeffirelli)	Film
1973	Timothy Dalton, Estelle Kohler (Terry Hands)	RST, Stratford (RSC)
1976	Ian McKellen, Francesca Annis (Trevor Nunn/Barry Kyle)	RST, Stratford (RSC)
1976	Peter McEnery, Sarah Badel (George Murcell)	St George's Elizabethan Theatre
1978	Patrick Ryecart, Rebecca Saire (Alvin Rakoff)	BBC-TV
1980	Anton Lesser, Judy Buxton (Ron Daniels)	RST, Stratford (RSC)
1986	Sean Bean, Niamh Cusack (Michael Bogdanov)	RST, Stratford (RSC)
1986	Kenneth Branagh, Samantha Bond (Kenneth Branagh)	Riverside Studios
1986	Ralph Fiennes, Sarah Woodward (Declan Donellan)	Regent's Park
1988	Carlton Chance, Janet Steel (Terry Keindl)	Albany Empire, London
1988	Peter MacNicol, Cynthia Nixon (Les Waters)	Public Theatre (New York Shakespeare Festival) NYSF
1988	David Harewood, Georgia Slowe (Alby James)	Contact, Manchester/ Young Vic (Temba Theatre Company)
1988	Edret Brinston, Amy Brenneman (Bill Rauch)	Cornerstone Theater Co., Port Gibson, Mississippi
1989	Mark Rylance, Georgia Slowe (Terry Hands)	Swan, Stratford (RSC)
1990	Roland Gift, Daphne Nayar (Bill Homewood)	Touring (Hull Truck)
1991	Michael Maloney, Clare Holman (David Leveaux)	RST, Stratford (RSC)
1992	Christopher Toba, Heather Imani (David Evans Rees)	Barons Court

Date	Principal actors (Director)	Venue (Company)
1993	Joe Dixon, Joanna Roth (Michael Bogdanov)	Touring (English Shakespeare Co.)
1993	Zubin Varla, Rebecca Callard (Judi Dench)	Regent's Park
1995	Zubin Varla, Lucy Whybrow (Adrian Noble)	RST, Stratford (RSC)
1996	Leonardo DiCaprio, Claire Danes (Baz Luhrmann)	Film
1997	Ray Fearon, Zoe Waites (Michael Attenborough)	Pit, London (RSC)
1997 (*Shakespeare's R&J*)	Greg Shamie, Daniel J. Shore (Joe Calarco)	John Houseman Studio Theatre, NY
1999	Ben Graetz, Bojana Novakovic (Wesley Enoch)	Bell Shakespeare Co., Sydney
1999	Christopher Morris, Maria Tusa (Sue Rider)	Kooemba Jdarra/La Boite, Brisbane
2000	David Tennant, Alexandra Gilbreath (Michael Boyd)	RST, Stratford (RSC)
2000	Chiwetel Ejiofor, Charlotte Randle (Tim Supple)	Olivier, Royal National Theatre

INTRODUCTION

Romeo and Juliet is not only one of the most popular of Shakespeare's plays, it is one of the most popular stories in the world. It is probably the most widely disseminated myth of romantic love; the very names of its heroes have become synonyms for young lovers. The image of a young woman on a balcony, conversing with her lover by moonlight, is a universally recognised icon. Romeo and Juliet are endlessly invoked in pop culture, in advertisements, TV shows, cartoons, and popular songs. The play has been filmed dozens of times and is probably second only to *Hamlet* as the most frequently performed of Shakespeare's works.

Yet while *Romeo and Juliet* has rarely been off the stage since Shakespeare's time, it has rarely – if ever – been there as Shakespeare wrote it. Wide discrepancies between the two quarto texts suggest a degree of instability in the play even in Shakespeare's day, and since the theatres reopened after the Restoration the play has undergone radical transformations. It has always been popular, but it has also always been edited, adapted, and rewritten. In spite, or perhaps because, of its enduring appeal as the definitive love story, *Romeo and Juliet* has been a dynamic and unstable performance text, endlessly reinvented to suit differing cultural needs.

Restoration adapters radically altered the text, adding a happy ending in James Howard's version, and a Roman political context in Thomas Otway's *Caius Marius*. A century later David Garrick, following Otway and others, added a passionate scene between Romeo and Juliet in the tomb. Garrick tailored the play to showcase his own histrionic powers, making it primarily a vehicle for Romeo: he and Spranger Barry had a celebrated rivalry in the role. By the nineteenth century, however, Romeo had become a role that actors avoided, and the play primarily a vehicle for actresses. Juliet became the signature part of Eliza O'Neill, Fanny Kemble, and Helena Faucit, and developed into an idealisation of Victorian womanhood. Even Romeo became a star part for actresses, especially Charlotte Cushman, who finally rejected the Garrick text in favour of Shakespeare's. This restoration coincided with the Victorian penchant for authenticity, which, together with technological and theatrical developments, shifted the play's focus from the lovers to their environment. Henry Irving's production used scrupulously detailed Veronese settings, expertly choreographed crowd scenes, and spectacular scenic effects to create an imaginative representation of Renaissance Italy in which he and Ellen Terry were awkwardly out of place.

The twentieth century has seen further shifts in the play's meaning. The influence of William Poel and Harley Granville-Barker led to fuller texts and leaner stagings, notably John Gielgud's celebrated production of 1935, in which he and Olivier alternated Romeo and Mercutio. The contrast between them marked a crucial change in modern acting styles, with Gielgud's poetic elegance giving way to Olivier's intense realism. This transition, continued by Peter Brook at Stratford, was fully realised with Zeffirelli's boisterous, earthily Italian production at the Old Vic in 1960, a seminal moment in the play's history. Zeffirelli made the play a celebration of youthful rebellion, in keeping with the cultural trends of the sixties and the rise of the teenager. The focus on recognisably modern youth in Zeffirelli's play and film, as well as in the stage and film versions of Leonard Bernstein's *West Side Story*, redefined *Romeo and Juliet* as a study of generational and cultural conflict. In the twentieth century *Romeo and Juliet* turned from a play about love into a play about hate. Modern-dress versions became increasingly common, as did settings in various contemporary blood-feuds such as Northern Ireland or Bosnia. Baz Luhrmann's 1996 film version sums up the contemporary approach with its urban nightmare world of gang violence, conspicuous consumption, and frenzied, lurid imagery.

While different aspects of *Romeo and Juliet* – its lyricism and bawdry, its comedy and tragedy, its politics and sentiment – have emerged at different times, it has remained a vivid index of cultural attitudes about romantic love and social crisis. This edition aims to trace the broad trends whereby performance has reinvented the play, as well as to detail the remarkable variety of individual choices actors and directors have made to bring life and death to Shakespeare's star-crossed lovers.

ROMEO AND JULIET ON SHAKESPEARE'S STAGE

About the first performances of *Romeo and Juliet* we know little that is concrete. We do not know when, where, or how often the play was performed, or who played the leading roles, although there has been much speculation on these subjects. The title page of the 1597 first quarto (Q1) records that 'it hath been often (with great applause) played publicly, by the right honorable the Lord of Hunsdon his servants'. This company was Shakespeare's, better known as the Lord Chamberlain's Men. The play must have been performed before 1597, but there is no conclusive evidence that it was written later than 1592; probably it dates from between 1594 and

1596.[1] At any rate, the Q1 title page suggests that it was a success, and it is among the plays Francis Meres cited in 1598 as examples of Shakespeare's mastery of tragedy.

Shakespeare almost certainly wrote *Romeo and Juliet* for the Theatre, the first home of the Chamberlain's Men and the first purpose-built theatre in London since Roman times. The Chamberlain's Men probably performed the play at the Curtain, their temporary home during the closure of the Theatre, in 1598, and at the Globe after their move there in 1599.[2] It is also likely that *Romeo and Juliet* was performed on tour; the company performed in Ipswich, Cambridge, Dover, Rye, Bath, and Bristol, among other towns, between 1594 and 1597.[3] The first quarto version of the play can be performed with doubling by a company of twelve, plus supers, such as might have been available for a provincial tour.[4]

The two quarto texts of *Romeo and Juliet* have occasioned much discussion as to their relation and provenance. The second quarto (Q2), published in 1599 and long regarded as the superior version, is the basis for all standard texts of the play. However, Q1, once dismissed as a 'bad quarto', has gained much esteem in recent years. Scholars have moved away from the idea of an authorially sanctioned 'authentic' Shakespearean text toward a notion of the text as merely one unstable element in the complex creation of Elizabethan theatre. Even if Q1 is a pirated version, reconstructed from memory (the traditional interpretation), it reflects something of Elizabethan playhouse practice. David Farley-Hills has argued that it is a shortened version adapted for provincial performance; Jay Halio concurs, and suggests the adapter was Shakespeare himself. Donald Foster has also argued, using a computer analysis of the text, that Q1 is Shakespeare's work, though Foster asserts that it precedes Q2.[5] Whatever its history, Q1 provides suggestive material for performance historians, including unusually precise stage directions. Before their wedding at the Friar's cell, 'Enter Juliet, somewhat fast, and she embraces Romeo' (Q1, 2.5.8 SD).[6] While Romeo is lamenting his banishment,

---

1 See Gurr, 'Date', p. 19.
2 Evans, Introduction, New Cambridge Shakespeare edition, p. 28.
3 Gurr, 'Date', p. 20, n. 14.   4 King, *Casting*, p. 82.
5 Farley-Hills, '"Bad" Quarto', p. 27; Halio, 'Handy-Dandy', p. 137; Foster, 'Webbing', p. 134. Critics supporting the memorial reconstruction theory include Hoppe, *The Bad Quarto*, and Irace, *Reforming the 'Bad' Quartos*. Jill Levenson, who includes both Q1 and Q2 in her 2000 Oxford edition, concludes her comprehensive discussion of the issue by saying that 'both early quartos of *Romeo and Juliet* can be viewed as important records of a tragedy that underwent many changes when first written and performed, beginning a process still vital after four centuries' (p. 125).
6 All citations of Q1 are from Jill Levenson's Oxford edition.

'Romeo offers to stab himself, and the Nurse snatches the dagger away' (3.3.98 SD). After Juliet drinks the potion, 'She falls upon her bed within the curtains' (4.5.98 SD). When Juliet is discovered, apparently dead, 'They all but the Nurse go forth, casting rosemary on Juliet and shutting the curtains' (4.5.80 SD).

As Andrew Gurr has pointed out, *Romeo and Juliet* makes considerable demands on the resources of the Elizabethan theatre.[7] It has a very large cast (especially in Q2), numerous properties, and very specific scenic requirements, notably an upper playing area, a curtained bed, and some representation of a tomb. A performance at the Theatre or Curtain would have made full use of Elizabethan staging conventions. Played in broad daylight, night scenes would have been identified by the torches carried by the actors, as before the Capulet ball (1.4). The unlocalised stage, a bare platform in front of the tiring-house façade, would have allowed fluid changes of scene, as when Romeo and his friends move from the street to the party without leaving the stage: 'they march about the stage, and servingmen come forth with napkins' (Q2, 1.4.114 SD). Sometimes the location could change even within a scene. In 3.5 Romeo and Juliet enter 'aloft' (Q2) or 'at the window'(Q1) of Juliet's bedroom, clearly at an upper level above the stage; then 'he goes down' to the main-stage platform (presumably using the rope ladder), where he converses with Juliet as from the Capulet orchard. After his exit Lady Capulet enters the platform, and Juliet 'goes down from the window' (Q1); when she reenters the platform, it is now presumed to be her bedroom. Such free changes of scene have frustrated many modern directors, but were easily managed on the Elizabethan stage.

The complex demands of the last few scenes must have required similar staging. Juliet's bed, which appears in 4.3 and 4.5, was either brought out from the tiring house, in which case it must have had its own curtains, or it was located in the discovery space in the tiring-house façade, and so curtained off; the former seems more likely, given sight-line constraints. If the bed was brought onto the stage, it clearly remained during the intervening scene in the Capulet household (4.4), and it may well have become the bier for 5.3.[8] The staging of the tomb scene raises multiple possibilities. Either the tomb was the discovery space; or the body of Juliet was brought up out of the trap; or she had remained onstage in her bed, which became a bier; or some form of tomb-structure was brought on.[9] Each of these solutions has its

7 Gurr, 'Date', p. 15.
8 Graham Holderness argues that the bed remained and became the bier, given the non–illusionistic nature of the Elizabethan stage, and the many metaphoric connections between Juliet's bed, the marriage bed, and the tomb. Holderness, *Romeo*, pp. 64–5.
9 Dessen, *Recovering*, p. 193.

adherents, and indeed each has been made to work, one way or another, in subsequent performances.

About the casting we know almost nothing. A bit of an elegy associating Richard Burbage with the role of Romeo is now generally discounted as inauthentic, though as the leading actor of Shakespeare's company he is the likeliest candidate.[10] In *The Organization and Personnel of the Shakespearean Company*, T. W. Baldwin argued that Richard Burbage played Romeo, Thomas Pope Mercutio, Robert Goffe Juliet, George Bryane Friar Lawrence, John Heminges Capulet, Augustine Phillips Benvolio, William Sly Tybalt, Will Kemp Peter, and Shakespeare the Prince.[11] Donald Foster, using computer analysis, has argued that Shakespeare played Friar Lawrence.[12] Only the assignment of Peter to Kemp has any direct evidence to support it. The Q2 text has the stage direction 'Enter Will Kemp' for Peter's scene with the musicians at 4.5.99. Beyond that, all we really know is that *Romeo and Juliet* was performed by a professional theatre company, of which Shakespeare was a member; that the women's roles were played by male actors; and that the play availed itself of such scenic resources as the Elizabethan playhouse afforded.

As to what Elizabethan audiences made of the play, there again we can only speculate. Stories of young lovers confronting parental opposition were familiar enough, though mainly limited to comedy; Shakespeare had used similar situations, and the same setting, for *The Two Gentlemen of Verona*. In *A Midsummer Night's Dream*, written either just before or just after *Romeo and Juliet*, he burlesqued the star-crossed lovers' story, both through the adventures of Lysander and Hermia and with the Mechanicals' version of *Pyramus and Thisbe*. In any event, *Romeo and Juliet* used a familiar narrative and dealt with issues of interest to the Elizabethans, notably marriage, family conflict, and civil disturbance. It did not, however, present a strict mirror of Elizabethan family life. Juliet's marriage at age thirteen, for instance, was not at all typical. Elizabethan women of the propertied classes usually married at twenty, the middle and lower classes even later.[13] Upper-class families certainly made arranged marriages, though the children's wishes were usually consulted. The notion of a love-match based purely on personal affection was something of a novel one, and Shakespeare's play may well have encouraged it. As Lawrence Stone observes, there was 'a clear conflict of values between the idealisation of love by some poets, playwrights and the authors of romances on the one hand, and its rejection as a form of imprudent folly

---

10 Evans, Introduction, New Cambridge Shakespeare edition, p. 28, n. 3.
11 Baldwin, *Organization*, pp. 268–9.   12 Foster, 'Webbing', p. 134.
13 L. Stone, *Family*, p. 46.

and even madness by all theologians, moralists, authors of manuals of conduct, and parents and adults in general'.[14] Shakespeare's sympathy for the lovers was not the only possible response; the preface to his source, Arthur Brooke's *Romeus and Juliet*, describes 'a couple of unfortunate lovers, thralling themselves to unhonest desire, neglecting the authority and advice of parents and friends . . . abusing the honorable name of lawful marriage to cloak the shame of stolen contracts, finally, by all means of unhonest life, hasting to most unhappy death'.[15] While Brooke's narrative itself isn't so harsh, such antipathy toward the lovers' 'unhonest' behaviour was certainly an available attitude.

At any rate, the conflict between love-matches and marriages arranged for family interest would have been a recognisable one to Elizabethans, particularly as many of the audience were likely to have been in their late teens and early twenties.[16] Another highly topical issue was duelling. Despite Tudor edicts against them, street fighting and violent feuds were a constant danger, and duelling was on the rise in the 1590s.[17] The late sixteenth century saw an invasion of Italian and Spanish fencing masters, with their stylish terminology and elaborate rules of etiquette.[18] Shakespeare's Mercutio, though ostensibly Italian himself, repeatedly mocks 'such antic, lisping, affecting phantasimes' (2.4.25) in his characterisation of Tybalt as 'the courageous captain of compliments . . . the very butcher of a silk button, a duellist, a duellist' (18–19, 21–2). Indeed, the play's presentation of duelling is a part of its curious admixture of things English and things Italian. Elizabethans certainly associated the Italians with violence and passion: Roger Ascham wrote in 1570 of 'private contention in many families, [and] open factions in every city'.[19] Yet English playwrights regularly used Italy as a mirror, and audiences would not have needed to look too hard to see themselves in Shakespeare's play. The domestic details of the Capulet household, with its servants Potpan, Sue Grindstone, and Nell, and its joint-stools, trenchers, log fires, and baked meats, suggest middle-class Elizabethan life rather than the aristocracy of the Italian Renaissance.

Elizabethan audiences certainly seem to have liked and remembered the play. It was reprinted three times before the 1623 Folio, and *The Shakspere Allusion-Book* cites thirty-six references to it before 1649, more than to any play except *Hamlet*. Several plays of the period echo or parody elements of *Romeo and Juliet*. Porter's *The Two Angry Women of Abingdon* and Dekker's

14 Ibid., p. 181.
15 In Evans's New Cambridge Shakespeare edition, pp. 215–16.
16 Novy, 'Violence', p. 368.   17 Levenson, '*Alla stoccado*', pp. 85–6.
18 Martinez, *Swords*, p. 109.   19 Quoted in Levith, *Italian Settings*, p. 55.

Blurt, Master Constable both include burlesqued balcony scenes, as well as deliberate verbal echoes.[20] John Ford's *'Tis Pity She's a Whore* (1631) invokes Shakespeare's tragedy in depicting a star-crossed love affair between a brother and sister, admonished by a Friar and aided by a Nurse. Robert Burton, discussing the dangerous effects of love in *The Anatomy of Melancholy*, cites Shakespeare's lovers, as though they had already, in 1624, become universally recognised emblems of tragic passion:

> Who ever heard a story of more woe,
> Than that of Juliet and her Romeo?[21]

ROMEO AND JULIET IN THE RESTORATION THEATRE

Romeo and Juliet returned to the stage, in some form, soon after the Restoration. Samuel Pepys records in his diary that he saw the premiere on 1 March 1662, given by William Davenant's company, the Duke's Men. Pepys was not impressed: 'It is the play of itself the worst that ever I heard in my life, and the worst acted that ever I saw these people do', largely because the actors didn't know their lines.[22] Mary Saunderson played Juliet, probably the first woman to take the role. Her future husband Thomas Betterton, the leading actor of the period, did not partner her, but played Mercutio, while Henry Harris was Romeo, according to the prompter John Downes.[23] Downes relates that the play was next revived in altered form: 'This tragedy of *Romeo and Juliet*, was made sometime thereafter into a tragicomedy by Mr James Howard, he preserving Romeo and Juliet alive; so that when the tragedy was revived again, 'twas played alternately, tragical one day, and tragicomical another, for several days together.'[24] No other account of this version exists, but the story isn't

---

20 Bly, 'Bawdy Puns', p. 97.
21 Burton, *The Anatomy of Melancholy*, 2nd edition, 1624, cited in Munro, *Shakspere Allusion-Book*, I, p. 324.
22 Pepys, *Diary*, 1 March 1662 (III, p. 39).
23 Downes, *Roscius Anglicanus*, p. 22. Downes goes on to relate the following anecdote: 'There being a fight and scuffle in this play, between the House of Capulet, and the House of Paris; Mrs Holden acting his wife, entered in a hurry, crying, "O my dear Count!" She inadvertently left out, "O," in the pronunciation of the word "Count!", giving it a vehement accent, put the house into such a laughter, that London Bridge at low-water was silence to it.' This story led Christopher Spencer to devise an elaborate theory about the lost play, related in ' "Count Paris's Wife": *Romeo and Juliet* on the Early Restoration Stage', *Texas Studies in Language and Literature* 7, 1966, 309–16.
24 Downes, *Roscius Anglicanus*, p. 22.

implausible: Howard was a writer of comedies, and Nahum Tate was soon to add a happy ending to *King Lear*. While *Romeo and Juliet* has seldom been played with the lovers surviving, several adaptations and non-English versions have had happy endings. In David Edgar's stage version of Dickens's *Nicholas Nickleby*, Vincent Crummles's troupe perform a hilarious *Romeo and Juliet* wherein the lovers come back to life singing a patriotic British anthem.[25] Sadly, I can find no evidence that any Victorian companies actually ended the play this way, though something similar does happen in Andrew Halliday's popular 1859 burlesque, *Romeo and Juliet Travestie: or, The Cup of Cold Poison*, wherein Queen Mab appears to reanimate the corpses.[26]

After Howard's version, the next important incarnation of *Romeo and Juliet* was in Thomas Otway's *Caius Marius*, 1679. Otway grafted much of Shakespeare's language and characterisation onto a story from Plutarch's Rome, renaming Romeo Young Marius, and turning Juliet into Lavinia, the daughter of a rival senator. Otway acknowledges, in a disarming prologue, that he has stolen from Shakespeare out of his own necessity, rather than trying to improve the material as other Restoration adapters had done:

> Like greedy beggars that steal sheaves away,
> You'll find h'has rifled him of half a play.
> Amidst this baser dross you'll see it shine
> Most beautiful, amazing and divine.[27]

In Otway's play the elder Marius is a demagogue who falls foul of the ruling party in Rome. Though he has himself proposed that his son marry Lavinia, daughter of his rival Metellus, he forbids the match when he learns that Young Marius loves her. Metellus meanwhile wishes Lavinia to marry Sylla, Marius' chief opponent. Otway gives Young Marius and Lavinia a fairly full version of Shakespeare's balcony scene – 'O Marius, Marius, wherefore art thou Marius?' – as well as much of the dawn parting. As in the French and Italian versions of the story, the lovers share a brief scene in the tomb, when Lavinia awakes from her trance before Young Marius dies:

> LAVINIA . . . Hadst thou not come, sure I had slept forever.
>   But there's a sovereign charm in thy embraces,
>   That might do wonders, and revive the dead.
> MARIUS Ill fate no more, Lavinia, now shall part us,
>   Nor cruel parents, nor oppressing laws.
>
> (5.5.379–83)

---

25 Edgar, *Nicholas Nickleby*, pp. 131–6.   26 Wells, *Shakespeare Burlesques*, III.
27 Otway, Prologue, 30–3. All references are to *Works*, ed. J. C. Ghosh.

After Young Marius dies, Lavinia has to watch Old Marius kill her own father before she stabs herself. Her suicide is an act of fury rather than pathos, as she rages at her former father-in-law:

> . . . You have my father butchered,
> The only comfort I had left on earth.
> The gods have taken too my husband from me.
> See where he lies, your and my only joy.
> This sword yet reeking with my father's gore,
> Plunge in my breast: plunge, plunge it thus.
> And now let rage, distraction and despair
> Seize all mankind, till they grow mad as I am.
>
> (450–7)

The political conflict remains unresolved; civil war once again threatens to engulf Rome. The play ends with the death of Sulpitius, Old Marius' henchman, who is based loosely on Mercutio but turned into a character of almost unmitigated brutality and cynicism:

> SULPITIUS A curse on all repentance! How I hate it!
>   I'd rather hear a dog howl than a man whine.
> GRANIUS You're wounded, sir: I hope it is not much.
> SULPITIUS No, 'tis not so deep as a well, nor so wide as a church-door.
>   But 'tis enough; 'twill serve; I am peppered I warrant, I warrant for
>   this world. A pox on all madmen hereafter, if I get a monument, let
>   this be my epitaph:
>   Sulpitius lies here, that troublesome slave,
>   That sent many honester men to the grave,
>   And died like a fool when he'd lived like a knave.
>
> (484–93)

Later critics have been very hard on Otway's adaptation, with some justification. Frederick Kilbourne, in 1906, refused 'to waste any time or words upon such a contemptible piece of thieving', while in 1927 Hazelton Spencer found it an 'abominable mixture of Roman and Renaissance', of which 'the execution . . . is as grotesque as its conception'.[28] Yet Otway's work deserves reappraisal, especially in the light of twentieth-century attempts to reinterpret *Romeo and Juliet*. For while Otway's setting the play in Rome may seem incongruous, he is in fact doing what many modern productions have done, in trying to give the play a contemporary political relevance. As Kerstin P. Warner has pointed out, Otway's play is not really concerned with ancient

28 Kilbourne, *Alterations*, p. 131; Spencer, *Shakespeare Improved*, p. 296.

Rome but with the politics of Restoration England.[29] Old Marius is a version of Lord Shaftesbury, a powerful Whig politician Otway saw as a dangerous demagogue. The scenes of civil conflict throughout are directly related to the Exclusion crisis; Otway feared that Whig attempts to keep the Catholic Duke of York from succession would lead to civil war. By using the story of Romeo and Juliet to protest, not the feuding of rival families, but a contemporary political crisis, Otway was anticipating many directors and adapters of much more recent times.

Two other features of Otway's version are notable, from the point of view of staging. Otway acknowledged in the Epilogue that some of his audience came 'Only for love of Underhill and Nurse Nokes' (18). These were two of the star performances, in the roles of Sulpitius (Mercutio) and the Nurse – then as now characters in danger of stealing the play from the leads. The Nurse was played by a man, James Nokes, in the Elizabethan tradition. This practice continued until at least 1727. Mrs Talbot was apparently the first female Nurse, at Lincoln's Inn Fields in 1735.[30] Otway and the actor Cave Underhill made Sulpitius a caustic and brutal swordsman. In the 1774 Bell edition, Francis Gentleman, comparing Otway's 'snarling cynic' with the 'vacant, swaggering blade' typical of eighteenth-century Mercutios, declared that 'Otway's conception of him is more consistent with nature and with Shakespeare.'[31] Otway's cynical Sulpitius was perhaps not so far from the violent gang-leader Mercutio often became in the twentieth century. Betterton played Old Marius; the lovers were William Smith and Elizabeth Barry, the leading tragic actress of the Restoration.

The play fared well with Restoration audiences, and proved Otway's third most popular: it was performed most seasons for the next fifty years.[32] Its success presumably inspired the staging of more Shakespearean versions in the 1740s, by Theophilus Cibber at the Haymarket, Thomas Sheridan in Smock Alley, Dublin, and finally David Garrick. Perhaps Otway's most important influence was the inclusion of a scene between the lovers in the tomb, which became standard practice for nearly 165 years.[33]

Theophilus Cibber's version, performed in 1744, restores a good deal of Shakespeare's text, though it also incorporates large sections of Otway and bits of *The Two Gentlemen of Verona*. There is no ball scene, as Romeo is in

29 Warner, *Thomas Otway*, p. 33.   30 *The London Stage*, III, I, p. 504.
31 Gentleman, *Bell's Edition*, p. 89.   32 Warner, *Thomas Otway*, p. 8.
33 A handwritten acting version prepared for a performance at the English College in Douai in 1694 includes Shakespeare's original ending (see G. Blakemore Evans, *Philological Quarterly* (41), pp. 158–72).

love with Juliet from the beginning. As in Otway, Romeo's father has previously considered a match between the two,

> Which so increas'd the anger of our wives
> (Whose quarrels we are ever apt to join in)
> That rage of civil war, broke out more fiercely.[34]

Almost all of Shakespeare's scenes appear in some form, generally abbreviated; the Mantua scene, 5.1, is reset 'near the walls of Verona' in accordance with the neoclassical unity of place. The tomb scene between the lovers is taken from Otway almost without alteration, though Juliet is given a more pathetic death speech:

> Come well-secreted dagger.
> This is thy sheath, there rust and let me die.
> 'Tis o'er; – my eyes grow dim. Where is my love?
> Have I caught you! now, now, we'll part no more.
>
> (p. 64)

Cibber, the dissolute and much-hated son of Colley Cibber, played Romeo himself, opposite his daughter Jane (Jenny), who was Juliet's age of fourteen at the time. Much of the Prologue to the play is devoted to begging indulgence for young Jenny, 'Who, full of modest terror, dreads t'appear, / But, trembling, begs a father's fate to share' (p. 74). By Cibber's own account, the play ran successfully for twelve nights at the Haymarket: 'Jenny nightly improved in the part of Juliet. Our audiences were frequently numerous, and of the politest sort' (p. 74). Other contemporary accounts are harsher. John Hill pitied Jenny Cibber for having to play opposite 'a person whom we could not but remember, at every sentence she delivered concerning him, to be too old for her choice, too little handsome to be in love with, and, into the bargain, her father'.[35] Such quasi-incestuous pairings were not uncommon among the theatrical dynasties of the eighteenth and nineteenth centuries, but the Cibbers came under particular attack. David Garrick was revolted: 'I never heard so vile and scandalous a performance in my life . . . the girl, I believe, may have genius; but unless she changes her preceptor, she must be entirely ruined.'[36] *Romeo and Juliet* did seem to catch the public's fancy, and would have played

---

34 Cibber, *Romeo*, p. 2. In Shakespeare, the wives specifically oppose their husbands' entry into the quarrel.

35 Hill, *The Actor* (1750), pp. 134–5.

36 Garrick, letter to Somerset Draper, 16 September 1744, quoted in Pedicord and Bergmann, *Garrick's Adaptations*, p. 407.

longer had not the owners of the two patent theatres invoked the Licensing Act to shut down the Haymarket performances.

The next revival of the play was by Garrick's sometime associate Thomas Sheridan in Dublin, opening 15 December 1746. Sheridan's performances, at the Smock Alley Theatre, were notable for their reattribution of the Queen Mab speech. According to Gentleman, Sheridan, who played Romeo, 'by an amazing stroke of injudicious monopoly annexed this whimsical picture to his own sighing, lovesick part'.[37] Sheridan gave the speech 'with all the melancholy solemnity of a sermon', according to Thomas Wilkes.[38] Juliet was George Anne Bellamy, a young Irish actress who would later partner Garrick. The play, 'written by Shakespeare with alterations', was grandly mounted; Sheridan added an elaborate funeral scene and raised his prices to cover 'a great deal of expense in decorations'.[39] The production managed a successful run of nine nights.

DAVID GARRICK AND THE 'BATTLE OF THE ROMEOS'

The most significant of the eighteenth-century adaptations was certainly that of David Garrick. First published and performed in 1748, Garrick's version was close to Shakespeare by eighteenth-century standards. As he explained in his preface, 'the alterations to the following play are few and trifling, except in the last act; the design was to clear the original, as much as possible, from the jingle and quibble which were always thought the great objections to reviving it'.[40] By jingle, Garrick meant rhymed verse, which he avoided by judicious substitutions. Speaking of Juliet's eyes, Garrick's Romeo observes, 'They'd through the airy region stream so bright / That birds would sing and think it were the morn' (rather than 'not night', as in 2.2.21–2). The sonnet shared by the lovers at the Capulet ball (1.5.92–105) is reduced to a seven-line exchange containing only one rhyme. By quibble, Garrick meant the punning and bawdry that offended eighteenth-century sensibilities. Garrick's Mercutio loses the quip about dying 'a grave man', for instance, and the sexual innuendo is increasingly curtailed in successive editions of the play. Garrick makes other concessions to decorum: Juliet's age is increased to eighteen, and in the 'Gallop apace' speech she loses her most explicit reflections on 'amorous rites' and 'stainless maidenhoods' (3.2.8–16). Nevertheless, in his first version of the play in 1748, Garrick

---

37 Gentleman, *Dramatic Censor*, p. 175.   38 Sheldon, *Thomas Sheridan*, p. 79.
39 Highfill, *Biographical Dictionary*, XIII, p. 341.
40 'To the Reader', 1748 edition, in Pedicord and Bergmann, *Garrick's Adaptations*, p. 77.

1 George Anne Bellamy and David Garrick in Garrick's added tomb scene, wherein
Juliet wakes after Romeo has taken the poison but before he dies, c. 1750.

included Romeo's love for Rosaline, in the face of public opinion: 'Many
people have imagined that the sudden change of Romeo's love from
Rosaline to Juliet was a blemish in his character, but an alteration of that
kind was thought too bold to be attempted; Shakespeare has dwelt
particularly upon it, and so great a judge of human nature knew that to be
young and inconstant was extremely natural.'[41] By 1750, however, Garrick
accepted his friend Dr Johnson's dictum that 'the drama's laws the drama's
patrons give', and wrote Rosaline out of the play, protesting only that he did
so 'with as little injury to the original as possible'.[42] Gentleman approved,
commenting: 'Making no mention of Rosaline, but rendering Romeo's love
more uniform, is certainly improving on the original, notwithstanding the
caprices of love.'[43]

In the last act, Garrick added a new scene between the lovers in the tomb,
even longer and more complex than the Otway–Cibber version (see Appendix, pp. 252–4). In a preface to his published text, Garrick cited literary
precedent to justify his alteration: 'Bandello, the Italian novelist, from whom

41 Ibid.
42 'Advertisement', 1750, in Pedicord and Bergmann, *Garrick's Adaptations*, p. 78.
43 Gentleman, *Bell's Edition*, p. 93.

Shakespeare has borrow'd the subject of this play, has made Juliet to wake in the tomb before Romeo dies: this circumstance Shakespeare has omitted not perhaps from judgement, but from reading the story in the French or English translation, both which have injudiciously left out this addition to the catastrophe.'[44] While it is unlikely that Shakespeare couldn't have thought of a tomb duet by himself, Garrick is perfectly correct in his account of the various versions. Garrick's own judicious 'addition to the catastrophe' afforded scope for the virtuoso display of alternating passions that was the hallmark of eighteenth-century acting. In 1746 Aaron Hill had codified the ten dramatic passions in an actor's arsenal as 'joy, grief, fear, anger, pity, scorn, hatred, jealousy, wonder, and love'.[45] Garrick's tomb scene allows for all of these, most in the seventy-line exchange with Juliet, as his happiness at her awakening gives way to the poison's effect, and he dies cursing his fate:

> 'Twixt death and love I'm torn, I am distracted!
> But death's strongest – and must I leave thee, Juliet?
> O, cruel, cursed fate! in sight of heaven –
>
> (5.4.125–7)

Garrick's ending, however, adds another dimension to the scene beyond the actor's self-display. Garrick's text brings the social causes of the tragedy into the tomb. 'Fathers have flinty hearts, no tears can melt 'em', Romeo cries. 'Nature pleads in vain – children must be wretched.' Shakespeare's lovers give little thought to the feud in their final moments, whereas Garrick's are bitterly aware of the reason for their fate, and die exclaiming against it. Accordingly, when the families enter the tomb at the end, the Prince's condemnation of them is even harsher and more explicit than in Shakespeare:

> Well may you mourn, my lords (now wise too late)
> These tragic issues of your mortal hate:
> From private feuds, what dire misfortunes flow,
> Whate'er the cause, the sure effect is WOE.

Garrick's ending certainly proved popular with contemporary critics. Francis Gentleman, in 1770, wrote, 'As to the catastrophe, it is so much improved, that to it we impute a great part of the success which has attended this tragedy of late years.'[46] In 1808 Thomas Davis asserted that the scene 'was written with a spirit not unworthy of Shakespeare himself'.[47] Charles

---

44 'To the Reader', 1748 edition, in Pedicord and Bergmann, *Garrick's Adaptations*, p. 77.

45 Quoted in Wright, *Romeo*, p. 65.   46 Gentleman, *Bell's Edition*, p. 83.

47 G. W. Stone, '*Romeo*', p. 193.

Wyndham used Garrick's text as late as 1875, and Fanny Kemble allegedly preferred Garrick: Clifford Harrison quotes her as saying, in 1879, 'I have played both; my father has played both; and I *know* which is best for the stage.'[48] Few would now make this claim; but in the twentieth century it again became common to have Juliet wake before Romeo's death. Julie Harris, in Michael Langham's 1960 Stratford, Ontario production, awoke in time to watch Romeo die, a moment described by one reviewer as 'electric in its impact'.[49] Trevor Nunn and Barry Kyle, at Stratford in 1976, made Juliet's awakening a central emblem of the production, and in Baz Luhrmann's 1996 film the lovers share a few moments of desperate anguish and even exchange some lines. The early awakening of Juliet can add not only pathos, but a defamiliarising shock that reminds the audience of the larger social circumstances responsible for the lovers' deaths.

Romeo and Juliet opened, under Garrick's direction, at Drury Lane on 29 November 1748. Well performed by Spranger Barry and Susanna Cibber (Theophilus' estranged second wife), the play ran successfully for eighteen performances. Two years later, however, Barry and Cibber decamped to the rival Covent Garden management of John Rich, who announced they would play Romeo and Juliet there. Garrick, anticipating the challenge, secretly prepared for the part of Romeo opposite George Anne Bellamy, who had acted Juliet at Covent Garden earlier in the year. The two productions opened simultaneously on 28 September 1750, beginning what was known as 'the Battle of the Romeos'. For twelve nights the productions ran head to head, until Cibber withdrew from fatigue or illness. Garrick played for one more night to mark his triumph, but audiences had grown tired of having a single play monopolise both patent theatres, as a verse in the *Daily Advertiser* attested:

> Well, what tonight, says angry Ned,
> > As up from bed he rouses,
> Romeo again! and shakes his head,
> > Ah! Pox on both your houses!
> > > I. H – tt[50]

There are a number of contemporary accounts of the relative merits of the two productions, all centring on the character of Romeo. According to William Cooke, 'Parties were much divided about which of the Romeos had the superiority; but the critics seemed to be unanimous in favour of Barry.

---

48 Harrison, *Stray Records*, p. 132.
49 Arnold Edinborough, 'Artistic Success in Canada', *SQ* 11:4 (1960), 455–9; p. 457.
50 12 October 1750, quoted in *The London Stage*, IV, I, p. 211.

Mr *Barry and . Miss . Nossiter .*
in the *Characters of Romeo and Juliet .*
Act 2.^d Scene 2.^d

2 Spranger Barry and Isabella Nossiter in the balcony scene, c. 1753. Hannah Pritchard commented, '. . . had I been Juliet to Barry's Romeo, – so tender and seductive was he, I should certainly have jumped down to him!'

His fine person, and silver tones, spoke the very voice of love.'[51] Some felt Barry was better in the love scenes of the first three acts, Garrick better in the tragic ending, and Cooke reports that 'some of them supported this opinion by frequently leaving Covent Garden in the middle of the play, to see it finish at Drury Lane'. While Garrick exhibited more tragic passion, he could not compete with the tall, good-looking Barry as a stage lover. Francis Gentleman gave a divided verdict based on careful study of both performances:

> As to figure, though there is no necessity for a lover being tall, yet we apprehend Mr Barry had a peculiar advantage in this point; his amorous harmony of features, melting eyes, and unequalled plaintiveness of voice, seemed to promise every thing we could wish, and yet the superior grace of Mr Garrick's attitudes, the vivacity of his countenance, and the fire of his expression, showed there were many essential beauties in which his great competitor might be excelled.[52]

Gentleman felt Barry was more successful in the balcony and parting scenes, Garrick with the Friar and Apothecary; he divided the play's end, awarding 'Mr Barry first part of the tomb scene, and Mr Garrick from where the poison operates to the end'. In conclusion he felt that 'Mr Garrick commanded most applause, Mr Barry most tears.'

John Hill likewise felt that their different gifts illuminated different aspects of Romeo, but that finally Barry was more suited to it:

> in parts where violence and fury are the great characteristics, Mr Garrick succeeds best, and Mr Barry in those distinguished by tenderness; and in the character of Romeo, where there is a great deal of both, they are both . . . amazingly eminent: if upon the whole, we see Mr Barry with the greatest pleasure, it is not because Mr Garrick is the inferior actor, but because Romeo is more distinguished by love than rage.[53]

One of the most succinct and oft-quoted comparisons is attributed to the actress Hannah Pritchard: 'Had I been Juliet to Garrick's Romeo, – so impassioned was he, I should have expected that he would have come up to me in the balcony; but had I been Juliet to Barry's Romeo, – so tender and seductive was he, I should certainly have jumped down to him!'[54] Katherine Wright observes that by his triumph as Romeo, Barry redefined the

51 Cooke, *Memoirs of Charles Macklin*, p. 160.
52 Gentleman, *Dramatic Censor*, p. 189.
53 Hill, *The Actor* (1755), p. 66.
54 Simpson and Braun, *Famous Actresses*, pp. 11–12.

character as a romantic lover rather than a tragic hero, leaving a mark on the play that would not be challenged until the twentieth century.[55]

As to their respective Juliets, Susanna Cibber, who had originally been directed by Garrick, was generally felt to be the more successful, particularly in the tragic passages. Thirty-six at the time of the rivalry, she possessed great beauty, skill, and stage presence, and excelled in tenderness and pathos. As John Hill wrote, 'What is the reason that nobody ever played Juliet so well as Mrs Cibber, but that Mrs Cibber has a heart better formed for tenderness than any other woman who ever attempted it . . . ?'[56] Bellamy, at nineteen, was a younger, more passionate Juliet, lacking Cibber's stature and depth of feeling. The actresses' offstage identities may have coloured the reception of their performances, as has often happened with this play. Susanna Cibber was the long-suffering wife of the hated Theophilus, and constantly plagued by ill-health, while Bellamy was a bold, vivacious beauty with many lovers and a reckless taste for gambling. The critic of the *Gentleman's Magazine* seems to reflect this perception in his assessment: 'Miss Bellamy, if she possesses not Mrs Cibber's softness, she makes a larger compensation by her variety . . . For my own part, I shed more tears in seeing Mrs Cibber, but I am more delighted in seeing Miss Bellamy.'[57] The partnerships were later reversed; Cibber returned to Drury Lane in 1753 and played Juliet opposite Garrick, though her health frequently kept her off the stage. Barry's new Juliet, the eighteen-year-old Maria Isabella Nossiter, made a sensational début in the role, but was replaced in 1757 by Bellamy. Nossiter remains the best documented of eighteenth-century Juliets, as an admirer (probably the critic MacNamara Morgan) wrote a detailed pamphlet praising her; he called Nossiter's potion scene 'the greatest acting that has been exhibited on the stage, by man or woman, since Betterton went off'.[58]

The rival Mercutios were also noteworthy. By far the more successful was Henry Woodward, who played with Garrick at Drury Lane. A master of high comedy, Woodward made Mercutio a graceful, whimsical fop. The high point of his performance was the Mab speech, treated as an extravagant flight of fancy; John Hill felt '. . . it is not more certain that none but Shakespeare could have wrote this speech, than that no man but Woodward can speak it'.[59] By contrast, Covent Garden's Mercutio was Charles Macklin, famous for turning Shylock from a low comic part to one of bitter tragedy. Macklin made Mercutio a coarse and cynical malcontent, along the lines of Otway's Sulpitius. Gentleman felt Macklin's 'saturnine cast of countenance,

55 Wright, *Romeo*, pp. 89–90.   56 Hill, *The Actor* (1750), p. 116.
57 October 1750, quoted in Highfill, *Biographical Dictionary*, II, p. 12.
58 *A Letter to Miss Nossiter*, p. 31.   59 Hill, *The Actor* (1750), p. 242.

sententious utterance, hollow toned voice, and heaviness of deportment, ill
suited the whimsical Mercutio'.[60] Yet he conceded that Macklin showed 'ten
times more art' than Woodward. The predominance of Woodward's
approach is evident in a comment by Macklin's friend and biographer
William Cooke: 'How Macklin could have been *endured* in a character so
totally unfitted to his powers of mind and body, is a question not easily
resolved at this day; particularly as Woodward played this character at the
other house, and played it in a style of excellence never perhaps before, or
since, equalled.'[61] Macklin's darker interpretation of the character would
have to wait for the twentieth century to become predominant.

As far as the staging goes, the Covent Garden and Drury Lane performances followed the conventions of the mid-eighteenth century. The theatres were proscenium houses seating well over a thousand, though the actors
shared the same light with the audience and could address them directly from
the forestage. While actors used conventional gestures to indicate the different passions, Garrick had led a revolution of 'real feeling' on the stage, and
both Cibber and Bellamy were known for crying real tears.[62] The scenery
was primarily two-dimensional, with wings and shutters pulled from the
theatre's stock of streets, palaces, churches, and groves. Costumes were
modern dress: long coats, knee-breeches, elegant gowns, and powdered wigs,
even a tricorne hat for Barry's gallant Romeo.[63] Both the Drury Lane and
Covent Garden productions added elaborate music and spectacle. In addition to a grandly staged masquerade dance at the Capulet ball, both productions included Juliet's funeral procession, accompanied by a solemn dirge.
The dirges were significant musical events, written by two of the leading
composers of the day; Drury Lane's was by William Boyce, Covent Garden's
by Thomas Arne, the brother of Susanna Cibber. Of this innovation Gentleman comments sardonically: 'Though not absolutely essential, nothing
could be better devised than a funeral procession, to render this play thoroughly popular; as it is certain that three-fourths of every audience are more
capable of enjoying sound and show, than solid sense and poetical imagination.'[64] The funeral dirge remained an important part of productions
through the nineteenth century, and was often more prominent on playbills
than the names of the actors.

Romeo and Juliet was performed 399 times between 1750 and 1800, more
than any other Shakespeare play.[65] Garrick went on playing Romeo until

60 Gentleman, *Dramatic Censor*, p. 190.
61 Cooke, *Memoirs of Charles Macklin*, p. 196.
62 Wright, *Romeo*, p. 97.   63 Halio, *Romeo*, p. 102.
64 Gentleman, *Dramatic Censor*, p. 185.
65 Hogan, *Shakespeare in the Theatre*, II, p. 716.

1761, when he switched to Mercutio; Barry played it continually until 1768, when he was nearly fifty. The play appeared in virtually every season, often at both theatres, through to 1800.

NINETEENTH-CENTURY FAILURES

By the end of the century the London theatre was dominated by the Kemble family, particularly John Philip Kemble and his sister, Sarah Siddons. Both excelled in lofty tragic roles, and were rather too statuesque for *Romeo and Juliet*. John Philip Kemble's marmoreal patrician demeanour was more suited to Coriolanus than to Romeo, whom he played for only three performances, without success. Even his loyal biographer James Boaden conceded that 'youthful love . . . was never well expressed by Kemble: the thoughtful strength of his features was at variance with juvenile passion'.[66] Kemble did carefully reedit the play, retaining most of Garrick's alterations, in what became the standard theatrical version for much of the century. Sarah Siddons played Juliet in the provinces in her youth, but only took the role once in London, opposite her brother on 11 May 1789. She was then thirty-four years old, and 'time and study had stamped her countenance . . . too strongly for Juliet'; besides, her cold and formal style was ill suited to the role.[67] Boaden felt her Juliet 'was exactly what might have been anticipated – too dignified and thoughtful to assume the childish ardours of a first affection; but, as the serious interest grew upon the character, impassioned, terrific, and sublime'. Nevertheless, 'she left fewer of her marks upon it, than she did upon any other character of equal force', and she never attempted it again.[68]

It was Charles Kemble, another brother, who had the best luck with the play. He had considerable success as Romeo opposite Eliza O'Neill, but truly distinguished himself when he switched to the role of Mercutio in 1829, in which part 'he walked, spoke, looked, fought, and died like a gentleman', according to one viewer.[69] He avoided the bullying cynicism of Macklin as well as the foppishness of Woodward, making Mercutio instead an elegant and courtly figure of high comedy. His Mab speech was famous for its freshness and spontaneity, the way each 'sudden burst of fancy' led to the next, 'till the speaker abandoned himself to the brilliant and thronging illustra-

---

66 Boaden, *Memoirs of J. P. Kemble*, I, p. 419.
67 Campbell, *Life of Mrs Siddons*, II, pp. 158–9.
68 Boaden, *Memoirs of J. P. Kemble*, I, p. 437.
69 Fitzgerald, *Lives of the Kembles*, II, p. 387.

tions which, amidst all their rapidity and fire, never lost the simple and spontaneous grace of nature in which they took rise'.[70] He was gallant and courtly
in his banter with the Nurse, and made a point of grasping Romeo's hand in
forgiveness even at the moment of his death. His 'heroic and courtly
humorist' was the definitive Mercutio of the nineteenth century.[71]

Among other actors of the period, William Charles Macready had some
success when he debuted as Romeo in 1810, but later audiences resisted his
Romeo because of his appearance. His 'want of personal attractions' was
noted in one review, which, according to Macready, observed that 'Nature
had interposed an everlasting bar to my success' by being 'unaccommodating
. . . in the formation of my face'.[72] He later found himself reduced to playing
Friar Lawrence, a part in which he found 'no direct character to sustain, no
effort to make'.[73]

The greatest actor of the age, Edmund Kean, failed disastrously as
Romeo; as William Hazlitt crushingly declared, 'His Romeo had nothing of
the lover in it. We never saw anything less ardent or less voluptuous . . . He
stood like a statue of lead.'[74] The Drury Lane committee, noting the success
Eliza O'Neill was having as Juliet at Covent Garden, decided to push their
star actor into the play; Kean reluctantly accepted, opposite Mrs Bartley.[75]
Hazlitt observed that Kean's remarkable powers, which he admired, were
particularly unsuited to Romeo: 'Mr Kean's imagination appears not to have
the principles of joy or hope or love in it. He seems chiefly sensible to pain, or
to the passions that spring from it.' Accordingly, while he was effective in the
Friar's cell and the tomb, he was unconvincing before Juliet's balcony: 'His
acting sometimes reminded us of the scene with Lady Anne [in *Richard III*]',
Hazlitt observed dryly, 'and we cannot say a worse thing of it, considering the
difference of the two characters.' After the first three performances a different Juliet was tried, Miss L. Kelly, but to no avail. The play was taken off after
nine performances, and Kean never attempted Romeo again.

The major English Shakespeareans of the Victorian period – Macready,
Samuel Phelps, Charles Kean, and Henry Irving – were all better suited to
tragic kingship than to the youthful ardour of Romeo. Phelps limited himself
to Mercutio, and Charles Kean attempted Romeo only a few times, to bruis-
ing reviews. The response to his debut in the role, opposite Miss C. Phillips,
is not atypical of nineteenth-century biases: 'Miss Phillips was a great

---

70 Marston, *Our Recent Actors*, I, p. 122.   71 Williamson, *Charles Kemble*, p. 118.
72 Macready, *Reminiscences*, I, p. 92.   73 Trewin, *Mr Macready*, p. 146.
74 Hazlitt, *Hazlitt on Theatre*, p. 32; subsequent quotations are from pp. 33, 32.
75 Hillebrand, *Edmund Kean*, pp. 141–2.

success, and Kean a great failure. He was consequently very much humiliated and distressed.'[76] Though the play remained popular, Romeo became a
role actors sought to avoid.

VICTORIAN ACTRESSES

For women it was a different story. Where virtually every important
nineteenth-century actor failed as Romeo, virtually every important
nineteenth-century actress succeeded as Juliet. In part this has to do with
the importance of Juliet in the canon of nineteenth-century women's parts;
it was typically a début role, and if one failed in it, one was unlikely to have
much of a subsequent career.

The position of actresses in the nineteenth-century theatre was an
ambiguous one. Tracy Davis, in *Actresses as Working Women*, has pointed out
the disproportionate hardships women faced in an ill-paid and highly com-
petitive industry where they were often regarded as little better than prosti-
tutes. Gail Marshall has argued that Victorian actresses were constrained by
a dominant cultural 'Galatea myth' that positioned them as sculptures, silent
and immobilised commodities for male visual and sexual appreciation. Kerry
Powell has asserted that the Victorian theatre 'conspired in producing
repressive codes of gender even as it provided women with a rare opportunity to experience independence and power'.[77] Yet women achieved increasing numbers and economic success on the stage in the nineteenth century,
and *Romeo and Juliet* was one of the chief vehicles by which they did so.
Indeed, the history of nineteenth-century theatre is a long catalogue of triumphant débuts as Juliet.

The first was Eliza O'Neill, who débuted at Covent Garden in 1814. She
was twenty-four but looked fifteen, and her performance called up hyperbole
in all who saw it. 'Through my whole experience hers was the only representation of Juliet I have seen,' gushed Macready, who later played opposite her.
'I left my seat in the orchestra with the words of Iachimo in my mind. "All of
her, that is out of door, most rich! . . . She is alone the Arabian bird." '[78] His
apparently unselfconscious quotation of Iachimo, the villain who lustfully
describes the beauties of the innocently sleeping Imogen in *Cymbeline*, says a
good deal about how nineteenth-century spectators viewed their Juliets.
Much of Macready's account has this same voyeuristic quality:

> It was not altogether the matchless beauty of form and face, but the spirit of
> perfect innocence and purity that seemed to glisten in her speaking eyes and

76 Armstrong, *Great Actors*, p. 290.   77 Powell, *Women*, p. xi.
78 Macready, *Reminiscences*, I, p. 98. The following quotation is from p. 97.

breathe from her chiseled lips . . . There was in her look, voice, and manner, an artlessness, an apparent unconsciousness (so foreign to the generality of stage performers) that riveted the spectator's gaze . . .

It is Juliet's eyes that speak, while her lips are those of a statue; she is unconscious and innocent, but rivets the (male) spectator's gaze. Macready's effusions are firmly in line with the 'Galatea aesthetic' Gail Marshall has identified. The most famous critic of the age, William Hazlitt, resisted O'Neill's performance, being partial to her great predecessor Sarah Siddons; but he did acknowledge her skill in 'the silent expression of feeling'.[79]

John Cole made an extended comparison between the two actresses that suggests much about the changing fashion between the eighteenth and nineteenth centuries:

> Inferior to Siddons in grandeur, and in depicting the more terrible and stormy passions of human nature, [Miss O'Neill] excelled that great mistress of her art in tenderness and natural pathos . . . Mrs Siddons presented a being exalted above humanity, to admire and gaze upon with wonder; but whom you hesitated to approach in familiar intercourse. Miss O'Neill invited sympathy, and while she suffered with intenseness, appeared incapable of retaliation.[80]

Eliza O'Neill, with her beauty, artlessness, susceptibility to 'familiar intercourse', and defenceless suffering, became the model for nineteenth-century Juliets. With her graceful figure, fair curls, and huge, easily weeping eyes, she was 'a perfect image of loveliness in distress', according to William Winter, and 'evoked prodigious sympathy, – as loveliness in distress always will'.[81] Fanny Kemble, who succeeded her in the role, archly commented that O'Neill 'was expressly designed for a representative victim'.[82] Nonetheless, accounts of Kemble's own début stress similarly vulnerable qualities. Kemble first played Juliet at the age of twenty, at Covent Garden, with her father Charles playing Mercutio and her mother as Lady Capulet. Her first appearance was a metatheatrical emblem of innocence suffering under an oppressive gaze:

> On her first entrance she seemed to feel very sensibly the embarrassment of the new and overwhelming task she had undertaken. She ran to her mother's arms with a sort of instinctive impulse, but almost immediately recovered

79 Hazlitt, *Hazlitt on Theatre*, p. 18.   80 Cole, *Life of Charles Kean*, I, p. 73.
81 Winter, *Shakespeare on the Stage*, p. 147.
82 Kemble, *Records of a Girlhood*, p. 195.

her composure . . . In the garden scene she gave the exquisite poetry of the part with a most innocent gracefulness . . . The scene with the Nurse was full of delightful simplicity.[83]

In spite of the critical emphasis on her timidity, Fanny Kemble was given credit for saving her family's management of Covent Garden. *Romeo and Juliet* was a tremendous success, and her career was launched. The vehement effusions of contemporary writers make it difficult to judge how Kemble actually played the role: Anna Jameson, for instance, says she did it 'as though every line and sentiment in Shakespeare had been transplanted into her heart, – had long been brooded over in silence, – watered with her tears, – to burst forth at last, like the spontaneous and native growth of her own soul'.[84] Interestingly, Kemble's writings reveal a degree of frustration with the character of Juliet, whom she calls a 'foolish child', and an intelligent and slightly cynical attitude toward the play: 'I have little or no sympathy with, though much compassion for, that Veronese young person.'[85] She also had little tolerance for traditional and sentimental stage business; when Ellen Tree, as Romeo, wanted to carry her to the footlights in the tomb scene, Kemble declared, 'If you attempt to lift or carry me down the stage, I will kick and scream till you set me down.'[86] Though she never again matched her initial success and was often a reluctant actress, Kemble was a perceptive critic and writer, full of insights into the role and the play. She observed to Clifford Harrison that 'Romeo represents the sentiment, Juliet the passion, of love. The pathos is his, the power hers.'[87] She made her mark on the role of Juliet and continued to give readings of it, in public and private, until she was at least seventy.

Helena Faucit also made her début as Juliet, and identified herself with the part for much of her early life. In her book, *On Some of Shakespeare's Female Characters*, she discusses her childish admiration for Juliet's courage, and her terror in reading the tomb scene. She recalls playfully acting the balcony scene opposite her sister in the empty Richmond Theatre, being overheard, and thus being invited to play Juliet there at the age of thirteen. She felt her youth worked against her; she was 'too near the age of Shakespeare's Juliet, considering the tardier development of an English girl, to understand so strong and deep a nature'.[88] In the potion scene, Faucit recalls, she was so overwrought that she crushed the vial in her hand, and then genuinely fainted at the sight of her own blood staining her dress.

---

83 *Times*, 6 October 1829.   84 Jameson, *Sketches*, p. 482.
85 Kemble, *Records of a Girlhood*, pp. 438–9.   86 Ibid., p. 201.
87 Harrison, *Stray Records*, p. 134.
88 Faucit, *Shakespeare's Female Characters*, p. 107.

THE ATTITUDES of MISS FANNY KEMBLE,
as JULIET.

3 Fanny Kemble, from her 1829 Covent Garden performances: with the Nurse, taking
the potion, and in Garrick's version of the tomb scene.

Whether accurate or not, Faucit's reminiscences embody the same combination of innocent fragility and unbidden, passive sexuality that made
O'Neill and Kemble so successful in the role. As Gail Marshall argues, the
story of *Romeo and Juliet*

enabled the display of, and contained its own solutions to the problems
raised by, theatrical representations of female sexuality. Juliet's youthfully
unconscious desirability is invoked by others only to be obliterated by death
. . . Juliet's sexual awakening is amply contained by the dimensions of the

tragedy, thus making the part the perfect vehicle for conveying the attractively malleable sexuality of the actress.[89]

Faucit gave a highly successful performance at Covent Garden in 1836, and continued to play Juliet regularly for the next thirty-five years. Her ability to embody the ideal of Victorian womanhood was an important aspect of her performance. According to her husband and biographer Theodore Martin, 'People saw in her not only a great actress, they felt themselves in the presence of one who was in herself the ideal woman of whom poets had written.'[90] Faucit to some extent played into this role, idealising Shakespeare's heroines as 'these sweet and noble representatives of our sex', and declaring that 'women are deeply in debt to Shakespeare for all the lovely noble things he has put into his women's hearts and mouths'.[91] But her detailed discussion of the play, in *On Some of Shakespeare's Female Characters*, reveals insights that go far beyond an idealised stereotype. For one thing, Faucit was rare in the nineteenth century in viewing the play in social terms rather than focusing solely on the protagonists; she felt Shakespeare's 'far wider and deeper' purpose was obscured if the play ended, as it often did, with the deaths of the lovers.

Faucit's account of the potion scene shows the pragmatic choices of an intelligent performer fully aware of the emotional demands of the role: 'What a scene is this – so simple, so grand, so terrible! What it is to act I need not tell you. What power it demands, and yet what restraint!' Her moment-by-moment account of the scene is full of vivid psychological details:

> I always felt a kind of icy coldness and stillness come over me after leaving the Friar's cell which lasted until this moment. The 'Farewell!' to Lady Capulet, – 'God knows when we shall meet again' – relaxed this state of tension.

> I could never utter these words [about Tybalt's corpse] without an exclamation of shuddering disgust accompanying them.

> At the mention of Romeo's name I used to feel all my resolution return.

By charting her own psychological journey through the scene, Faucit asserted a degree of creative autonomy, and to some extent transcended the objectification to which her performance on stage was subject. The writings of actresses like Faucit, together with other women like Mary Cowden Clarke (*The Girlhood of Shakespeare's Heroines*) and Anna Jameson

---

89 Marshall, *Actresses*, pp. 107–8.   90 Martin, *Helena Faucit*, pp. 125–6.
91 Faucit, *Shakespeare's Female Characters*, pp. viii, 118. Subsequent quotations are from pp. 153, 145, 143, 144, 145.

(*Shakespeare's Heroines*), fleshed out the conception of Juliet that had been offered to the gaze of Victorian spectators. These character-studies, though in many ways false to the play, enabled women to lay claim to Juliet's inner life, and insist on her depth and complexity.

CHARLOTTE CUSHMAN'S ROMEO, 1845

If Victorian women were able, through their performances and writings, to give cultural prominence and variety to Shakespeare's Juliet, they were also able to best their male counterparts in the role of Romeo. A variety of actresses played Romeo on the Victorian stage, including Caroline Rankley, Felicita Vestvalli, Fanny Vining, Margaret Leighton, Esmé Beringer, and Ellen Tree.[92] Tree played Romeo at Covent Garden in 1829, opposite Fanny Kemble, who described it as the 'only occasion on which I ever acted Juliet to a Romeo who looked the part'.[93] According to John Cole, Tree's 'hazardous attempt' achieved 'singular success, all the newspapers being unanimous in her praise'.[94] Other female Romeos were less enthusiastically received: William Archer felt Esmé Beringer was 'a clever young lady, and made a graceful, inoffensive and even intelligent Romeo . . . but for my part, I hold such travesties, in their very nature, unprofitable and unattractive'.[95] Nonetheless, the most acclaimed Romeo of the century – male or female – was the American actress Charlotte Cushman. Cross-dressing actresses had been common on the English stage since the Restoration, but in the nineteenth century women were able to transcend the crude bodily display that initially made 'breeches parts' popular. Actresses like Cushman who could convincingly embody male characters 'dissociated breeches roles from their tradition of sexual titillation', according to Sandra Richards.[96] Cushman defied and transcended gender roles even in female characters like Lady Macbeth, according to a contemporary critic, William Winter: 'She was not a theatrical beauty. She neither employed, nor made pretence of employing, the soft allurements of her sex. She was incarnate power: she dominated by intrinsic authority: she was a woman born to command.'[97]

---

92 William Winter records fourteen female Romeos in the US between 1827 and 1869, but notes that 'In description of their performances the chronicles of our Theatre are comparatively barren' (*Shakespeare on the Stage*, p. 201).

93 Kemble, *Records of a Girlhood*, p. 200.   94 Cole, *Life of Charles Kean*, I, p. 322.

95 Archer, *Theatrical 'World' of 1896*, p. 155. Clement Scott, by contrast, felt that 'a more ideal Romeo has seldom been seen' (Winter, *Shakespeare on the Stage*, p. 200).

96 Richards, *Rise of the English Actress*, p. 93.

97 Winter, *Other Days*, pp. 152–3.

Cushman ostensibly took the role of Romeo in order to showcase her sister Susan, who played Juliet; she wrote that she wanted to give Susan 'the support I knew she required and would never get from any gentleman that could be got to act with her'.[98] The arrangement caused some concern among the citizens of Edinburgh, where they played before coming to London; her friend and fellow-actor John Coleman reports that 'her amorous endearments were of so erotic a character that no man would have dared to indulge in them'.[99] Such comments were actually quite rare, though Lisa Merill has convincingly argued that Cushman's performance enacted a passionate lesbian sexuality – which the public mostly took great pains to ignore.[100] Cushman defended herself by citing the precedent of Ellen Tree, and claiming that her performance opposite her sister was less indelicate than Fanny Kemble's, who played Juliet to her father's Romeo on a US tour. In any event, when *Romeo and Juliet* opened in London in December 1845, it was clear not only that Cushman's Romeo was acceptable to the public, but that she was the star of the production; Susan's Juliet passed almost unnoticed.

Cushman's Romeo was noteworthy in part because she used Shakespeare's original text instead of Garrick's. She was not the first to do so; Madame Vestris had apparently attempted it, without success, in 1840.[101] Cushman herself had played the Garrick text in the US, but for the Haymarket she insisted on reverting to Shakespeare. Cushman's version was not by any means complete, and indeed she made many of the same cuts as Garrick and Kemble. According to the Lacy edition of 1855, she cut the Prologue, the servants' bawdry and the entry of the Capulet and Montague wives in 1.1, much of the discussion of Rosaline's chastity, most of the Nurse's story of Juliet's childhood, most of the bawdy jesting of Mercutio, Benvolio's report of the duel in 3.1, some of the lamentations in the 'banished' scenes, and much of the Friar's counsel, much of the mourning for Juliet in 4.5, the Musicians, and a certain amount of the final recapitulation and sorting of evidence. Perhaps not surprisingly, her version favoured the part of Romeo at the expense of nearly everyone else. Her return to Shakespeare had the crucial effect of expanding Romeo's character by including his early passion

98 Leach, *Bright Particular Star*, p. 170.   99 Coleman, *Fifty Years*, II, p. 363.
100 Merill, *When Romeo Was a Woman*, pp. 126–30. One critic, George Fletcher, did object strongly to 'the disgustingly monstrous grossness of such a perversion'; though his invective was directed not only at 'the hysterical sobbing and blubbering' and 'coarse, unmodulated vehemence' of Cushman's performance, but also at 'the nasal utterance and awkward vowel pronunciation of her country' (*Studies of Shakespeare*, pp. 379–81).
101 Odell, *Shakespeare from Betterton to Irving*, II, p. 191.

for Rosaline. Passion was the keynote of her performance; as one review remarked, 'Miss Cushman has suddenly placed a living, breathing, burning Italian upon boards where we have hitherto had an unfortunate and some-what energetic Englishman.'[102] *The Times* concurred: 'For a long time Romeo has been a convention. Miss Cushman's Romeo is a creative, a living, breathing, animated, ardent human being' (30 December 1848). James Sheridan Knowles compared her Romeo to Kean's Othello, citing 'the genuine heart-storm' of the banishment scene: 'not simulated passion, – no such thing; real, palpably real'.[103] Several critics commented that Cushman was restoring a previously lost role:

> The character, instead of being shown to us in a heap of *disjecta membra*, is
> exhibited by her in a powerful light which at once displays the proportions
> and the beauty of the poet's conception. It is as if a noble symphony,
> distorted and rendered unmeaning by inefficient conductors, had suddenly
> been performed under the hand of one who knew in what *time* the composer
> intended it should be taken.

While her unified and passionate grasp of the role was widely praised, her gender certainly didn't pass without comment. Queen Victoria herself went to see her, and was surprised by her authentically masculine performance:

> Miss Cushman took the part of Romeo, and no one would ever have
> imagined she was a woman, her figure and her voice being so masculine, but
> her face was very plain. Her acting is not pleasing, though clever, and she
> entered well into the character, bringing out forcibly its impetuosity.[104]

In the one surviving photo of Cushman as Romeo, taken in the 1850s, she looks obviously female and middle-aged, but in 1845 audiences had no difficulty responding to her as a passionate young man.[105] Joseph Leach summarises the contemporary response: 'Few Romeos in London's memory had looked young enough and passionately agile enough to be convincing, but watching this fiery young gallant, one witness was soon exclaiming that this Miss Cushman seemed "just *man* enough to be a *boy*!"'[106]

At some level, Cushman was able to succeed as Romeo, where men failed, because of her gender. One reviewer, commenting on recent male perfor-mances, observed that 'there is no part more difficult to sustain efficiently than Romeo. At one time we have seen it a lifeless, sickly, and repulsive

---

102 Unidentified review quoted in Levenson, *Romeo* (1987), p. 38.
103 Quoted in Clement, *Charlotte Cushman*, p. 45; the following quotation is from p. 46.
104 Rowell, *Queen Victoria*, p. 74. 105 Merill, *When Romeo Was a Woman*, p. 116.
106 Leach, *Bright Particular Star*, p. 175.

4 Charlotte Cushman, the most successful woman to take the role,
in her costume as Romeo, c. 1855.

conception; at another a rough, indelicate, animal picture.'[107] The character of Romeo, as understood in the nineteenth century, was incompatible with Victorian notions of masculinity. As an article in *Britannia* observed, in reference to Cushman's performance, 'It is open to question whether Romeo may not best be impersonated by a woman, for it is thus only that in actual representation can we view the passionate love of this play made real and palpable.'[108] Indeed, Victorian productions of *Romeo and Juliet* seem to suggest a rare case where gender bias, in a small way, liberated women and hindered men. Where Victorian women used a range of performances, and their considerable writings on the play, to assert a degree of female subjectivity and independence, their male counterparts repeatedly failed as Romeo; and failed, at least in part, because they just weren't sexy enough. Emma Stebbins, companion and biographer of Charlotte Cushman, thought that Victorian actors were simply too old and ugly for Romeo: 'Who could endure to see a man with the muscles of Forrest, or even the keen intellectual face of Macready, in the part of a gallant and loving boy?' Turning the tables on an oft-repeated aphorism about Juliet, Stebbins put male actors firmly in their place: 'When a man has achieved the experience requisite to *act* Romeo, he has ceased to be young enough to *look* it.'[109] For most of the nineteenth century, the English theatre-going public seems to have agreed.

HENRY IRVING AND ELLEN TERRY AT THE LYCEUM, 1882

Cushman's success broke the hold of the Garrick–Kemble version of *Romeo and Juliet*, but it by no means meant a return to full Shakespearean texts. Not only were the many sexual references consistently censored, but theatrical conventions prompted heavy cutting for various reasons. London's two patent theatres had greatly increased in size and scenic capabilities. After fires in 1808 and 1809, Covent Garden and Drury Lane were rebuilt with seating capacities of 3,044 and 3,611 respectively, roughly twice the size they had been in Garrick's day. In such a cavernous theatre, the nimble banter of Mercutio could have much less impact than a rhetorical set piece like Juliet's potion speech, and the play was cut accordingly. The need for slower, more demonstrative playing increased as a series of renovations reduced and eventually eliminated the stage apron, leaving a picture-frame opening measuring 12.8 metres (42 feet) across at

---

107 Quoted in Levenson, *Romeo* (1987), p. 31.
108 3 January 1846, quoted in Merill, *When Romeo Was a Woman*, p. 110.
109 Stebbins, *Charlotte Cushman*, p. 59.

Covent Garden, with wings of 6 metres (20 feet).[110] Through this proscenium audiences viewed more and more elaborate scenery, complemented, after 1817, by gas lighting. New scenes, rather than stock flats, came to be employed (and advertised) for major new productions; the painter's art was increasingly supplemented by that of the carpenter, as more and more elaborate three-dimensional structures were employed. The difficulty in changing these caused managers to cut and rearrange scenes in order to simplify the staging; for instance, 4.2 and 4.4 were regularly cut, so that the only sets needed for the fourth act were the Friar's cell and Juliet's bedroom. A representative production was that of Charles Kean, the antiquarian son of Edmund, who played Romeo opposite his wife Ellen Tree at the Haymarket in 1841. Charles Marshall designed thirteen separate scenes that carefully reproduced the art and architecture of the Italian Renaissance; the brief Mantua scene, 5.1, even had a recognisably different architectural style from the Verona scenes.

One exception to the prevailing trend was Samuel Phelps. After the Theatre Regulation Act of 1843 abolished the monopoly of the patent houses, Phelps took over the management of the unfashionable Sadler's Wells Theatre, where he staged all but four of Shakespeare's plays, emphasising acting and poetry over scenic spectacle. He played Mercutio with William Creswick and Laura Addison in 1846, using a remarkably full text unrivalled until the twentieth century. The Nurse's story was complete (except for her reference to 'a young cock'rel's stone', 1.3.54), Phelps allowed himself most of Mercutio's banter, and every scene of Shakespeare's play was included in some form. Both Benvolio and the Friar retained their accounts of past events, and the mourning for Juliet in 4.5 was included, with only the Musicians gone. In a smaller theatre, with less scenery to change, Phelps was able to give a virtually complete performance of the play, anticipating the 'Shakespeare revolution' led by William Poel and Harley Granville-Barker at the beginning of the next century.

Phelps had few imitators, however, and the other London theatres continued to opt for spectacle. The culmination of the Victorian pictorial tradition came with Henry Irving's production of *Romeo and Juliet* at the Lyceum, opening 8 March 1882. Irving's conception of the play, from the beginning, was visual. According to Ellen Terry, he observed that '*Hamlet* could be played anywhere on its acting merits. It marches from situation to situation. But *Romeo and Juliet* proceeds from picture to picture. Every line suggests a picture. It is a dramatic poem rather than a drama, and I mean to treat it from that point of view.'[111]

110 Styan, *Shakespeare Revolution*, p. 15.   111 Terry, *Story of My Life*, p. 227.

Accordingly, Irving created a theatrical experience of unprecedented splendour and expense. The play was given in twenty-two scenes, most of which had different sets, solidly constructed in three dimensions. He made innovative use of lighting to enhance his changes of scenery, producing 'a sort of richness of effect and surprise as the gloom passes away and a gorgeous scene steeped in effulgence and colour is revealed'.[112] The production clearly used every resource the Victorian theatre could afford. Clement Scott responded to the combination of scenery, lighting, and music by which Irving created an Italian world:

> Such scenes as these – the outside of Capulet's house lighted for the ball, the sunny pictures of Verona in summer, the marriage chant to Juliet changed into a death dirge, the old, lonely street in Mantua where the Apothecary dwells, the wondrous solid tomb of the Capulets – are as worthy of close and renewed study as are the pictures in a gallery of paintings.[113]

In the costumes, which Irving designed along with Alfred Thompson, he sought to convey 'the rich harmonies and bold compositions of the Italian masters'.[114] Sir Julius Benedict provided accompanying music in the Italian manner.

Much of Irving's direction seems to have been theatrically effective. Irving had seen the Duke of Saxe-Meiningen and his company play in London the previous year, and imitated his method of directing crowd movement. The opening fight was particularly gripping, according to Bram Stoker, as the Montagues pushed the Capulets downstage over a bridge: 'they used to pour in on the scene down the slope of the bridge like a released torrent, and for a few minutes such a scene of fighting was enacted as I have never seen elsewhere on the stage'.[115] Ellen Terry, though dissatisfied with her own performance as Juliet, agreed that the production was visually breathtaking:

> In it Henry first displayed his mastery of crowds. The brawling of the rival houses in the streets, the procession of girls to wake Juliet on her wedding morning, the musicians, the magnificent reconciliation of the two houses which closed the play, every one on the stage holding a torch, were all treated with a marvellous sense of pictorial effect.[116]

In this last scene, Irving achieved a *coup de théâtre* that demonstrated his confident marshalling of Victorian stage techniques. Not content with a

---

112 Fitzgerald, *Henry Irving*, p. 141.   113 *The Theatre*, 1 April 1882.
114 Irving, *Henry Irving*, p. 388.   115 Stoker, *Personal Reminiscences*, I, p. 99.
116 Terry, *Story of My Life*, p. 227.

single image for churchyard and tomb, he divided 5.3 into two distinct scenes. Romeo killed Paris in a moonlit gothic churchyard, from which Irving moved the scene into the tomb with an almost cinematic dissolve, as one critic later recalled:

> Seizing his torch and dragging after him the lifeless form of his antagonist, Romeo disappeared, descending into the vault below. While the flare of his torch still reddened the damp walls of the entrance, the picture faded from view. Silently it came; as silently it vanished . . . Again the darkness became luminous, and the outlines of a deep cavern, hewn in solid rock, grew before the eye. It was the crypt in which rested the Capulet dead. High up in the background was seen an entrance from which a staircase, rudely fashioned in the rock, wound downward on the left to the cavern floor, and through which the moonlight streamed and fell upon the form of Juliet lying upon a silken covered bier in the foreground. Immediately the scene was developed Romeo appeared at the entrance leading from the churchyard above, bearing his flaming torch, and with the corpse of Paris in his arms, descended the rocky stairway to the bottom of the tomb.[117]

Irving spent hours practising how best to carry the body; in the end he substituted a dummy for the actor of Paris, but insisted that it be the appropriate weight and dimensions.[118] His care paid off, as this became the most memorable effect of the production. Even Shaw, no fan of Irving's, was haunted by the image years later: 'One remembers Irving, a dim figure dragging a horrible burden down through the gloom "into the rotten jaws of death".'[119]

Irving prepared his own version of the text, cutting the bawdry as usual, judiciously eliminating all references to Juliet's age (Ellen Terry was thirty-six, Irving forty-four), and dropping 4.2 and 4.4 to accommodate the scenery. Following Cushman, he retained and even emphasised Romeo's love for Rosaline: 'Its value can hardly be over-appreciated, since Shakespeare has carefully worked out this first baseless love of Romeo as a palpable evidence of the subjective nature of the man and his passion.'[120] He even carefully chose a tall dark actress to play Rosaline at the ball. 'Can I ever forget his face,' Terry asked rhetorically, 'when in pursuit of *her* he saw *me*.'[121]

By a good margin, the performances were less successful than the stage effects. The one triumph was Mrs Stirling's Nurse, a definitive performance for the era. The young and handsome William Terriss played a vigorous

117 *The Era*, 7 December 1907, quoted in Vardac, *Stage to Screen*, p. 99.
118 Stoker, *Personal Reminiscences*, I, p. 99.
119 Shaw, *Our Theatres in the Nineties*, III, p. 212.
120 Irving, Acting Edition, Preface, v.   121 Terry, *Story of My Life*, p. 233.

Mercutio, and many felt he should have been Romeo, as indeed he was in Mary Anderson's Lyceum production two years later. Irving achieved a few powerful effects in scenes of melancholy and despair; his reception of the news of Juliet's death, and his subsequent visit to the Apothecary, were his best moments. But Irving's age, his intellectuality, his bony figure and hoarse voice, all precluded a successful characterisation of the young lover. As Henry James observed, 'How little Mr Irving is Romeo it is not worth while even to attempt to declare; he must know it of course, better than anyone else, and there is something really touching in so extreme a sacrifice of one's ideal.'[122] A less charitable critic compared Irving to 'a pig who has been taught to play the fiddle. He does it very cleverly, but he would be better employed in squealing.'[123] Irving's inadequacy did not, however, prevent the production from running for over a hundred performances.

Terry's Juliet was not a success, though it was not quite so great a failure as Irving's Romeo. One of the chief complaints against Terry was that she was simply 'too English', in Henry James's phrase. Her Victorian heroine lacked 'the joy of this passionate young Italian', as Terry characterised her.[124] One critic wrote, 'Miss Ellen Terry is very charming, but she is not Juliet; and when really tragic passion is wanted for the part, it is not forthcoming.'[125] Ironically, Terry's relative lack of success as Juliet seems to have been due in part to the ideal of Victorian womanhood she embodied. She was unable to compete with a new conception of Juliet that went beyond the fragile, unconscious sexuality of O'Neill and her followers. In several reviews, Terry was compared unfavourably with the darkly passionate, doom-laden Juliet of Adelaide Neilson.[126]

FOREIGN JULIETS OF LATE-VICTORIAN TIMES

In the latter part of the nineteenth century, several actresses succeeded as Juliet by playing against the English conception of the role. Capitalising on the Imperial fascination with the exotic and foreign, and the licence associated with other cultures, Adelaide Neilson, Stella Colas, and Helena Modjeska achieved considerable success and extended the possibilities for performing Juliet.

Neilson, who played Juliet from 1865 to 1879, was actually from working-class Leeds, but she wrapped herself in an aura of illicit Mediterranean sexuality. Allegedly the natural daughter of a Spanish artist and an English

122 Quoted in Salgado, *Eyewitnesses*, p. 201.
123 Quoted in Terry, *Story of My Life*, p. 231. 124 Terry, *Four Lectures*, p. 138.
125 Hiatt, *Ellen Terry*, p. 166. 126 Ibid., p. 167.

gentlewoman, raised at Saragossa and educated in Italy, she owed to this upbringing 'the richness of her voice, the depth of expression in her dark eyes, the sensuous grace of her movements, the burning energy of passion which she displays as the tragedy progresses'.[127] Her phoney origins, her dark beauty, and her death at the age of thirty-two all contributed to her legend, but she clearly was a remarkable performer. What critics chiefly comment on is her very un-Victorian passion. William Winter writes that 'her performances were duly planned, and her rehearsals of them conscientious; but at moments in the actual exposition of them her voice, countenance and demeanor would undergo such changes, because of a surge of feeling, that her person became transfigured, and she was more like a spirit than a woman'.[128] None of her competitors could match her in 'manifesting the bewildering, exultant happiness of Juliet, or her passion, or her awestricken foreboding of impending fate'. These notes of open sexuality and tragic doom made her Juliet distinctively different from the innocent heroines who had preceded her. Her supposed otherness enabled her to stretch the role of Juliet beyond the conventional Victorian expectations for the part.

Several other actresses succeeded as Juliet in Victorian London by exploiting their foreign origins. Stella Colas, a French actress, had a period of success in the role, both in London (first in 1863) and at the Tercentenary celebrations in Stratford in 1864. Colas had a thick French accent, was considered a great beauty, and performed with 'a strong voice and much force, volitive and physical'.[129] Her merits as an actress were much debated. Clement Scott commended her youth, beauty, and passion in the early scenes, and the tragic force of her potion speech. In the balcony scene, he felt, 'her foreign origin enabled her to delight us with those tricks, fantastic changes, coquettings, poutings, and petulance which come with such difficulty from the Anglo-Saxon temperament'.[130] In the potion scene, by contrast, she 'turned positively green with fear, and became prematurely old, ugly, and haggard', uttering a terrifying shriek as she lapsed into momentary madness. Henry Morley thought her coquetry in the balcony scene 'abominable', and her shrieking at Tybalt's ghost a 'claptrap stage effect' done with 'a great deal of misdirected force'.[131] George Henry Lewes found her lacking in spontaneity and tiresomely over-emphatic: 'With all her vehemence, she is destitute of passion; she "splits the ears of the groundlings", but moves no

127 Wright, *Romeo*, p. 172.
128 Winter, *Other Days*, p. 284. The following quotation is from p. 286.
129 Winter, *Shakespeare on the Stage*, p. 151.
130 Scott, *Yesterday and Today*, II, p. 301.   131 Morley, *Journal*, p. 278.

human soul'.[132] Her accent hindered her somewhat, but her beauty, energy, and non-English passion seem to have compensated for it, at least for the popular audience.

Helena Modjeska, a Polish actress who later emigrated to America, first acted in *Romeo and Juliet* in 1866 at the Imperial Theatre, Warsaw. After giving some performances in English in the United States, she played Juliet at the Court Theatre in 1881, in a well-cast revival featuring Wilson Barrett's highly praised Mercutio and the Romeo of the young Johnston Forbes-Robertson. Responses to her performance were mixed. Having studied the role outside the English tradition, Modjeska brought many original touches; rather than playing the 2.5 exchange with the Nurse as comic wheedling, she alternately wept with anxiety and laughed with joy.[133] Odell found the love scenes 'sweetly and sympathetically played', and Winter praised her 'ingeniously devised and expertly used' stage business, such as her frenzied recoil from Tybalt's ghost.[134] One of the striking features of her performance was her emphasis on the increasing disorder of Juliet's mental state. 'If in her hands Juliet's mind is not completely shattered like Ophelia's', one critic wrote, 'it is at least unhinged and strained to a point bordering closely on the very confines of madness.'[135] Her undeniable technical skill impressed many critics, but seemed inappropriate for Juliet: 'she could scarcely have lighted on a character less suited to her physique, temperament, and histrionic method'.[136] In her forties, she expressed Juliet's youth 'by crossing the stage now and again with a certain skipping, ambling, skittish gait', and her 'airs of ingenuousness became almost grimaces'. Reception of her Juliet was in part coloured by her most famous role, in Dumas's *Camille*; though her European origins gave her a licence beyond that of English actresses, she was perhaps too much of a sophisticated and experienced woman of the world.

Another important late-Victorian Juliet was also a foreigner, the American actress and producer Mary Anderson. She engaged the Lyceum for her London début only two years after the Irving–Terry production, and borrowed two prominent members of its cast: William Terriss, who graduated from Mercutio to Romeo, and Mrs Stirling, who repeated her definitive Nurse. Further, Anderson sought to rival Irving's production in pictorial effect. She consulted with the painter Lawrence Alma-Tadema on the visual

132 Quoted in Mullin, *Victorian Actors*, p. 129.
133 Shattuck, *American Stage*, II, p. 127.
134 Odell, *Shakespeare from Betterton to Irving*, II, p. 377; Winter, *Shakespeare on the Stage*, p. 172.
135 Altemus, *Helena Modjeska*, pp. 130–1.
136 Dutton Cook, *Nights at the Play*, II, p. 311. The following quotations are from p. 312.

design, and even travelled to Verona to study the architecture; every scene was set in a recognisable Veronese location. Her efforts as producer may have hindered her performance, which she herself felt was crude and disappointing.[137] Several critics denounced the production as vulgar, attacking Anderson's American speech and her overplaying of the potion scene. Clement Scott found her 'artificial to the last degree . . . modern, unideal, and exaggerative in every tender scene', and thought the production was 'a melodrama . . . not a poem'.[138] Yet Anderson had her defenders also; Winter, who saw her play Juliet thirty-five times, thought her performance exceeded Terry, Neilson, and Modjeska in being 'saturated with the force and color of tragedy'.[139] Odell found her 'self-conscious and at times declamatory, but her faults were faults of exuberance. One never had to complain of her performances that they were too quiet or too "naturalistic." And how melodiously she read the verse!'[140] The production was a success with the public, in part because of the beauty of the designs. Their splendour led to a debate in the press about the value of pictorial Shakespeare. Scott opined, 'We are gradually overdoing spectacle so much that poetry must suffer in the long run . . . Acting is more and more made subordinate to mere scenic success.'[141] Such reservations would lead, within a few years, to the bare-stage experiments of William Poel.

Undeterred by the mixed reviews in London, Anderson took the production to the US the following year, adding a new Romeo, Johnston Forbes-Robertson. After his debut opposite Modjeska in 1881, he had quickly risen to be recognised as the definitive Romeo of the period; he was the first successful male actor in the role since Charles Kemble. Tall and handsome, with a beautiful voice and elegant classical profile, he played Romeo 'with a chivalrous grace and a subdued ardor equally rare and delightful', according to Westland Marston.[142] He also apparently achieved a marked freshness and naturalism in his speaking of Shakespearean verse, though recordings made in his later life suggest otherwise. The critic of the *Athenaeum* of 28 September 1895 proclaimed, 'It is doubtful whether since the days of Spranger Barry a Romeo more satisfactory than Mr Forbes-Robertson has been seen. The delivery of the lines is perfect; not a single mannerism mars speech or disfigures gesture. The attitudes and bearing are natural, and yet heroical.' In

137 Anderson, *A Few Memories*, p. 184.
138 Quoted in Shattuck, *American Stage*, II, p. 106.
139 Winter, *Shakespeare on the Stage*, p. 177.
140 Odell, *Shakespeare from Betterton to Irving*, II, p. 434.
141 Clement Scott, *Dramatic Notes*, November 1884, quoted in Odell, *Shakespeare from Betterton to Irving*, II, p. 434.
142 *The Critic*, 4 June 1881.

1895 Forbes-Robertson was at the Lyceum, in his own production, opposite the undistinguished Juliet of Mrs Patrick Campbell. His Romeo combined the handsome gentleman lover of the Barry tradition with the doomed melancholy of Irving. William Archer found him rather too restrained: 'It is neither thought nor understanding that is lacking in his performance, but that lyric rapture, that throb and flush of youth, which no intensity of thought can compass.'[143] Forbes-Robertson emphasised Romeo's premonitions of his fate 'yet hanging in the stars', and allowed these to temper his love scenes; he used a restrained delicacy before Juliet's balcony. He played the duel with Tybalt with resignation rather than rage, and the despair in the Friar's cell 'without extravagance'.[144] The tomb scene was the most famous part of his performance. He played it with great dignity and pathos, with none of the gothic extravagance of Irving's version. With Juliet's bier downstage centre, Forbes-Robertson could make his farewell an intimate and tender one, and 'bring out to the full the romance, the poetry, and the sadness of the scene'.[145]

ROMEO AND JULIET IN EUROPE

Romeo and Juliet has always been popular outside the English-speaking world. The play's overwrought rhetorical conceits are easily dispensed with in translation, and the story has immediacy and power across a wide range of cultures. *Romeo and Juliet* was one of the first Shakespeare plays staged outside England, part of the repertory of the 'Englische Komödianten', who toured the Continent beginning in the late sixteenth century, giving performances of Elizabethan plays in English and eventually German. Some version of the play was performed as early as 1604 in Nördlingen; *Eine Tragœdia von Romeo und Julietta* was played at court in Dresden on 1 June and 29 September 1626. A Dutch version was apparently given in Amsterdam in 1634. The earliest German text in existence is an undated manuscript from the Imperial Library in Vienna; it may or may not reflect the performances of the Komödianten but is typical of the period. It follows the story almost scene by scene, and incorporates direct translations of some poetic passages. It is considerably shortened and simplified: Romeo's love for Rosaline remains, for instance, but there is no trace of the Queen Mab speech; Juliet's taking of the potion and her supposed death occur offstage. But the German version is most notable for the intrusions of

---

143 Archer, *Theatrical 'World' of 1895*, pp. 287–8.
144 Winter, *Shakespeare on the Stage*, p. 137.
145 *The Theatre*, 1 January 1876, quoted in Wright, *Romeo*, p. 169.

the low-comic clown *Pickl Häring*, a standard character in plays of the period. He takes on some of Mercutio's role in mocking Romeo's love for Rosaline, though his main concern, inevitably, is to procure food for himself. He adds some low comedy to the duel scene, ordering the dead Tybalt to go with him to the Duke: 'But look what a parcel of snot is this? Zounds, it is Tybalt, bleeding like a pig.'[146] He brings the news of Tybalt's death to Juliet in garbled fashion, thus accounting for her confusion as to who exactly has been killed; likewise, he takes the Nurse's place during Romeo's scene in the Friar's cell. It is certainly a crude piece of work, reproducing merely the outlines of Shakespeare's plot; its Victorian editor, Albert Cohn, complains with some justice that the adaptation is spoiled 'by the omission of all the finer motives of this magnificent tragedy, as also by the insertion of comic scenes which are utterly devoid of taste, and by their disgusting coarseness obliterate even the very small amount of tragic feeling of which this author is capable'.[147] A more decorous, but even less Shakespearean version appeared in 1767: Christian Felix Weisse's *Romeo und Julie*, subtitled 'a bourgeois tragedy'. A friend of Lessing, Weisse turned the play into a tightly focused domestic drama set almost wholly within the household of Herr and Frau von Capellet. The play hinges on the relationship between Julie and her parents; the feud, and even the love story, are secondary to this family tragedy, which proved compelling and successful in the theatre.[148] Goethe produced his own adaptation of *Romeo and Juliet* in his theatre at Weimar in 1812. He concentrated wholly on the love story, making Romeo a mature figure of idealised dignity. Goethe virtually eliminated the feud, as well as the 'many disharmonious trivialities' which he felt disrupted the tragic mood of Shakespeare's play.[149] A more faithful translation by A. W. Schlegel was published in 1797, enjoying regular revivals into the twentieth century.

A French version by J.-F. Ducis played at the Comédie-Française in 1772, and soon became the most popular Shakespeare play in France, enjoying seven revivals in the period leading up to the revolution. To call it a Shake-speare play is misleading, since Ducis knew no English, and significantly altered the story to conform to the decorum of the French neoclassical theatre. All the comedy of Mercutio and the Nurse is cut; there is neither ball nor balcony scene; Friar Lawrence is omitted altogether. Ducis borrows from Corneille's *Le Cid* the conflict between love and family duty: Romeo is torn between his love for Juliet and his desire to avenge his own father, who has

146 Cohn, *Shakespeare in Germany*, pp. 367–8.   147 Ibid., p. cxxiv.
148 Williams, *German Stage*, p. 61.   149 Quoted in Williams, *German Stage*, p. 101.

suffered terribly at the hands of the Capulets. The overall emphasis of the play is on the horror of the feud, and Romeo and Juliet deliberately sacrifice themselves in order to end it; there is no sleeping potion, only a solemn double suicide among the tombs. This final scene, with its gothic setting, brought out the best in the scenic artist Brunetti, who provided the Comédie-Française with fourteen separate tombs of marble, porphyry, and bronze, some of enormous size, centred on a mausoleum twenty-four feet high and topped with a pyramid.[150] Mercier wrote a prose adaptation in 1782, *The Tombs of Verona*, in which Juliet awoke at the last minute and averted the tragedy.[151] Two musical versions of *Romeo and Juliet* premiered in 1792 and 1793. The first was written by J.-M. B. de Monvel, the actor who had played both Romeo and the Duke in Ducis's play; the second by J.-A. de Ségur. Both were romantic fantasies, with the nightingale and lark duet set to music, elaborately floral funeral scenes, and happy endings in which both lovers survive. Both were very successful, and Ségur's played well into the nineteenth century.

In Italy, *Romeo and Juliet* was first played in the late eighteenth century, in a version based on Mercier's French adaptation. Madame de Staël, who promoted the translation of Shakespeare, wrote that in Italian *Romeo and Juliet* seemed returned 'to its maternal language'.[152] The Veronese quickly recognised the value of the play to the tourist industry; Juliet's supposed balcony became a popular nineteenth-century pilgrimage site.[153] *Romeo and Juliet* has been mounted regularly in Verona's Roman amphitheatre; Eleanora Duse played Juliet there as a teenager.[154] The play was also immensely popular in Italy's puppet theatres, with the *commedia dell'arte* characters Brighella and Arlecchino joining the cast.[155] The famous tragedian Ernesto Rossi played Romeo, both in Italy and on tours throughout Europe and the United States, for nearly thirty years, though many critics felt his 'massive head and portly figure ill accord[ed] with anybody's notion of a love-sick boy'.[156] Nonetheless, Italians responded eagerly to Rossi and to the play, which, along with *Othello*, became Shakespeare's most popular in Italy.[157]

150 Monaco, *French Stage*, p. 96.   151 Jusserand, *Shakespeare in France*, p. 444.

152 Collison-Morley, *Shakespeare in Italy*, p. 80.

153 Bradbrook, 'Romeo', pp. 70–1; Weaver, *Duse*, p. 21.

154 Grebanier, *Then Came Each Actor*, p. 328.

155 Young, *Shakespeare Manipulated*, pp. 31, 107.

156 Frederick Wedmore in the *Academy*, 3 June 1876, quoted in Carlson, *The Italian Shakespearians*, p. 162.

157 Collison-Morley, *Shakespeare in Italy*, p. 164.

MUSICAL ADAPTATIONS OF *ROMEO AND JULIET*

Romeo and Juliet has been from the beginning a favourite work for adaptation into musical form. The love story, the feud, the fanciful Mab speech of Mercutio, the pacific impulse of Friar Lawrence, the power of the Prince – all lend themselves readily to musical interpretation. Not surprisingly, perhaps, most of these versions have come from continental Europe, where music can provide a way to translate Shakespeare when his original language is unavailable.

The first important operatic version of *Romeo and Juliet*, in 1830, was related to its Italian heritage; indeed, it was something of an attempt to reclaim the lovers for Italy. Vincenzo Bellini and his librettist, Felice Romani, bypassed Shakespeare altogether and went back to the original Italian sources of the tale. The title, *I Capuleti e i Montecchi*, reflects Romani's interest in the feuding families, who are linked both to the Guelphs and the Ghibellines of Dante's time and to the political factionalism that still divided Italy in the early nineteenth century. Romeo is the captain of the Ghibelline faction, and has killed the son of Capellio before the action begins; Juliet is engaged to be married to the Guelph Tebaldo. For all the politics of the story, Bellini's music is pure bel canto, filled with tender, lingering melodies of great beauty. Bellini wrote the part of Romeo for a mezzo-soprano, Giuditta Grisi, though in 1966 Claudio Abbado adapted it for a male tenor at La Scala.[158] Bellini gives his female lovers a gorgeous duet in the tomb, ending in a simultaneous *Liebestod*, when they sink down together, in Peter Conrad's phrase, 'languid casualties of Romantic sensibility'.[159]

Hector Berlioz, in his dramatic symphony *Roméo et Juliette*, returns to Shakespeare, though in Garrick's version. Berlioz had seen Harriet Smithson, his future wife, play Juliet in Paris in 1827, and was instantly smitten with her and with the play. His musical adaptation, first performed in 1839, follows the general outlines of Garrick's version. It begins with an orchestral rendering of the opening brawl, followed by a choral version of the Prologue. Many of the main events of the play are represented, in music or song: the Capulet ball, the balcony scene, even Garrick's funeral procession and tomb scene. The admonitions of Friar Lawrence are sung, as is Mercutio's Mab speech. But Berlioz leaves out the voices of Romeo and Juliet themselves, representing them only through the orchestra; instrumental language, he argued in his preface, 'is richer, more varied, less punctuated, and thanks to its very indefinition, incomparably more powerful'.[160]

---

158 Sadie, *New Grove*, p. 106.   159 Conrad, *To Be Continued*, p. 65.
160 Quoted in Bate, *Genius of Shakespeare*, p. 233.

Charles Gounod brought the lovers into the realm of grand opera in 1867. His *Roméo et Juliette*, which follows Shakespeare more closely than either the Bellini or Berlioz versions, enjoyed a series of Paris revivals and was spectacularly staged at the Opéra in 1888. It begins in grand style at the Capulet party, a lavish affair reflecting the materialistic *nouveaux riches* of Second Empire Paris. The meeting of Romeo and Juliet is a minuet-like duet, reflecting the formality of their sonnet exchange in the play.[161] The action progresses through the balcony scene, the wedding at Frère Laurent's cell, the fight in which Mercutio and Tybalt are killed, and the dawn parting of the lovers, all accompanied by sumptuous music. Gounod's Juliette doesn't faint from the potion in the privacy of her bedroom, but in the midst of a grandiose wedding to Paris. Even the lovers' deaths, again staged as a duet, are a 'delicious reverie . . . lush, upholstered, comfortable'.[162] *Roméo et Juliette* was an immediate success and remains the most popular operatic version of the play. Frederick Delius' opera, *A Village Romeo and Juliet* (1907), is based not on Shakespeare but on Gottfried Keller's story of a love-suicide in a Swiss village.

Pyotr Ilyich Tchaikovsky's version of *Romeo and Juliet* is a purely orchestral 'Fantasy Overture' (1869), in which he dramatises the tension between love and power. Written under the spell of his infatuation with a fifteen-year-old boy, Eduard Zak, Tchaikovsky's *Romeo and Juliet* reflects a dominant theme in his work, 'the psychological drama of unfulfilled and frustrated love and of impossible youthful passion consumed by omnipresent death'.[163] Perhaps reflecting his own anxiety and guilt over his homosexuality, Tchaikovsky's work gives the lovers 'only a brief, fugitive interval of lyricism' between the solemnity of Friar Lawrence and the destructive energy of the feud.[164] The lovers' melody is quickly overwhelmed by the tumult of conflict and death. The love theme is last heard, in Tchaikovsky's revisions of 1880, 'twisted, broken, and accompanied by a lacerating dissonance'; with his grim, concluding B minor chords, Tchaikovsky 'drove home the fatalism' of this despairing masterpiece.[165]

Serge Prokofiev's ballet similarly oppresses the lovers between the thrusting rhythms of the feud and the frightening crash of state power, with the threatening Prince, perhaps, standing in for Stalin.[166] Prokofiev and his Soviet scenarists had contemplated a happy ending in which the lovers were spared and the Capulet and Montague factions chastened and subdued.[167]

---

161 Sadie, *New Grove*, p. 549.   162 Conrad, *To Be Continued*, p. 81.

163 Poznansky, *Tchaikovsky*, p. 119.   164 Conrad, *To Be Continued*, p. 81.

165 Brown, *Tchaikovsky*, p. 195.   166 Conrad, *To Be Continued*, p. 82.

167 Clarke and Crisp, *Ballet Goer's Guide*, p. 237.

The final result was something much darker; according to John Gruen, 'for the first time in ballet under Soviet rule, a work went beyond the precepts of Socialist realism to the heart of human tragedy'.[168] The production by Leonid Lavrosky, with Galina Ulanova as Juliet, was staged first at the Kirov in 1940, then at the Bolshoi in 1946, finally appearing in the West at Covent Garden in 1956 and in New York in 1959. It featured staggering spectacle, with a massive force of dancers and thrilling swordplay. The Royal Ballet staged its own version in 1965, with Margot Fonteyn and Rudolf Nureyev, in Kenneth Macmillan's choreography. Prokofiev's music ranks among the greatest orchestral works derived from Shakespeare, along with the *Romeo and Juliet* compositions of Berlioz and Tchaikovsky.[169]

ROMEO AND JULIET IN AMERICA

The first recorded Shakespeare performance on the American continent was *Romeo and Juliet*. It was produced in 1730 by an amateur troupe under the direction of a New York doctor, one Joachimus Bertrand, while Otway's version still held sway in London. Bertrand himself played the Apothecary, joking in his advertisement that he hoped his performance of this role would 'be kindly taken and looked upon as a great condescension in a physician'.[170] In 1752, when Lewis Hallam brought an itinerant company of actors from England, Garrick's version of *Romeo and Juliet* was part of the repertoire. For several years the Hallams performed at various makeshift theatres around the colonies, with Mrs Hallam, the company's leading lady, playing Juliet opposite William Rigby, and eventually opposite her own son, Lewis Jr. *Romeo and Juliet* proved, along with Cibber's *Richard III*, to be the most popular play in the colonies during the period preceding the Revolutionary War.[171] The play held the stage during the growth of the new nation, though even then most American Shakespeareans were born and trained in England. After the War of 1812, English stars began to make frequent American tours. Charles Kean played Romeo in New York, Boston, and Philadelphia, as did Charles Kemble, opposite his daughter Fanny. The first great American Shakespearean, the muscular and commanding Edwin Forrest, was wholly unsuited to Romeo and never attempted it. The first native Romeo of distinction was Charlotte Cushman, who played the role first in Albany in 1837, reprising it regularly around the country until at least 1860.

168 Gruen, *World's Great Ballets*, p. 171.
169 Fiske, 'Shakespeare in the Concert Hall', p. 241.
170 Rankin, *Theatre in Colonial America*, p. 23.
171 Grebanier, *Then Came Each Actor*, p. 50.

Perhaps the most significant American production of the play in the nineteenth century was that with which Edwin Booth opened his grand theatre in New York in 1869. Determined to make the American stage the equal of the British, Booth had spared no expense in constructing one of the most lavishly equipped playhouses in the world. Seating 1,750, with standing room for many more, Booth's Theatre had the most elaborate stage machinery that had ever been seen in the United States.[172] Booth chose *Romeo and Juliet* for his opening production, perhaps under the influence of his infatuation with Mary McVicker, a young Chicago actress to whom he was engaged. From an acting perspective, it was a disastrous choice. McVicker was unequal to a leading tragic role, having 'a face that is too small to be expressive, and too attenuated to be pleasing, and a voice deficient in quality and power'.[173] Booth was equally unsuited to Romeo; his accustomed princely dignity was lost in his effusions of youthful passion, which the critic of the *Herald* described as 'ludicrous by-play under the arch of the balcony, which suggested the active, bustling, glittering harlequin of the pantomime'.[174] His adoption of a blond wig probably didn't help. Like Irving, he was more effective in tragic scenes – the killing of Tybalt, the Friar's cell, the tomb – but Booth still considered it one of his worst performances.[175] The production was sumptuous and elaborate, though there were long waits between scenes on the opening night. The scenery was the most ambitious ever seen in the US, with a sweeping, solidly constructed loggia for Juliet's balcony, and a Romanesque church 12 metres (40 feet) high for the backdrop to Mercutio's death. Booth's direction was highly praised, his crowd scenes particularly: he used over a hundred well-trained fighters for the opening mêlée, and a full *corps de ballet* for the Capulet ball. In spite of the mediocre performances, the production ran successfully for ten weeks. Unfortunately, theatre on this scale was a great financial risk, and Booth declared bankruptcy only five years later.

The New York stage produced several undistinguished revivals. A production at the Union Square Theatre in 1885 achieved popular success but was attacked by critics as showy and artificial; Margaret Mather, as Juliet, was best remembered for rolling down a flight of steps after taking the poison.[176] William Winter called her 'a commonplace person fortuitously placed in a prominent public position'.[177] Another lightweight actress, Cora Brown Potter, was similarly o'er-parted in the 1888 production at the Grand

172 Odell, *Annals*, VIII, p. 423.
173 *New York World*, 4 February 1869, quoted in Shattuck, *American Stage*, I, p. 139.
174 1 March 1869, quoted in Shattuck, *American Stage*, I, p. 140.
175 Winter, *Shakespeare on the Stage*, p. 165.   176 Odell, *Annals*, XIII, p. 25.
177 Winter, *Shakespeare on the Stage*, p. 182.

Opera House, though Kyrle Bellew won some praise as a 'handsome, ir-resolute, romantic Romeo'.[178] Charles Frohman's production of 1899 was a notable disaster: Maude Adams, though successful in light popular drama, 'showed herself unsuited to tragedy and woefully out of place as Juliet, giving a performance which ceased to be frivolous only when it became mildly hysterical'.[179]

Edwin Booth's mantle as the leading American exponent of Shakespeare fell to Julia Marlowe. She first played Juliet, to considerable acclaim, in 1887, but it was her production with her eventual husband, E. H. Sothern, that became an American institution. They first acted *Romeo and Juliet* together in Chicago in 1904, and continued to perform it for twenty years, until Marlowe was fifty-seven and Sothern sixty-five. She was generally recog-nised as the bigger talent, and the production was designed to showcase her. As a producer, Marlowe was unimaginative, opting for rich spectacle and star glamour. She crowded the stage with business – for instance, creating elabo-rate comic by-play for the masquers attending the Capulet ball – and resisted none of the sentimental details that through nineteenth-century tradition had gradually come to clutter the role of Juliet. At the ball, she dropped a flower for Romeo to pick up; she kissed rose petals and dropped them to him from the balcony; she gave her mother a furtive farewell kiss before her potion speech. This scene was crowded with 'points' in the nineteenth-century manner, notably surrounding her vision of Tybalt's ghost, as her promptbook records:

> Juliet starts up looks toward C then as if satisfied that it was only her imagination looks away – then as if conscious of some thing beside her, she turns and her eye seems to rest on some moving form . . . Juliet springs up as if to intercept and then as if she had failed she utters a piercing scream and sinks back against the post of the bed for support –[180]

When the production played in New York, the *New York Times* doubted 'whether the English-speaking stage has any two actors who could surpass the present performance'.[181] Marlowe and Sothern were respectfully received in London in 1907, though Gordon Crosse noted a good deal of ad-libbing and paraphrasing among the company. He thought Marlowe 'undistinguished at first', but felt she 'rose with the character and gave a strong wild rendering of it which was very effective'.[182] The

178 Brereton, *Romeo*, p. 31.   179 Winter, *Shakespeare on the Stage*, p. 189.
180 Promptbook, s70.   181 18 October 1904, Shattuck, *American Stage*, II, p. 266.
182 Crosse, *Diaries*, IV (1907), pp. 65–6.

Sothern–Marlowe production of *Romeo and Juliet* was seen by thousands of people across the US over two decades, and remained the dominant popular image of the play for over a generation.

The first half of the twentieth century saw three big New York successes all centring on star Juliets: Jane Cowl, Eva Le Gallienne, and Katherine Cornell. Cowl's production ran for a record-breaking 174 consecutive performances in 1923. An immensely popular actress in light contemporary drama, Cowl impressed critics with the depth and lyricism of her Juliet. With thick dark hair and huge dark eyes, 'she was convincing to the eye as few Juliets have the good fortune to be', though she was thirty-nine years old.[183] Bernard Grebanier called the look with which she fell in love with Romeo at the ball 'a miracle of acting'.[184] Cowl played Juliet with tenderness and simplicity rather than showy passion; according to the *New York Times*, in the tomb scene she 'rose to that rare height where gesture is impotent and speech most effective when most subdued' (25 January 1923). Rollo Peters, as Romeo, and Dennis King, as Mercutio, gave effective support, but the focus was clearly on Cowl; beyond her performance, Stark Young complained, the production lacked 'a single stamp of invention or idea'.[185]

Eva Le Gallienne, an important director as well as actress, staged *Romeo and Juliet* as part of her Civic Repertory Theatre season in 1930. At the first rehearsal, she told her cast that the play 'had been written by a young man just a few days before. It's a young, vital, gay, passionate and romantic play, and it isn't the Bible'.[186] The production began vigorously with a drum roll and the Capulet/Montague fight spilling out onto the apron; the Prologue was cut. Le Gallienne herself designed the effective unit set of stairways and platforms, along with her collaborator Aline Berstein. The production built up tragic momentum as the play progressed. According to Brooks Atkinson, both Donald Cameron's Romeo and Edward Bromberg's Mercutio were best in their death scenes, and Le Gallienne herself '[grew] steadily in dignity and command as the tragedy unfold[ed]' (*New York Times*, 22 April 1930). He considered Juliet the 'finest and most elastic performance of her career' to date.

The Cornell production, while centred on its star actress, also capitalised on a rich array of native and imported talent in the other roles. In its first New York run in 1934, it featured Edith Evans as the Nurse, Brian Aherne as Mercutio, and the nineteen-year-old Orson Welles as Tybalt. Welles had actually played Mercutio in the out-of-town tryouts, but accepted the demotion in

---

183 *New Republic*, 14 February 1923.   184 Grebanier, *Then Came Each Actor*, p. 452.
185 Ibid.   186 Schanke, *Shattered Applause*, p. 83.

order to make his Broadway début; he also spoke the Prologue, in a gold mask.[187] Romeo was played initially by Basil Rathbone, then by Maurice Evans in the production's second season. Ralph Richardson took over as Mercutio, Tyrone Power played Benvolio, and Florence Reed played the Nurse. The sets, by Jo Mielziner, were among the more inventive of that period. Though they featured fairly standard arrangements of low steps and arched openings for the various interior scenes, they employed painted drops by Mielziner that ranged from the fanciful to the expressionist. The brief Mantua scene, for instance, showed a huge, menacing aqueduct towering in distorted perspective over the characters of Romeo and the Apothecary.

The director, Cornell's husband Guthrie McClintic, emphasised the lightness, speed, and youth of the play. When touring the play in the previous year, he had used the heavily cut Sothern–Marlowe promptbook; for New York he restored all the scenes, cutting only the Musicians and some of the servants' bawdry. Mielziner's sets and McClintic's pacing allowed for fast changes of scene, with no lapses for audience applause. The thirty-six-year-old Cornell emphasised Juliet's youth through an exuberant, athletic physicality. She ran offstage at the end of all her scenes; Richard Lockridge described her as 'an eager child, rushing toward love with arms stretched out'.[188] John Mason Brown called her 'free-limbed and lovely, with enchanting and seemingly unconscious grace'; she seemed to move 'with the rapidity of thought': 'Her Juliet is innocent and unawakened yet hotly eager for love. Later she is vibrant with the all-consuming passion which seizes upon her. Girlish as she is, her heart and mind are mature enough to do justice to the poetic beauty and human anguish Shakespeare wrote into the character of his fourteen-year-old maiden.' Cornell's *Romeo and Juliet* ran for ninety-seven performances in 1934, made a national tour in 1935, and returned to Broadway for a special two-week Christmas engagement that year. It was the most critically acclaimed American production of the century. In its full text, lightness of touch, and fast, fluid staging, it was in many ways comparable to its English contemporary and parallel, John Gielgud's 1935 production at the New Theatre.

WILLIAM POEL AND THE ELIZABETHAN REVIVAL

The twentieth century saw a shift toward fuller texts, leaner stagings, and an attempt to return to the conventions of Shakespeare's theatre. This 'Shakespeare revolution', as J. L. Styan termed it, was led above all by the

187 Brady, *Citizen Welles*, p. 65.
188 Quoted in Brown, *Dramatis Personae*, p. 218. The following quotation is from p. 219.

scholar, actor, and director, William Poel, who devoted his life to rescuing Shakespeare from the proscenium-arch pictorialism of Irving and Beerbohm Tree. Poel's productions for the Elizabethan Stage Society, performed on reconstructed stages in various London halls, were remarkable and sometimes eccentric events. He experimented with boy actresses and 'bad quarto' texts; he put spectators on the stage in Elizabethan dress; he insisted on a rapid and musical delivery of the verse according to something he called 'tuned tones'.[189] But his insistence on letting Shakespeare's scenes flow rapidly and naturally on an open, uncluttered stage had a great impact on twentieth-century production.

Poel's last production for the Elizabethan Stage Society was *Romeo and Juliet*, given at the Royalty Theatre on 5, 6, 9, and 11 May 1905. Poel cast two very young actors, Esmé Percy and Dorothy Minto, as the lovers (Percy would later be Poel's Hamlet). Recalling the performance, Shaw quipped that Poel had

> the ridiculous habit of going to see what Shakespeare said. When he found that a child of fourteen was wanted, his critics exclaimed, 'Ah – but she was an Italian child, and an Italian child of fourteen looks exactly the same as an Englishwoman of forty-five.' Mr Poel did not believe it. He said, 'I will get a child of fourteen', and accordingly he performed *Romeo and Juliet* in that way and for the first time it became endurable.[190]

The young lovers had pathos and passion, and the play moved quickly, with few cuts, on a bare Elizabethan stage constructed within the Royalty's proscenium. In *The Stage-Version of 'Romeo and Juliet'*, Poel argued emphatically for the inclusion of scenes regularly cut from Victorian productions. He insisted on the dramatic effectiveness of the normally cut scenes in the Capulet household that frame the famous potion speech, calling the alteration of these scenes 'perhaps the most dramatic episode in the whole play':

> We are shown Capulet's household busy with preparations for the marriage-feast, and the father, now bent on having a 'great ado' . . . While the poor child lies prostrate upon her bed in the likeness of death, we are shown the dawn of the morning, the rousing and bustle of the household; we hear the bridal march in the distance . . .[191]

Poel also emphasised the great public scenes of the feud, which give context and meaning to the lovers' tragedy. Complaining that Irving had cut all but

---

189 Styan, *Shakespeare Revolution*, p. 49.
190 Speaight, *William Poel*, p. 192.
191 Poel, *Stage-Version*, pp. 19–20. The following quotation is from p. 26.

a few lines following the lovers' deaths, Poel wrote that 'no stage-version of *Romeo and Juliet* is consistent with Shakespeare's intentions that does not give prominence to the hatred of the two houses and retain intact the three "crowd scenes" – the one at the opening of the play, the second in the middle, and the third at the end'.

An interesting reemergence of the Poel tradition occurred in 1976, when George Murcell directed a nearly uncut *Romeo and Juliet* at St George's Theatre, London, an Elizabethan-style playhouse recreated by C. Walter Hodges (*SQ* 28: 2, Spring 1977). With Elizabethan costumes and staging techniques, the production provided an effective realisation of Poel's methods. Night scenes were conveyed without light changes, by actors carrying torches; the tomb problems were easily solved by using the perimeter of the large stage to suggest the churchyard. Murcell did use actresses in the women's roles; Sarah Badel played Juliet to Peter McEnery's Romeo. The real centre of the production, however, was Joseph O'Conor's magisterial Friar Lawrence, one of the most distinguished recent performances of the role.

Poel's most influential follower, Harley Granville-Barker, never directed *Romeo and Juliet*, though his *Preface* to the play shows Poel's influence, and in turn affected many subsequent productions. Granville-Barker is particularly stern on the subject of cutting the text:

> To omit the final scurry of Montagues and Capulets and citizens of Verona to the tomb and the Friar's redundant story for the sake of finishing upon the more poignant note of Juliet's death is, as we have seen, to falsify Shakespeare's whole intention; and to omit the sequel to the drinking of the potion is as bad and worse![192]

As to the scenery, Granville-Barker remarks that the producer 'must devise such scenery as will not deform, obscure, or prejudice its craftsmanship or its art'.

Poel's impact on the play was gradual. In 1913 Beerbohm Tree staged it in a traditional Victorian manner, with elaborate scenery and a cut and rearranged text. In his diary, Gordon Crosse, a convert to Poel's approach, complained that 'there is no excuse for playing I iv as a continuation of I ii, and then I iii and v as a single scene – it is merely rearranging Shakespeare for stage convenience'.[193] The nineteenth-century tradition of cumbersome realistic scenery passed more quickly on the Continent, because of the

192 Granville-Barker, *Prefaces*, IV, p. 67. The following quotation is from p. 65.
193 Crosse, *Diaries*, V (1913), p. 157.

general aesthetic tendencies of modernism and the influence of designer–theorists Adolphe Appia and Edward Gordon Craig. Alexander Tairov, at Moscow's Kamerny Theatre, used a constructivist unit set for his 1921 *Romeo and Juliet*, so that the action swirled around a dynamic arrangement of steps and platforms that filled the stage.[194] Jean Cocteau staged an experimental, poetic version of the play in Paris in 1924, with a mobile set derived from Italian futurism that could 'decompose and rebuild like a house of cards'.[195] In Warsaw, Arnold Szyfman used an expressionist combination of soaring, nonrealistic spaces and starkly angled lighting for the Polish Theatre production of 1931.[196] The eccentric and visionary director Terence Gray brought modernist inventiveness to Britain in 1929 with a production of *Romeo and Juliet* at his Cambridge Festival Theatre. Using a permanent set of five medieval-style mansions, continuous action, and colourful flamenco costumes inspired by the films of Rudolph Valentino, Gray and his designer Doria Paston created a playful visual spectacle that broke radically with the Victorian tradition.[197]

Even mainstream British *Romeo and Juliet* productions in the twenties and early thirties came to embrace the revolution in staging methods. Gordon Crosse praised Barry Jackson's 1924 production, with the young John Gielgud and Gwen Ffrangcon-Davies, for the full text and rapid pace allowed by a single unit set: 'the columns of the public place of I i remained in place as the pillars of Capulet's hall . . . the musicians' gallery in that hall reappeared as Juliet's balcony'.[198] Crosse noted ' how happily the dialogue of Peter and the musicians (which I don't think I have ever heard on the stage before) relieved the tension just at the right places. Sh. always justifies himself when the manager (and actors) will let him.'[199]

Gielgud himself felt the scenery 'was hard and rather crude, though it solved the problem of speed very satisfactorily , and the production was commendably free from cuts or extraneous business'.[200] Ffrangcon-Davies was the recognised star of the production, highly praised for her childlike simplicity and beautiful speech. Gielgud was unhappy with his own performance: 'I had neither the looks, the dash, nor the virility to make a real success of it, however well I spoke the verse and felt the emotion'; in addition, Gielgud felt that he 'looked a sight . . . a mixture of Rameses of Egypt and a

---

194 Kennedy, *Looking at Shakespeare*, pp. 94–6.
195 Oxenhandler, 'Theatre of Jean Cocteau', p. 130.
196 Kennedy, *Looking at Shakespeare*, pp. 103–4.
197 Ibid., pp. 117–18.   198 Crosse, *Diaries*, VIII (1924), p. 151.
199 Ibid., p. 153.
200 Gielgud, *Early Stages*, p. 51. The following quotation is from p. 50.

Victorian matron'. Nonetheless, he was converted to the Poel method of Elizabethan-style playing, and adopted it when he directed the play at Oxford in 1932.

Gielgud directed a cast of male undergraduates, with two professionals brought in for the female leads: Peggy Ashcroft and Edith Evans. Molly MacArthur's set used a backdrop of three curtained arches, which could be preset for various locations, allowing the production to proceed quickly from scene to scene; the open space in front was used for large crowd scenes. The costumes were by the design team Motley (Margaret and Sophia Harris and Elizabeth Montgomery). Among the undergraduate cast members were Christopher Hassall as Romeo, George Devine (later director of the Royal Court) as Mercutio, Hugh Hunt as the Friar, and Terence Rattigan as one of the Musicians. Gielgud rehearsed the cast rigorously to develop a quick and poetic delivery of the verse, and capitalised on their youth for a swift and energetic production. After a successful run in Oxford, the company gave a single Sunday performance at the New Theatre in London, where Gielgud's historic revival would take place three years later.

GIELGUD AND OLIVIER, 1935–1936

Gielgud's *Romeo and Juliet* at the New Theatre in 1935–6 has become a landmark in the history of the play. It was at the time the single most successful run of any Shakespeare play, with 183 performances. Many aspects of the Oxford production remained. The swiftly alternating scenes, on a single variable set, were repeated, though this time Motley designed both set and costumes. Ashcroft and Evans repeated their roles, further developing their highly successful characterisations. Gielgud played Mercutio to the Romeo of Laurence Olivier, exchanging parts, by design, after the first six weeks of the run.

The production was put together in only three weeks. The Motley design provided a variety of acting spaces that could be curtained off when not in use. There were two arched alcoves on either side of a central tower, which had both upper and lower acting areas. Each scene was given in a clearly defined location, occupying one or two of the acting spaces; the full stage was used for large scenes such as the Capulet party or the opening brawl. Gordon Crosse described it as a 'remarkably effective piece of modern staging . . . a reproduction under modern conditions of the upper and lower stages . . . The arrangement of IV iii, iv, v, without any change or even the drawing of a curtain, was one of the most Elizabethan things I have seen.'[201] Juliet's

201 Crosse, *Diaries*, xv (1935), pp. 93–5.

bedroom was on a raised dais in one of the side alcoves, allowing it to remain visible while Romeo descended from the balcony in 3.5, and after Juliet took the potion in 4.3.

The only drawbacks of the setting were that it made the small stage of the New Theatre rather cramped, and the black velvet curtains muted any sense of Italian heat; Gielgud later added a strip of blue sky to the brawl scenes. Both scenery and costumes were elegantly decorated with colourful patterns in the style and palette of the Italian Renaissance. The Montagues, conceived by Gielgud as more aristocratic, wore rich reds and greens, while the bourgeois Capulets wore darker colours, with the exception of Juliet. Peggy Ashcroft's costumes alluded to the *Primavera* of Botticelli, making her a figure of freshness and youth in floral-printed green.[202] Romeo went from moody blue and grey to tragic crimson velvet for the end.

The fluid staging allowed Gielgud to play a nearly full text, almost unprecedented in productions of the play. Aside from the second chorus and the Musicians' banter, little was cut; with one interval after Mercutio's death, the production ran over three hours, but the pace was fast and grew faster over the course of the run.

The remarkable cast included Glen Byam Shaw as Benvolio, Harry Andrews as Tybalt, George Devine as Peter, and the young Alec Guinness as the Apothecary. Edith Evans's Nurse was considered by many to be the finest modern performance of the role: 'I have never seen a better Nurse than Edith Evans. And I don't believe anyone ever has . . . Coarse, garrulous, wordy, dominant, massive with the accretions of an experience that has left her fundamentally shallow-pated, it is a mighty achievement in characterization.'[203] Evans used a coarse country accent and a wheezing, shambling walk; W. A. Darlington called her 'the most real old woman you ever saw, earthy as a potato, slow as a carthorse, cunning as a badger' (*Daily Telegraph*, 18 October 1935). G. W. Stonier thought her the core of the production: 'Whenever she was on the stage, reprimanding, soothing, or merely getting her breath, the lovers both seemed children, and it needed her magnificently vital presence to give their story depth' (*New Statesman*, 26 October 1935). Evans played the Nurse again twenty-six years later at Stratford, and made an audio recording of the part the same year.[204]

Ashcroft was also very well received, playing Juliet as 'a child who in love, and in nothing but love, is a woman', according to *The Times* (18 October 1935). 'She has not had time to think, only to feel . . . The petals have hardly

202 Levenson, *Romeo* (1987), p. 61.   203 Farjeon, *Shakespearean Scene*, p. 122.
204 Shakespeare Recording Society SRS-M 228, 1961 (with Albert Finney and Claire Bloom).

5 Laurence Olivier and Peggy Ashcroft in John Gielgud's production at the New Theatre, 1935, featuring Motley's flexible set with a central tower flanked by archways. According to Gielgud, Olivier's 'beautiful pose as he stood beneath the balcony expressed the essence of the character to perfection'.

opened when the flower is crushed.' Although twenty-eight at the time of the performance, Ashcroft looked very young, and she emphasised the childlike aspect of the character. Accordingly, most critics found her better in the first half of the play; James Agate felt 'the eager and touching childishness could not be bettered . . . I found the performance heartrending until it came to the part where the heart should be rent' (*Sunday Times*, 20 October 1935). However, Stephen Williams, in the *Evening Standard* (18 October) wrote, 'I cannot imagine a sweeter, sincerer or more melting Juliet.' The *New York Times* critic felt that 'the lovely eagerness of the child moves perpetually hand in hand with the passionate eagerness of the woman, and this entirely unrealistic treatment of the character gives it a reality that is purely poetic' (17 November 1935).

As to the leading men, Gielgud had greater success with the critics in both roles, but Olivier's influence came to dominate the role of Romeo in the twentieth century. The two have come to be seen as representing two distinct acting traditions, Gielgud harking back to the poetic beauties of the nineteenth century (Ellen Terry was his great-aunt), Olivier forward to the naked emotional realism of the post-war era. In an interview with Kenneth Tynan, Olivier compared himself with Gielgud:

> I've always though that we were the reverses of the same coin, perhaps . . .
> the top half John, all spiritual, all spirituality, all beauty, all abstract things;
> and myself as all earth, blood, humanity . . . when I was playing Romeo
> I was carrying a torch, I was trying to sell realism in Shakespeare. I believed
> in it with my whole soul and I believed that Johnny was not doing that
> enough. I thought that he was paying attention – to the exclusion of the
> earth – to all music, all lyricism, and I was for the other side of the coin. I
> dived for that.[205]

Olivier opened as Romeo, playing him as an exuberant, passionate Italian adolescent, suntanned and athletic. Alec Guinness thought him 'undoubt-edly glamorous' and 'remarkably beautiful', but felt his performance was 'a bit cheap – striving after theatrical effects and so on – and making nonsense of the verse'.[206] Most critics concurred: 'His voice has neither the tone nor the compass and his blank verse is the blankest I ever heard' (*Evening Standard*, 18 October 1935). Yet he had his defenders: 'Mr Olivier, it is true, never made his lines ring, so far as speech went all his effects were obtained by prose; and yet he seemed to me an excellent Romeo – abrupt, passionate, ill-fated – how well he looked!' (*New Statesman*, 26 October 1935). St John Ervine in the *Observer* thought him the best Romeo he had seen: '. . . here at last is a young and gallant Romeo, a manly Romeo, a lad to take a girl by storm, and be taken so himself . . . I have seen few sights so moving as the spectacle of Mr Olivier's Romeo, stunned with Juliet's beauty, fumbling for words with which to say his love' (3 November 1935).

Gielgud was felt to be 'the Mercutio of tradition. He lived like a rake and died like a gentleman' (*Evening Standard*, 18 October 1935). He drew praise for his elegantly poetic Mab speech, 'the words fluttering from Mercutio's brain as lightly as the elfin vision that they draw'.[207] But most of the London critics were happier when the actors traded roles after six weeks:

> Now that John Gielgud and Laurence Olivier have changed parts, the
> production, which could hardly have gained in emotional effect, gains
> greatly in artistic balance. Mr Gielgud's Romeo is more romantic than was
> Mr Olivier's, has a much greater sense of the beauty of the language, and
> substitutes a thoughtfulness that suits the part for an impetuosity that did
> not. And if there were doubts as to whether Mr Olivier was well cast as

205 Quoted in Hayman, *Gielgud*, p. 97.   206 Quoted in Gourlay, *Olivier*, p. 56.
207 Dent, *Nocturnes*, p. 13.

Romeo, there can be none about his Mercutio. This is a brilliant piece of work – full of zest, humour, and virility.

Daily Telegraph, 29 November 1935

Some of the discussion of Gielgud's Romeo, however, had an edge of faint praise about it, as though critics were beginning to acknowledge Olivier's achievement: 'As Romeo Mr Olivier was about twenty times as much in love with Juliet as Mr Gielgud is. But Mr Gielgud speaks most of the poetry far better than Mr Olivier.'[208] 'Mr Olivier's Romeo showed himself very much in love but rather butchered the poetry, whereas Mr Gielgud carves the verse so exquisitely . . . but I have the feeling that this Romeo never warms up to Juliet till she is cold' (*Sunday Times*, 1 December 1935).

Over the years, Olivier's performance has had the greater impact. Gielgud himself said, 'I knew I was more lyrically successful as Mercutio in the Queen Mab scene, but his virility and panache in the other scenes, his furious and skilful fencing and the final exit to his death, were certainly more striking in the part than anything I was able to achieve, while his performance as Romeo was infinitely romantic. His beautiful pose as he stood beneath the balcony expressed the essence of the character to perfection.'[209] The production, with its contrasting leads, marked a division between the late nineteenth-century conception of a melancholy and poetic Romeo and the modern emphasis on youth, sexuality, and violence.

PETER BROOK AT STRATFORD, 1947

Romeo and Juliet played frequently at Stratford-upon-Avon from the opening of the Shakespeare Memorial Theatre in 1879, but there were few performances of distinction. The first Stratford production to make a real mark in the history of the play was one that initially displeased nearly all the critics. It was directed in 1947 by the twenty-one-year-old *enfant terrible*, Peter Brook. Having established himself the previous year with an enchanting *Love's Labour's Lost*, Brook now took on *Romeo and Juliet*. He made his intentions clear in a press conference, reported in the *Birmingham Post* of 10 March 1947:

> It is our job . . . to forget the conventions of painted curtains and traditional business, and to do everything to make you feel that the play is something new . . . we must make you feel this is not the *Romeo and Juliet* you have all loved and read but that you have come into an unknown theatre in an unknown town prepared for a new experience . . . To present Shakespeare

208 Farjeon, *Shakespearean Scene*, p. 123.   209 Gielgud, *Acting Shakespeare*, p. 48.

alive without being vulgar, and exciting without being crude is the function
of the Shakespearean producer.

Brook's was the most highly anticipated production of the season. His
interpretation was much discussed in the press even before the production
opened: 'Intense hate, violent passion, and no sentimentality are Peter
Brook's theme which he constantly instils into the actors, and which he has
distilled from what he maintains is the play's most telling line – "For now,
these hot days, is the mad blood stirring"' (*Leamington Spa Courier*, 21
March 1947). After a highly publicised search, Brook cast an eighteen-year-
old, Daphne Slater, as Juliet; his Romeo, Laurence Payne, was twenty-six.
He conceived Romeo and Juliet as 'as two children lost among the warring
fury of the Southern houses'.[210] Many of the critics thought they *were* lost.
The Times found Slater 'childlike and nothing more', and called Payne
'a Romeo with scarcely a note of music in him' (7 October 1947). Harold
Hobson found Payne an utter failure and thought Slater's Juliet too immature to communicate Juliet's passion: 'As the hot words burn her mouth she
seems like a precocious child babbling of things she doesn't understand.'[211]
The performance that gained most notice was the young Paul Scofield as an
unusually grave Mercutio, 'who really has seen the fairies and wishes,
perhaps, that he had not' (*Sunday Times*, 6 April 1947). One of the most
memorable moments of the production was the Mab speech, which Scofield
gave 'lying on the stage in the torchlight, arms raised and eyes rapt as he he let
the words flower into the silence of the grotesquely-visaged masquers'.[212]
Brook's setting, designed by Rolf Gérard, used a broad empty space surrounded by miniature crenellated walls, suggesting an Italian town baking
under a 'great tent of Mediterranean blue'.[213] Unit set pieces were introduced for the central scenes, so that Juliet's bedroom and balcony could
remain visible from 3.5 to 4.5. Brook expended great effort on the atmosphere and the crowd scenes: 'Hot arid, bare, brown and enclosed, [Brook's
Verona] resembles . . . old Baghdad, thronged with negroes, Jews and water-
sellers' (*Theatre World*, 13, June 1947, p. 29). *The Times* acknowledged that
Brook 'invariably achieves decorative significance with crowded rooms or
street scenes, and surely never have the factions brawled with more vigour or
verisimilitude' (7 April 1947). Hobson also felt that 'all the life of this production is packed into the burning pavements under the glaring sun'.[214]
Brook's text was also unconventional and corresponded to his interests in
the play. There were some deep cuts: after Juliet's death the play ended, with

---

210 Trewin, *Shakespeare on the English Stage*, p. 205.   211 Hobson, *Theatre*, p. 145.
212 Trewin, *Shakespeare on the English Stage*, p. 206.   213 Ibid.
214 Hobson, *Theatre*, p. 144.

6 Daphne Slater and Laurence Payne, under the 'great tent of Mediterranean blue' in Peter Brook's hot-blooded, controversial Stratford production. Shakespeare Memorial Theatre, 1947.

the Chorus speaking the Prince's final words. The scene wherein the Friar gives Juliet the potion (4.1) was at first cut entirely, and later reinstated in an abridged version (*Times*, 7 October 1947). The wedding scene, 2.6, was replaced with the version in the first quarto. On the other hand, Brook included many scenes that had usually been cut, including the bawdy jesting of the servants in 1.1 and Mercutio and friends in 2.4, Benvolio's recapitulation of the fight in 3.1, and most of Romeo's ravings in the Friar's cell (3.3). Brook originally included even the Musicians from 4.5, but cut them just before opening.

Summing up the critical response to the production, *The Times* of 7 October 1947 reported, 'It was considered that the poetry and passion of the tragedy were by no means well lost for the sake of much clever stagecraft. Yet the stagecraft, with its realistic crowd scenes and elaborate duelling, pleased festival audiences, and the spectacle arranged by Mr Peter Brook became the most popular thing of the year.' Brook felt vindicated:

> If my production of *Romeo and Juliet* has done nothing else, it has at least aroused controversy, which in itself is a good thing . . . What I have attempted is to break away from the popular conception of *Romeo and Juliet* as a pretty-pretty, sentimental love story, and to get back to the violence, the passion, and the excitement of the stinking crowds, the feuds, the intrigues. To recapture the poetry and the beauty that arise from the Veronese sewer, and to which the story of the two lovers is merely incidental.[215]

The idea that the lovers could be 'merely incidental' to the play was indeed a radical one, but one that was borne out by many productions in the remaining half of the century.

A series of significant British productions in the 1950s extended Brook's influence. Sets became more streamlined and settings more Italian; the lovers grew younger and the fights grew fiercer. In 1952, Hugh Hunt's Old Vic production to some extent vindicated Brook's innovations, gaining almost universal praise for its sun-drenched porticos, youthful cast, and dangerous, exciting fights. Critics who had damned him as Brook's Romeo heaped praise on Laurence Payne, who not only choreographed the duels but played a Tybalt 'of smouldering rage and fierce passions' (*Times*, 16 September 1952), 'the night's one completely flawless performance' (*Daily Sketch*, 24 September 1952). The twenty-one-year-old Claire Bloom was 'childlike and touching' in the love scenes (*Times*) but criticised for poor verse-speaking; 'As a romantic child the Juliet is more affecting than as a tragic woman' (*Punch*, 1 October 1952). Kenneth Tynan, however, called her the best Juliet he had ever seen, insisting 'that what Shakespeare demands is not verse-speaking but verse-acting', and praising her for being 'impatient and mettlesome, proud and vehement, not a blindfold child of milk'.[216] Alan Badel's Romeo lacked traditional romantic good looks but was convincing as 'an adolescent Romeo wildly extravagant in his love' (*Times*). One critic, who

215 Brook, *Shifting Point*, p. 71.   216 Tynan, *Curtains*, pp. 32–3.

thought him the best Romeo since Olivier, praised his 'resolve to act the part with a Southern intensity, to shun a false restraint, and for once to give the passionate speeches their full weight and drive' (*Daily Sketch*). Above all, critics applauded the 'atmosphere of lusty and hot-blooded youth which pervades the production'; the very thing Brook had been attacked for five years before (*Daily Telegraph*, 16 September 1952).

A pair of Stratford productions by Glen Byam Shaw, in 1954 and 1958, carried on the new tradition, though with less complete success. In the first, film star Laurence Harvey was a dashing young Romeo to the dimpled Juliet of twenty-year-old Zena Walker in a smooth, swift, nearly uncut production. What was missing was the Italian heat of Hunt's production. The set, by Motley, was an updated, streamlined version of their setting for Gielgud: an elegant, symmetrical construction of unpainted wood that could accommodate fluid scene changes. To critics, however, it suggested 'a Swedish furnishing store rather than hot, sandy Verona' (*Manchester Guardian*, 29 April 1954). Derek Granger complained, 'Here we have a Verona that seems almost cool in Midsummer and though the pace has the appropriately ardent rapidity the effect of the stage picture throughout is one of pale neatness' (*Financial Times*, 28 April 1954). The 1958 version likewise had youth and pace, but lacked fire. Richard Johnson was a handsome and vigorous Romeo; Dorothy Tutin made a noteworthy Stratford début as a 'touchingly childlike' Juliet (*Times*, 9 April 1958). The Motley designs were more decorative than in 1958, and while they allowed a well-paced and stylish production, they still reflected the general aesthetic of the Gielgud version nearly twenty-five years before. The definitive new version, the next major milestone after Gielgud and Brook, was to come two years later at the Old Vic, in the legendary production of the young Italian director Franco Zeffirelli.

ZEFFIRELLI, 1960

Franco Zeffirelli's production achieved what Brook had attempted: to free *Romeo and Juliet* from lyricism, prettiness, and the weight of the past, and present it as a vivid and immediate play about youth. It is no coincidence that it opened in 1960, ushering in a decade wherein young people gained a political, cultural, and economic status they had never had before. Zeffirelli commented on the historical ironies of the production in his autobiography. When he first met his young cast in London, he had to browbeat the men into growing their hair long:

> at first the boys were embarrassed, they wore their hair under berets on the underground and were galled by the jokes their friends made. But when they

started to act they saw the point – instead of the posing a wig brings with it they acted freely, moving their heads likes lions tossing their manes . . . by a strange coincidence, at the end of the run the fashion for long hair was in full swing, so our curious cast came to seem more and more in tune with the youngsters who packed the gallery and the gods. Romeo and Juliet slotted neatly into the world of the Beatles, of flower-power and peace-and-love.[217]

Of course, the way for Zeffirelli's production was paved, not only by Brook, Hunt, and Byam Shaw, but by John Osborne and Leonard Bernstein. *Look Back in Anger* had alerted the British theatre to the power of angry youth, and indeed Zeffirelli's Mercutio, Alec McCowen, was often compared to Osborne's misanthropic Jimmy Porter. *West Side Story*, which opened on Broadway in 1957, achieved startling contemporary relevance by resetting *Romeo and Juliet* amid the youth gangs of New York City. The importance of *West Side Story*, in redefining Shakespeare's play as a story of youth violence and generational conflict, cannot be overstressed. Meanwhile, in London, a revolution in acting styles was under way, as vigorous young talent poured out of drama schools with regional dialects intact, privileging feeling and authenticity over classical technique. Zeffirelli, an Italian opera director then in his thirties, seized the moment for a production that remained the dominant influence on the play for the rest of the twentieth century.

Zeffirelli designed his own settings, of peeling whitewashed walls that could double for indoor and outdoor scenes. Compared to the spare, elegant unit sets then in fashion, Zeffirelli's looked heavy, solid and earthy. The Montagues and Capulets were not sumptuously dressed aristocrats but middle-class Italians; in place of the traditional open white shirt, dark wig, and velvet cloak, John Stride's Romeo wore 'comfortable, hard-wearing, familiar clothes' in which he 'could sit, squat, run, or stroll; he could run his hand through his hair or look insignificant among a crowd'.[218] Judi Dench, who played an eager young Juliet, recalled that 'the audience gasped when the curtain went up because it was all misty in this very real-looking Italian street and people were throwing out sheets to air: nothing as realistic had been seen for a very long time in Shakespeare'.[219] Zeffirelli's neorealist environment complemented his approach to the characters, who were, in Kenneth Tynan's phrase, 'neither larger nor smaller than life; they were precisely life-size, and we watched them living, spontaneously and unpredictably' (*Observer*, 9 October 1960).

217 Zeffirelli, *Zeffirelli: The Autobiography*, pp. 162–3.
218 Brown, *SS* 15 (1962), p. 147.
219 Dench, in Bate and Jackson, *Shakespeare*, p. 201.

7 Joanna Dunham and John Stride as passionate young lovers in the international tour of Franco Zeffirelli's celebrated Old Vic production (1960–2).

The street life of Verona was at the centre of the production, with wholly convincing scenes of young people idling, playing, fighting, and making love: ' they ate apples and threw them, splashed each other with water, mocked, laughed, shouted'.[220] The fights were not swashbuckling swordplay but adolescent scrapping; Mercutio was killed accidentally after his fight with Tybalt was more or less over. The lovers were equally prosaic; Judi Dench 'was made

220 Brown, *SS* 15 (1962), p. 148.

to flop over the rail of the balcony, like a sulky child who doesn't agree that it's bedtime', while John Stride scrambled awkwardly up a tree in order to kiss her.[221] Some critics felt such choices undermined the dignity of the play, but Zeffirelli defended them in relation to his overall goal: 'to make the audience understand that the classics are living flesh'.[222] Many critics approved: Henry Hewes, reviewing the New York tour, noted that 'instead of the usual poetic and static reciting of sentiments, we have two hot-blooded kids trying to get at each other, with all the awkwardness and embarassment of inexperienced lovers. The result is highly entertaining and predominantly humorous' (*Saturday Review*, 3 March 1962). John Stride and Joanna Dunham, who took over the role of Juliet for the tour, succeeded in conveying 'consuming young love with its desire, sweetness and uncontainable rashness', according to Howard Taubman (*New York Times*, 14 February 1962).

Even the production's defenders conceded that it was weaker in the later scenes. The prosaic style was at odds with the long speeches of formalised despair and lamentation; Zeffirelli clearly had less interest in the figures of adult authority than in the youth of the streets, and, as Tynan put it, 'in the tangible, credible reality that he has created, magic potions have no place' (*Observer*, 9 October 1960). Further, some of his cuts were very severe; the production moved directly from Juliet's supposed death to Romeo's line, 'Is it e'en so? then I defy you, stars!' (5.1.24). Even Judi Dench felt that Zeffirelli 'had no respect for the verse at all, and cut it appallingly, hacking at it, for which he was rightly criticized. He left the text to the actors, and it didn't survive at all well.'[223] Long speeches, such as Queen Mab and Juliet's potion speech, were broken up with stage business, muting their rhetorical force. Yet the lovers 'made their own clarity and their own modern cut-down poetry', according to one critic.[224] The production overcame its shortcomings, and initially bad reviews, to achieve a huge international success, extended by Zeffirelli's 1968 film. Kenneth Tynan called it 'a revelation, even perhaps a revolution', and it proved to be both in the history of the play.

MODERN PRODUCTIONS WORLDWIDE

Romeo and Juliet was performed around the world in the twentieth century, and the most interesting productions were often in countries where English was not the native language. The New York stage has not had a notable

---

221 Speaight, *SQ* 12 (1961), p. 426.
222 Quoted in Loney, *Staging Shakespeare*, p. 252.
223 Dench, in Bate and Jackson, *Shakespeare*, p. 201.
224 *Plays and Players*, November 1960, quoted in Levenson, *Romeo* (1987), p. 97.

success since Cornell's in the thirties. Laurence Olivier and Vivien Leigh mounted a disastrous revival in 1940. Encumbered by a slow-moving set and heavy costumes, the production dragged along, and Olivier was unable to recreate the fiery Romeo of his London performance. Equally unsuccessful was a 1951 production featuring Olivia de Havilland. The traditional American model of a production designed to showcase a major star clearly no longer worked. A more youth-orientated production, showing the Zeffirelli influence, failed at Circle in the Square in the early seventies, and *Romeo and Juliet* was a particularly limp entry in Joseph Papp's Shakespeare Marathon at the Public Theatre in the eighties. Peter MacNicol was miscast as Romeo opposite Cynthia Nixon's fresh but unmoving Juliet. Courtney B. Vance contributed a brave performance, playing Mercutio as flamboyantly gay, but could infuse little life into Les Waters's lacklustre production, which Frank Rich condemned as 'so devoid of pulse that it seems a form of indentured servitude' (*New York Times*, 25 May 1988). Some of the more successful American versions of *Romeo and Juliet* have come from the regional repertory theatre scene. In the 1980s a number of distinguished actresses led successful regional productions: Tovah Feldshuh in San Diego, Mary Beth Hurt at the Long Wharf Theatre, Amy Irving at Seattle Repertory, Amanda Plummer at La Jolla Playhouse.[225]

In Canada, *Romeo and Juliet* has been performed regularly at the Stratford Festival in Ontario. Michael Langham's 1960 production was in the traditional vein, with bright Renaissance costumes and a touch of idealisation, led by Christopher Plummer as a dashing and romantic Mercutio. Julie Harris's voice was not ideally suited to the demands of Juliet, but her grave and introspective stage presence gave her performance great impact. With her realistic modern acting, she was the emotional centre for the production's pageantry. Bruno Gerussi made a strong Stratford début as a virile and tender Romeo. The unlocalised Elizabethan stage of the Stratford Festival Theatre allowed effective solutions to the traditional staging problems of bedroom, balcony, and tomb. The tomb scene featured two arresting pieces of business. Juliet awoke in time to watch Romeo die, in the Garrick tradition, though without additional dialogue. At the end, the two families rushed jealously forward to reclaim their dead children, only to find that the bodies still clung together in death; only then did the impulse toward reconciliation emerge.[226]

A subsequent Stratford production (1968) explored the ethnic and cultural divisions in Canada by using a French Canadian actress, Louise Marleau, opposite Christopher Walken's Romeo. A Napoleonic setting

225 Londré, '*Romeo*', p. 628.   226 Ibid., p. 639.

brought the action out of Renaissance prettiness but ill suited the play. Douglas Campbell's staging used a raised platform in the centre of the Stratford stage, which served both for Juliet's bed and her bier, as well as a seating area for the street scenes; it was rather awkwardly in the way during the ball. The lovers actually made little impression; the most memorable performance came from Leo Ciceri's Mercutio. Much older than Romeo, a battle-hardened soldier with physical and emotional scars, he gave a tragic power to the play's ordinarily comic first half. Ciceri, noting connections between Mercutio and Jaques in *As You Like It*, played the Queen Mab speech as a sardonic catalogue of human folly, which 'suddenly brings him face to face with his own realities and his own memories of his life as a soldier when the glamour and the glory is drowned in fear, filth, rapine and horror'. [227] Mercutio's impulse to fight Tybalt was suicidal, a product of his disillusionment at finding the world of peace no different from that of war. He died cursing both houses as an embittered veteran – a powerful statement in 1968, at the height of the Vietnam conflict.

Productions outside the English-speaking world were even more aggressive in their use of the play to make political statements. As Dennis Kennedy has argued, directors who present Shakespeare in translation are often much freer to take strong interpretive lines. [228] Felicia Harrison Londré has observed that *Romeo and Juliet* was particularly popular in Central and Eastern Europe during the cold war era. [229] At the Vakhtangov Theatre in Moscow, Iosif Rapoport staged the play as a political drama, with the hapless lovers destroyed by social forces. The depiction of the Prince as violently abusive to his subjects represented an overt critique of medieval tyranny, and perhaps a more subtle one of Stalinism. Otomar Krejca's Czech production also had submerged political implications, though the general tone was lyrical and elegiac. Mercutio's cry, 'A plague a'both your houses!' (3.1.97), resonated powerfully in 1963 Prague, which was struggling to find an alternative to both Western capitalism and Soviet totalitarianism. The production was distinguished by a remarkable design by Josef Svoboda, which allowed fluid and graceful interplay between highly expressive lighting and moving scenic units. A 1970 Moscow production by Anatoly Efros condemned commercial greed, represented by a fat bourgeois Capulet, but also upheld the youthful idealism of the lovers against a cynical and life-denying world. Tamás Major's overtly political Hungarian production of 1971 made

---

227 In Raby, *The Stratford Scene*, p. 162.
228 Kennedy, *Foreign Shakespeare*, p. 16.
229 Londré, '*Romeo*', p. 625. The following discussion is much indebted to her catalogue of productions.

the love of the protagonists merely a symbol of resistance; the feud was an outright civil war, and the Prince represented a crushing military authority.

THE ROYAL SHAKESPEARE COMPANY, 1960–2000

While British productions have not been as explicitly political as those on the Continent, they have followed the same general interpretive trend. In the latter half of the twentieth century, *Romeo and Juliet* was transformed, in production and perception, from a play about love into a play about hate. Modern productions have tended to emphasise the feud over the love story, and have used it to comment on a variety of social ills: from the competitiveness and greed of the parents, to the sexual aggression of the young men, to ethnic or cultural difference as a source of conflict. The productions of the Royal Shakespeare Company, from its inception in 1960 to the end of the century, illustrate this trend clearly.

Peter Hall directed the play, in what some critics termed an 'anti-Zeffirelli production', in 1961.[230] Staged with Hall's trademark coolness and clarity, on a cumbrous, gothic revolving set, the production couldn't match the Southern fire of its London rival. Part of the problem was that it was actually Benvolio and Juliet: Hall's Romeo, the young Pakistani actor Zia Mohyeddin, had left the production six days before opening, leaving Brian Murray to take over. Whatever the intended force of Mohyeddin's casting, his departure made the central pairing blandly English. Murray spoke the verse well, but there was little chemistry between him and Dorothy Tutin, who gave her second Stratford Juliet in three years. Robert Speaight called her the best English Juliet since Peggy Ashcroft, and the comparison was frequently made, partly because she played opposite Ashcroft's Nurse, the legendary Dame Edith Evans. Like Ashcroft, Tutin 'was a child who grew into a woman', according to Speaight; her birdlike delicacy, youthful innocence, and exquisite poetry all resembled Ashcroft's Juliet, as did her essentially English characterisation. Ian Bannen's sophisticated, poetic Mercutio also drew critical praise, though the highest accolades were reserved for Evans's definitive Nurse. In general, the production connected solidly back to the old Gielgud tradition.

In 1973, Terry Hands directed a very different *Romeo* at Stratford, one that fully established the preoccupations of modern versions. The set, designed by Farrah, was an austere metallic structure on which the actors played out a grim spectacle of fate and violent death. Hands's motto for the

230 Speaight, *SQ* 12 (1961), p. 436.

production was 'these violent delights have violent ends'; he emphasised the speed and impulsiveness with which the lovers fling themselves into tragedy, as well as the cruel tricks of fate that hasten their doom.[231] The Apothecary, a sinister embodiment of Destiny, brooded over crucial points of the action from a metal catwalk high over the stage. Verona was a cold and violent world. In place of the traditional costumes of the Italian Renaissance, the young men of the play wore leather jerkins and trousers, vaguely seventeenth-century but bristling with the straps and studs of contemporary biker culture. The leader of this gang of thugs was Bernard Lloyd's Mercutio. Aggressively misogynist and presumably homosexual, he carried around a life-size female dummy, which he dismembered obscenely during the conjuration by Rosaline. The fights, led by David Suchet's sadistic, macho Tybalt, were given with shocking violence.

Estelle Kohler's Juliet was an earthy, physical, wholly unidealised girl, far removed from the fragile child–woman of Tutin and Ashcroft. With her open face, strong voice, and evident physical vitality, she made a vivid impression from the beginning of the play, laughing delightedly at the Nurse's bawdy story. She was very much involved in the domestic tasks of the Capulets' middle-class household, taking washing in, beating carpets, and the like, and her 'impetuous stretching, twisting, reaching, lunging gestures' revealed her eager and impulsive character.[232] Some critics found her frankness unappealing: 'In the early scenes she indicates a man-hunting voraciousness beyond her years and in her latter scenes we have visions of a tiresome shrew she might have become in middle age had not death saved her' (*Evening Standard*, 29 March 1973). However, she drew praise for her shift to sudden maturity at the Nurse's betrayal, and her defiance in the Friar's cell. Her performance was strong and original and she made much more of an impression than did Timothy Dalton, who was 'remarkably unobtrusive as Romeo, a gentle victim of the production's violence'.[233] While plausible as the romantic lover with his good looks and physical grace, he was unable to meet the emotional and vocal demands of the latter half of the play. Hands managed numerous striking stage effects, particularly in the later scenes. The mourning speeches over Juliet's supposed death were overlapped, creating a formal ritual of lamentation; the bizarre, parodic effect was heightened by the presence of the grotesquely masked Musicians. At the end of the scene Juliet's bed stayed onstage to become her bier; the Mantua scenes were played up on the metal catwalks, while Juliet remained visible

---

231 David, *Shakespeare in the Theatre*, p. 107.
232 Ibid., p. 109. 233 Thompson, *SS* 27 (1974), p. 151.

below. The final moments of the play were shocking, with Juliet's lifeless body sprawled in gore, an image that disturbed the 'glooming peace' of the Prince's lines.

Trevor Nunn and Barry Kyle directed the play in 1976, again focusing attention on violence, in this case within rather than between the families. John Woodvine's Capulet was a brutal patriarch, 'the source and fountain of the hate and violence that runs through the play', according to Michael Billington (*Guardian*, 2 April 1976). He beat Juliet, kicked Romeo's corpse in the tomb, and turned a dagger on the bumbling Friar.[234] By contrast, the young men were fairly amiable, with Michael Pennington's Mercutio 'no gang-leader but the adored funny-man in a group of more casual companions'.[235] Even Paul Shelley's Tybalt was a courteous and affectionate young man, who strove to maintain a patient dignity against Mercutio's provocations. Their duel was 'pure game', according to Irving Wardle, 'very fast and sexy, with Pennington playing clown to Shelley's straight man, and receiving the death blow as he leaps into Tybalt's arms to kiss him' (*Times*, 5 April 1976). Even Mercutio did not realise the seriousness of the wound at first; his joking was genuine. Tragedy came not from the violence of youth, but from the fatal gulf between youth and age.

In a production emphasising the generation gap, Ian McKellen and Francesca Annis seemed a little too old for the lovers. McKellen tried to compensate through an excess of adolescent energy, bounding about the stage and bursting into tears at the slightest provocation. His despair over Rosaline was exaggerated to comic absurdity; his infatuation with Juliet was equally extreme, and played out through physical exuberance: 'He jumped on and off stools, popped up unexpectedly in various balconies, and finally made a jet-landing from the staircase stage left to snatch Juliet for their first meeting.'[236] Annis also stressed Juliet's youth, giggling at the Nurse and chattering nervously in the balcony scene, which had comic energy but little passion. The later scenes of separation and despair successfully contrasted the frenzied abandon of the lovers with the blunt incomprehension of the older generation. Woodvine's Capulet even yanked Juliet's unconscious body to the floor on the morning of her marriage to Paris, thinking initially that she was staying in bed out of spite.

One of the most distinctive moments in the production came in the tomb scene, where Nunn and Kyle, like Hands, stressed the cruel mischance that continually plagues the lovers. The tomb was merely a trap door in the stage, which had been redesigned for the season as a modified Elizabethan theatre.

234 Dawson, *Watching Shakespeare*, p. 131.
235 David, *Shakespeare in the Theatre*, p. 115.   236 Ibid., p. 116.

8 The moment of Juliet's awakening, just before Romeo drinks the poison, in Trevor Nunn and Barry Kyle's Royal Shakespeare Company production with Francesca Annis and Ian McKellen. Royal Shakespeare Theatre, 1976.

McKellen's Romeo brought Juliet up out of the trap and carried her around with him in his farewell speech, which he delivered with a quiet gravity in sharp contrast to his earlier animation. As he sat to drink the poison, with Juliet still in his arms, her fingers began to flutter into life behind his head, though he was too deep in his grief to notice.[237] This striking image, reproduced on the production's poster, recalled the heightened pathos of Garrick's adaptation, where Juliet wakes before Romeo dies.

Ron Daniels's 1980 production returned to the masculine violence of Hands's version, though placed in a more recognisably modern context. Ralph Koltai's set of two bare, peeling walls suggested 'a faceless precinct for urban violence, where rival gangs lounged, hands in pockets'.[238] The young men's costumes, though not specifically contemporary, were made from black leather and worn with surly modern swagger. Tybalt and Mercutio fought with heavy sticks, from which they produced sword-blades as the duel escalated out of control. Daniels stressed not only the violence but the camaraderie of the young men, their wit-contests punctuated with hand-claps and playful wrestling matches. Jonathan Hyde's Mercutio turned the Capulet party into a raunchy disco as he led an impromptu masque featuring

237 Holding, *Romeo*, p. 62.   238 Warren, *SS* 34 (1981), pp. 149–50.

a grotesquely endowed pink Cupid doll. As a pale and neurotic Romeo, Anton Lesser gave an incisive performance very much against the romantic tradition, 'wild, frenetic, careless of dignity'.[239] With his wiry build, intense dark eyes, and high raspy voice, Lesser was equally convincing as a member of the down-market male gang and as 'an intemperate, ferocious adolescent poleaxed by love'.[240] Judy Buxton made less of an impression on the critics, perhaps because her tremulous childish Juliet didn't fit clearly into Daniels's contemporary world of aggressive masculinity. Brenda Bruce drew praise, however, as an unusually young and lively Nurse, with long silk dress and red curls, actively enjoying the sexual teasing of the young men. Daniels seems to have focused, in rehearsal, on creating the distinctive male and female worlds of the play, so that the love of Romeo and Juliet was less convincing than the antics of Romeo and his friends or the evolving relationship of Juliet and the Nurse.[241] When the production transferred to London, Daniels went so far as to get rid of the balcony, a choice that displeased critics: 'having the lovers clutch each other at ground level in what looks like a shabby alley, deprives the situation of all its symbolism', according to Milton Shulman (*Evening Standard*, 10 October 1981). In any event, Daniels's production provided another tough modern take on the play.

The impulse toward a contemporary urban *Romeo and Juliet*, where the lovers contend against the crassness of a bankrupt culture, had not yet run its course, and Michael Bogdanov injected it with vigorous life in a sensationally successful production in 1986. Set in contemporary Italy, the production made the lovers victims of their parents' materialism. After Juliet's supposed death, Robert Demeger, as a tough young urban Friar, attacked the Capulets' values with the line, 'The most you sought was her *promotion*' (4.5.71). The conspicuous consumption of the idle rich was everywhere evident. The cast wore chic Italian fashions, mostly in black and white. Chris Dyer's revolving set was a hideous faux-marble and chrome construction of stairs and plat-forms. The Prince was a sinister Mafia don, the Apothecary a drug pusher. Hugh Quarshie's Tybalt even drove a red convertible onto the stage, causing Michael Billington to nickname the production 'Alfa-Romeo and Juliet' (*Guardian*, 10 April 1986).

Bogdanov handled the big public scenes with enormous verve. The fights mixed convincing violence with uproarious comedy; at one point, Michael Kitchen's Mercutio evaded the chain-wielding Tybalt by sprawling across the bonnet of his car, causing Tybalt to desist for fear of scratching the paint job. At the Capulets' party, Mercutio and his dance partner jumped into a

---

239 Michael Billington, quoted in Crowl, *Shakespeare Observed*, p. 119.
240 Ibid.   241 Crowl, *Shakespeare Observed*, p. 104.

9 Michael Bogdanov's stylish modern-dress production, nicknamed 'Alfa-Romeo and
Juliet'. Hugh Quarshie as Tybalt, Martin Jacobs as Benvolio, Michael Kitchen as
Mercutio. Royal Shakespeare Theatre, 1986.

swimming pool to the accompaniment of a jazz-rock band. Kitchen played
the part as a drunken roué, too old to be cavorting with Romeo and his
friends, and without a very convincing emotional connection to them. He
delivered the Queen Mab speech as a sort of parodic bedtime story, taking
Romeo onto his lap; this choice got a couple of big laughs but otherwise sacri-
ficed the whole effect of the speech. The Capulets were more plausibly
updated as a *nouveau riche* couple, with Dilys Laye as a surprisingly unsym-
pathetic Nurse, a sycophantic social climber in pink suits and high heels.

The lovers, Sean Bean and Niamh Cusack, were less obviously modernised, though both retained non-standard regional dialects. In the balcony
scene, though they emphasised feeling at the expense of poetry, they conveyed a timeless sexual ardour removed from the gimmickry of the production. Bean found a balance between machismo and sensitivity, and Cusack
conveyed both Juliet's wide-eyed youth and her growing maturity. Both were
attractive and sympathetic according to the standards of the mid-eighties,
and young audiences flocked to the production.

Bogdanov's most striking and controversial choice involved the ending.
When the production opened, Romeo committed suicide by injecting
himself with a hypodermic syringe, though Bogdanov later switched to con-
ventionally administered poison. At any rate, after the deaths of the two

lovers, Bogdanov made a sudden cut to the final tableau. This was a sort of press conference at the dedication of the statues of Romeo and Juliet, which were represented by the actors themselves, wearing golden metallic gowns and masks. As cameras rolled and flashbulbs popped, the bored Mafioso Prince read a brief speech from cue cards. His words were the first eight lines of the Prologue (which had earlier been cut), converted to the past tense: 'Two households, both alike in dignity, / In fair Verona, where we laid our scene', and so forth. Capulet and Montague shook hands for the photographers; their reconciliation was a business merger or media event rather than a true recognition of their responsibility for their children's deaths. This choice annoyed many critics: 'an ending doubtless to the taste of modern sceptics, but a grotesque distortion of Shakespeare, who wanted to suggest that out of love, pain, death, good might come' (Benedict Nightingale, *New Statesman*, 18 April 1986). Actually, Bogdanov's ending allowed the play to conclude on a note of hip postmodern irony rather than timeless sorrow; and indeed, the whole production was informed less by Bogdanov's critique of capitalism than by his youth-friendly theatrical verve. Nothing in Bogdanov's approach to the play was especially original – there had been many angry modern productions in the nearly three decades since *West Side Story* – but he carried it off with such flair, energy, and fun that this *Romeo and Juliet* became probably the most influential since Zeffirelli's.

None of the RSC's remaining twentieth-century productions matched its success. In 1989 Terry Hands staged the play again in the new Swan Theatre, using virtually no scenery beyond the bare stage and wooden galleries of the Swan. Hands employed many of the same staging techniques he had used in 1973, such as the choral mourning, and the presence of the 'dead' Juliet throughout Act 5, while scenes were played on the levels above. Georgia Slowe was a very youthful Juliet, skipping about the stage in the early scenes and responding to Romeo with eager delight. Her parents continued to treat her as a child throughout; in a disturbing and effective moment, Bernard Horsfall's towering Capulet picked her up and spanked her when she refused to marry Paris. Mark Rylance's striking Romeo was closely connected to his neurotic Hamlet of the same season. Stooped and soft-spoken, Rylance was a tortured adolescent, haunted by death from the beginning of the play: he delivered his despairing Petrarchan oxymorons with chilling conviction. For once it seemed that he, rather than the feuding families, might be the source of the tragedy. It was an odd and powerful performance that grounded an otherwise somewhat unfocused production.

David Leveaux's main-stage production in 1991 was initially a disaster. The critics assailed it for a dark and cumbersome set and a lack of chemistry between Michael Maloney and Clare Holman. It was also very long, with a nearly uncut text playing close to four hours. The production was certainly distinctive, eschewing the now-traditional Italian heat in favour of a Caravaggiesque world of brooding shadowy interiors. The darkness extended to the characterisations, with Maloney's pensive Romeo matched by Tim McInnerny's psychotic Mercutio. When the production transferred to London, it was shorter, faster, and lighter in tone and atmosphere, and better pleased critics and audiences.

Adrian Noble's production in 1995 took its lessons to heart, and kept the tone light for much of the play. Noble used a nineteenth-century Italian setting, with clothes-lines strung in the narrow streets, espresso served at pavement cafés, and frock-coats, parasols, and crinolines for the citizens of Verona. His lovers were not only young, they were children: immature, self-dramatising, tantrum-throwing. By not treating the play as an idealised love story, Noble breathed a good deal of freshness into it, but at the expense of tragic impact. Zubin Varla's petulant, foot-stamping Romeo and Lucy Whybrow's Alice-in-Wonderland Juliet, who gave her 'Gallop apace' speech from a garden swing, were interesting but too rarely moving. Many of the other characterisations were also original. Christopher Benjamin was an unusually sympathetic Capulet, kindly and befuddled. Mark Lockyer was a sweet-tempered, youthful, and giddy Mercutio who wore drag to the Capulet party (an elaborately staged Italian festa featuring Verdi's *brindisi* from *La Traviata*). The dominant performance came from Julian Glover's Scots Friar Lawrence, who went from confident authority to eager meddling to shocking cowardice in his flight from Juliet's tomb.

The most successful RSC version of the 1990s was directed by Michael Attenborough at the Pit, the company's small studio theatre in the Barbican Centre, before going on tour in 1997–8. Attenborough capitalised on the intimate space and a simple, effective design to create a hot-blooded and original take on the play. The production was set, not in Renaissance Verona or a modern city, but in a small Sicilian village in the early twentieth century. The set was a sun-baked, tiled piazza backed by a single crumbling wall; Juliet's little balcony featured green shutters and a potted geranium. A water-pump added to the homely detail of the town square; a rectangular stone plinth served for Juliet's bed and tomb, as well as seating for the townsfolk. The Capulets and Montagues were not aristocrats, but working country people; Mercutio came from the fields, scythe in hand, and Juliet chopped parsley in the kitchen while talking to the Nurse and her mother. The Capulet party featured accordion music, a string of electric light bulbs, and red wine from unmarked bottles.

In this setting both the passion and the violence of the play flourished. The fights were scrappy and unchivalric; Chook Sibtain's insolent, mean-

10 Ray Fearon and Zoe Waites in Michael Attenborough's production, typical of many
    late twentieth-century productions in its emphasis on violence and sexuality and its
    racially mixed cast. Royal Shakespeare Company, the Pit and the Swan theatres, 1997.

spirited Mercutio taunted Tybalt with a broomstick. The bawdry of the
young men was continually reinforced with crotch-grabbing and pelvic
thrusting. The love of Romeo and Juliet lacked lyricism but was convincingly
carnal. Zoe Waites played a young woman ripe with sexual hunger: she
danced a sensuous tango with Paris and writhed on her bed in anticipation of
her wedding night. Ray Fearon's Romeo was ardent and muscular, and the
lovers' scenes had a sweaty intensity that matched the earthy design of the
production. It is also worth noting that this was the RSC's first production to
cast the lovers across racial lines (Fearon is black, Waites white, and they
played Othello and Desdemona the next season). There was no attempt to
represent the Montague/Capulet conflict as racially motivated – this was
merely 'colour-blind' casting such as the RSC often used – but it added to the
production's impact, and linked it to the many contemporary productions
that use the play to comment on ethnic or cultural conflict.

The RSC again staged *Romeo and Juliet* in the Royal Shakespeare Theatre
in 2000, in a dark and pessimistic production by Michael Boyd. A stark grey
set of high, curved walls, colourless costumes, expressionist lighting, and
brutal, relentless violence created a world in which the lovers were doomed
from the start. The Prologue was delivered, in the midst of the opening
brawl, by a pale, spectral figure who turned out to be Romeo himself, perhaps

already dead. David Tennant's nervous, Hamlet-like Romeo and Alexandra Gilbreath's huskily sensual Juliet were unable to generate much warmth in the grim surroundings of the production, but many of Boyd's images were vivid and compelling. He depicted the violence depopulating Verona as a literal plague, so that by the end of the play all the characters were wearing surgical masks to try to avoid infection. The presiding spirit of this Verona was not the Prince, an enervated old man hobbling on two canes, but rather Paris, a strapping, black-clad sadist, always accompanied by a band of armed retainers, who nearly raped Juliet in the Friar's cell. The final attempt to establish a 'glooming peace' was a hollow one. While the families wallowed in self-pity and made futile gestures of reconciliation, Romeo and Juliet emerged eerily from the tomb and walked out through the audience, noticed only by Friar Lawrence. The diseased world of Verona was far from ready to receive or even understand them, and the play ended on a note of fatalism and despair.

FILM

Romeo and Juliet has been one of the most popular plays for adaptation to film and video, rivalled only by *Hamlet*, *Othello*, and *Macbeth*. In the silent era it was the most frequently filmed of all Shakespeare's plays, inspiring such adaptations as *Romeo in Pajamas*, *Romeo in the Stone Age*, Mack Sennett's Western *Roping Her Romeo*, Fatty Arbuckle's *A Restless Romeo*, and *Doubling for Romeo*, in which Will Rogers plays a clumsily amorous cowboy who dreams himself into the play.[242] There were numerous feature films of the play itself, including a 1916 Fox version in which Theda Bara played Juliet in her characteristic vamp style: the *New York Tribune* critic described her as 'a Juliet with a sensuous mouth and provocative arms . . . beautiful but oh! so knowing' (23 October 1916). This picture was defeated at the box office by a rival Metro production starring Francis X. Bushman and Beverly Bayne; both films are now unfortunately lost. Of the silent versions remaining, the earliest is William Ranous's 1908 Vitagraph production, a fifteen-minute one-reeler, which experiments with a variety of outdoor locations around New York City; Romeo and Tybalt fight their duel in Central Park.[243] The Thanhouser production of 1911, of which only the second reel survives, incorporates more of Shakespeare's plot, but George A. Lessey's bulky middle-aged Romeo is hard to take seriously: ''A bears him like a portly gentleman' (1.5.65). Lo Savio's Italian version of the same year (Film d'Arte Italiana, 1911), uses extensive and elegant location

---

242 Ball, *Shakespeare on Silent Film*, pp. 218, 268.   243 Rothwell, *History*, p. 8.

shooting; the funeral of Juliet is staged as an elaborate procession across a square and up the great steps of a church. The film also features a really memorable performance of Juliet from Francesca Bertini, well partnered by Gustavo Serena. Their scenes together are charming and sexy, and Juliet's final scene – she wakes while Romeo is dying – is truly haunting.

The first major sound version, George Cukor's 1936 MGM film, has been often cited as an example of how not to film Shakespeare.[244] With its $2 million dollar budget, elaborate sets and costumes, reverential tone, and dowdy middle-aged leads, it was such a colossal failure that Hollywood produced no more Shakespeare for nearly twenty years.[245] Romeo was the 44-year-old Leslie Howard; Juliet the 36-year-old Norma Shearer, wife of producer Irving Thalberg. Neither really gives a bad performance, but their scenes have little passion or romance. John Barrymore's hammy Mercutio is easily outclassed by Basil Rathbone's sinister Tybalt. The film has its moments: an elaborate if slightly kitschy ballroom scene choreographed by Agnes de Mille, and a very beautiful slow tracking shot as Romeo approaches Juliet's balcony through a moonlit garden along the edge of a reflecting pool.

Renato Castellani's film of 1954 used authentic Italian settings of remarkable beauty, in which his English actors seem slightly stiff and out of place. Indeed, the whole film has a rather chilly feeling; the architecture is made to look rigid and imposing, in spite of its beauty, and Robert Krasker's photography is clinically cool, with long takes and little camera movement. The lovers are kept remote from the audience. The face of Susan Shentall's Juliet looks like a mask of porcelain, and Laurence Harvey, as Romeo, has the brainwashed quality he later used effectively in *The Manchurian Candidate*. The film has considerable power and restraint, however, with an insistent sense of doom from the beginning. Though the lovers generate little emotional warmth, Castellani achieves some striking images, as when they perform their wedding ceremony from the opposite sides of a metal grating, while an ominous plainchant is sung in the background. During her potion speech, Juliet is menaced by her enormous wedding dress, on a dummy standing in the corner of her darkened bedroom. The grim atmosphere is unrelieved by action or humour. The fights are short and clumsy. Mercutio, deprived of Queen Mab, does little to lighten the tone, and Flora Robson's Nurse is sturdy and pragmatic rather than warm and bawdy. Only Friar

244 Laurence Olivier credits the film with inspiring his directorial approach to *Henry V*, which combined theatrical acting and cinematic techniques. Watching Norma Shearer's potion scene, which moves into close-up as it nears its climax, Olivier came to believe that 'cinematic' acting is at odds with the full play of Shakespeare's language. Manvell, *Shakespeare and the Film*, pp. 37–8.
245 Rothwell, *History*, p. 44.

11 The accidental killing of Mercutio (John McEnery) in Franco Zeffirelli's 1968 Paramount film, with Michael York as Tybalt and Leonard Whiting as Romeo.

Lawrence is played, oddly, for comedy. Friar John's quarantine with the plague victim is developed into an elaborate set piece. John Gielgud opens the film as a Chorus rather absurdly made up to look like Shakespeare.

The 1968 film by Franco Zeffirelli extended and developed the tendencies of his stage version. It seems earthily realistic next to Castellani's, with dusty streets packed with extras, and long-haired teenagers bounding with hormonal energy. Flooded with sunshine, with indoor scenes warmed by torchlight, it is a vivid and colourful film, washed with Nino Rota's cloying but effective romantic score. The characters are colour-coded: the Montagues wear blues, the Capulets reds and oranges; when the dead bodies of Romeo and Juliet are carried across the square at the end of the film, they wear muted lavenders and pinks combining the colours of their houses. As in the stage production, the leads are very young; unlike that production, they are untrained and can give no vocal life to the lines. Zeffirelli cut the potion speech – once the most famous in the play – because Olivia Hussey was unable to make it work.[246] The film's most striking performance is John McEnery's neurotic Mercutio, whose descent into madness during the Mab speech created an abiding cliché for late twentieth-century performers of the role. As in Zeffirelli's stage version, Mercutio is killed accidentally in an essentially playful fight; his companions fail to realise he is wounded until he collapses at the end of a furious denunciation of both houses. The film collapses with him; the tragic scenes are heavily cut, perfunctory, and drowned in Rota's music. But the film overall conveys the exuberant youth and rich visual detail that made Zeffirelli's stage production such a landmark.

Romeo and Juliet has been broadcast on television a number of times. A 1955 BBC-TV version with Tony Britton and Virginia McKenna is well acted but awkwardly crowded into tight studio settings. Laurence Payne – who on stage was Peter Brook's Romeo and Hugh Hunt's Tybalt – is here an effective, sardonic Mercutio. The 1978 television version for the BBC/Time–Life *Shakespeare Plays* was one of the first and least successful of that series. Fourteen-year-old Rebecca Saire is convincingly young and innocent as Juliet, but lacks chemistry with Patrick Ryecart's lacklustre Romeo. Anthony Andrews gives a mannered, campy performance as Mercutio, and Alan Rickman is a surprisingly bland Tybalt. The older characters are given much better, more interesting realisations. Joseph O'Conor repeats his near-definitive Friar Lawrence from the St George's production, though with slightly less effect in the smaller-scaled medium. Michael Hordern gives a richly engaging and likeable portrait of Capulet, affable and bewildered, wholly lacking in patriarchal authority. Jacqueline Hill is an affectionate Lady Capulet, who plainly wants what is best for her daughter. Celia Johnson is a dignified and sympathetic Nurse. According to the director, Alvin Rakoff, 'It's very important to realise that the Capulet family is a happy family . . . If the family unit is tight it heightens the tragedy.'[247] The television close-ups are effective in conveying this sense of a close-knit family unit; the more public scenes are less successful. The plywood soundstage Verona looks cheap and uninhabited, without the degree of imaginative stylisation that works for some of the BBC projects.

Along with straightforward film and television productions, *Romeo and Juliet* has inspired countless spin-offs, with the star-crossed lovers adapted

246 Loney, *Staging Shakespeare*, p. 260.   247 Fenwick, 'Production', p. 23.

to other settings. *West Side Story*, the most influential of these (filmed in 1961), has led to numerous films about young lovers trying to cross social divides in American cities, such as Duncan Gibbons's *Fire with Fire* (1986), Abel Ferrara's *China Girl* (1987), and the Jet Li martial arts picture *Romeo Must Die* (2000). The play has also lent itself to comic parody, as in the polymorphously perverse Troma Films production *Tromeo and Juliet* (1996). Directed by Lloyd Kaufman, *Tromeo* is a tongue-in-cheek retelling loaded with soft-core sex, cartoonish violence, crude humour, and occasional wit. The young lovers eventually discover that they are brother and sister, as in Ford's *'Tis Pity She's a Whore*; they decide to live happily ever after anyway, and in the last scene are shown at a cheerful backyard barbecue surrounded by their malformed, inbred children.

Some international variations on the theme have been more sophisticated. *Les Amants de Vérone* (1948), scripted by Jacques Prévert as a début vehicle for the 16-year-old Anouk Aimée, portrays two young understudies for a film of *Romeo and Juliet* who end up living out the play's conflicts. *Romeo, Juliet, and Darkness* (Czechoslovakia, 1959), set during the Nazi occupation, tells of young Czech boy trying to protect a Jewish schoolgirl. *Shakespeare-Wallah* (India, 1965), an early Merchant–Ivory picture, depicts the doomed interracial romance of an Indian prince and a young English actress who is part of a travelling Shakespearean troupe. *Romeu y Julieta* (Brazil, 1982) is a free adaptation set in the mining town of Ouro Preto; *Torn Apart* (Israel, 1990) tells of an Israeli Romeo and Arab Juliet, while in *Henna* (India, 1992) the lovers are a Pakistani Muslim and an Indian Hindu.[248] No doubt the twenty-first century will see more such films, as old hatreds continue to plague young loves across the world.

ROMEO AND JULIET AFTER THE TWENTIETH CENTURY

The theme of ethnic or social hatred has become the dominant one in *Romeo and Juliet*. The play has come to symbolise bitter blood-feuds everywhere. In Sarajevo in 1993, a Muslim woman and Serb man died in each other's arms, gunned down by snipers while trying to flee the city. Bosko Brkic and Admira Ismic became known around the world as 'the Bosnian Romeo and Juliet' (*New York Times*, 8 May 1994). Their fate, and that of others like them, has moved countless theatre companies to try to address contemporary conflicts through productions of *Romeo and Juliet*. In June 1994, Palestinian and Israeli theatre companies in Jerusalem

248 Rothwell, *History*, p. 170.

worked together on a joint production. The Montagues were Arab, the Capulets Jewish. Rehearsals began only three days after a Jewish settler had massacred twenty-nine Arab worshippers in Hebron, and continued through two suicide bombings that killed thirteen Israelis (*Jerusalem Post*, 24 June 1994). The production made some direct allusions to the conflict; stones were thrown onstage during the opening brawl, and Tybalt and Mercutio fought with the kind of knives used during the Intifada (*The Jerusalem Report*, 14 July 1994). But the text was largely unaltered except through translation. In the balcony scene Romeo (Halifa Natur) spoke Arabic and Juliet (Orna Katz) replied in Hebrew. Despite death-threats to the actors and repeated disruptions, the production played successfully in Jerusalem and toured internationally.

In late twentieth-century Britain there were several productions that used racial division as the basis for the Capulet/Montague feud. Some were very much in the *West Side Story* mode, using contemporary urban settings. A 1990 production by the Hull Truck theatre company featured Roland Gift, lead singer of the Fine Young Cannibals, as a black Romeo opposite Daphne Nayar's Asian Juliet. Interestingly, both were represented as the products of racially mixed unhappy marriages. The production, aimed at young audiences, made Romeo's friends into loutish hooligans who illustrated their bawdy banter explicitly, with the help of an inflatable banana (*Independent*, 11 June 1990). A more sophisticated approach was taken by Temba Theatre Company, which set the play in 1870s Cuba under Spanish colonial rule. The Capulets were intermarried Spaniards and Cubans, the Montagues descendants of African slaves. Romeo was David Harewood, Juliet Georgia Slowe, who would go on to play the role at Stratford the following year. The actors gaining most praise were Joe Dixon as a dreadlocked, acrobatic Mercutio and Elin Morgan as a flamenco-dancing Rosaline. Live Spanish guitar music accompanied the action throughout. A production at the Albany Empire the same year was set in 1930s Trinidad, with the Capulets as well-to-do Indians and the Montagues as Afro-Caribbeans. Another, in Barons Court in 1992, had white colonial Montagues confronting black native Capulets on an African island. The Royal National Theatre used race-specific casting for its 2000 production of *Romeo and Juliet*, directed by Tim Supple. The production suggested a postcolonial African state, with white Capulets, black Montagues, and machetes carried in military holsters. Though plagued by production problems that caused it to open late, the National's *Romeo* established the postcolonial approach to the play as mainstream fare, and it featured appealing performances by Chiwetel Ejiofor and Charlotte Randle in the lead roles (*Independent*, 8 October 2000).

Tensions associated with colonialism were also central to two Australian productions from 1999. In Sydney, the Bell Shakespeare Company set indigenous Montagues against European Capulets in a modern-dress production directed by Wesley Enoch. At almost the same time, a Brisbane production, sponsored jointly by La Boite Theatre and Kooemba Jdarra Indigenous Performing Arts, used racially opposite casting. Director Sue Rider began the play with a tense, silent meeting around a conference table where the two families had gathered for an attempted reconciliation. This table later served as the balcony on which Maria Tusa's Juliet, dressed in pyjamas, apostrophised Romeo in her diary. The indigenous Capulets were led by a domineering matriarch, Roxanne McDonald, and their deaths were underscored by didgeridoo music (*The Australian*, 27 April 1999).

In the United States, a community-based production by Cornerstone Theater Company brought Verona's warring houses to the town of Port Gibson, Mississippi in 1988. The Harvard-based troupe took up residence for several months and incorporated dozens of locals into the production. Edret Brinston, an 18-year-old black high school student, played Romeo opposite Cornerstone's Amy Brenneman, later the creator and star of the television series *Judging Amy*. By using a racially divided company drawn from the community, Cornerstone addressed – and confronted – the severe racial tensions plaguing the town. The text was adapted to local realities, sometimes rather crudely, as when Tybalt challenged Romeo with, 'the love I bear thee can afford/ No better term than this: thou art a nigger'.[249] Mercutio's dying curse was 'A plague on both your races.' The play has been similarly invoked in response to racial problems in America's inner cities. In the 1997 Oscar-nominated documentary *Colors Straight Up*, a group of black and Latino teenagers in Los Angeles adapt the play as a response to, and a defence against, their culture of broken families and drive-by shootings. *Rome and Jewels*, a hip-hop adaptation by Rennie Harris's Puremovement company, reset the story in Philadelphia and used differing urban dance styles to depict the confrontation between two gangs, the Caps and the Monster Qs (*Los Angeles Times*, 30 October 2000). In Washington DC, a joint production combined students from historically black Howard University, as the Capulets, and predominantly white Catholic University, as the Montagues (*Washington Post*, 1 November 2000).

Questions of gender and sexuality, rather than race, were at the centre of another successful American adaptation, Joe Calarco's *Shakespeare's R&J*. First performed off-Broadway in 1997, *R&J* depicts *Romeo and Juliet* performed by four male parochial school students as an act of creative rebellion. After a prologue evoking the repressive routine of the school, the play uses

---

249 Coe, 'Verona, Mississippi', p. 52.

only Shakespeare's text, as the boys confront questions of homoerotic desire and gendered role-playing. When one of the boys first assumes the role of Juliet, his friends are nervous and uncomfortable with his earnest portrayal. At the Capulet ball, the verbal fencing and erotic tension of the shared sonnet take on a new subtext: the boy playing Juliet, at first, is reluctant to take his performance into the realm of sexuality. Romeo and Juliet begin fully to inhabit their roles in a passionate balcony scene, so that the other two boys are alarmed by their performance. The hostility of Tybalt and Mercutio to Romeo's love becomes layered with the two schoolboys' homophobia, which temporarily threatens to break off the impromptu performance of the play.

When the boys finally accept the homoeroticism of the cross-gender casting, the frame story fades from view. The second half of the play is a straightforward but inventive small-cast version of *Romeo and Juliet*, with a strong emphasis on the young lovers at the expense of the other characters. In the New York production all the adults were played with varying degrees of parody and stylisation; Capulet and the Prince, in particular, were sinister, inhuman forces of adult authority, their lines barked by all the boys together. The younger characters, by contrast, were played with Method intimacy, especially Daniel J. Shore's sensitive Juliet and Sean Dugin's Mercutio. The production not only applied *Romeo and Juliet* to questions of homoeroticism and homophobia, it made a convincing argument for the effectiveness of cross-gender casting. Even when issues of sexuality were not foregrounded, Shore's Juliet carried absolute conviction. Calarco's *R&J* thus provided an original and contemporary approach to the conflicts in the play as well as an exploration of the Elizabethan convention of the boy actress. It established once again how *Romeo and Juliet* can be adapted to a variety of social circumstances, and to many kinds of love and hate.

The cultural position of *Romeo and Juliet* at the beginning of the twenty-first century may be summed up by two films from the late 1990s, *William Shakespeare's Romeo + Juliet* and *Shakespeare in Love*. The former brings Shakespeare's play into a grim postmodern world of greed and violence; the latter wishfully projects contemporary values back into an idealised Elizabethan England. *William Shakespeare's Romeo + Juliet* is very much in the tradition of late twentieth-century stage productions, with its emphasis on the masculine aggression of the feud and its condemnation of the materialism and insensitivity of the older generation. The film is set in 'Verona Beach', a near-future urban dystopia combining elements of Los Angeles, Miami, and Mexico City. Social organisation is a mixture of capitalism, Catholicism, and feudalism: the smoggy skyline is dominated by a monumental statue of Christ flanked by the skyscrapers of the Capulet and Montague empires. The rival youths carry high-tech sidearms marked with the

12 Mercutio (Harold Perrineau) urges Romeo (Leonardo DiCaprio) to fight Tybalt in
Baz Luhrmann's 1996 Twentieth-Century Fox film, *William Shakespeare's
Romeo + Juliet*.

family crests, while Captain Prince, the chief of police, tries to maintain
order with helicopters and riot squads. Within this apocalyptic setting,
Romeo and Juliet are played in conventional post-Zeffirelli style as eager,
earnest adolescents misunderstood by their crass and selfish parents.

Director Baz Luhrmann succeeds admirably in creating his frenzied contemporary setting, using MTV editing rhythms, lurid colours, and endless
pop-culture references. Some of the characterisations are vivid and immediate. John Leguizamo is a Latino gang-leader Tybalt; Diane Venora a pill-
popping, chain-smoking Lady Capulet; Paul Rudd a blandly smiling Paris,
who attends the Capulet party in an astronaut costume. Harold Perrineau's
Mercutio comes to the party in drag and does a flashy *Paris is Burning*-style
dance number. Luhrmann whips up an atmosphere of frantic excess, with
pounding music, drug trips, car chases, and gunfights. The whole film is
clearly marked as postmodern spectacle, beginning and ending as a television
news broadcast.

The lovers, however, are to some extent kept apart from the chaos of
Verona Beach. Leonardo DiCaprio and Claire Danes, though they give little
depth to the poetry, are easy and natural on screen, and play their love scenes
with gravity and innocence. Luhrmann repeatedly associates them with
quiet, stillness, and water; they play their balcony scene in a swimming pool.
Though they are recognisably modern kids, Luhrmann links them with a

mythic past of courtly love: they attend the party dressed as a young King Arthur and a Botticelli angel. They play their tomb scene in a shimmering candlelit church that seems miles from the raucous present of the rest of the film, and their suicide is accompanied by the *Liebestod* from *Tristan und Isolde*. Only the final frames of the film thrust us back into the present, with a grainy television news image of two shrouded corpses being loaded into an ambulance.

There is a clear ambivalence in Luhrmann's film, a tension between a wish to throw modern gang violence and ethnic hatreds into the face of the audience, and a desire to retain the sense of Romeo and Juliet's love as a timeless ideal. Directors may want the play to comment on our world, but audiences still want the lovers to remain above it. *Shakespeare in Love* is, in a sense, the other side of the coin from Luhrmann's *Romeo + Juliet*. The 1998 Academy Award Winner for Best Picture, scripted by Marc Norman and Tom Stoppard and directed by John Madden, *Shakespeare in Love* reinvests the play with the cultural authority of Shakespeare in a unique way. The film's conceit is that Shakespeare not only wrote the play, he lived it. *Shakespeare in Love* posits a star-crossed romance between young Will Shakespeare and a court lady, Viola de Lesseps. The course of the affair parallels and inspires Shakespeare's writing of *Romeo and Juliet*. The film makes numerous witty connections between the events and incidents of the play and the world of Elizabethan theatre that produced it. 'A plague a'both your houses' is prompted by the street-corner imprecations of a Puritan against the Rose and the Curtain, the rival theatres of the Admiral's and Chamberlain's Men. The death of Mercutio is paralleled by the death of Marlowe, for which Shakespeare mistakenly feels responsible. In the end, the opening production of *Romeo and Juliet* is rather implausibly performed by Shakespeare and Viola; earlier, a cross-dressing Viola had played the balcony scene, effectively, with a male Juliet. The film's reauthenticating of *Romeo and Juliet* as the true experience of Shakespeare, and its subsequent popularity, suggest how much audiences have invested in this originary myth of romantic love. *Shakespeare in Love* gives *Romeo and Juliet* the sanction, not only of Shakespearean authorship, but of Shakespeare's own experience; it reconfirms the play's status as the ultimate love story.

The huge success of both of these films provides a test case of how *Romeo and Juliet* has evolved with the times while always retaining its unique importance as the central love myth of Western culture. Much as the play has changed over the years, it has continued to hold its central place, at least since the eighteenth century. Whether the focus has been on Romeo or Juliet; on the comedy of the Nurse or the anger of Capulet; on the poetry of the balcony scene, the bawdy wit of Mercutio, or the violence of the feud, the play has remained on the world stage. *Romeo and Juliet* has rarely been regarded as one of Shakespeare's greatest works, but it continues to function admirably as 'equipment for living', in Kenneth Burke's phrase.[250] The latest appropriations of *Romeo and Juliet* are part of a long history of reinvention, whereby successive cultures have used the play to figure their own civil brawls and death-marked loves.

250 Burke, *Philosophy*, p. 253; see Montrose, *Purpose of Playing*, p. 40.

LIST OF CHARACTERS

CHORUS
ESCALES, *Prince of Verona*
PARIS, *a young nobleman, kinsman to the Prince*
MONTAGUE } *heads of two houses at variance with each other*
CAPULET
COUSIN CAPULET, *kinsman to Capulet*
ROMEO, *son to Montague*
MERCUTIO, *kinsman to the Prince, and friend to Romeo*
BENVOLIO, *nephew to Montague, and friend to Romeo*
TYBALT, *nephew to Lady Capulet*
PETRUCHIO, *a (mute) follower of Tybalt*
FRIAR LAWRENCE } *Franciscans*
FRIAR JOHN
BALTHASAR, *servant to Romeo*
ABRAM, *servant to Montague*
SAMPSON
GREGORY } *servants to Capulet*
CLOWN
PETER, *servant to Juliet's Nurse*
PAGE *to Paris*
APOTHECARY
Three MUSICIANS

LADY MONTAGUE, *wife to Montague*
LADY CAPULET, *wife to Capulet*
JULIET, *daughter to Capulet*
NURSE to *Juliet*

GENTLEMEN *and* GENTLEWOMEN, MASKERS, TORCH-BEARERS,
    OFFICERS *of the Watch, other* CITIZENS, SERVINGMEN, *and*
    ATTENDANTS

SCENE: *Verona, Mantua*

Note
The List of Characters was first given in published form by Rowe (1709),
although an earlier list appears in the Douai MS. (1694).

THE TRAGEDY OF
ROMEO AND JULIET

Before the twentieth century, it was customary to omit the Prologue in performance. Helena Faucit would supposedly sometimes speak it herself before playing Juliet, wearing a silk domino over her dress (Wingate, *Shakespeare's Heroines*, p. 20). Irving is generally credited with having restored it, at the Lyceum in 1882. Howard Russell, costumed as Dante, delivered the Prologue in front of fantastically embroidered curtains (*The Theatre*, 1 April 1882). Twentieth-century versions have used a variety of approaches. In his 1935 production, John Gielgud spoke it himself in a gold mask (Hayman, *Gielgud*, p. 95). Orson Welles also wore a gold mask for the Prologue of Katherine Cornell's production, in which he played Tybalt (Brady, *Citizen Welles*, p. 65). Peter Brook had the actor of Benvolio, John Harrison, speak from 'a darkened stage in grey midnight mists', with 'tranquil and musical' voice (*Sunday Times*, 6 April 1947). In the 1976 St George's Theatre production, which emulated Elizabethan staging, Joseph O'Conor's Friar Lawrence gave the Prologue. In modern productions it is most often spoken by the Prince, as in Terry Hands's 1973 RSC version. In this staging the entire company stood arrayed on Farrah's metallic, three-tiered set, with the fateful figure of the Apothecary on the highest level (David, *Shakespeare*, p. 107). In Michael Attenborough's 1997 RSC production, the Prologue accompanied a gloomy tableau of the lovers' funeral, complete with black overcoats and umbrellas (*Times*, 7 November 1997). In the Castellani film, John Gielgud, made up as Shakespeare, speaks directly to the camera with a book in his hand. In Zeffirelli's film, Laurence Olivier's offscreen voice intones the Prologue over early-morning shots of Tuscan hill towns. Baz Luhrmann uses an elaborate opening wherein the Prologue is spoken twice, first by a banal television news anchor, then offscreen over a montage of images of urban violence and conspicuous consumption.

[*Enter*] CHORUS.

Two households, both alike in dignity,
In fair Verona (where we lay our scene),
From ancient grudge break to new mutiny,
Where civil blood makes civil hands unclean.
From forth the fatal loins of these two foes   5
A pair of star-crossed lovers take their life;
Whose misadventured piteous overthrows
Doth with their death bury their parents' strife.
The fearful passage of their death-marked love,
And the continuance of their parents' rage,   10
Which but their children's end nought could remove,
Is now the two hours' traffic of our stage;
The which if you with patient ears attend,
What here shall miss, our toil shall strive to mend.   [*Exit*]

ACT 1   SCENE 1

Enter SAMPSON *and* GREGORY, *with swords and bucklers,*
of the house of Capulet.

SAMPSON   Gregory, on my word, we'll not carry coals.
GREGORY   No, for then we should be colliers.
SAMPSON   I mean, and we be in choler, we'll draw.
GREGORY   Ay, while you live, draw your neck out of collar.
SAMPSON   I strike quickly, being moved.   5

1.1 The first scene clearly occurs in the morning in a public place, and since the nineteenth
century it has been an occasion for elaborate scenic design and stage business. Irving accu-
rately recreated the marketplace of Verona, with a central fountain, shady fruit-trees, and a
bridge at the back of the stage, as well as live donkeys and children (*Macmillan's Magazine*,
XLVI, 1882, p. 326; *The Theatre*, 1 April 1882). Peter Brook established a Mediterranean piazza
bustling with 'chattering coloured crowds, dotted with Jew and Ethiope', according to the
Manchester Guardian review (7 April 1947); Gordon Crosse felt 'the opening scene was
spoiled by the dialogue of the servants being accompanied by the laughter of a crowd of
fantastically dressed supers' (*Diaries*, XIX, 1947 p. 53). Zeffirelli's stage and film versions both
featured a bustling marketplace full of fruit vendors. In Michael Bogdanov's 1986 RSC production, street youths crossed the space on roller skates, bicycles, and motorbikes; the
Apothecary, a drug pusher, skulked around looking for customers, while the Prince, a Mafia
Don, surveyed his domain, flanked by two bodyguards. In Terry Hands's 1989 production, by
contrast, the stage was bare except for the characters who were speaking. Michael Attenborough updated the play to a rural Italian setting, 'a world of flat caps, dirty vests and knives
tucked into belts . . . In the tiled piazza, figures pit olives, scrub clothes in a tub and doze in
the sun' (*Independent on Sunday*, 9 November 1997). Baz Luhrmann set the scene at an
urban petrol station for his 1996 film.

1–28 The servants' quarrel has rarely been played in its full form. Before the twentieth century, the
bawdy double-entendres were regularly cut because of their obscenity (by, for instance,
Garrick, Kemble, Irving); now they are usually retained, and often graphically enacted, but
much of the other wordplay is cut because of its obscurity. Terry Hands, in 1973, began at line
7; Bogdanov 1986 at line 37. Francis Gentleman, in 1770, deplored the servants' quibbling as
'a farcical prelude to grave events, not unlike a merry andrew skipping before a funeral'
(*Dramatic Censor*, p. 172).

5 Terry Hands's 1989 Swan production began with uncharacteristic deliberateness and low-
key humour. Sampson and Gregory lay lazily on the stage; after a long pause Sampson said
lethargically, 'Gregory . . . [pause] I strike quickly . . . [pause] . . . being moved.' From this
sluggish beginning the fight built in carefully modulated waves to a full-scale mêlée

GREGORY But thou art not quickly moved to strike.

SAMPSON A dog of the house of Montague moves me.

GREGORY To move is to stir, and to be valiant is to stand: therefore
if thou art moved thou runn'st away.

SAMPSON A dog of that house shall move me to stand: I will take the   10
wall of any man or maid of Montague's.

GREGORY That shows thee a weak slave, for the weakest goes to the
wall.

SAMPSON 'Tis true, and therefore women being the weaker vessels are
ever thrust to the wall: therefore I will push Montague's men from   15
the wall, and thrust his maids to the wall.

GREGORY The quarrel is between our masters, and us their men.

SAMPSON 'Tis all one, I will show myself a tyrant: when I have fought
with the men, I will be civil with the maids; I will cut off their
heads.   20

GREGORY The heads of the maids?

SAMPSON Ay, the heads of the maids, or their maidenheads, take it in
what sense thou wilt.

GREGORY They must take it in sense that feel it.

SAMPSON Me they shall feel while I am able to stand, and 'tis known   25
I am a pretty piece of flesh.

GREGORY 'Tis well thou art not fish; if thou hadst, thou hadst been
poor-John. Draw thy tool, here comes of the house of Montagues.

Enter two other SERVINGMEN, [*one being* ABRAM].

SAMPSON My naked weapon is out. Quarrel, I will back thee.

GREGORY How, turn thy back and run?   30

SAMPSON Fear me not.

GREGORY No, marry, I fear thee!

occupying all three levels of the Swan Theatre (*Independent*, 7 April 1989). Michael Boyd's
2000 RSC production also began at this line, with a chair flung violently in from offstage,
followed by the furious Sampson.

28 SD Luhrmann reversed the roles in the quarrel, turning Sampson and Gregory into Montagues
and making Abram 'Abra', a tough Latino with silver-capped teeth. The other servingman is
often Balthasar (following Rowe's 1709 suggestion), though this identification seems at odds
with Balthasar's grave, pacific presence in Act 5.

28–9a Irving cut 'Draw thy tool', and 'My naked weapon is out', along with the preceding
discussion of maidenheads.

29 In Les Waters's 1988 New York Shakespeare Festival production, Sampson got a laugh by
retiring behind a pillar while urging Gregory, 'Quarrel, I will back thee.'

SAMPSON Let us take the law of our sides, let them begin.

GREGORY I will frown as I pass by, and let them take it as they list.

SAMPSON Nay, as they dare. I will bite my thumb at them, which is   35
disgrace to them if they bear it.

ABRAM Do you bite your thumb at us, sir?

SAMPSON I do bite my thumb, sir.

ABRAM Do you bite your thumb at us, sir?

SAMPSON [*Aside to Gregory*] Is the law of our side if I say ay?   40

GREGORY [*Aside to Sampson*] No.

SAMPSON No, sir, I do not bite my thumb at you, sir, but I bite my
thumb, sir.

GREGORY Do you quarrel, sir?

ABRAM Quarrel, sir? No, sir.   45

SAMPSON But if you do, sir, I am for you. I serve as good a man as
you.

ABRAM No better.

SAMPSON Well, sir.

Enter BENVOLIO.

GREGORY [*Aside to Sampson*] Say 'better', here comes one of my   50
master's kinsmen.

SAMPSON Yes, better, sir.

ABRAM You lie.

SAMPSON Draw, if you be men. Gregory, remember thy washing blow.
They fight.

35 In the 1989 Cornerstone Theater production, reset in contemporary Mississippi, Sampson's offensive gesture was modernised to an upraised middle finger (Coe, 'Verona, Mississippi', p. 16).

36 Peter Brook marked the sudden escalation of the quarrel through the reaction of his supernumeraries; after the thumb-biting, his promptbook reads 'crowd freeze to silence' (S100).

37 The thumb-biting is generally comic, but in Michael Boyd's 2000 RSC production this line was spoken very quietly, as the scene took on a sudden deadly earnestness.

42–3 Often, as in Bogdanov 1986, Abram has begun to walk away before Sampson completes his line, 'but I bite my thumb, sir.'

49 SD Gentleman (1770) notes that 'Benvolio requires but moderate requisites in exhibition; a distinct, easy, natural delivery, with gentility of person and deportment, will suffice' (*Bell's Edition*, p. 89).

54 SD Terry Hands's 1989 production established class distinctions by carefully differentiating the

BENVOLIO   Part, fools!   55
       Put up your swords, you know not what you do.
               [*Beats down their swords.*]

             Enter TYBALT.

TYBALT   What, art thou drawn among these heartless hinds?
       Turn thee, Benvolio, look upon thy death.
BENVOLIO   I do but keep the peace. Put up thy sword,
       Or manage it to part these men with me.   60
TYBALT   What, drawn and talk of peace? I hate the word,
       As I hate hell, all Montagues, and thee.
       Have at thee, coward.
            [*They fight.*]

Enter [*several of both houses, who join the fray, and*] *three or four Citizens* [*as*
OFFICERS *of the Watch,*] *with clubs or partisans.*

weapons: the servants fought with sword and buckler, the young gentlemen with rapiers, and the older generation, as suggested by the text, with longswords.

55–6 In Luhrmann's modern-dress film, while a gun-wielding Benvolio orders the servants to put up their 'swords', a close-up of his automatic pistol reveals the legend 'Sword 9 mm', establishing the convention for the film's weaponry.

56 In a Margaret Anglin production from the early twentieth century (s61), the play began at this line. In place of the preceding servants' quarrel, the audience listened to thirty seconds of fighting sounds before the curtain rose to show Tybalt and Benvolio facing off, each at the head of about twenty men.

56 SD Though he has barely thirty lines, Tybalt invariably makes a large impression. Among distinguished Tybalts were Orson Welles (New York 1934), Laurence Payne (Old Vic 1952), and Keith Michell (Stratford 1954), who was described by Ivor Brown as 'king of panthers' rather than 'Prince of Cats' (2.4.18), (*Shakespeare Memorial Theatre*, p. 4). Tybalt's personality – fiery, or feline, or both – is usually reflected in his costume; in Zeffirelli's film Michael York's hat suggests a cat's pointed ears.

57 In David Leveaux's 1991 RSC production, Tybalt was present from the beginning of the fight, but looked on with boredom until Benvolio, his social equal, got involved. Benvolio started to leave at Tybalt's 'Have at thee', then turned and attacked when Tybalt hissed 'coward'.

63 SD The Q2 stage direction, 'Enter three or four Citizens', reflects the degree to which Shakespeare's whole company was already involved in the scene. Victorian productions were not so economical; Irving used over a hundred extras. The fight took place across a narrow stone bridge, over which the Montagues 'used to pour in . . . like a released torrent' in such a violent fight that 'there was never a day when there was not at least one of the young men in the hospital' (*The Era*, 7 December 1907, quoted in Vardac, *Stage to Screen*,

OFFICERS Clubs, bills, and partisans! Strike! Beat them down!
　　　　　 Down with the Capulets! Down with the Montagues!   65

Enter old CAPULET *in his gown, and his wife* [LADY CAPULET].

CAPULET What noise is this? Give me my long sword, ho!
LADY CAPULET A crutch, a crutch! why call you for a sword?
CAPULET My sword, I say! old Montague is come,
　　　　　 And flourishes his blade in spite of me.

Enter old MONTAGUE *and his wife* [LADY MONTAGUE].

MONTAGUE Thou villain Capulet! – Hold me not, let me go.   70
LADY MONTAGUE Thou shalt not stir one foot to seek a foe.

Enter PRINCE ESCALES *with his train.*

PRINCE Rebellious subjects, enemies to peace,
　　　　 Profaners of this neighbour-stainèd steel –
　　　　 Will they not hear? – What ho, you men, you beasts!

p. 98). Modern productions also generally create vivid and elaborate brawls. In Bogdanov's
1986 production, Hugh Quarshie's Tybalt, clad in black leather, attacked Benvolio from
behind with a chain; loud rock music and sirens accompanied the fight. David Leveaux's
1991 production used a stylised fight of back-lit freeze-frame poses so that all of the lines of
the elder Capulets and Montagues were audible. In Michael Boyd's 2000 production, the
fight became silent and stylised while David Tennant's Romeo entered to deliver the
Prologue; the line 'Two households, both alike in dignity' was thus highly ironic.

66–71 Garrick cut the entrance of the wives, as did most nineteenth-century productions, including
those of Phelps, Irving, Mary Anderson, and Forbes-Robertson. When included, the wives
have often been used for comic effect, as in the 1955 BBC-TV production, where they
physically grapple with their belligerent husbands.

71 SD Irving brought in the Prince to the accompaniment of trumpeters, who silenced the fighting
citizens (*Macmillan's Magazine*, XLVI, 1882, p. 327). Zeffirelli had the Prince's speech backed
up by a muffled rolling drum offstage; in his film Robert Stephens is on horseback (*SS* 15,
1962, p. 150). The Prince is ordinarily a figure of order and authority, but in the late
twentieth century he often had a sinister quality. In a Soviet production of 1956, he was a
violent young man who used a whip to beat the mob into submission; a 1971 Hungarian
version had him supported by storm-troopers (Londré, '*Romeo*', pp. 638, 645). In
Bogdanov's 1986 production he was a Mafia Don. In Joe Calarco's adaptation, *R & J*, he was
a figure of fascistic authority whose lines were spoken by all the cast members in unison, as
they held their fists up in rigid salute. In Michael Boyd's 2000 RSC production, by contrast,
he was a weak old man, completely devoid of authority.

74a In Terry Hands's 1989 RSC production, Paris and Mercutio established their kinship with the

That quench the fire of your pernicious rage   75
With purple fountains issuing from your veins:
On pain of torture, from those bloody hands
Throw your mistempered weapons to the ground,
And hear the sentence of your movèd prince.
Three civil brawls, bred of an airy word,   80
By thee, old Capulet, and Montague,
Have thrice disturbed the quiet of our streets,
And made Verona's ancient citizens
Cast by their grave beseeming ornaments
To wield old partisans, in hands as old,   85
Cankered with peace, to part your cankered hate;
If ever you disturb our streets again,
Your lives shall pay the forfeit of the peace.
For this time all the rest depart away:
You, Capulet, shall go along with me,   90
And, Montague, come you this afternoon,
To know our farther pleasure in this case,
To old Free-town, our common judgement-place.
Once more, on pain of death, all men depart.
                  Exeunt [all but Montague, Lady Montague, and Benvolio]
MONTAGUE Who set this ancient quarrel new abroach?   95
Speak, nephew, were you by when it began?
BENVOLIO Here were the servants of your adversary,
And yours, close fighting ere I did approach:
I drew to part them; in the instant came
The fiery Tybalt, with his sword prepared,   100
Which, as he breathed defiance to my ears,
He swung about his head and cut the winds,
Who, nothing hurt withal, hissed him in scorn;
While we were interchanging thrusts and blows,
Came more and more, and fought on part and part,   105
Till the Prince came, who parted either part.

Prince by helping to break up the fight. Paris intervened between Capulet and Montague,
Mercutio between Tybalt and Benvolio.
94 SD Charlotte Cushman's promptbook marked this exit with a threat of renewed hostilities, as
'Tybalt and Benvolio encounter each other's glances. They each draw their swords and
remain in attitude' (531).

LADY MONTAGUE O where is Romeo? saw you him today?
        Right glad I am he was not at this fray.
BENVOLIO Madam, an hour before the worshipped sun
        Peered forth the golden window of the east,   110
        A troubled mind drive me to walk abroad,
        Where underneath the grove of sycamore,
        That westward rooteth from this city side,
        So early walking did I see your son;
        Towards him I made, but he was ware of me,   115
        And stole into the covert of the wood;
        I, measuring his affections by my own,
        Which then most sought where most might not be found,
        Being one too many by my weary self,
        Pursued my humour, not pursuing his,   120
        And gladly shunned who gladly fled from me.
MONTAGUE Many a morning hath he there been seen,
        With tears augmenting the fresh morning's dew,
        Adding to clouds more clouds with his deep sighs,
        But all so soon as the all-cheering sun   125
        Should in the farthest east begin to draw
        The shady curtains from Aurora's bed,
        Away from light steals home my heavy son,
        And private in his chamber pens himself,
        Shuts up his windows, locks fair daylight out,   130
        And makes himself an artificial night:
        Black and portentous must this humour prove,
        Unless good counsel may the cause remove.
BENVOLIO My noble uncle, do you know the cause?
MONTAGUE I neither know it, nor can learn of him.   135
BENVOLIO Have you importuned him by any means?
MONTAGUE Both by myself and many other friends
        But he, his own affections' counsellor,

122–33 Bogdanov's Montague was grumpy and impatient, contemptuous of Romeo's behaviour
      (RSC 1986); in Adrian Noble's Victorian setting, Montague seemed embarrassed by his son's
      lack of manliness (RSC 1995). In Hands's 1989 production, by contrast, both Montague and
      his wife were notably sympathetic and concerned.
   131 Philip Voss's Benvolio laughed knowingly at this report of Romeo's behaviour; he seemed to
      understand his friend's condition better than he let on (St George's, 1976).

Is to himself (I will not say how true)
But to himself so secret and so close,   140
So far from sounding and discovery,
As is the bud bit with an envious worm
Ere he can spread his sweet leaves to the air,
Or dedicate his beauty to the sun.
Could we but learn from whence his sorrows grow,   145
We would as willingly give cure as know.

Enter ROMEO.

BENVOLIO See where he comes. So please you step aside,
    I'll know his grievance or be much denied.
MONTAGUE I would thou wert so happy by thy stay
    To hear true shrift. Come, madam, let's away.   150
Exeunt [Montague and Lady Montague]

146 SD Romeo's appearance and dress have changed dramatically over the centuries. Burbage presumably wore an Elizabethan doublet; Garrick and Barry wore long eighteenth-century coats and wigs (Halio, *Romeo*, p. 102). Cushman wore a thigh-length tunic that revealed her commanding, but obviously female, figure (Merill, *When Romeo Was a Woman*, p. 116). Dark hair has been standard since the nineteenth century: Edwin Booth's blond wig was considered an aberration (Ruggles, *Prince of Players*, p. 222). Victorian Romeos often wore early Renaissance costumes based on Italian paintings. Irving wore a grey-green tunic and a hat with a sprig of crimson oleander (*The Theatre*, 1 April 1882; Terry, *Story of My Life*, p. 233). Not all attempts at historical costuming have been flattering to actors. John Gielgud was ill suited to the Italian Renaissance style: in a page-boy wig for Barry Jackson's 1924 production, he felt he looked 'a mixture of Rameses of Egypt and a Victorian matron', while in tights in 1935, he was said to have 'the most meaningless legs imaginable' (*Early Stages*, p. 50). Olivier cut a particularly striking figure, very much the Italian youth, with dark good looks, open white shirt, short doublet and tights: 'he won half his battle as soon as Romeo, olive-skinned, impetuous adolescent, entered straight from Renaissance Italy, a world of hot sun, sharp swords, and brief lives' (Trewin, *Shakespeare on the English Stage*, p. 153). The romantic figure of Olivier has given way, since the 1960 Zeffirelli production, to plainer, tougher, more realistic young Romeos. John Stride, in rough-textured, practical woollen clothing, with a mop of brown hair, was 'an emotional but extremely normal young man . . . one of the gang' (*Saturday Review*, 3 March 1962). Stride's Romeo made a long, slow, silent entrance, which 'showed his solitary and self-absorbed nature at the cost of narrative pressure' (*SS* 15, 1962, p. 154).

BENVOLIO   Good morrow, cousin.
ROMEO   Is the day so young?
BENVOLIO   But new struck nine.
ROMEO   Ay me, sad hours seem long.
       Was that my father that went hence so fast?
BENVOLIO   It was. What sadness lengthens Romeo's hours?
ROMEO   Not having that, which, having, makes them short.   155
BENVOLIO   In love?
ROMEO   Out –
BENVOLIO   Of love?
ROMEO   Out of her favour where I am in love.
BENVOLIO   Alas that Love, so gentle in his view,   160
       Should be so tyrannous and rough in proof!
ROMEO   Alas that Love, whose view is muffled still,
       Should, without eyes, see pathways to his will!
       Where shall we dine? O me! what fray was here?
       Yet tell me not, for I have heard it all: 165
       Here's much to do with hate, but more with love:

151a–229 In the Garrick version, this scene, much abbreviated, takes place in 'a Wood near Verona' and includes Mercutio, who gives the Queen Mab speech. In modern productions this dialogue generally continues the previous action, though some change of time or mood may be indicated. In the Bogdanov and Noble RSC productions, for instance, Romeo and Benvolio sat at a pavement café and drank espresso.

151b Romeo may speak with genuine lovesick confusion, bitter irony, or self-aware mockery. Laurence Harvey, sitting beside a canal in the Castellani film, seems grateful at being roused from his reverie.

155 Peter MacNicol spoke this line with petulant irony, as if the trouble were obvious and Benvolio foolish to miss it (NYSF 1988).

164a On this line, by his sly change of mood, Ian McKellen (RSC 1976) acknowledged the role-playing aspect of Romeo's lovesick behaviour, causing a 'ripple of laughter and understanding' in the audience (*SQ* 29, 1978, p. 223).

164b Romeo generally notices weapons discarded from the fight; sometimes Benvolio has been slightly wounded (Sprague, *Shakespeare and the Actors*, p. 298). In Michael Boyd's 2000 production, Romeo observed a smear of blood left on the wall where one of the servants' faces had been smashed against it. In Luhrmann's film Romeo sees a television news report showing Benvolio and Tybalt being arrested by riot police.

165–6 Peter Brook's Romeo, Laurence Payne, walked about the stage kicking the swords and staves from the fight (s100).

166 Romeo's 'Here' usually makes reference to the evidence of the feud, but Michael Maloney touched his own breast, referring to the conflict within him (Leveaux, RSC 1991).

Why then, O brawling love, O loving hate,
O any thing of nothing first create!
O heavy lightness, serious vanity,
Misshapen chaos of well-seeming forms, 170
Feather of lead, bright smoke, cold fire, sick health,
Still-waking sleep, that is not what it is!
This love feel I, that feel no love in this.
Dost thou not laugh?
BENVOLIO   No, coz, I rather weep.
ROMEO Good heart, at what?
BENVOLIO   At thy good heart's oppression. 175
ROMEO Why, such is love's transgression:
Griefs of mine own lie heavy in my breast,
Which thou wilt propagate to have it pressed
With more of thine; this love that thou hast shown
Doth add more grief to too much of mine own. 180
Love is a smoke made with the fume of sighs,
Being purged, a fire sparkling in lovers' eyes,
Being vexed, a sea nourished with loving tears.
What is it else? a madness most discreet,

167–73 Romeo's Petrarchan oxymorons are often mocked by actors, as an opportunity to display the shallowness of Romeo's attachment to Rosaline. Irving was said to 'distinguish . . . well between the more subjective and fanciful infatuation' for Rosaline and the passion for Juliet. John Gielgud played the early couplets with a degree of academic detachment, as though Rosaline was an abstract ideal like Petrarch's Laura (Wright, *Romeo*, p. 210). This choice disconcerted the *New York Times* critic: 'You begin by thinking: "Good heavens! He's going to play it *cold*!" ' (29 December 1935). Olivier took these passages 'a little heavily', failing to reveal any 'underlying note of character' (*Times*, 18 October, 1935). Mark Rylance gave these lines with conviction; his Romeo was a death-haunted, melancholy poet, suffering deeply over Rosaline. In Luhrmann's film Leonardo DiCaprio is seen laboriously writing out the oxymorons in a journal, a cigarette dangling from his mouth; he later dazzles Benvolio with his verbal dexterity by seeming to produce them spontaneously.

173 David Tennant referred to a bloodstain remaining from the fight, and thus metonymically to the feud itself, on 'This love feel I, that feel no love in *this*.' His line therefore became, not a paradox, but a statement of opposition between his love and the hatred of the feud (Boyd, RSC 2000).

176 Tony Britton, with a smile, broke out of his self-absorption into genuine concern for his friend (BBC-TV 1955); conveyed in televised close-up, the moment made Romeo more appealing to the audience than he often is at this point in the play.

184 In Ron Daniels's leather-clad production, Anton Lesser's Romeo hammered out these

A choking gall, and a preserving sweet.   185
Farewell, my coz.
BENVOLIO   Soft. I will go along;
And if you leave me so, you do me wrong.
ROMEO Tut, I have lost myself, I am not here,
This is not Romeo, he's some other where.
BENVOLIO Tell me in sadness, who is that you love?   190
ROMEO What, shall I groan and tell thee?
BENVOLIO   Groan? why, no;
But sadly tell me, who?
ROMEO Bid a sick man in sadness make his will –
A word ill urged to one that is so ill:
In sadness, cousin, I do love a woman.   195
BENVOLIO I aimed so near, when I supposed you loved.
ROMEO A right good mark-man! and she's fair I love.
BENVOLIO A right fair mark, fair coz, is soonest hit.
ROMEO Well, in that hit you miss: she'll not be hit
With Cupid's arrow, she hath Dian's wit;   200
And in strong proof of chastity well armed,
From Love's weak childish bow she lives uncharmed.
She will not stay the siege of loving terms,
Nor bide th'encounter of assailing eyes,
Nor ope her lap to saint-seducing gold.   205
O, she is rich in beauty, only poor
That when she dies, with beauty dies her store.
BENVOLIO Then she hath sworn that she will still live chaste?
ROMEO She hath, and in that sparing makes huge waste;
For beauty starved with her severity   210

definitions with pained effort; 'a *madness*' was 'barked out desperately, an internal version of the violence around him' (*SS* 34, 1981, p. 151). Cornerstone Theater had Romeo rap out his lovesick lines to the rhythmic beat of a basketball bounced by one of the Montague boys (Coe, 'Verona, Missisippi', p. 17).

187 Peter Brook ended the scene at this line, leaving out Romeo's account of Rosaline's chastity (s100).

195 Usually a joke, but Sean Bean (1986) played it seriously and sadly, unconscious of the irony; the audience laugh was at his expense, not Benvolio's. Mark Rylance (1989) was so anguished that the line passed without a laugh. Peter MacNicol played the line sadly, and Benvolio got the laugh on his wryly understated response (NYSF 1988).

205 The more explicit aspects of Romeo's discussion of Rosaline's chastity were almost invariably cut before the twentieth century, though Samuel Phelps included them (s26).

Cuts beauty off from all posterity.
She is too fair, too wise, wisely too fair,
To merit bliss by making me despair.
She hath forsworn to love, and in that vow
Do I live dead, that live to tell it now.   215
BENVOLIO Be ruled by me, forget to think of her.
ROMEO O teach me how I should forget to think.
BENVOLIO By giving liberty unto thine eyes,
Examine other beauties.
ROMEO   'Tis the way
To call hers (exquisite) in question more: 220
These happy masks that kiss fair ladies' brows,
Being black, puts us in mind they hide the fair;
He that is strucken blind cannot forget
The precious treasure of his eyesight lost;
Show me a mistress that is passing fair,   225
What doth her beauty serve but as a note
Where I may read who passed that passing fair?
Farewell, thou canst not teach me to forget.
BENVOLIO I'll pay that doctrine, or else die in debt.

Exeunt

229b For both Bogdanov and Noble, Benvolio's 'or else die in debt' made reference to the café
      bill, which Benvolio hastily returned to pay under the eyes of a disgruntled waiter (RSC
      1986, 1995).

ACT 1   SCENE 2

Enter CAPULET, COUNTY PARIS, *and the Clown*
[SERVANT *to Capulet*].

CAPULET But Montague is bound as well as I,
  In penalty alike, and 'tis not hard, I think,
  For men so old as we to keep the peace.
PARIS Of honourable reckoning are you both,
  And pity 'tis, you lived at odds so long.   5
  But now, my lord, what say you to my suit?
CAPULET But saying o'er what I have said before:
  My child is yet a stranger in the world,
  She hath not seen the change of fourteen years;
  Let two more summers wither in their pride,   10
  Ere we may think her ripe to be a bride.
PARIS Younger than she are happy mothers made.
CAPULET And too soon marred are those so early made.

1.2 Victorian productions played this scene on the same set as the previous one, or in front of the curtain while Juliet's chamber was being prepared. In the 1978 BBC-TV production Michael Hordern's Capulet is going through the market buying produce for the party. In Bogdanov's 1986 RSC production, Richard Moore's Capulet, a self-satisfied Northern industrialist with a cigar, played the scene behind an imposing desk. Film allows even greater licence; Luhrmann places Capulet and Paris in a sauna.

 3 In Terry Hands's 1973 production, Capulet's pacific magnanimity was immediately undercut as he kicked his sleeping servant at the end of his line (promptbook, SCL).

 4 According to John Gielgud in 1935, Paris 'is usually played as a foolish fop. I make him a rather pitiful figure – a simple boy who contrasts with the more mature Romeo' (*Evening Standard*, 10 October 1935). Most modern productions have given Paris some dignity; indeed, Alan Dent felt that Laurence Payne's Romeo was 'a dishclout' to Donald Sinden's noble, courtly Paris in Peter Brook's 1947 production (*News Chronicle*, 11 April 1947). In their RSC production of 1976, Trevor Nunn and Barry Kyle used 'a goofy Paris, an Aguecheek, instead of the straight but dull young noble the action demands', according to Richard David (*Shakespeare in the Theatre*, p. 117). Michael Boyd, in 2000, made an unusual choice in presenting Paris as a very powerful and sinister figure to whom the Capulets wish to link their family.

 13 In the Zeffirelli film, a quick zoom to a frowning Lady Capulet across the courtyard makes it evident that Capulet is speaking from bitter experience about the bad effects of early marriage on young women.

Earth hath swallowed all my hopes but she;
She's the hopeful lady of my earth.   15
But woo her, gentle Paris, get her heart,
My will to her consent is but a part;
And she agreed, within her scope of choice
Lies my consent and fair according voice.
This night I hold an old accustomed feast,   20
Whereto I have invited many a guest,
Such as I love, and you among the store,
One more, most welcome, makes my number more.
At my poor house look to behold this night
Earth-treading stars that make dark heaven light.   25
Such comfort as do lusty young men feel
When well-apparelled April on the heel
Of limping winter treads, even such delight
Among fresh fennel buds shall you this night
Inherit at my house; hear all, all see;   30
And like her most whose merit most shall be;
Which on more view of many, mine, being one,
May stand in number, though in reck'ning none.
Come go with me. [*To Servant*] Go, sirrah, trudge about
Through fair Verona, find those persons out   35
Whose names are written there [*Gives a paper.*], and to
      them say,
My house and welcome on their pleasure stay.
                                                        Exit [*with Paris*]
SERVANT Find them out whose names are written here! It is written
   that the shoemaker should meddle with his yard and the tailor with
   his last, the fisher with his pencil and the painter with his nets;   40
   but I am sent to find those persons whose names are here writ, and

29 In Bogdanov's 1993 English Shakespeare Company production, which used the Q1 reading
     'fresh female buds', Paris giggled with nervous excitement at this line (*Guardian*, 1 June
     1993).
38 Generally the servant is Peter, who was played by Will Kemp in Shakespeare's company.
     Traditionally he is a lazy buffoon who spends his onstage time falling asleep or catching
     flies, as in Edwin Booth's production (s35). Peter Brook made him a 'merry-quipped, quick-
     footed, black-faced servant whose movements weave a rhythmic thread through several
     scenes' (*Birmingham Post*, 10 April 1947).

can never find what names the writing person hath here writ. I must
to the learnèd. In good time!

Enter BENVOLIO *and* ROMEO.

BENVOLIO Tut, man, one fire burns out another's burning,
    One pain is lessened by another's anguish;   45
    Turn giddy, and be holp by backward turning;
    One desperate grief cures with another's languish:
    Take thou some new infection to thy eye,
    And the rank poison of the old will die.
ROMEO Your plantain leaf is excellent for that.   50
BENVOLIO For what, I pray thee?
ROMEO   For your broken shin.
BENVOLIO Why, Romeo, art thou mad?
ROMEO Not mad, but bound more than a madman is:
    Shut up in prison, kept without my food,
    Whipt and tormented, and – God-den, good fellow.   55
SERVANT God gi' god-den. I pray, sir, can you read?
ROMEO Ay, mine own fortune in my misery.
SERVANT Perhaps you have learned it without book; but I pray, can
    you read any thing you see?
ROMEO Ay, if I know the letters and the language.   60
SERVANT Ye say honestly, rest you merry.
ROMEO Stay, fellow, I can read.

He reads the letter.

42–3 In the 1955 BBC-TV production, Peter yawned before 'I must to the learnèd', then made 'In good time!' an excuse for taking a nap first; Benvolio and Romeo only entered after he had curled up to sleep.

43 SD In Bogdanov's 1986 production Benvolio and Romeo entered on a motorbike, with Romeo leaning on his friend's back in an attitude of lovelorn misery.

51 Sometimes Romeo kicks Benvolio in the shin, as in Leveaux's RSC production (1991).

54–5 Mark Rylance (RSC 1989) made these lines an outburst of genuine anguish, which he undercut slightly in his quick, embarrassed response to Peter. Peter's interruption of the scene often has a comic, deflationary effect, as in Boyd's 2000 RSC production, where he insinuated himself gradually between Benvolio and Romeo until his unexplained presence could no longer be ignored.

62 One nineteenth-century promptbook (S23) has a note, 'Peter gives paper upside down to Romeo': classic low-comic business that may well date back to Will Kemp and is still regularly used (e.g. St George's 1976).

'Signior Martino and his wife and daughters,
County Anselme and his beauteous sisters,
The lady widow of Vitruvio,   65
Signior Placentio and his lovely nieces,
Mercutio and his brother Valentine,
Mine uncle Capulet, his wife and daughters,
My fair niece Rosaline, and Livia,
Signior Valentio and his cousin Tybalt,   70
Lucio and the lively Helena.'
A fair assembly: whither should they come?

SERVANT Up.

ROMEO Whither? to supper?

SERVANT To our house.   75

ROMEO Whose house?

SERVANT My master's.

ROMEO Indeed I should have asked thee that before.

SERVANT Now I'll tell you without asking. My master is the great rich
Capulet, and if you be not of the house of Montagues, I pray come   80
and crush a cup of wine. Rest you merry.   [*Exit*]

BENVOLIO At this same ancient feast of Capulet's

---

63   Tony Britton began the list deliberately, while Peter ticked off each name on his fingers, then
he purposely accelerated his reading, to Peter's consternation and Benvolio's delight, until
he was suddenly stopped cold by Rosaline's name (BBC-TV 1955). Incidentally, the fact that
Rosaline is Capulet's niece (and possibly even Tybalt's sister) makes Romeo's initial love as
dangerous as his subsequent one, though few productions have made anything of this
point.

67   The first mention of Mercutio offers an opportunity for foreshadowing; in the 1995 RSC
production, Romeo spoke this name with pointed meaning to Benvolio, suggesting some
interest in wangling an invitation to the party.

69   Actors usually mark the mention of Rosaline somehow. Samuel Phelps had Romeo kiss the
letter; Irving used the same business (s27, Sprague, *Shakespeare and the Actors*, p. 299). A
much-used nineteenth-century promptbook (s23) has 'Benvolio laughs' next to Rosaline's
name. Mark Rylance (RSC 1989) read the list quickly and tonelessly until he came to her
name, and then began again brokenly after a long pause. In the 1991 RSC production
Benvolio interrupted Romeo's reading with a knowing 'Aaah!' In Forbes-Robertson's Lyceum
production, Peter took advantage of Romeo's pause at Rosaline's name to commit at least
one of the invited guests to his memory: 'Peter downs a finger indicating he has that one at
any rate' (s63). Some pantomime of painful memorisation is inevitable on Peter's part; Terry
Hands's 1973 promptbook has merely 'Peter recall biz' after the letter is read.

        Sups the fair Rosaline whom thou so loves,
        With all the admirèd beauties of Verona:
        Go thither, and with unattainted eye   85
        Compare her face with some that I shall show,
        And I will make thee think thy swan a crow.
ROMEO When the devout religion of mine eye
        Maintains such falsehood, then turn tears to fires;
        And these who, often drowned, could never die,   90
        Transparent heretics, be burnt for liars.
        One fairer than my love! the all-seeing sun
        Ne'er saw her match since first the world begun.
BENVOLIO Tut, you saw her fair, none else being by,
        Herself poised with herself in either eye;   95
        But in that crystal scales let there be weighed
        Your lady's love against some other maid
        That I will show you shining at this feast,
        And she shall scant show well that now seems best.
ROMEO I'll go along no such sight to be shown,   100
        But to rejoice in splendour of mine own.

                                              [Exeunt]

ACT 1   SCENE 3

Enter CAPULET'S WIFE *and* NURSE.

LADY CAPULET   Nurse, where's my daughter? call her forth to me.
NURSE   Now by my maidenhead at twelve year old,
      I bade her come. What, lamb! What, ladybird!
      God forbid, where's this girl? What, Juliet!

Enter JULIET.

0 SD   The nurse is usually matronly and sometimes ancient, though as Juliet's wet-nurse she shouldn't be much over fifty. Dame Edith Evans looked like a peasant woman from a Dutch painting, with her white head-scarf and voluminous skirts (*Evening Standard*, 18 October 1935). In Peter Brook's production, according to Alan Dent, Beatrix Lehmann's Nurse was 'the most frightening and least funny I ever hope to see . . . racked by every ailment known to pathology from dropsy downwards' (*News Chronicle*, 11 April 1947). In late twentieth-century productions the Nurse became younger and more openly sexual. For Ron Daniels (RSC 1980) Brenda Bruce played her as a frank, energetic, unfussy woman 'with blood still flowing strongly enough to recognize the call of the young's sexual attraction' (Crowl, *Shakespeare Observed*, p. 120). Dilys Laye, for Bogdanov (RSC 1986), made her an opportunistic social climber in a pink suit and heels. In Karin Beier's Düsseldorf production, she was 'a gorgeous young blonde in an evidently lesbian relationship to her charge' (*Spectator*, 29 October 1994).

4 SD   Francis Gentleman, writing of eighteenth-century performers, argued that 'Juliet should either be, or nearly look, as young as she is described; of middling stature, rather than either of the extremes; with soft, melting, but expressive features, and a musical, yet powerful voice' (*Bell's Edition*, p. 94). In the eighteenth and nineteenth centuries, audience scrutiny of the entrance of Juliet often conflated actor and character, particularly when a young actress made her début. The author of *A Letter to Miss Nossiter* comments: 'Her unaffected fear, when she came on, was felt by every heart. So fine a girl, in such distress, was an object of real pity' (p. 5). When Fanny Kemble made her début at Covent Garden in 1829, the reviewer similarly described her as a vulnerable young woman threatened by the audience's gaze: 'On her first entrance she seemed to feel very sensibly the embarrassment of the new and overwhelming task she had undertaken. She ran to her mother's arms with a sort of instinctive impulse, but almost immediately recovered her composure' (Pascoe, *Dramatic List*, p. 209). In the nineteenth century, Juliet traditionally appeared first in a white satin gown bordered with gold, as Ellen Terry did at the Lyceum (*Times*, 9 March 1882). Mary Anderson, at the Lyceum in 1884, made a celebrated appearance: 'at "Madam, I am here", she thrust aside a curtain and was seen standing on a stair framed in an arched

JULIET How now, who calls? 5
NURSE Your mother.
JULIET Madam, I am here, what is your will?
LADY CAPULET This is the matter. Nurse, give leave a while,
      We must talk in secret. Nurse, come back again,
      I have remembered me, thou s' hear our counsel. 10
      Thou knowest my daughter's of a pretty age.
NURSE Faith, I can tell her age unto an hour.
LADY CAPULET She's not fourteen.
NURSE   I'll lay fourteen of my teeth –
      And yet to my teen be it spoken, I have but four –
      She's not fourteen. How long is it now 15
      To Lammas-tide?
LADY CAPULET   A fortnight and odd days.
NURSE Even or odd, of all days in the year,
      Come Lammas-eve at night shall she be fourteen.
      Susan and she – God rest all Christian souls! –
      Were of an age. Well. Susan is with God, 20

doorway' (Shattuck, *American Stage*, II, p. 106). Several twentieth-century productions have used Juliet's entrance to establish her youth. Peggy Ashcroft played the scene as an eager child, radiant with expectation (Wright, *Romeo*, pp. 231–2). Daphne Slater, in Brook's production, sat on her Nurse's knee in a blue nightgown, looking like a little girl (*Sunday Times*, 6 April 1947). Dorothy Tutin expressed 'sunny, childlike gaiety . . . given over to the excitement of being grown-up, and the new dress and the first party' (*SQ* 9, 1958, p. 519). The exceptionally young Juliet portrayed by Rebecca Callard (Regent's Park 1993) appeared carrying a rag doll (*Guardian*, 21 June 1993). By contrast, in Michael Attenborough's rural Italian production for the RSC, Zoe Waites's practical, homey Juliet was chopping parsley to add to the stew for the Capulet party (*Financial Times*, 10 November 1997).

9–10 The recalling of the Nurse is always a comic moment; the standard business goes back at least to the nineteenth century. One Victorian promptbook (S23) has 'Nurse approaches to listen' just before Lady Capulet's 'give leave awhile', followed by 'Nurse is going away sulkily . . . Juliet goes to her, puts her arms round her neck to comfort her – Nurse appears pleased to be recalled.'

13 Garrick increased Juliet's age to nearly eighteen. Irving, with Ellen Terry, cut all references to Juliet's age. More recently, the age references were cut in Michael Boyd's 2000 RSC production with Alexandra Gilbreath.

17 ff. The Nurse's story was cut entirely by Cushman, and Irving left only enough to establish Juliet's age – the joke about falling backwards was cut in virtually all nineteenth-century productions. Phelps allowed it, cutting only the reference to 'a young cock'rel's stone' (S26).

20–1 The Nurse often gets sentimental over Susan, presumably her daughter. Mrs Stirling, the

She was too good for me. But as I said.
On Lammas-eve at night shall she be fourteen,
That shall she, marry, I remember it well.
'Tis since the earthquake now aleven years,
And she was weaned – I never shall forget it – 25
Of all the days of the year, upon that day;
For I had then laid wormwood to my dug,
Sitting in the sun under the dove-house wall.
My lord and you were then at Mantua –
Nay, I do bear a brain – but as I said, 30
When it did taste the wormwood on the nipple
Of my dug, and felt it bitter, pretty fool,
To see it tetchy and fall out wi'th'dug!
'Shake!' quoth the dove-house; 'twas no need, I trow,
To bid me trudge. 35
And since that time it is aleven years,
For then she could stand high-lone; nay, by th'rood,
She could have run and waddled all about;
For even the day before, she broke her brow,
And then my husband – God be with his soul, 40
'A was a merry man – took up the child.
'Yea', quoth he, 'dost thou fall upon thy face?
Thou wilt fall backward when thou hast more wit,
Wilt thou not, Jule?' And by my holidam,
The pretty wretch left crying, and said 'Ay'. 45
To see now how a jest shall come about!
I warrant, and I should live a thousand years,
I never should forget it: 'Wilt thou not, Jule?' quoth he,

Nurse to Ellen Terry and Mary Anderson at the Lyceum, 'lowered her voice, spoke absently, and crossed herself' (Sprague, *Shakespeare and the Actors*, p. 299). The promptbook s23 says the Nurse 'Weeps. Juliet embraces her and dries her eyes with her apron.' The 1995 RSC production undercut this sentimental tendency by having the other women cross themselves very wearily, along with the Nurse, at the mention of Susan; Juliet dropped back in exasperation onto the bed, as if to say 'Not Susan again!'

27 Garrick changed the Nurse's 'dug' to her 'breast'.

31–3 When Anne Meara, as the Nurse in the 1988 NYSF production, reached the detail about how little Juliet 'did . . . tetchy and fall out wi'th'dug', she grabbed Juliet's hand and slapped it back and forth against her breast several times in a comic reenactment of the moment.

38 Georgia Slowe (RSC 1989), a young and playful Juliet, ran and waddled about in illustration of the Nurse's story.

And, pretty fool, it stinted, and said 'Ay'.
LADY CAPULET Enough of this, I pray thee hold thy peace.   50
NURSE Yes, madam, yet I cannot choose but laugh,
       To think it should leave crying, and say 'Ay':
       And yet I warrant it had upon it brow
       A bump as big as a young cock'rel's stone,
       A perilous knock, and it cried bitterly.   55
       'Yea', quoth my husband, 'fall'st upon thy face?
       Thou wilt fall backward when thou comest to age,
       Wilt thou not, Jule?' It stinted, and said 'Ay'.
JULIET And stint thou too, I pray thee, Nurse, say I.
NURSE Peace, I have done. God mark thee to his grace,   60
       Thou wast the prettiest babe that e'er I nursed.
       And I might live to see thee married once,
       I have my wish.
LADY CAPULET Marry, that 'marry' is the very theme
       I came to talk of. Tell me, daughter Juliet,   65
       How stands your dispositions to be married?
JULIET It is an honour that I dream not of.

49 In the detailed notes he kept of Katherine Cornell's production, the American novelist
    Fitzroy Davis observed dryly that the audience 'generally laughs rather in sympathy with the
    Nurse's laughter, than with amusement at the incident' (595).
50 In Leveaux's production (RSC 1991), Lady Capulet uncharacteristically enjoyed the Nurse's
    story, and was physically affectionate with Juliet; Terry Hands's 1973 production also had
    Lady Capulet stifling laughter (Holding, *Romeo*, p. 53).
58 Clare Holman (RSC 1991) said 'Ay!' along with the Nurse, in imitation of her childhood self.
61 Anne Meara tearfully held Juliet's hand against her breast (NYSF).
64 ff. As Juliet has little to say in this scene, much of the impact of her performance depends on
    her reactions to her mother and the Nurse. Austin Brereton wrote that Eliza O'Neill's Juliet
    'made a fine distinction between her reverence for her mother and her fascinating
    condescension to the nurse, never forgetting in either instance that she was the child of a
    noble house' (*Romeo*, p. 23). Henry Morley complained that Stella Colas tried to steal too
    much focus: 'Mdlle Colas perks her head, grins, twists, ambles from one side of the chair to
    the other, and looks obtrusively conscious of every part of herself' (*Journal*, pp. 277–8).
    Modern productions often highlight Juliet's awkward and premature transition to
    adulthood. In Karin Beier's 1994 Düsseldorf production, Lady Capulet gave Juliet a pair of
    high-heeled shoes, which she tried on eagerly but couldn't walk in; nonetheless, her mother
    refused to give her old shoes back (*Times*, 1 November 1994). During Lady Capulet's speech
    in the 1995 RSC production, the Nurse removed Juliet's childish pinafore and dressed her in
    a more womanly party frock.

NURSE   An honour! were not I thine only nurse,
        I would say thou hadst sucked wisdom from thy teat.
LADY CAPULET   Well, think of marriage now; younger than you,   70
        Here in Verona, ladies of esteem,
        Are made already mothers. By my count,
        I was your mother much upon these years
        That you are now a maid. Thus then in brief:
        The valiant Paris seeks you for his love.   75
NURSE   A man, young lady! lady, such a man
        As all the world – Why, he's a man of wax.
LADY CAPULET   Verona's summer hath not such a flower.
NURSE   Nay, he's a flower, in faith, a very flower.
LADY CAPULET   What say you, can you love the gentleman?   80
        This night you shall behold him at our feast;
        Read o'er the volume of young Paris' face,
        And find delight writ there with beauty's pen;
        Examine every married lineament,
        And see how one another lends content;   85
        And what obscured in this fair volume lies
        Find written in the margent of his eyes.
        This precious book of love, this unbound lover,
        To beautify him, only lacks a cover.
        The fish lives in the sea, and 'tis much pride   90

72–5 These lines can be played for comedy if Lady Capulet is obviously older than twenty-eight.
      In the Luhrmann film, Diane Venora is visibly exasperated by Juliet's reticence.

75 Katherine Cornell was evidently pleased on being told Paris sought her for his love; Fitzroy
    Davis's notes read 'Juliet puts palms together, looks idyllically to gallery' (s95).

79 Margaret Courtenay's bawdy rustic Nurse in Hands's 1989 production made 'in faith, a very
    flower' a *sotto voce* double-entendre, drawing an audience laugh.

80–95 In Declan Donellan's Edwardian Production (Regent's Park 1986), Sarah Woodward's Juliet,
       a bookish Shavian New Woman, was reading and ignoring her mother's praise of County
       Paris, so that, according to Jack Tinker, 'Philippa Gail's picture-postcard Edwardian hostess
       is reduced to snatching the volume from her indifferent daughter and expounding the
       Count's virtues in terms of literary metaphors to make her point' (*Daily Mail*, 3 June 1986).
       Linda Spurrier's stiffly unmaternal Lady Capulet developed an amusing reading of the
       speech in Hands's 1989 production. She began her long speech very formally, then lost her
       way in the image of the book, and awkwardly started over, speaking as to a child, with 'The
       fish lives in the sea . . .' In Michael Boyd's production, by contrast, Caroline Harris
       whispered sensually in Juliet's ear, trying to arouse her. On the line 'For fair without the fair
       within to hide', she placed Juliet's hands over her crotch (RSC 2000).

> For fair without the fair within to hide;
> That book in many's eyes doth share the glory
> That in gold clasps locks in the golden story:
> So shall you share all that he doth possess,
> By having him, making yourself no less.   95
> NURSE No less! nay, bigger women grow by men.
> LADY CAPULET Speak briefly, can you like of Paris' love?
> JULIET I'll look to like, if looking liking move;
> But no more deep will I endart mine eye
> Than your consent gives strength to make it fly.   100

Enter SERVINGMAN.

SERVINGMAN Madam, the guests are come, supper served up, you
  called, my young lady asked for, the Nurse cursed in the pantry,
  and every thing in extremity. I must hence to wait, I beseech you
  follow straight.   [*Exit*]
LADY CAPULET We follow thee. Juliet, the County stays.   105
NURSE Go, girl, seek happy nights to happy days.

Exeunt

96 The Nurse's jest was regularly cut from Garrick until the twentieth century.

98–100 In Bogdanov's 1986 production, Niamh Cusack's reply was 'guarded and ambiguous'
  (Cusack, 'Juliet', p. 125).

101 Gentleman deplored the comedy of this moment: the 'familiar, low comic message which
  concludes the scene, is totally inconsistent with common English decorum, much more the
  pride and diffidence of Italian quality; Nurse, from her station, may claim some liberty, but
  such headlong behaviour from other servants is very censurable' (*Dramatic Censor*, p. 176).

102 In the Sothern–Marlowe production, the Nurse was indignant at being cursed in the pantry;
  Juliet comforted her while Peter suppressed a laugh (S70).

106 The Nurse's exit line was too bawdy for Victorian audiences, and was regularly cut until the
  twentieth century.

106 SD The Victorian promptbook S23 records traditional stage business: 'Juliet is following [Lady
  Capulet]. Nurse coughs – Juliet returns and takes her off kindly.' Julia Marlowe also gave
  attention to the Nurse: 'Nurse starts to dance in time with the music, but gets a pain in her
  side and Juliet laughing comforts her' (S70). Mary Anderson herself began 'a little dance
  movement with her feet as she follow[ed] her mother to the ball' (Sprague, *Shakespeare
  and the Actors*, p. 299). Katherine Cornell rushed offstage 'ecstatically' with 'cries of joy'
  (S95). Modern Juliets are likely to show more ambivalence, as Claire Danes does in the
  Luhrmann film. In Michael Boyd's production, while Juliet hesitated centre stage, the sinister
  figures of the maskers from 1.4 appeared over the walls and dropped down to the stage,
  thus creating an ominous ending to the scene (RSC 2000).

ACT 1   SCENE 4

Enter ROMEO, MERCUTIO, BENVOLIO, *with five or six other*

MASKERS, TORCH-BEARERS.

ROMEO What, shall this speech be spoke for our excuse?
　　　　Or shall we on without apology?
BENVOLIO The date is out of such prolixity:
　　　　We'll have no Cupid hoodwinked with a scarf,
　　　　Bearing a Tartar's painted bow of lath,　　　　　　　　　　　5
　　　　Scaring the ladies like a crow-keeper,
　　　　Nor no without-book prologue, faintly spoke
　　　　After the prompter, for our entrance;
　　　　But let them measure us by what they will,
　　　　We'll measure them a measure and be gone.　　　　　　　10
ROMEO Give me a torch, I am not for this ambling;
　　　　Being but heavy, I will bear the light.
MERCUTIO Nay, gentle Romeo, we must have you dance.
ROMEO Not I, believe me. You have dancing shoes
　　　　With nimble soles, I have a soul of lead　　　　　　　　15
　　　　So stakes me to the ground I cannot move.

1.4 SD Mercutio has almost always cut an impressive figure on his first entrance, though the
character has been played in many different ways. With Garrick, Henry Woodward was an
elegant fop with a big feather in his tricorne hat (Wright, *Romeo*, p. 123). Charles Macklin,
who played with Spranger Barry at Drury Lane, was a surly malcontent (Gentleman,
Dramatic Censor, p. 190). Charles Kemble, the most famous nineteenth-century Mercutio,
was a courtly, noble gentleman (Williamson, *Charles Kemble*, p. 118). In the 1935 New
Theatre production, Gielgud upheld the tradition of gentlemanly, poetic Mercutios, while
Olivier was 'a bold, agreeably dirty-minded, and quite jolly young man' (*Evening News*, 29
November 1935). Paul Scofield, in Brook's production, was a melancholy poet 'who really
has seen the fairies and wishes, perhaps, that he had not' (*Sunday Times*, 6 April 1947). Leo
Ciceri was a battle-scarred veteran in the 1968 Stratford, Ontario production. Michael
Kitchen, for Bogdanov (RSC 1986), was a dissipated playboy in a sharp black suit; he
entered holding a champagne flute. Joe Dixon, in Alby James's Cuban-set Temba
production, was a tall, graceful Rastafarian in dreadlocks (*Observer*, 10 July 1988). In
modern productions, race may serve to affiliate Mercutio either with the Montagues or with
the Prince. In the 2000 Royal National Theatre production, Mercutio was white, the
Montagues black; in the Luhrmann film Mercutio and the Prince are black, the Montagues
white.

MERCUTIO You are a lover, borrow Cupid's wings,
    And soar with them above a common bound.
ROMEO I am too sore enpiercèd with his shaft
    To soar with his light feathers, and so bound   20
    I cannot bound a pitch above dull woe:
    Under love's heavy burden do I sink.
MERCUTIO And to sink in it should you burden love,
    Too great oppression for a tender thing.
ROMEO Is love a tender thing? it is too rough,   25
    Too rude, too boist'rous, and it pricks like thorn.
MERCUTIO If love be rough with you, be rough with love:
    Prick love for pricking, and you beat love down.
    Give me a case to put my visage in, [*Puts on a mask.*]
    A visor for a visor! what care I   30
    What curious eye doth cote deformities?
    Here are the beetle brows shall blush for me.
BENVOLIO Come knock and enter, and no sooner in,
    But every man betake him to his legs.
ROMEO A torch for me: let wantons light of heart   35
    Tickle the senseless rushes with their heels;
    For I am proverbed with a grandsire phrase,
    I'll be a candle-holder and look on:
    The game was ne'er so fair, and I am done.
MERCUTIO Tut, dun's the mouse, the constable's own word.   40
    If thou art Dun, we'll draw thee from the mire,
    Or (save your reverence) love, wherein thou stickest
    Up to the ears. Come, we burn daylight, ho!

27–8 Michael Kitchen delivered these lines angrily, betraying a resentment of Romeo's passion for Rosaline. He took a swig from a hip flask and moved upstage away from the group, returning only gradually and in an ill humour.

30 This was a key line for Leo Ciceri's Mercutio (Stratford, Ontario, 1968); his face bore both physical and emotional scars from his years of soldiering (Raby, *The Stratford Scene*, p. 162). Tim McInnery (RSC 1991) said 'a visor for a visor' with wistful self-knowledge; John McEnery, in the Zeffirelli film, with self-mocking bravado. Mark Lockyer (RSC 1995) played the line with false sentiment, parodying one fishing for sympathy; his friends responded with derisive sighs.

32 The 'beetle brows' generally belong to Mercutio's grotesque mask; however, in Terry Hands's 1973 production, they were the face of the life-size female doll Bernard Lloyd carried around as a focus for his psychotic misogyny.

ROMEO Nay, that's not so.
MERCUTIO   I mean, sir, in delay
           We waste our lights in vain, like lights by day.   45
           Take our good meaning, for our judgement sits
           Five times in that ere once in our five wits.
ROMEO And we mean well in going to this mask,
           But 'tis no wit to go.
MERCUTIO   Why, may one ask?
ROMEO I dreamt a dream tonight.
MERCUTIO   And so did I.   50
ROMEO Well, what was yours?
MERCUTIO   That dreamers often lie.
ROMEO In bed asleep, while they do dream things true.
MERCUTIO O then I see Queen Mab hath been with you:

50b Michael Kitchen's Mercutio got a laugh even before his line, simply from the look of disdain
     with which he responded to Romeo's 'I dreamt a dream tonight' (Bogdanov, RSC 1986).

53   Peter Brook included, from Q1, the question 'Queen Mab, what's she?', attributing it not to
     Benvolio but to Romeo (s100). In Ron Daniels's postmodern gangland setting, where fairy
     lore seemed out of context, Mercutio's very young page asked the question, 'to which
     Mercutio improvised an increasingly imaginative explanation, illustrated in mime by the
     others' (*SS* 34, 1981, p. 149).

53 ff. Charles Kemble, the most celebrated Mercutio of the nineteenth century, began the Mab
     speech off-handedly; the first line 'was uttered without a touch of formal rhetoric or *pose* –
     by no means as a prelude to a set description, but as a simple, whimsical thought springing
     from mere buoyancy of heart', according to Westland Marston (Marston, *Our Recent Actors*,
     I, pp. 121–2). Wilson Barrett, another distinguished nineteenth-century Mercutio, showed
     'possibly too great a tendency to illustrate the text by physical signs and gestures', according
     to Clement Scott (*Yesterday and Today*, II, p. 305). William Terriss, in Irving's production,
     was likewise condemned for 'so very literally "suiting the action to the word . . ." ' (*The
     Theatre*, 1 April 1882). In Forbes-Robertson's 1895 Lyceum production, Charles Coghlan
     played the speech 'half drunk and lolling on the stone seat . . . to repeat a tipsy rigmarole
     about nothing', much to G. B. Shaw's disgust (*Our Theatres*, III, p. 210). Ralph Richardson
     (1935) began slowly and magically but built to frantic energy, leaping backwards up the
     staircase of Jo Mielziner's abstract set (s95). In Peter Brook's 1947 production, Paul Scofield
     lay on the stage in torchlight and quietly entranced his hearers (*Sunday Times*, 6 April
     1947). Bernard Lloyd, at Stratford in 1973, took the speech at a furious pace, making it the
     'frenzied and quite terrifying' rant of 'an increasingly isolated sociopath' (Holding, *Romeo*,
     p. 55). Michael Kitchen, in Bogdanov's 1986 production, teased Romeo by making the
     speech a mocking bedtime story suitable for Romeo's childish imagination. He drew out his

She is the fairies' midwife, and she comes
In shape no bigger than an agate-stone   55
On the forefinger of an alderman,
Drawn with a team of little atomi
Over men's noses as they lie asleep.
Her chariot is an empty hazel-nut,
Made by the joiner squirrel or old grub,   60
Time out a'mind the fairies' coachmakers:
Her waggon-spokes made of long spinners' legs,
The cover of the wings of grasshoppers,
Her traces of the smallest spider web,
Her collars of the moonshine's wat'ry beams,   65
Her whip of cricket's bone, the lash of film,
Her waggoner a small grey-coated gnat,
Not half so big as a round little worm
Pricked from the lazy finger of a maid.
And in this state she gallops night by night   70
Through lovers' brains, and then they dream of love,
O'er courtiers' knees, that dream on cur'sies straight,
O'er lawyers' fingers, who straight dream on fees,
O'er ladies' lips, who straight on kisses dream,
Which oft the angry Mab with blisters plagues,   75
Because their breaths with sweetmeats tainted are.

vowels as though speaking to a child, and took Romeo onto his lap on 'the fairies' coach-makers'. By contrast, Tim McInnery only occasionally acknowledged the performative nature of the speech, getting wrapped up in his own private world, so that the speech built in intensity but not volume (Leveaux, RSC 1991).

56 In Baz Luhrmann's film, 'Queen Mab' is introduced as a drug, a tablet marked with a heart which Harold Perrineau's Mercutio holds out on his fingertip.

71–4 Ralph Richardson drew out the first part of each of these lines (identifying the dreamer) with a lifting, magical cadence, then deflated it with a prosy mundane tone in recounting the subject of the dream (curtsies, fees, kisses) (595).

74 Jean Cocteau, who played Mercutio in his own 1924 production, ended the speech at this point; he also left out the details of Queen Mab's coach and train (Cocteau, *Roméo et Juliette*, p. 83). Given Cocteau's interest in dreams and the fantastic, his cuts are surprising, but outside the English-speaking world the speech doesn't have the same reputation as an inviolable classic. In the undated German version, possibly played by the English Comedians at Dresden in 1626, this scene is translated almost verbatim, but the Mab speech is cut entirely (Cohn, *Shakespeare in Germany*, pp. 330–1).

Sometime she gallops o'er a courtier's nose,
And then dreams he of smelling out a suit;
And sometime comes she with a tithe-pig's tail
Tickling a parson's nose as 'a lies asleep,   80
Then he dreams of another benefice.
Sometime she driveth o'er a soldier's neck,
And then dreams he of cutting foreign throats,
Of breaches, ambuscadoes, Spanish blades,
Of healths five fathom deep; and then anon   85
Drums in his ear, at which he starts and wakes,
And being thus frighted, swears a prayer or two,
And sleeps again. This is that very Mab
That plats the manes of horses in the night,
And bakes the elf-locks in foul sluttish hairs,   90
Which, once untangled, much misfortune bodes.
This is the hag, when maids lie on their backs,
That presses them and learns them first to bear,
Making them women of good carriage.
This is she –

ROMEO   Peace, peace, Mercutio, peace!   95

81 Mercutio may adopt a sacerdotal tone and cross himself, as John McEnery and Laurence
    Payne did (Zeffirelli film, BBC-TV 1955).

87 The soldier's prayer may transport Mercutio to a disturbing soldierly past, as it did for Leo
    Ciceri at Stratford, Ontario (Raby, *The Stratford Scene*, p. 162). Laurence Payne (BBC-TV
    1955) merely played the comic contrast between his startled waking and his subsequent
    complacent sleep, thus drawing a laugh from his friends. Adrian Schiller (Boyd 2000) flung
    Romeo to the stage on this line, then straddled him for the subsequent lines of sexual
    aggression.

90 David Collings, unusually light-hearted and comic for a modern Mercutio, pulled his own
    long hair on end to illustrate 'the elf-locks' (St George's, 1976).

93 Laurence Payne made 'learns them first to bear' a giggled dirty joke, which his companions
    enjoyed, then returned to ostentatious propriety for 'making them women of good carriage'
    (BBC-TV 1955).

91–4 For Mercutio to descend into sexually violent psychosis at the end of the speech has now
    virtually become standard, since John McEnery's performance in the Zeffirelli film. Harold
    Perrineau gives almost the same reading of the lines in Luhrmann. Colm Feore, in Richard
    Monette's Ontario production, played with this convention by making Mercutio's madness
    an act, and responding quickly and lightly with 'True, I talk of dreams . . .', breaking the
    tension and getting a laugh at his friend's expense. Ralph Richardson, in the 1935 Katherine
    Cornell production, remained 'in idyllic–romantic strain' for 'I talk of dreams' (s95).

Thou talk'st of nothing.

MERCUTIO   True, I talk of dreams,
Which are the children of an idle brain,
Begot of nothing but vain fantasy,
Which is as thin of substance as the air,
And more inconstant than the wind, who woos   100
Even now the frozen bosom of the north,
And being angered puffs away from thence,
Turning his side to the dew-dropping south.

BENVOLIO This wind you talk of blows us from ourselves:
Supper is done, and we shall come too late.   105

ROMEO I fear too early, for my mind misgives
Some consequence yet hanging in the stars
Shall bitterly begin his fearful date
With this night's revels, and expire the term
Of a despisèd life closed in my breast,   110
By some vile forfeit of untimely death.
But He that hath the steerage of my course
Direct my sail! On, lusty gentlemen.

BENVOLIO Strike, drum.
They march about the stage [and stand to one side].

106–13 Romeo's premonition is often given as an aside, with his friends either self-occupied or
offstage (as in NYSF 1988); however, Michael Maloney, in 1991, gave it full volume and
intensity, deeply disturbing his companions. In Henry Irving's production, Romeo gave the
speech under what Ellen Terry called 'his favourite "fate" tree', an ominous stage property
that also turned up in the Apothecary scene (*Story of My Life*, p. 234). In the St George's
production, Romeo spoke aside to the audience from the lip of the Elizabethan stage, while
his companions donned their costumes up near the façade; as he finished his prediction of
'untimely death', they turned back toward him, revealing their skull-like masks to chilling
effect (1976). Peter Brook used a 'general laugh' from the maskers to counterpoint Romeo's
'untimely death' (s100). In the Luhrmann film, the premonition is interspersed with five brief
flash-forward clips of Romeo approaching Juliet's body in the tomb.

112–13 Mark Rylance made this a rather forced attempt to reassure his friends, who were disturbed
at his outburst (RSC 1989).

114 SD If the quarto stage direction reflects stage practice, it seems that the maskers merely
progressed around the outside rim of the Elizabethan stage while the servants entered
bantering to establish the Capulet hall. For Victorian productions with an elaborate hall set
this staging was obviously impractical, but few modern directors have adopted it either.

ACT 1   SCENE 5

And SERVINGMEN *come forth with napkins.*

FIRST SERVINGMAN Where's Potpan, that he helps not to take away?
He shift a trencher? he scrape a trencher?
SECOND SERVINGMAN When good manners shall lie all in one or two
men's hands, and they unwashed too, 'tis a foul thing.
FIRST SERVINGMAN Away with the join-stools, remove the court-   5
cupboard, look to the plate. Good thou, save me a piece of
marchpane, and as thou loves me, let the porter let in Susan
Grindstone and Nell.

> [*Exit Second Servingman*]

Anthony and Potpan!

> [*Enter two more* SERVINGMEN.]

THIRD SERVINGMAN Ay, boy, ready.   10
FIRST SERVINGMAN You are looked for and called for, asked for and
sought for, in the great chamber.
FOURTH SERVINGMAN We cannot be here and there too. Cheerly, boys, be
brisk a while, and the longer liver take all.

> [*They retire behind*]

Enter [CAPULET, LADY CAPULET, JULIET, TYBALT *and his Page*, NURSE,
COUSIN CAPULET, *and*] *all the Guests and Gentlewomen to the Maskers.*

1–14 The opening of this scene, with the Capulet servants, has generally been cut in performance,
as by Garrick and Irving. Edwin Booth's promptbook, however, bears the telling note: 'This
scene must be kept up by Peter, until set is ready' (s39). To fill time, Booth here inserted
most of the Musicians' dialogue with Peter from 4.5, with all references to mourning cut.
Peter Brook also kept this brief exchange (s100). At any rate, Capulet's house is one of the
settings on which scenic designers have traditionally lavished their skills. In Irving's
production, 'the gaudy peacocks just removed from the banquet table, the minstrel's gallery
crowded with musicians, the sedilia of blue and silver, on which sat the black-haired, pale-
faced Rosaline, the trees of azalea, the overhanging drapery of silver brocade, the pages,
and the dancers, so distracted the attention that the play was for the moment lost' (*The
Theatre*, 1 April 1882).

14 SD The revelry at the Capulet party has inspired a range of choices from modern directors.
Peter Brook introduced a 'grim masque' with a touch of the grotesque (*Manchester
Guardian*, 7 April 1947). In Ron Daniels's RSC production, the scene was dominated by 'a

CAPULET Welcome, gentlemen! Ladies that have their toes   15
             Unplagued with corns will walk a bout with you.
             Ah, my mistresses, which of you all
             Will now deny to dance? She that makes dainty,
             She I'll swear hath corns. Am I come near ye now?
             Welcome, gentlemen! I have seen the day   20
             That I have worn a visor and could tell
             A whispering tale in a fair lady's ear,
             Such as would please; 'tis gone, 'tis gone, 'tis gone.

naked blindfold Cupid with a huge sexual organ' carried aloft by the maskers (*Guardian*, 10 October 1981). Bogdanov's 1986 ball scene was a jazz-rock party, complete with coloured disco lighting and introduced by Tybalt playing a riff from the Andrew Lloyd-Webber song, 'Memory', on the saxophone (a theatrical in-joke making Tybalt the Prince of *Cats* – the musical). During the dancing, Mercutio played a showy guitar solo with the band, then engaged in a wild swing dance that ended with him and his partner falling into the onstage swimming pool. In Alby James's Caribbean Temba production (1988), Elin Morgan's Rosaline performed 'a fiery, skirt-swishing flamenco amid cries of "Arriba, Arriba" from the Capulets' party guests' (*Evening Standard*, 7 July 1988). In Terry Hands's 1989 production, Mercutio and friends did a sword dance on their entry, to the applause of the Capulet clan. Adrian Noble's 1995 RSC production, set in nineteenth-century Italy, featured the *brindisi* from Act I of *La Traviata*, played by a small onstage band. In Michael Attenborough's down-market production, the ball comprised merely 'a string of light-bulbs, an accordian, clarinet and horn, and some local plonk' (*Independent on Sunday*, 9 November 1997). Michael Boyd, in 2000, used a clattering stick-dance that suggested the aggression of the feud. In the Luhrmann film the party is a raucous fancy-dress carnival, with the characters all in symbolic costumes. Romeo and Juliet, harking back to an idealised courtly love, are a knight in armour and a Botticelli angel, while the all-American Paris is an astronaut. Capulet and Lady Capulet, in toga and Egyptian wig, call to mind Shakespeare's dissipated middle-aged lovers, Antony and Cleopatra.

15 Capulet used regularly to be played as a basically comic character. In Gielgud's production, Frederick Lloyd made him 'a genuine, lovable old martinet . . . One realised why Juliet loved him and what she inherited from him' (*Morning Post*, 18 October 1935). Michael Hordern was a similarly lovable Capulet (BBC-TV 1978), thoroughly drunk and enjoying the party. In Peter Brook's 1947 production, Walter Hudd surprised Gordon Crosse by being 'not comically fussy but stern and vigorous in a really good style' (*Diaries*, XIX, 1947, p. 57). Most modern Capulets are violent and abusive characters almost from the beginning, as Jonathan Newth was for Leveaux (RSC 1991).

22-3 In Hands 1989, Bernard Horsfall kissed Lady Capulet on the cheek, showing that his lines recalled a decorous courtship rather than misspent youth.

You are welcome, gentlemen. Come, musicians, play.

Music plays.

A hall, a hall, give room! and foot it, girls.

And they dance.   25

More light, you knaves, and turn the tables up;
And quench the fire, the room is grown too hot.
Ah, sirrah, this unlooked-for sport comes well.
Nay, sit, nay, sit, good Cousin Capulet,
For you and I are past our dancing days.   30
How long is't now since last yourself and I
Were in a mask?

COUSIN CAPULET   Berlady, thirty years.

CAPULET What, man, 'tis not so much, 'tis not so much:
'Tis since the nuptial of Lucentio,
Come Pentecost as quickly as it will,   35
Some five and twenty years, and then we masked.

COUSIN CAPULET 'Tis more, 'tis more, his son is elder, sir;
His son is thirty.

CAPULET   Will you tell me that?
His son was but a ward two years ago.

25 SD Victorian productions often went all-out for spectacle. Edwin Booth used a trained *corps de ballet*; Irving provided 'a blaze of splendour with every accessory consistent with the period', taking care 'in blending the colours of the costumes so that the seeming chance-mingling shall bring together no incongruities' (*Macmillan's Magazine*, XLVI, 1882, p. 328). Irving also had Ellen Terry's Juliet take time out from the dancing for some 'natural unobtrusive toying with the children' (ibid). George Bernard Shaw reported that Mrs Patrick Campbell 'danced like the daughter of Herodias', and that her dancing was the most memorable part of her performance; the critic of the *Athenaeum* concurred that her 'performance of the *pavane* [was] beyond praise' (*Our Theatres*, III, pp. 212–13; *Athenaeum*, 28 September 1895).

29–39 Cousin Capulet was traditionally cut in the nineteenth century; Edwin Booth restored him in 1869 (Winter, *Shakespeare on the Stage*, p. 162). In David Leveaux's 1991 RSC production, Capulet and his cousin were isolated downstage for this little exchange. It was played seriously and with real poignancy, like the exchange between Shallow and Silence in *2 Henry IV* about the aging and death of their friends.

39 Hugh Hunt's 1952 Old Vic production gave Capulet the first quarto line, 'Oh, youth's a jolly thing!' just at the moment when Romeo and Juliet came face to face for the first time and fell instantly in love. According to one critic, 'As we watch them with Capulet's tossed-off words in our ears, we remember also the fateful lines of the Chorus about the "star-crossed lovers"

ROMEO [*To a Servingman*] What lady's that which doth enrich the
        hand 40
        Of yonder knight?
SERVINGMAN I know not, sir.
ROMEO O she doth teach the torches to burn bright!
        It seems she hangs upon the cheek of night
        As a rich jewel in an Ethiop's ear – 45
        Beauty too rich for use, for earth too dear:
        So shows a snowy dove trooping with crows,
        As yonder lady o'er her fellows shows.
        The measure done, I'll watch her place of stand,
        And touching hers, make blessèd my rude hand. 50

and "the fearful passage of their death-marked love" ' (*Illustrated London News*, 27 September 1952).

42 In the Krejca–Svoboda Czech production of 1963, this line was spoken as a deliberate lie by Peter, who was secretly in love with Juliet and jealous of Romeo's interest in her (Londré, 'Romeo', p. 642). It does seem implausible that a servant in Capulet's household would not recognise his daughter; productions have sometimes reassigned the servant's line, to Balthasar, Mercutio's page, even Benvolio (Levenson, Oxford edition, p. 192n.)

43 Laurence Olivier made Romeo's sudden love for Juliet one of the key strokes of his interpretation, displaying 'the fervour of a boy turned man' with 'clumsy grace'; 'stunned with Juliet's beauty, fumbling for words with which to say his love' (*Observer*, 3 November 1935).

49–50 These lines indicate that Romeo does not dance with Juliet, but merely watches her. In the 1997 RSC production, Zoe Waites danced a sensuous tango with Paris; when she saw Romeo, the music suddenly ceased, 'as if the only music for her now is her new interest in Romeo, whom she keeps trying to regard, this way or that, over Paris's shoulder' (*Financial Times*, 10 November 1997). Dorothy Tutin, at Stratford in 1958, went on dancing by herself for a moment after the music had stopped, 'for the sheer delight of it' (*SQ* 9, 1958, p. 520). Some directors can't resist having the lovers meet on the ballroom floor; Olivier 'cut in' to dance with Vivien Leigh's Juliet in his 1940 Broadway production (Wright, *Romeo*, p. 212). The formal *pavane* of the Zeffirelli film, with the dancers exchanging partners until the lovers meet with their hands raised together, has become something of a cliché (it is invoked in the film *Shakespeare in Love* for the first meeting of Joseph Fiennes and Gwyneth Paltrow). Zeffirelli, in representing Rosaline at the Capulet ball in his film, builds on a long stage tradition. Ellen Terry thought Irving had invented it: 'It is not usual, I think, to make much of the Rosaline episode. Henry Irving chose with great care a tall dark girl to represent Rosaline at the ball. Can I ever forget his face when suddenly in pursuit of *her* he saw *me*. . . .' (*Story of My Life*, p. 233). At any rate, the lovers' first sight of each other is

Did my heart love till now? forswear it, sight!
For I ne'er saw true beauty till this night.
TYBALT   This, by his voice, should be a Montague.
Fetch me my rapier, boy.   [*Exit Page*]
                What dares the slave
Come hither, covered with an antic face,   55
To fleer and scorn at our solemnity?
Now by the stock and honour of my kin,
To strike him dead I hold it not a sin.
CAPULET   Why, how now, kinsman, wherefore storm you so?
TYBALT   Uncle, this is a Montague, our foe: 60
A villain that is hither come in spite,
To scorn at our solemnity this night.
CAPULET   Young Romeo is it?
TYBALT   'Tis he, that villain Romeo.
CAPULET   Content thee, gentle coz, let him alone,

always an important moment in production. Ellen Terry's studybook has the note, 'Loves him in a minute. Look at each other all the while. Can't help it' (s47). John Rankin Towse wrote of Julia Marlowe, 'There was more than a trace of coquetry in the responsive glances with which she ogled – the word is deliberately chosen – Romeo at her first encounter with him at the ball' (Towse, *Sixty Years*, p. 396). Marlowe dropped a rose, which E. H. Sothern's Romeo picked up and pressed to his lips (s70). Eleanora Duse also dropped a rose; Modjeska dropped her fan, which Romeo returned to her (Weaver, *Duse*, p. 21, Sprague, *Shakespeare and the Actors*, p. 299). Jane Cowl used similar business. She entered with Paris, then stopped at first sight of Romeo, while Paris moved on for a few steps without noticing; Romeo unmasked, the lovers gazed at each other for a moment, and Juliet dropped a white flower, looking back to see Romeo pick it up as she rejoined Paris (s91). Bernard Grebanier felt that in the one look she exchanged with Rollo Peters's Romeo, Cowl 'managed the miracle: to project with her eyes and her entire countenance, and her hands suddenly dropped to her sides, that she had fallen completely in love' (*Then Came Each Actor*, p. 435).

54 In the 1955 BBC-TV production, the Page brought the rapier midway through the quarrel, and Capulet and Tybalt grappled over it to comic effect.

55 Romeo is usually masked for at least part of the scene, unmasking for the sonnet exchange with Juliet. In the nineteenth century (Irving, Sothern–Marlowe) through to Gielgud's 1935 production he often wore a pilgrim's white gown for his costume, sometimes with a palm staff, in allusion to the sonnet's chief metaphor (production photographs, TM). Even Peter Brook, in his iconoclastic 1947 production, used the traditional pilgrim's disguise for Romeo (*Theatre World*, 13, 1947, p. 30).

'A bears him like a portly gentleman;   65
And to say truth, Verona brags of him
To be a virtuous and well-governed youth.
I would not for the wealth of all this town
Here in my house do him disparagement;
Therefore be patient, take no note of him;   70
It is my will, the which if thou respect,
Show a fair presence, and put off these frowns,
An ill-beseeming semblance for a feast.

TYBALT It fits when such a villain is a guest:
I'll not endure him.

CAPULET   He shall be endured.   75
What, goodman boy, I say he shall, go to!
Am I the master here, or you? go to!
You'll not endure him? God shall mend my soul,
You'll make a mutiny among my guests!
You will set cock-a-hoop! you'll be the man!   80

TYBALT Why, uncle, 'tis a shame.

CAPULET   Go to, go to,
You are a saucy boy. Is't so indeed?
This trick may chance to scathe you, I know what.
You must contrary me! Marry, 'tis time. –
Well said, my hearts! – You are a princox, go,   85
Be quiet, or – More light, more light! – For shame,
I'll make you quiet, what! – Cheerly, my hearts!

TYBALT Patience perforce with wilful choler meeting
Makes my flesh tremble in their different greeting:
I will withdraw, but this intrusion shall,   90
Now seeming sweet, convert to bitt'rest gall.   *Exit*

65 Garrick emended 'portly' to 'courtly', to avoid unintended comedy.

75 In Hands 1989, the previously avuncular Capulet suddenly struck Tybalt, showing his
capacity for impulsive violence. In the Castellani film, Sebastian Cabot's Capulet veers
comically between blustering anger and joviality. Lady Capulet, noticing the quarrel, gives
Romeo a mask and warns him to leave.

85 Zeffirelli seems to have been the first to introduce a sexual affair between Tybalt and Lady
Capulet; it is now quite common on stage, as in Bogdanov's 1993 production (*Times*, 31 May
1993). In Zeffirelli's film, Lady Capulet interrupts the quarrel, sexily admonishing Tybalt with
the line, 'You are a princox, go.' In Luhrmann's film, Diane Venora's rapacious Lady Capulet
seems involved with both Tybalt and Paris.

ROMEO   [*To Juliet*] If I profane with my unworthiest hand
       This holy shrine, the gentle sin is this,
       My lips, two blushing pilgrims, ready stand
       To smooth that rough touch with a tender kiss.   95
JULIET Good pilgrim, you do wrong your hand too much,
       Which mannerly devotion shows in this,
       For saints have hands that pilgrims' hands do touch,
       And palm to palm is holy palmers' kiss.
ROMEO Have not saints lips, and holy palmers too?   100

92 ff. From 1748 onwards, for nearly a century, the lovers' sonnet was replaced by Garrick's abbreviated version:

> If I profane with my unworthy hand
> This holy shrine, the gentle fine is this.
> J Good pilgrim, you do wrong your hand too much,
> For palm to palm is holy palmer's kiss.
> R Have not saints lips, and holy palmers too?
> J Ay pilgrim, lips that they must use in prayer.
> R Thus then, dear saint, let lips put up their prayers. (Pedicord and Bergmann, *Garrick's Adaptations*, p. 95)

One effect of this shortened exchange was to obviate the need for an indecorous kiss on the lips. Indeed, Romeo seems merely to have kissed Juliet's hand in most nineteenth-century productions; the Italian Ernesto Rossi (1876) and Otis Skinner (1890) were both noted for their daring kisses on the lips (Sprague, *Shakespeare and the Actors*, p. 300). Productions often used stage business to separate Juliet and Romeo from the other actors. Phelps had the lovers leave the scene separately during the Capulet/Tybalt quarrel and return together, having met offstage (s26). Mercutio deliberately distracted both Paris and the Nurse in the Sothern–Marlowe version (s70). Many modern directors have cleared the stage entirely to leave Romeo and Juliet alone (e.g. Brook, Hall, Nunn). If other dancers remain, they are often held in the background by darkness and stylised movement, as in the film of *West Side Story*. Declan Donnellan, in his Edwardian-style production, used 'a Charleston revel slowed to a decorative cakewalk as the lovers get to first base' (*Financial Times*, 3 June 1986). Mark Rylance, for Terry Hands in 1989, impulsively seized Juliet's hand as she was about to leave the stage; as they touched, the rest of the dancers froze and the lovers were caught in a follow-spot. Surprisingly, in Noble's 1995 RSC production, Romeo and Juliet did not face each other until the kiss at the end of the scene; he stood behind her as both faced the audience.

96 Eliza O'Neill (using the Garrick text) made her replies to Romeo 'peculiarly elegant and modest', avoiding 'hoydenish wantonness', according to Charles Jones (*Memoirs*, p. 13).

JULIET   Ay, pilgrim, lips that they must use in prayer.
ROMEO   O then, dear saint, let lips do what hands do:
        They pray, grant thou, lest faith turn to despair.
JULIET   Saints do not move, though grant for prayers' sake.
ROMEO   Then move not while my prayer's effect I take.   105
        Thus from my lips, by thine, my sin is purged.
                   [*Kissing her.*]
JULIET   Then have my lips the sin that they have took.
ROMEO   Sin from my lips? O trespass sweetly urged!
        Give me my sin again.
                 [*Kissing her again.*]
JULIET   You kiss by th'book.
NURSE   Madam, your mother craves a word with you.   110
ROMEO   What is her mother?
NURSE   Marry, bachelor,
        Her mother is the lady of the house,
        And a good lady, and a wise and virtuous.
        I nursed her daughter that you talked withal;
        I tell you, he that can lay hold of her   115
        Shall have the chinks.
ROMEO   Is she a Capulet?
        O dear account! my life is my foe's debt.

101 Ellen Terry was 'grave' on this line (s47). Cynthia Nixon (NYSF 1988) reinforced the line with an amusing gesture, taking Romeo's hand away from her face and placing it up against his other hand in an attitude of prayer.

104 Ellen Terry spoke this line with a tremor (s47).

108 Anton Lesser broke this line up colloquially for comic effect, winning an audience laugh: 'Sin? From my lips? Oh! Trespass sweetly urged' (*SS* 34, 1981, p. 151).

109b Niamh Cusack (RSC 1986) played the line as a quick parting shot. Zoe Waites (RSC 1997) spoke with 'enthusiastic approval', as 'one who has done a lot of homework on the subject' (*Observer*, 9 November 1997). Alexandra Gilbreath, by contrast, admonished Romeo for not being more imaginative (RSC 2000).

110 In nineteenth-century productions, the Nurse's efforts to get Juliet away from Romeo could be the occasion for elaborate slapstick. One promptbook reads: 'Lady Capulet sends Nurse. Mercutio, wishing to aid Romeo, runs to the left of Nurse and drags her away by the dress from the lovers, then gets between them and her' (s28).

114 The Nurse often gives a disapproving pause before '*talked* withal', as in Bogdanov (1986).

117 In the Sothern–Marlowe production, Romeo's sudden discomfiture was highlighted by stage business; one of the maskers, dressed as a devil, alarmed a lady, causing her to scream (s70).

BENVOLIO Away, be gone, the sport is at the best.
ROMEO Ay, so I fear, the more is my unrest.
CAPULET Nay, gentlemen, prepare not to be gone,   120
   We have a trifling foolish banquet towards.
       [*They whisper in his ear.*]
   Is it e'en so? Why then I thank you all.
   I thank you, honest gentlemen, good night.
   More torches here, come on! then let's to bed.
   Ah, sirrah, by my fay, it waxes late,   125
   I'll to my rest.
      [*Exeunt all but Juliet and Nurse*]
JULIET Come hither, Nurse. What is yond gentleman?
NURSE The son and heir of old Tiberio.
JULIET What's he that now is going out of door?
NURSE Marry, that I think be young Petruchio.   130
JULIET What's he that follows here, that would not dance?
NURSE I know not.
JULIET Go ask his name. – If he be marrièd,
   My grave is like to be my wedding bed.
NURSE His name is Romeo, and a Montague,   135

120 While Capulet is often a 'jolly host' as in Katherine Cornell's production (Davis, s95), Paul
  Gaffney made a striking choice by having him speak the lines with gently threatening irony,
  while menacing retainers appeared behind him (University of Texas, 1984). In Michael
  Boyd's production, Capulet and his men threatened the gate-crashers until Mercutio
  removed his mask; thereafter they fawned obsequiously on him as the Prince's kinsman.
121 SD In the 1955 BBC-TV production, following the Q1 stage direction, Mercutio here whispered an
  excuse for their exit, causing Capulet to giggle with lascivious and conspiratorial mirth.
127–31 Fanny Kemble carefully distinguished her three curtsies to the parting guests. The first was
  to Benvolio; the second, to 'young Mercutio' (who replaces Petruchio in Garrick's version)
  was 'distinctly marked, as though in him she recognized the chosen friend of Romeo'. The
  third, to Romeo himself, she defined by 'the bashful sinking of the whole figure, the
  conscious drooping of the eyelids, and the hurried, yet graceful recovery of herself . . .'
  (Jameson, *Sketches*, p. 480).
133–4 Of Adelaide Neilson: 'there was a thrilling tremor in her voice that enhanced the pathos of
  the words, and as her riveted glance followed the vanishing Romeo she suddenly raised her
  left hand and kissed the spot that he, a moment earlier, had kissed, in parting from her'
  (Winter, *Shakespeare on the Stage*, p. 154).
135 Flora Robson's Nurse (BBC-TV 1955), having overheard the quarrel between Capulet and
  Tybalt, knew perfectly well who Romeo was; when Juliet pressed her to seek his name, she

       The only son of your great enemy.
JULIET My only love sprung from my only hate!
       Too early seen unknown, and known too late!
       Prodigious birth of love it is to me,
       That I must love a loathèd enemy.   140
NURSE What's tis? what's tis?
JULIET   A rhyme I learnt even now
       Of one I danced withal.
          One calls within, 'Juliet!'
NURSE   Anon, anon!
       Come let's away, the strangers all are gone.

                    Exeunt

       [*Enter*] CHORUS.

       Now old desire doth in his death-bed lie,
       And young affection gapes to be his heir;   145
       That fair for which love groaned for and would die,

did not need to go to enquire, and merely stated it disapprovingly. In the Zeffirelli film, the Nurse gets the news of Romeo's identity from Tybalt himself. Phelps had the Nurse encounter three musicians, who were exiting when 'stopped by the Nurse, who whispers them' (s26).

137–8 Adelaide Neilson's dark, doom-haunted Juliet (1865) used these lines to establish her original conception of the character. 'The sudden overclouding of her love, even in the first act, was full of sinister omen', according to Westland Marston. 'Her bending eagerness in inquiring as to Romeo's identity was suddenly exchanged for an erect and arrested attitude, while her look seemed to realize the tragic "future in the instant" ' (*Our Recent Actors*, II, p. 234). Julia Marlowe 'sat and looked far into space on the gathering fates' (Russell, *Julia Marlowe*, p. 231).

141b–2a Niamh Cusack made this line merely a hasty, nervous excuse; after all she had not danced with Romeo. Katherine Cornell's voice grew faint at the end of the line, as if she were herself struck by the pathos of her words (s95). Eliza O'Neill remained 'riveted to the ground . . . till her loquacious attendant drags her away. Even then her eye is seen to look to the door through which [Romeo] passed' (Jones, *Memoirs*, p. 13).

144–57 The second chorus is almost invariably cut in performance. Peter Brook, surprisingly, used it in 1947, even though his Chorus, John Harrison, doubled as Benvolio and had to appear in the next scene. The second chorus is also included in the 1978 BBC-TV version, presumably because John Gielgud was available to speak it. In Michael Boyd's 2000 RSC production, it was sung mockingly by a group of the male supporting actors who lurked on the walls after the ballroom scene; their menacing presence heightened the feeling of dread with which Juliet learned of Romeo's identity.

With tender Juliet matched is now not fair.
Now Romeo is beloved, and loves again,
Alike bewitchèd by the charm of looks;
But to his foe supposed he must complain,   150
And she steal love's sweet bait from fearful hooks.
Being held a foe, he may not have access
To breathe such vows as lovers use to swear,
And she as much in love, her means much less
To meet her new-belovèd any where: 155
But passion lends them power, time means, to meet,
Temp'ring extremities with extreme sweet.   [*Exit*]

ACT 2 SCENE 1

Enter ROMEO *alone.*

ROMEO Can I go forward when my heart is here?
　　　　Turn back, dull earth, and find thy centre out.

　　　　　　　　　　　　　　　　　　　　　[*Romeo withdraws*]

Enter BENVOLIO *with* MERCUTIO.

BENVOLIO Romeo! my cousin Romeo! Romeo!
MERCUTIO 　　　　　　　　　　　　　　He is wise,
　　　　And on my life hath stol'n him home to bed.
BENVOLIO He ran this way and leapt this orchard wall.　　　　5
　　　　Call, good Mercutio.
MERCUTIO 　　　　　　　　　Nay, I'll conjure too.
　　　　Romeo! humours! madman! passion! lover!
　　　　Appear thou in the likeness of a sigh,
　　　　Speak but one rhyme, and I am satisfied;
　　　　Cry but 'Ay me!', pronounce but 'love' and 'dove',　　　10
　　　　Speak to my gossip Venus one fair word,
　　　　One nickname for her purblind son and heir,
　　　　Young Abraham Cupid, he that shot so trim
　　　　When King Cophetua loved the beggar-maid.
　　　　He heareth not, he stirreth not, he moveth not,　　　15
　　　　The ape is dead, and I must conjure him.

2 SD The business of Romeo's alleged leaping of the orchard wall has troubled many editors and
confused many directors. In Elizabethan performances it is likely that Romeo merely
concealed himself behind one of the stage pillars, and that the stage became simultaneously
the Capulet orchard and the lane outside it where Mercutio and Benvolio conjure for Romeo
(Evans, New Cambridge Shakespeare edition, pp. 30–1). More representational settings
have provided a real wall for Romeo to leap. In Charles Frohman's 1899 New York
production, the wall had a large gate through which Benvolio and Mercutio could be seen
during their exchange (Winter, *Shakespeare on the Stage*, p. 188). In Michael Bogdanov's
1986 production, Sean Bean's Romeo set off a security alarm when he leapt the orchard
wall, and had to hide while a guard investigated with a flashlight.

3 In the 1990 Hull Truck modern-dress production, Romeo's friends were drunken louts who
chanted 'Romeo, Romeo' to the tune of "Ere we go, 'ere we go, 'ere we go', a chant favoured
by football hooligans (*Independent*, 11 June 1990).

13–16 Cut by Garrick, Phelps, Irving, Mary Anderson, and most others throughout the twentieth
century.

        I conjure thee by Rosaline's bright eyes,
        By her high forehead and her scarlet lip,
        By her fine foot, straight leg, and quivering thigh,
        And the demesnes that there adjacent lie,   20
        That in thy likeness thou appear to us.
BENVOLIO And if he hear thee, thou wilt anger him.
MERCUTIO This cannot anger him; 'twould anger him
        To raise a spirit in his mistress' circle,
        Of some strange nature, letting it there stand   25
        Till she had laid it and conjured it down:
        That were some spite. My invocation
        Is fair and honest: in his mistress' name
        I conjure only but to raise up him.
BENVOLIO Come, he hath hid himself among these trees   30
        To be consorted with the humorous night:
        Blind is his love, and best befits the dark.
MERCUTIO If love be blind, love cannot hit the mark.
        Now will he sit under a medlar tree,

17–20 In the Garrick version, used until 1845, Mercutio conjures by 'thy mistress' bright eye', since there has been no mention of Rosaline. Garrick kept lines 19–20, but they were cut in almost all nineteenth-century productions, and many in the twentieth, including those of William Poel, Katherine Cornell, and Eva Le Gallienne. Bernard Lloyd's misogynistic Mercutio (Hands 1973) dismembered a life-size female doll with obscene violence as he enumerated Rosaline's body parts (*Evening Standard*, 29 March 1973). Michael Kitchen (Bogdanov 1986) knelt drunkenly and roared these lines like a Southern evangelist preacher: 'Ah conjure thee . . . !' Mark Lockyer's youthful, winning Mercutio (Noble 1995) ventriloquised his conjuration with a hand puppet.

20–1 Kitchen's Mercutio, while referring to Rosaline's 'demesnes', shook up the champagne bottle he was carrying, which he let erupt orgasmically at the end of line 21.

23–7 Tim McInnery (1991) illustrated the quibbles on 'raise', 'stand', and 'laid' with a phallic fist thrust up between Benvolio's legs. The bawdy quibbling was cut throughout the nineteenth century.

33 Ralph Richardson, writing to Olivier about playing Mercutio, commented on the 'sudden delicacy' of this line (O'Connor, *Ralph Richardson*, p. 79).

33–8 Mercutio's remarkable obscenities were cut by Garrick and throughout the nineteenth century. Gordon Crosse noted that when Olivier took over Mercutio from Gielgud in the 1935 production, 'he was allowed to speak more of the ropery (including, I am sorry to say, the Poperin couplet) than Mr Gielgud, perhaps as a compensation for losing the longer part – and he did it very well' (*Diaries*, XV, 1936, p. 127). Twentieth-century productions generally opted for the euphemistic 'open etcetera', from Q1, but 'open-arse' became more usual after

And wish his mistress were that kind of fruit   35
As maids call medlars, when they laugh alone.
O Romeo, that she were, O that she were
An open-arse, thou a pop'rin pear!
Romeo, good night, I'll to my truckle-bed,
This field-bed is too cold for me to sleep.   40
Come, shall we go?
BENVOLIO   Go then, for 'tis in vain
To seek him here that means not to be found.

Exit [with Mercutio]

the sixties (e.g. in Bogdanov 1986, Luhrmann). David O'Hara, in Hands's 1989 production, tried the pronunciation 'pop-her-in' for 'poperin'.

39b–40 This line often marks a return to sobriety for Mercutio. For Leo Ciceri, in Stratford, Ontario (1968), it recalled his military past (Raby, *The Stratford Scene*, p. 162). Nicholas Pennell, in a 1977 Ontario production, 'had the future in his bones', according to Ralph Berry (*SQ* 29, 1978, p. 223). Michael Kitchen (1986) spoke the line quickly and bitterly after a scene of drunken hilarity. The momentarily chilling effect was broken by the crudely comic business of Benvolio urinating off the back of a staircase.

2.2 The so-called 'balcony scene' is the most famous scene in the play, and indeed one of the most famous in world literature. Its traditional name is perhaps inaccurate; it used to be known as the orchard scene or garden scene. The word 'balcony' certainly does not appear in the play, and the lines suggest that Juliet is to be imagined at a window. It is clear that a physical distance between the lovers is intended. The Elizabethan Juliet appeared 'aloft', presumably in some sort of gallery such as the one indicated in the DeWitt drawing of the Swan (see the reconstruction of this scene by C. Walter Hodges in Evans's New Cambridge Shakespeare edition). Some twentieth-century productions have made do without a balcony, notably Ron Daniels's 1981 London RSC production (*Evening Standard*, 10 October 1981). Paul Gaffney's 1984 University of Texas production had the lovers playing across a large gap in the stage; a Dutch production of 1999 had them both facing the audience, with a beam of light dividing them; Joe Calarco's *Shakespeare's R&J* had them holding opposite ends of a long piece of red silk (*Shakespeare Bulletin*, Winter 2000, p. 37). The 1988 Temba production played the scene in reverse, with Juliet on floor level and Romeo looking down from a parapet above (*Independent*, 4 July 1988). *West Side Story* famously reset this exchange on a fire escape, but it was not the first production to do so; a Harlem adaptation called *Romey and Julie* used the same business as early as 1936, in a production by the Federal Theatre Negro Unit #2 (Hill, *Shakespeare in Sable*, p. 112). The nature of the setting does much to define the tone of the scene. In the nineteenth century, the development of atmospheric lighting and scenery construction made this scene a favourite, with moonlit foliage and an elaborate Renaissance loggia; Edwin Booth's production actually had two balconies enclosing a grand courtyard (Ruggles, *Prince of Players*, p. 221). This tradition has been perpetuated in films of the play; one of the most famous and beautiful shots in the 1936 Cukor MGM film is of Leslie Howard walking along a silvery reflecting pool, through an orchard of cypresses, to the Capulet palazzo. Zeffirelli continues the tradition with a lush scene shot at the Palazzo Borghese, Artena, and Luhrmann spoofs it with a witty parody. In Luhrmann's film Leonardo DiCaprio wanders across a dreamy, moonlit Renaissance courtyard very like Zeffirelli's; suddenly he trips over the poolside furniture and sets off the motion-sensitive security lights. Because the scene is now so heavily laden with romantic associations, it is often played for comedy. There is a good deal of humour in Shakespeare's text, but further, deflationary business is often added. In the Luhrmann film, for instance, Romeo climbs up to the balcony only to encounter Juliet's middle-aged Nurse and fall down in horror; *Shakespeare in Love* uses the same business.

[ROMEO *advances.*]

ROMEO He jests at scars that never felt a wound.
Bur soft, what light through yonder window breaks?
It is the east, and Juliet is the sun.
Arise, fair sun, and kill the envious moon,
Who is already sick and pale with grief   5
That thou, her maid, art far more fair than she.
Be not her maid, since she is envious;
Her vestal livery is but sick and green,
And none but fools do wear it; cast it off.

[JULIET *appears aloft as at a window.*]

It is my lady, O it is my love: 10
O that she knew she were!
She speaks, yet she says nothing; what of that?
Her eye discourses, I will answer it.

---

1 Bernard Grebanier complained that Olivier, in 1940, 'popped up like a jack-in-the-box' from the far side of the orchard wall to say this line (*Then Came Each Actor*, p. 495).

3 Charles Macklin, who played Mercutio to Barry's Romeo during the rivalry with Garrick, humorously contrasted their manner of approaching the balcony: 'Barry comes into it, Sir, as great as a lord, swaggering about his love . . .', while Garrick, 'sensible that the family are at enmity with him and his house, . . . comes creeping in upon his toes, whispering his love, and looking about him *just like a thief in the night*' (Cooke, *Memoirs of Charles Macklin*, p. 205).

7–9 Cut in almost all productions before the mid-twentieth century, presumably because of the sexual suggestiveness of the lines.

9 SD Many Juliets enter earlier, after line 1 or 2. In the 1976 St George's production, Romeo responded to a light in Juliet's room, though in the quasi-Elizabethan staging there was no light change. He turned away, somewhat disappointed, for the apostrophe of lines 4–9, during which Juliet entered (to cello accompaniment) as though called forth by his words; but he only turned to see her at line 10. Historically, this scene was transformed by the development of limelight, and later electric light; the Victorian promptbook s23 has the simple technical note, 'Calcium on Juliet'.

10 When William Terriss played Romeo opposite Mary Anderson in 1884, he inflected the line, 'It *is* my lady, O it is *my love*', according to his studybook. Mark Rylance (RSC 1989) stressed 'It *is* my lady!', rather surprised to see her – his language before had been pure hyperbole. Sean Bean (RSC 1986) said 'O, it is me luv!', using his Northern accent to colloquial comic effect.

12 Katherine Cornell formed Romeo's name silently with her lips (s95).

I am too bold, 'tis not to me she speaks:
Two of the fairest stars in all the heaven,   15
Having some business, do entreat her eyes
To twinkle in their spheres till they return.
What if her eyes were there, they in her head?
The brightness of her cheek would shame those stars,
As daylight doth a lamp; her eyes in heaven   20
Would through the airy region stream so bright
That birds would sing and think it were not night.
See how she leans her cheek upon her hand!
O that I were a glove upon that hand,
That I might touch that cheek!

JULIET   Ay me!

ROMEO [*Aside*]   She speaks.   25
O speak again, bright angel, for thou art
As glorious to this night, being o'er my head,
As is a wingèd messenger of heaven
Unto the white-upturnèd wond'ring eyes
Of mortals that fall back to gaze on him,   30
When he bestrides the lazy puffing clouds,
And sails upon the bosom of the air.

JULIET O Romeo, Romeo, wherefore art thou Romeo?
Deny thy father and refuse thy name;
Or if thou wilt not, be but sworn my love,   35
And I'll no longer be a Capulet.

ROMEO [*Aside*] Shall I hear more, or shall I speak at this?

22 Terry Hands used a very slight sound effect of birds twittering (RSC 1989).

24–5a Describing Irving's Romeo in this moment, Edward Russell wrote, 'the keynote is worship – yearning, tremulous worship' (*Macmillan's Magazine*, XLVI, 1882, p. 329).

25c Sean Bean's awed delivery of this line, as though her speaking were a miraculous achievement, was winningly comic (Bogdanov 1986).

33 Though most actresses understand what 'wherefore' means, one still regularly hears this famous line misinflected in television advertisements and the like, as though Juliet were enquiring as to Romeo's whereabouts. Alexandra Gilbreath gave a fresh, effective reading of the line in Michael Boyd's production. Rather than speaking with romantic yearning, she laid her head in her crossed arms on the balcony and groaned with exasperation, frustrated that something as trivial as a name should keep Romeo from her (RSC 2000).

33–6 Edmund Kean smiled on overhearing Juliet's confession, but according to Hazlitt, 'the smile was less like that of a fortunate lover who unexpectedly hears his happiness confirmed, than of a discarded lover, who hears of the disappointment of a rival' (*Hazlitt on Theatre*, p. 32).

JULIET   'Tis but thy name that is my enemy;
      Thou art thyself, though not a Montague.
      What's Montague? It is nor hand nor foot,   40
      Nor arm nor face, nor any other part
      Belonging to a man. O be some other name!
      What's in a name? That which we call a rose
      By any other word would smell as sweet;
      So Romeo would, were he not Romeo called,   45
      Retain that dear perfection which he owes
      Without that title. Romeo, doff thy name,
      And for thy name, which is no part of thee,
      Take all myself.
ROMEO   I take thee at thy word:
      Call me but love, and I'll be new baptised;   50
      Henceforth I never will be Romeo.
JULIET   What man art thou that thus bescreened in night
      So stumblest on my counsel?
ROMEO   By a name
      I know not how to tell thee who I am.
      My name, dear saint, is hateful to myself,   55
      Because it is an enemy to thee;
      Had I it written, I would tear the word.
JULIET   My ears have yet not drunk a hundred words

39–42   Cut by Garrick and many nineteenth-century producers, perhaps because of the sexual possibility of 'nor any other part / Belonging to a man'; Charlotte Cushman excised only this phrase, singularly out of place in a production with a female Romeo. Many recent Juliets have played this hint quite explicitly, including Niamh Cusack in 1986 and Claire Danes in the Luhrmann film.

49a   Fanny Kemble's delivery of this line was notable for 'the grace and *abandon* in the manner, and the softness of accent' according to Anna Jameson (*Sketches*, p. 487).

49b   Romeo's self-revelation may result in a shriek of alarm from Juliet; in the Luhrmann film, he so startles her that they both fall in a swimming pool.

49–51   Edmund Kean was not a success in his encounter with Juliet; Hazlitt dryly observed: 'His acting sometimes reminded us of the scene with Lady Anne [in *Richard III*], and we cannot say a worse thing of it, considering the difference of the two characters' (*Hazlitt on Theatre*, p. 32).

52–3a   Stella Colas peeped out at Romeo coquettishly through a cluster of roses gathered about the window (Brereton, *Romeo*, p. 26).

55   Juliet often demonstrates her sudden recognition of Romeo at his phrase 'dear saint' (as in Zeffirelli, Leveaux).

Of thy tongue's uttering, yet I know the sound.
Art thou not Romeo, and a Montague?   60
ROMEO Neither, fair maid, if either thee dislike.
JULIET How cam'st thou hither, tell me, and wherefore?
The orchard walls are high and hard to climb,
And the place death, considering who thou art,
If any of my kinsmen find thee here.   65
ROMEO With love's light wings did I o'erperch these walls,
For stony limits cannot hold love out,
And what love can do, that dares love attempt:
Therefore thy kinsmen are no stop to me.
JULIET If they do see thee, they will murder thee.   70
ROMEO Alack, there lies more peril in thine eye
Than twenty of their swords. Look thou but sweet,
And I am proof against their enmity.
JULIET I would not for the world they saw thee here.
ROMEO I have night's cloak to hide me from their eyes,   75
And but thou love me, let them find me here;
My life were better ended by their hate,
Than death proroguèd, wanting of thy love.
JULIET By whose direction found'st thou out this place?
ROMEO By Love, that first did prompt me to enquire: 80

64–5 Modjeska was noted for her 'repeated and cautious look round the garden' and her
constant awareness of the danger to Romeo (*The Critic*, 4 June 1881).

66 Ian McKellen 'flapped his long arms as though ready to fly', to grotesque parodic effect
(Holding, *Romeo*, p. 59).

75 In Mary Anderson's Lyceum production, the lighting apparently came to Romeo's aid at this
point; the promptbook reads, 'Cloud passes over moon' (s49).

80 Olivier stood against the balcony with a pose 'so natural, so light, so animally correct, that
you feel the whole quality of Italy and of the character of Romeo and of Shakespeare's
impulse', according to Ralph Richardson, as recalled by John Gielgud (Wright, *Romeo*,
p. 217). When Olivier played the role in his own production in 1940, his physical expressions
of Romeo's love were criticised as 'so deliberate and so exhibitionistic as to be almost
indecent . . . he leaps continually about the stage and tops off every important speech
either by some sort of pirouette or by extending his arms high above his head in a gesture
which is not a lifting of the hands to heaven but a sort of voluptuous stretch' (*Nation*, 25
May 1940, quoted in Wright, *Romeo*, p. 214). Gielgud, by contrast, was graceful and poetic
even in his exaltation: 'the exaltation itself is of a peculiar kind – not hot, not animal, but
lyrically passionate, having precisely the same relationship to physical desire as a song has
to a prose piece with the same subject' (*New York Times*, 29 December 1935).

He lent me counsel, and I lent him eyes.
I am no pilot, yet wert thou as far
As that vast shore washed with the farthest sea,
I should adventure for such merchandise.
JULIET   Thou knowest the mask of night is on my face,   85
Else would a maiden blush bepaint my cheek
For that which thou hast heard me speak tonight.
Fain would I dwell on form, fain, fain deny
What I have spoke, but farewell compliment.
Dost thou love me? I know thou wilt say 'Ay';   90
And I will take thy word; yet if thou swear'st,
Thou mayst prove false: at lovers' perjuries
They say Jove laughs. O gentle Romeo,
If thou dost love, pronounce it faithfully;
Or if thou think'st I am too quickly won,   95
I'll frown and be perverse, and say thee nay,
So thou wilt woo, but else not for the world.
In truth, fair Montague, I am too fond,
And therefore thou mayst think my behaviour light:
But trust me, gentleman, I'll prove more true   100
Than those that have more coying to be strange.

85–106 Helena Faucit, writing of her own performance, said, 'I considered this speech one of the most difficult in the play, and loved and dreaded it equally . . . Watch all the fluctuations of emotion which pervade it and you will understand what a task is laid upon the actress to interpret them, not in voice and tone only, important as these are, but also in manner and action . . .' (*Shakespeare's Female Characters*, p. 119). Julia Marlowe was criticised for 'too frequent betrayals of artful premeditation' (Towse, *Sixty Years*, p. 396). Eliza O'Neill was praised for the 'chaste simplicity' of her delivery; she gave the speech with 'honourable frankness', avoiding 'a forwardness . . . which neither nature, nor Juliet's elevated rank justifies' (Jones, *Memoirs*, pp. 14–15).

89b Hubert Griffith objected to Gwen Ffrangcon-Davies's delivery of this line to Gielgud in Barry Jackson's 1924 production. He felt that 'farewell compliment' was 'something to be spoken as an aside, almost under the breath . . . Miss Ffrangcon-Davies caught fire at this simple sentence, raised her arms to it, let her voice ring out, and spoke it as though she were at the head of an army' (*Observer*, 25 May 1924).

93b–94 Helena Faucit gave this line 'kneeling on the balcony and leaning, both arms extended towards him' (s14).

95 In Zeffirelli's production, the balcony was the full width of the stage; accordingly, Juliet could 'scamper . . . back and forth laterally, as prompted by her emotional impulses, to give the scene a Punch-and-Judy-show quality' (*Saturday Review*, 3 March 1962).

I should have been more strange, I must confess,
But that thou overheard'st, ere I was ware,
My true-love passion; therefore pardon me,
And not impute this yielding to light love, 105
Which the dark night hath so discoverèd.

ROMEO　Lady, by yonder blessèd moon I vow,
That tips with silver all these fruit-tree tops –

JULIET　O swear not by the moon, th'inconstant moon,
That monthly changes in her circled orb, 110
Lest that thy love prove likewise variable.

ROMEO　What shall I swear by?

JULIET　　　　　　　　Do not swear at all;
Or if thou wilt, swear by thy gracious self,
Which is the god of my idolatry,
And I'll believe thee.

ROMEO　　　　　　　　If my heart's dear love – 115

JULIET　Well, do not swear. Although I joy in thee,
I have no joy of this contract tonight,
It is too rash, too unadvised, too sudden,
Too like the lightning, which doth cease to be
Ere one can say 'It lightens'. Sweet, good night: 120
This bud of love, by summer's ripening breath,

107　In Daniels's grim urban production of 1980, 'yonder blessèd moon' 'was a grotesque parody, all flailing arms' (*SS* 34, 1981, p. 151).

109　Stella Colas was coquettish and artful in refusing Romeo's oath; Clement Scott felt that 'her foreign origin enabled her to delight us with those tricks, fantastic changes, coquettings, poutings, and petulance which come with such difficulty from the Anglo-Saxon temperament' (*Yesterday and Today*, II, p. 301). Helena Modjeska gave the line 'with delicious archness, with that playful feigned coquetry in which passion seeks relief from its own excess' (*The Critic*, 4 June 1881). For Adelaide Neilson's death-haunted Juliet, by contrast, this injunction 'was no mere raillery, as it is with some actresses, but a superstitious misgiving' (Marston, *Our Recent Actors*, II, p. 235).

112　David Tennant's earnest young Romeo paused, momentarily at a loss, before stressing 'What *shall* I swear by?' to good comic effect – Romeo feels he must swear by *something* (RSC 2000).

117–20　Neilson spoke these lines 'with all the conviction and settled melancholy of a prophecy. You saw it was for her lover's sake, rather than her own, that Juliet rallied herself' with the lines that followed (Marston, *Our Recent Actors*, II, p. 235).

121–2　Nineteenth-century producers, apparently thinking this metaphor needed illustration, had the following business: 'Takes a flower from her bosom and throws it to him after kissing it'

        May prove a beauteous flower when next we meet.
        Good night, good night! as sweet repose and rest
        Come to thy heart as that within my breast.
ROMEO O wilt thou leave me so unsatisfied?   125
JULIET What satisfaction canst thou have tonight?
ROMEO Th'exchange of thy love's faithful vow for mine.
JULIET I gave thee mine before thou didst request it;
        And yet I would it were to give again.
ROMEO Wouldst thou withdraw it? for what purpose, love?   130
JULIET But to be frank and give it thee again,
        And yet I wish but for the thing I have:

      (s23); Helena Faucit, Helena Modjeska, and Julia Marlowe were among those who used this business (s14; Modjeska, *Memories and Impressions*, p. 137; s70). William Winter thought Adelaide Neilson had invented it (*Shakespeare on the Stage*, p. 155). Rossi's Juliet lowered a scarf, which he kissed (Carlson, *The Italian Shakespearians*, p. 165).

124 Daphne Nayar's brash young Juliet took the line literally, actually flashing her bare breasts at Roland Gift's Romeo in Hull Truck's iconoclastic 1990 production (*Financial Times*, 4 September 1990). Ivo Van Hove's 1999 Dutch production also featured a topless balcony scene (*Shakespeare Bulletin*, Winter 2000, p. 37).

125 In modern productions this line usually comes across with a sexual meaning, often unintended by Romeo but shocking to Juliet (and amusing to the audience). In 1991 Michael Maloney, realising he had alarmed Juliet with this apparently frank expression of desire, took a long pause, then reached out his hands toward her on the balcony. After shrinking back in momentary apprehension, she leaned down and placed her face in his hands as he began his line about the exchange of vows.

126 Helena Faucit delivered this line 'coyishly', according to her promptbook (s14).

128–9 Katherine Cornell said the first line in a prose tone, then went into an 'ecstatic flight' on the second, with a tremolo on the word 'yet' (s95).

131 ff. In both the stage and film productions, Zeffirelli had his lovers engage in a lot of kissing and physical contact, arousing the ire of many critics. Robert Speaight complained, of the stage production, that 'Romeo was made to scramble up a tree and start a petting-match with Juliet', while 'Miss Judi Dench was made to flop over the rail of the balcony, like a sulky child who doesn't agree that it's bedtime' (*SQ* 12, 1961, pp. 425, 426.) Defending his position, Zeffirelli suggested that Shakespeare's separation of the lovers had to do with the fact that both were male (Loney, *Staging Shakespeare*, p. 252). Earlier productions had generally kept the lovers apart, though there were sometimes attempts at contact, as in the 1881 Court Theatre production with Modjeska and Forbes-Robertson. According to Westland Marston, 'as the passion deepens, and Juliet . . . so leans from the balcony that her outstretched fingertips almost touch Romeo's, a point of intensity is reached by an action all the more

My bounty is as boundless as the sea,
My love as deep; the more I give to thee
The more I have, for both are infinite. 135
     [*Nurse calls within.*]
I hear some noise within; dear love, adieu! –
Anon, good Nurse! – Sweet Montague, be true.
Stay but a little, I will come again.   [*Exit above*]
ROMEO O blessèd, blessèd night! I am afeard,
Being in night, all this is but a dream, 140
Too flattering-sweet to be substantial.

    [*Enter Juliet above.*]

JULIET Three words, dear Romeo, and good night indeed.
If that thy bent of love be honourable,
Thy purpose marriage, send me word tomorrow,
By one that I'll procure to come to thee, 145
Where and what time thou wilt perform the rite,
And all my fortunes at thy foot I'll lay,
And follow thee my lord throughout the world.
NURSE [*Within*] Madam!
JULIET I come, anon. – But if thou meanest not well, 150
I do beseech thee –
NURSE [*Within*]   Madam!
JULIET   By and by I come –
To cease thy strife, and leave me to my grief.
Tomorrow will I send.
ROMEO So thrive my soul –
JULIET   A thousand times good night!
           [*Exit above*]

successful because its simple eagerness has a touch of the humorous' (*The Critic*, 4 June 1881).

142 Of Zeffirelli's Old Vic production: 'In the balcony scene after Juliet (Miss Judi Dench) has been called away, there was a still silence on her return before she dared speak again or Romeo dared come out of hiding: this was given meaning by Romeo's preceding soliloquy. . . And by illustrating their mutual sense of awe and fear, their response to the seemingly precarious nature of their new-found reality which at this time needs each other's presence to be substantiated, the still silence gave added force to the memory of Romeo's words' (*SS* 15, 1962, p. 148).

152 Katherine Cornell's voice caught in her throat on the word 'grief' (S95).

153 Georgia Slowe (Hands 1989) made 'Tomorrow will I send' a small, nervous question, to which Mark Rylance's Romeo replied reassuringly with 'So thrive my soul!'

ROMEO A thousand times the worse, to want thy light. 155
      Love goes toward love as schoolboys from their books,
      But love from love, toward school with heavy looks.
              [*Retiring slowly.*]

          Enter Juliet again [above].

JULIET Hist, Romeo, hist! O for a falc'ner's voice,
      To lure this tassel-gentle back again:
      Bondage is hoarse, and may nor speak aloud, 160
      Else would I tear the cave where Echo lies,
      And make her airy tongue more hoarse than mine
      With repetition of my Romeo's name.
ROMEO It is my soul that calls upon my name.
      How silver-sweet sound lovers' tongues by night, 165
      Like softest music to attending ears!
JULIET Romeo!
ROMEO   My nïesse?
JULIET   What a'clock tomorrow
      Shall I send to thee?
ROMEO   By the hour of nine.
JULIET I will not fail, 'tis twenty year till then.
      I have forgot why I did call thee back. 170

156–7 The schoolboy couplet was cut by Garrick, as part of the play's unattractive 'jingle and quibble'.

158 Mark Rylance lay back on the stage in darkness, luxuriating in Juliet's love and making no attempt to let her know of his presence (Hands, RSC 1989).

164–6 William Terriss, playing Romeo opposite Mary Anderson in 1884, seems to have given this entire speech from offstage, reentering only at the end (studybook, 1884).

167a Helena Modjeska expressed her 'thrill of delight' in finding Romeo again 'by a half-startled and stifled cry and an impulsive leaning forward and darting downwards of the hands' (Altemus, *Helena Modjeska*, p. 127).

167b Garrick said 'My sweet', Cushman and Irving 'my dear'; most productions have used one or the other of these emendations, though 'nïesse' is now frequently heard (e.g. Hands 1989, Boyd 2000).

170 William Hazlitt criticised Eliza O'Neill's playing of this moment (1814): 'the expression of tenderness bordered on hoydening, and affectation . . . She ought not to laugh when she says, "I have forgot why I did call thee back" as if conscious of the artifice, nor hang in a fondling posture over the balcony . . . the whole expression of her love should be like the breath of flowers' (*Hazlitt on Theatre*, p. 19). In Peggy Ashcroft's performance, 'there was in her voice a happy realisation that any reason Juliet may have given herself for recalling

ROMEO Let me stand here till thou remember it.
JULIET I shall forget, to have thee still stand there,
              Rememb'ring how I love thy company.
ROMEO And I'll still stay, to have thee still forget,
              Forgetting any other home but this.   175
JULIET 'Tis almost morning, I would have thee gone:
              And yet no farther than a wanton's bird,
              That lets it hop a little from his hand,
              Like a poor prisoner in his twisted gyves,
              And with a silken thread plucks it back again,   180
              So loving-jealous of his liberty.
ROMEO I would I were thy bird.
JULIET   Sweet, so would I,
              Yet I should kill thee with much cherishing.
              Good night, good night! Parting is such sweet sorrow,
              That I shall say good night till it be morrow.   [*Exit above*]   185
ROMEO Sleep dwell upon thine eyes, peace in thy breast!

Romeo had been no more than an excuse'; accordingly, her delivery of this line 'was rewarded with a burst of sympathetic and spontaneous laughter' (W. A. Darlington, quoted in Levenson, *Romeo* (1987), p. 53). According to Kenneth Tynan, Claire Bloom (Old Vic 1952) spoke the line 'with a grave amazement: there are no simpers or blushes in this dedicated young creature' (*Curtains*, p. 33).

170-1 Rather than showing 'rhetorical neatness, or passionate emphasis, or fanciful humour', 'in [Zeffirelli's] production the reply was frank and happy, appropriate to the quick sensations of the situation and suggesting a mutual response' (*SS* 15, 1962, p. 149).

175 In Terry Hands's 1989 RSC production, the lovers stood staring at each other in silence for nearly thirty seconds, until a sound effect of birds chirping prompted Juliet's line, ''Tis almost morning.'

179 This grim image was cut in Garrick's version.

184-5 Of Peggy Ashcroft's Juliet, in Gielgud's Oxford production: 'the superb farewell that follows can never have been spoken with a lovelier gravity . . . Not to hear Miss Ashcroft's farewells to Romeo . . . is to miss a part of the history of this play' (*Times*, 11 February 1932). By the end of the century, however, the farewell became hard to deliver seriously. In Declan Donellan's 1986 Regent's Park production, Ralph Fiennes and Sarah Woodward's playful Edwardian lovers mocked their own romantic enthusiasm, turning Juliet's line into a joke 'instead of the usual sniffling whine' (*Today*, 3 June 1986). Similarly, Michael Boyd's production got an anti-romantic, comic effect on the lines. Alexandra Gilbreath said, 'Good night . . . *Good night*', pointedly stressing the second in order to get the lovestruck Romeo out of his trance and on his way (RSC 2000).

> Would I were sleep and peace, so sweet to rest!
> Hence will I to my ghostly sire's close cell,
> His help to crave, and my dear hap to tell.   *Exit*

189 In his own 1940 production, Olivier completed his intensely physical playing of the scene
     with a running leap over the orchard wall (Wright, *Romeo*, p. 215).

ACT 2   SCENE 3

Enter FRIAR [LAWRENCE] *alone, with a basket.*

FRIAR LAWRENCE
    The grey-eyed morn smiles on the frowning night,
    Check'ring the eastern clouds with streaks of light;
    And fleckled darkness like a drunkard reels
    From forth day's path and Titan's fiery wheels:
    Now ere the sun advance his burning eye,   5
    The day to cheer, and night's dank dew to dry,
    I must upfill this osier cage of ours
    With baleful weeds and precious-juicèd flowers.
    The earth that's nature's mother is her tomb;
    What is her burying grave, that is her womb;   10
    And from her womb children of divers kind
    We sucking on her natural bosom find:
    Many for many virtues excellent,
    None but for some, and yet all different.

2.3 SD The Friar used traditionally to be played as a rather feeble old man (Trewin, *Going to Shakespeare*, p. 94). The twentieth century produced many younger Friars, especially in modern-dress productions. In Kurt Hübner's Bremen production of 1964, the Friar was an intellectual young monk in steel-rimmed glasses, 'an outsider who is trusted by young people' (Londré, '*Romeo*', p. 642). In the racially divided Cornerstone Theater version, the Friar was a liberal urban priest who wore a Martin Luther King T-shirt under his jacket (Coe, 'Verona, Mississippi', p. 55). Pete Postlethwaite, in the Luhrmann film, is hard-drinking and weather-beaten, with a large cross tattooed on his suntanned back.

1–30 This long speech has often been cut down in performance. Garrick and Irving both cut 3–4 and 9–14. Bogdanov (RSC 1986) made this scene an early-morning conversation between Friar Lawrence and Friar John, both on bicycles setting off about the day's business. They shared coffee from a thermos flask, Lawrence raising his cup to toast the 'true qualities' of plants (16). Adrian Noble set this scene at a pavement café, just opening for the day, where the Friar had a cup of espresso before going off to gather herbs. '. . . this weak flower' was a foxglove from the vase on the table (RSC 1995). Luhrmann has Postlethwaite explain the flower's effect to a pair of altar boys in his rooftop greenhouse. Michael Boyd, following Q2–4 and F, had Romeo begin this speech at the end of the previous scene, with the Friar only entering and beginning to speak at line 4 (RSC 2000).

14 Zeffirelli, in the stage production, broke up the speech by having an offstage bell ring, at which the Friar knelt and crossed himself (*SS* 15, 1962, p. 151).

O mickle is the powerful grace that lies 15
In plants, herbs, stones, and their true qualities:
For nought so vile, that on the earth doth live,
But to the earth some special good doth give;
Nor ought so good but, strained from that fair use,
Revolts from true birth, stumbling on abuse. 20
Virtue itself turns vice, being misapplied,
And vice sometime by action dignified.

Enter ROMEO.

Within the infant rind of this weak flower
Poison hath residence, and medicine power:
For this, being smelt, with that part cheers each part, 25
Being tasted, stays all senses with the heart.
Two such opposèd kings encamp them still
In man as well as herbs, grace and rude will;
And where the worser is predominant,
Full soon the canker death eats up that plant. 30
ROMEO Good morrow, father.
FRIAR LAWRENCE   Benedicite!
What early tongue so sweet saluteth me?
Young son, it argues a distempered head
So soon to bid good morrow to thy bed:
Care keeps his watch in every old man's eye, 35
And where care lodges, sleep will never lie;
But where unbruisèd youth with unstuffed brain
Doth couch his limbs, there golden sleep doth reign.

22 Robert Demeger, in Bogdanov 1986, vocally set off 'sometime', as if saying vice was only
rather rarely dignified by action.
22 SD From Q1. Alan Dessen defends Romeo's early entry at line 22, suggesting that the Friar's
discussion of the weak flower, containing both grace and rude will, makes Romeo into a
stage emblem (*Recovering*, p. 66). Romeo entered here in Noble (RSC 1995), but usually
Romeo has not entered until his first line (Garrick, Cushman, Irving). In Michael Boyd's
production, Des McAleer's Friar did not acknowledge Romeo's early, upstage entry, but he
evidently noticed him; for the rest of the speech, though he seemed merely to be thinking
aloud, he was clearly delivering a lesson for Romeo's benefit (RSC 2000).
23 In Beerbohm Tree's 1913 production, the Friar gave this speech in a street; a young girl came
by and gave him the flower on which he moralised (Crosse, *Diaries*, v, 1913, p. 159). In the
Castellani film, the hapless comic Friar (Mervyn Johns) is harried by church bells that
repeatedly interrupt him, so he has to make three attempts to finish this line.

Therefore thy earliness doth me assure
Thou art uproused with some distemp'rature; 40
Or if not so, then here I hit it right,
Our Romeo hath not been in bed tonight.

ROMEO That last is true, the sweeter rest was mine.

FRIAR LAWRENCE God pardon sin! wast thou with Rosaline?

ROMEO With Rosaline. my ghostly father? no; 45
I have forgot that name, and that name's woe.

FRIAR LAWRENCE That's my good son, but where hast thou been
then?

ROMEO I'll tell thee ere thou ask it me again:
I have been feasting with mine enemy,
Where on a sudden one hath wounded me 50
That's by me wounded; both our remedies
Within thy help and holy physic lies.
I bear no hatred, blessèd man; for lo,
My intercession likewise steads my foe.

FRIAR LAWRENCE Be plain, good son, and homely in thy drift, 55
Riddling confession finds but riddling shrift.

ROMEO Then plainly know, my heart's dear love is set
On the fair daughter of rich Capulet;
As mine on hers, so hers is set on mine,
And all combined, save what thou must combine 60

41–2 In Garrick, Kemble, Irving, and others, the Friar's speech is complete except for these last two lines; in modern productions, these lines, which get a laugh, are the whole purpose of the speech, which may be heavily cut before them.

43–7 Necessarily cut in the Garrick version, which makes no mention of Rosaline.

46 In Zeffirelli's production, Romeo blurted out 'I have forgot that name' as a sudden realisation, 'a thought which had, at that instant, come to him for the first time' (*SS* 15, 1962, p. 149).

47 In the 1988 NYSF production, Peter MacNicol absently started to put the poisonous flower in his mouth, and Milo O'Shea's Friar had to snatch it way on 'That's my good son.' In Bogdanov 1986, Robert Demeger spoke 'where *hast* thou been then?' with sudden comic alarm, as though fearing that Romeo's nocturnal activities were even worse than a tryst with Rosaline.

55 In the 1976 St George's production, both Romeo and the Friar knelt as though in a confessional; the latter held up his hand to screen his face.

58 David Tennant's Romeo rushed through his identification of Juliet, embarrassed at his sudden change of affection and its unlikely object (RSC 2000).

By holy marriage. When and where and how
We met, we wooed, and made exchange of vow,
I'll tell thee as we pass, but this I pray,
That thou consent to marry us today.
FRIAR LAWRENCE Holy Saint Francis, what a change is here!   65
Is Rosaline, that thou didst love so dear,
So soon forsaken? Young men's love then lies
Not truly in their hearts, but in their eyes.
Jesu Maria, what a deal of brine
Hath washed thy sallow cheeks for Rosaline!   70
How much salt water thrown away in waste,
To season love, that of it doth not taste!
The sun not yet thy sighs from heaven clears,
Thy old groans yet ringing in mine ancient ears;
Lo here upon thy cheek the stain doth sit   75
Of an old tear that is not washed off yet.
If e'er thou wast thyself, and these woes thine,
Thou and these woes were all for Rosaline.
And art thou changed? Pronounce this sentence then:
Women may fall, when there's no strength in men.   80
ROMEO Thou chid'st me oft for loving Rosaline.
FRIAR LAWRENCE For doting, not for loving, pupil mine.
ROMEO And bad'st me bury love.
FRIAR LAWRENCE   Not in a grave,
To lay one in, another out to have.
ROMEO I pray thee chide me not. Her I love now   85
Doth grace for grace and love for love allow;
The other did not so.
FRIAR LAWRENCE   O she knew well
Thy love did read by rote, that could not spell.

61–4 Mark Rylance eagerly picked up the Friar's stool and basket and tossed him his sandals in his hurry to make preparations for his marriage (RSC 1989).

65–80 Necessarily cut in the Garrick version, which eliminates Rosaline; instead the Friar warns Romeo about his 'rash ungovernable passions'. In the 1988 NYSF production, Romeo tried repeatedly to interrupt the Friar's string of platitudes, in the end speaking along with him on 'when there's no strength in men'; clearly he had heard this lecture before.

68 Pete Postlethwaite, in the Luhrmann film, takes a brief pause before 'eyes', as though about to suggest that young men's love lies elsewhere in their anatomy.

88 Mark Rylance's Romeo started to leave angrily, prompting the Friar to stop him and reassure him (RSC 1989).

But come, young waverer, come go with me,
In one respect I'll thy assistant be: 90
For this alliance may so happy prove
To turn your households' rancour to pure love.
ROMEO O let us hence, I stand on sudden haste.
FRIAR LAWRENCE Wisely and slow, they stumble that run fast.

Exeunt

89 In the Zeffirelli film, the Friar's change of heart is prompted by a tolling bell and the sight of a crucifix; in Luhrmann's by imagined newspaper headlines proclaiming the end of the feud, and featuring the Friar's role in bringing about its resolution.

94 The Friar's exit line often provokes rather obvious business: in the Zeffirelli film, it is the Friar that stumbles, whereas Luhrmann has his rash young Romeo trip over an altar candlestick in his hurried exit. In the 1988 NYSF production, Romeo hastily pulled the Friar offstage, thus causing him to stumble.

ACT 2   SCENE 4

Ener BENVOLIO *and* MERCUTIO.

MERCUTIO Where the dev'l should this Romeo be?
　　Came he not home tonight?
BENVOLIO Nor to his father's, I spoke with his man.
MERCUTIO Why, that same pale hard-hearted wench, that Rosaline,
　　Torments him so, that he will sure run mad.　　　　　　　　　5
BENVOLIO Tybalt, the kinsman to old Capulet,
　　Hath sent a letter to his father's house.
MERCUTIO A challenge, on my life.
BENVOLIO Romeo will answer it.
MERCUTIO Any man that can write may answer a letter.　　　　　10
BENVOLIO Nay, he will answer the letter's master, how he dares,
　　being dared.
MERCUTIO Alas, poor Romeo, he is already dead, stabbed with a white
　　wench's black eye, run through the ear with a love-song, the very
　　pin of his heart cleft with the blind bow-boy's butt-shaft; and is　　15
　　he a man to encounter Tybalt?
BENVOLIO Why, what is Tybalt?
MERCUTIO More than Prince of Cats. O, he's the courageous captain
　　of compliments: he fights as you sing prick-song, keeps time,
　　distance, and proportion; he rests his minim rests, one, two, and　　20
　　the third in your bosom; the very butcher of a silk button, a duellist,

---

2.4 Adrian Noble made this scene continuous with the previous one, both taking place at a
　　pavement café. Mercutio entered with an ice-bag on his head, nursing a hangover, and
　　winced when the waiter loudly dropped a tray on the table. Hangovers are common among
　　modern Mercutios; in Bogdanov 1986, Michael Kitchen dropped Alka-Seltzer into his glass
　　of wine.
17 Philip Voss spoke this line with contempt rather than interest or alarm; an unusually tough
　　and cynical Benvolio, he had held his own in the earlier combat with Tybalt, and thought
　　him no great threat (St George's 1976).
18–31 Mercutio's mockery of Tybalt often incorporates a parodic, stereotyped effeminacy. Ralph
　　Richardson used a 'mock courtier's bow' and 'feline falsetto' on 'these pardon-me's', for
　　instance (s95). Courtney B. Vance, who played Mercutio as homosexual, oddly mocked in
　　Tybalt the same high, affected voice and campy gestures he had himself been using (NYSF
　　1988).

a duellist; a gentleman of the very first house, of the first and second
cause. Ah, the immortal 'passado', the 'punto reverso', the 'hay'!

BENVOLIO The what?

MERCUTIO The pox of such antic, lisping, affecting phantasimes, these   25
new tuners of accent! 'By Jesu, a very good blade! a very tall man!
a very good whore!' Why, is not this a lamentable thing, grandsire,
that we should be thus afflicted with these strange flies, these
fashion-mongers, these pardon-me's, who stand so much on the
new form, that they cannot sit at ease on the old bench? O their   30
bones, their bones!

Enter ROMEO.

BENVOLIO Here comes Romeo, here comes Romeo.

MERCUTIO Without his roe, like a dried herring: O flesh, flesh, how
art thou fishified. Now is he for the numbers that Petrarch flowed
in. Laura to his lady was a kitchen wench (marry, she had a better   35
love to berhyme her), Dido a dowdy, Cleopatra a gipsy, Helen and
Hero hildings and harlots, Thisbe a grey eye or so, but not to the
purpose. Signior Romeo, 'bon jour'! there's a French salutation
to your French slop. You gave us the counterfeit fairly last night.

ROMEO Good morrow to you both. What counterfeit did I give you?   40

MERCUTIO The slip, sir, the slip, can you not conceive?

ROMEO Pardon, good Mercutio, my business was great, and in such a
case as mine a man may strain courtesy.

MERCUTIO That's as much as to say, such a case as yours constrains
a man to bow in the hams.   45

---

23 Mercutio often executes some flamboyant fencing moves; in Luhrmann's modern setting,
Harold Perrineau does some quick-draw twirling of his automatic pistol.

27–31 Mercutio sometimes mimics a crusty old codger, as in Zeffirelli's film. For Tim McInnery's
melancholy Mercutio, however, the 'grandsire' speech was not tossed-off silliness but a
grave and meaningful flight of fancy (Leveaux, RSC 1991).

38 Many Mercutios, including Charles Kemble and Ralph Richardson, have kissed Romeo in an
exaggeratedly continental fashion after 'bon jour' (Williamson, *Charles Kemble*, p. 114; s95).

44–82 Cut by Garrick, Kemble, Cushman, Forbes-Robertson, and many others; Irving kept eight
more lines of wordplay (to line 50), as well as Mercutio's important lines 72–4a, praising
Romeo's return to his sociable self. Phelps kept all but the lines on the 'wit of cheverel' and
the 'bauble in a hole' (s26). Terry Hands (1973) took this exchange at a furious pace, 'with
each verbal thrust and parry accompanied by a jump to a new formal posture' (David,

ROMEO Meaning to cur'sy.

MERCUTIO Thou hast most kindly hit it.

ROMEO A most courteous exposition.

MERCUTIO Nay, I am the very pink of courtesy.

ROMEO Pink for flower. 50

MERCUTIO Right.

ROMEO Why then is my pump well flowered.

MERCUTIO Sure wit! Follow me this jest now, till thou hast worn out
    thy pump, that when the single sole of it is worn, the jest may
    remain, after the wearing, solely singular. 55

ROMEO O single-soled jest, solely singular for the singleness!

MERCUTIO Come between us, good Benvolio, my wits faints.

ROMEO Swits and spurs, swits and spurs, or I'll cry a match.

MERCUTIO Nay, if our wits run the wild-goose chase, I am done; for
    thou hast more of the wild goose in one of thy wits than, I am sure, 60
    I have in my whole five. Was I with you there for the goose?

ROMEO Thou wast never with me for any thing when thou wast not
    there for the goose.

MERCUTIO I will bite thee by the ear for that jest.

ROMEO Nay, good goose, bite not. 65

MERCUTIO Thy wit is a very bitter sweeting, it is a most sharp sauce.

ROMEO And is it not then well served in to a sweet goose?

MERCUTIO O here's a wit of cheverel, that stretches from an inch
    narrow to an ell broad!

ROMEO I stretch it out for that word 'broad', which, added to the goose, 70
    proves thee far and wide a broad goose.

Shakespeare in the Theatre, p. 111). In Daniels's 1980 production the wit-contest 'was played
as street-corner gang in-joking, with no attempt to get laughs off the faded quibbles
themselves' (*SS* 34, 1981, p. 151).

50 Michael Kitchen's Mercutio took a pink carnation from the vase at their café table and stuck
it behind Benvolio's ear (RSC 1986).

52 Sean Bean put his shoe on the café table to demonstrate the surface meaning of this quip;
Leonardo DiCaprio grabbed his crotch to suggest another meaning. In Byam Shaw's 1954
production, Romeo lifted his foot to show off his shoe; Mercutio caught it and Romeo fell
(promptbook, SCL).

58 In Peter Brook's production Romeo and Mercutio actually fenced with rapiers during the
duel of wits; Romeo disarmed Mercutio at this line. In Terry Hands's 1989 production,
unusually, Mercutio was sulky and slow to participate in the wit-contest; Romeo's high
spirits eventually cheered him up.

MERCUTIO Why, is not this better now than groaning for love? Now
    art thou sociable, now art thou Romeo; now art thou what thou
    art, by art as well as by nature, for this drivelling love is like a great
    natural that runs lolling up and down to hide his bauble in a hole.   75
BENVOLIO Stop there, stop there.
MERCUTIO Thou desirest me to stop in my tale against the hair.
BENVOLIO Thou wouldst else have made thy tale large.
MERCUTIO O thou art deceived; I would have made it short, for I was
    come to the whole depth of my tale, and meant indeed to occupy   80
    the argument no longer.
ROMEO Here's goodly gear!

Enter NURSE *and her man* [PETER].

    A sail, a sail!

MERCUTIO Two, two: a shirt and a smock.
NURSE Peter!   85
PETER Anon.
NURSE My fan, Peter.
MERCUTIO Good Peter, to hide her face, for her fan's the fairer face.
NURSE God ye good morrow, gentlemen.
MERCUTIO God ye good den, fair gentlewoman.   90
NURSE Is it good den?
MERCUTTO 'Tis no less, I tell ye, for the bawdy hand of the dial is
    now upon the prick of noon.

72–81 Courtney Vance's gay Mercutio became very physical in this exchange, embracing both
    Romeo and Benvolio (to their embarrassment) and grabbing Romeo's crotch (NYSF 1988).
83 Romeo's line is often prompted by some billowing piece of the Nurse's apparel, as in the
    Zeffirelli film.
85 In Jane Cowl's 1923 production, according to the promptbook: 'Peter enters first, six feet
    ahead of the Nurse, whom he is fanning, but as he is too far away to be of any benefit to her,
    she calls him back with "My fan, Peter" ' (s91).
93 Though Ralph Richardson pointed his right arm up on 'the prick of noon', Fitzroy Davis
    observed that the 1935 audience 'never gets this dirt' (s95). More recent audiences have
    been unable to miss it. John McEnery, in the Zeffirelli film, artfully acknowledged the
    multiple meanings of 'prick' by pretending to be doing embroidery on his handkerchief,
    then thrusting his hand up under the fabric in a phallic gesture. Michael Kitchen, in 1986,
    placed the Nurse's hand on his crotch, while Margaret Courtenay, in 1989, hit Mercutio's
    crotch without prompting. In the 1990 Hull Truck production, the line was illustrated even
    more colourfully with a large inflatable banana (*Independent*, 11 June 1990).

NURSE Out upon you, what a man are you?

ROMEO One, gentlewoman, that God hath made, himself to mar.   95

NURSE By my troth, it is well said: 'for himself to mar', quoth'a?
   Gentlemen, can any of you tell me where I may find the young
   Romeo?

ROMEO I can tell you, but young Romeo will be older when you have
   found him than he was when you sought him: I am the youngest   100
   of that name, for fault of a worse.

NURSE You say well.

MERCUTIO Yea, is the worst well? Very well took, i'faith, wisely,
   wisely.

NURSE If you be he, sir, I desire some confidence with you.   105

BENVOLIO She will indite him to some supper.

MERCUTIO A bawd, a bawd, a bawd! So ho!

ROMEO What hast thou found?

MERCUTIO No hare, sir, unless a hare, sir, in a lenten pie, that is
   something stale and hoar ere it be spent.   110

[He walks by them and sings.]

94 In the Zeffirelli film Pat Heywood's Nurse laughs with relish at Mercutio's joke, then catches
    herself and feigns shocked disdain.

95 In Declan Donnellan's Regent's Park production (1986), Nicholas Wolff's Mercutio, who was
    in love with Romeo, was deeply pained by this line; it represented Romeo's final, unwitting
    betrayal of his affection (*Observer*, 22 June 1986).

97 In response to the Nurse's enquiry about Romeo's whereabouts, Benvolio and Mercutio in
    Katherine Cornell's production pretended ignorance, putting their hands to their chins and
    repeating 'Romeo?' quizzically (s95).

99 Peter McEnery began this rather laboured joke amused at his own wit, but soon realised
    that the Nurse wasn't catching on and gave up, declaring his identity in mild embarrassment
    (St George's, 1976). Mark Rylance, still in the rowdy mood of the wit-contest, hid behind his
    friends as though afraid the Nurse had her own designs on him; he actively participated in
    the mocking of the Nurse and only became serious when she explained she had come on
    Juliet's instructions.

100 In Irving's production, Romeo did not recognise the Nurse until after this line: he was sitting
    on a shaded bench in casual conversation with Benvolio, the preceding bawdy banter
    having been cut. Hence Irving avoided the 'great little absurdity' of 'Romeo's non-
    recognition of the Nurse whom he perfectly well knows, and at the sight of whom all his
    faculties would be on the alert' (*Macmillan's Magazine*, XLVI, 1882, p. 333).

107 In Noble's 1995 production, all the young men drew imaginary bows at the Nurse upon
    Mercutio's hunting cry.

An old hare hoar,
And an old hare hoar,
Is very good meat in Lent;
But a hare that is hoar
Is too much for a score,   115
When it hoars ere it be spent.
Romeo, will you come to your father's? We'll to dinner thither.
ROMEO I will follow you.
MERCUTIO Farewell, ancient lady, farewell, lady, [*Singing.*] 'lady,
lady'.   120

Exeunt [Mercutio and Benvolio]

NURSE I pray you, sir, what saucy merchant was this that was so full
of his ropery?
ROMEO A gentleman, Nurse, that loves to hear himself talk, and will
speak more in a minute than he will stand to in a month.
NURSE And 'a speak any thing against me, I'll take him down, and 'a   125
were lustier than he is, and twenty such Jacks; and if I cannot, I'll
find those that shall. Scurvy knave, I am none of his flirt-gills, I

111 Some physical abuse of the Nurse has been standard business in the scene for some time;
Fitzroy Davis wrote that in 1935 Ralph Richardson's Mercutio 'whisk[ed] under her skirts, as
if to goose her'. In David Leveaux's 1991 RSC production, Benvolio picked the Nurse up from
behind so that Tim McInnery's Mercutio could get between her legs in a grotesque mock-
coupling which the Nurse seemed rather to enjoy; she fanned herself afterwards as if
aroused.

117 Mark Lockyer's young Mercutio made 'will you come to your father's?' a hasty exit line,
fearing the resentful Nurse's threatening advance (RSC 1995). In the Luhrmann film, Harold
Perrineau asks with a kind of jealous desperation, as though Mercutio knows the Nurse's
business will draw Romeo away from him.

119 Charles Kemble's gentlemanly Mercutio had generally avoided open derision, assuming 'a
grave, though somewhat exaggerated, courtesy towards the ancient lady, as if to mask his
ridicule from her, while enhancing it towards his comrades' (Marston, *Our Recent Actors*, I,
p. 123). He did, however, mimic her by saying, 'Peter, my fan', just before his exit
(Williamson, *Charles Kemble*, p. 115). A nineteenth-century promptbook has Benvolio using
his cap to fan Mercutio, who hobbles offstage with his sword as a walking-stick (S43).

120 Laurence Payne, in the 1955 BBC-TV version, spoke his 'lady, lady' with a cluck of the tongue,
a wink, and a toss of the head, as though inviting the Nurse to accompany him offstage for
an assignation.

am none of his skains-mates. [*She turns to Peter, her man.*] And thou
must stand by too and suffer every knave to use me at his pleasure!

PETER I saw no man use you at his pleasure; if I had, my weapon should　130
quickly have been out. I warrant you, I dare draw as soon as another
man, if I see occasion in a good quarrel, and the law on my side.

NURSE Now afore God, I am so vexed that every part about me quivers.
Scurvy knave! Pray you, sir, a word: and as I told you, my young
lady bid me enquire you out; what she bid me say, I will keep to　135
myself. But first let me tell ye, if ye should lead her in a fool's
paradise, as they say, it were a very gross kind of behaviour, as they
say; for the gentlewoman is young; and therefore, if you should deal
double with her, truly it were an ill thing to be offered to any
gentlewoman, and very weak dealing.　140

ROMEO Nurse, commend me to thy lady and mistress. I protest unto
thee –

NURSE Good heart, and i'faith I will tell her as much. Lord, Lord, she
will be a joyful woman.

ROMEO What wilt thou tell her, Nurse? thou dost not mark me.　145

127–8 In Hands's 1989 production, according to Michael Billington, Margaret Courtenay spoke this
line with exceptional dignity, 'like a Duchess disdaining a pass by the footman' (*Guardian*, 7
April 1989).

128–9 'Stage policy, to please the upper regions, generally presents Peter as bearing an enormous
fan before his mistress; skipping also and grinning like a baboon; the beating which he gets
for not resenting Mercutio's raillery, is a very mean, pantomimical, yet sure motive of
laughter', according to Francis Gentleman in 1770 (*Bell's Edition*, p. 180). Such business
continued through the nineteenth century; the Victorian promptbook s23 has 'Peter laughs.
Nurse strikes him with fan', followed by another standard routine: 'Peter draws a small toy
sword from a large scabbard, catches a fly and cuts its head off.'

130 In Leveaux's 1991 production, Peter was unaware of the bawdy significance of his protest
that 'my weapon should quickly have been out', but in drawing his dagger to demonstrate,
he caught it inside the front of his long smock, giving the effect of a huge erection. The Q1
reading suggests that in the original performances Will Kemp was fairly explicit with his
business: 'You know my tool is as soon out as another's, if I see time and place' (2.3.130–1).

134–5 In Ivo Van Hove's 1999 Dutch production, the Nurse took it upon herself to examine Romeo
and assess his fitness for marriage, even taking down his trousers during their interview
(*Shakespeare Bulletin*, Winter 2000, p. 37).

NURSE I will tell her, sir, that you do protest, which, as I take it, is a
gentleman-like offer.
ROMEO Bid her devise
Some means to come to shrift this afternoon,
And there she shall at Friar Lawrence' cell   150
Be shrived and married. Here is for thy pains.
NURSE No truly, sir, not a penny.
ROMEO Go to, I say you shall.
NURSE This afternoon, sir? Well, she shall be there.
ROMEO And stay, good Nurse, behind the abbey wall: 155
Within this hour my man shall be with thee,
And bring thee cords made like a tackled stair,
Which to the high top-gallant of my joy
Must be my convoy in the secret night.
Farewell, be trusty, and I'll quit thy pains.   160
Farewell, commend me to thy mistress.
NURSE Now God in heaven bless thee! Hark you, sir.
ROMEO What say'st thou, my dear Nurse?
NURSE Is your man secret? Did you ne'er hear say,
'Two may keep counsel, putting one away'?   165
ROMEO 'Warrant thee, my man's as true as steel.
NURSE Well, sir, my mistress is the sweetest lady – Lord, Lord! when
'twas a little prating thing – O, there is a nobleman in town, one
Paris, that would fain lay knife aboard; but she, good soul, had as
lieve see a toad, a very toad, as see him. I anger her sometimes,   170
and tell her that Paris is the properer man, but I'll warrant you,

153 Inevitably, the Nurse doth protest too much, and then happily accepts the offered gratuity.
In Samuel Phelps's Sadler's Wells production (1846), 'Nurse continues repeating 'Not a
penny' until she gets the purse fully in her possession' (S26). In the Zeffirelli film Pat
Heywood impulsively snatches Romeo's coin just as he is about to drop it into the offering
box in the church where they are meeting. At the Lyceum in 1884, Mrs Stirling used
elaborate business, recalled by her Juliet, Mary Anderson: 'when she had taken the money,
she would cross the stage, chinking the coins as she went, with her hands under her chin,
until "Peter" was within reach of her stick. Then it was thwack! thwack! thwack: – chink,
chink, chink – quite legitimate business, that every night would set the house in a roar'
(Allen, *Mrs Stirling*, p. 215).
168 In Bogdanov 1986, Dilys Laye's Nurse began to launch into an ad lib retelling of little Juliet's
bumping her head, then checked herself and went on with the speech.

when I say so, she looks as pale as any clout in the versal world.
Doth not rosemary and Romeo begin both with a letter?
ROMEO Ay, Nurse, what of that? Both with an R.
NURSE Ah, mocker, that's the dog-name. R is for the – no, I know it   175
begins with some other letter – and she hath the prettiest sententious
of it, of you and rosemary, that it would do you good to hear it.
ROMEO Commend me to thy lady.
NURSE Ay, a thousand times.

                                                        [Exit Romeo]
                             Peter!
PETER Anon.   180
NURSE *[Handing him her fan.]* Before and apace.

                                           Exit [after Peter]

173 The Nurse's prattlings about Juliet have almost always been cut. The virtually uncut St George production included them, with Romeo making repeated false exits only to be called back by some further irrelevant detail.

174 After 'Both with an R', Peter McEnery demonstrated the sound – 'rrrr'–prompting the Nurse's remark about the dog's name (St George's 1976).

175 In Boyd 2000, Eileen McCallum managed to convey this obscure quibble by eliding 'R is' into something that sounded like 'arse'.

179 In Edwin Booth's production, according to the promptbook, Peter was 'asleep at left wing or catching flies – Nurse hits his head with her stick' (S37). In Henry Irving's detailed Italian setting, 'Instead of standing with a meaningless leer on his face while the Nurse conversed with Romeo, Peter seize[d] the occasion to stretch his limbs and bask in the sunshine' (*Athenaeum*, 11 March 1882).

Enter JULIET.

JULIET   The clock struck nine when I did send the Nurse;
           In half an hour she promised to return.
           Perchance she cannot meet him: that's not so.
           O, she is lame! Love's heralds should be thoughts,
           Which ten times faster glides than the sun's beams,   5
           Driving back shadows over low'ring hills;
           Therefore do nimble-pinioned doves draw Love,
           And therefore hath the wind-swift Cupid wings.
           Now is the sun upon the highmost hill
           Of this day's journey, and from nine till twelve   10
           Is three long hours, yet she is not come.
           Had she affections and warm youthful blood,
           She would be as swift in motion as a ball;
           My words would bandy her to my sweet love,
           And his to me.   15
           But old folks, many feign as they were dead,
           Unwieldy, slow, heavy, and pale as lead.

Enter NURSE [*with* PETER].

           O God, she comes! O honey Nurse, what news?
           Hast thou met with him? Send thy man away.

2.5   At the beginning of this scene Fanny Kemble 'was discovered in a picturesque attitude
       standing leaning on the back of a chair, earnestly looking out of a tall window opening onto
       a garden, as if eager to catch the first approach of the expected messenger . . .' (Charles and
       Mary Cowden Clark, *Recollections of Writers*, quoted in Salgado, *Eyewitnesses*, p. 201). By
       contrast, Estelle Kohler (Hands 1973) energetically worked off her impatience by beating a
       carpet while awaiting the Nurse's return (promptbook, SCL).
13   In the MGM film George Cukor felt it necessary to illustrate this simile; the published
       shooting script contains the stage direction, 'She imitates the stroke of a racquet' (Farjeon,
       Shakespearean Scene, p. 124).
16–17 In the Shakespeare at Winedale production of 2000, the Nurse entered in time to overhear
       this couplet, a choice that motivated her teasing of Juliet.

NURSE Peter, stay at the gate.   20

                                                    [*Exit Peter*]

JULIET Now, good sweet Nurse – O Lord, why look'st thou sad?
            Though news be sad, yet tell them merrily;
            If good, thou shamest the music of sweet news
            By playing it to me with so sour a face.

NURSE I am a-weary, give me leave a while.   25
            Fie, how my bones ache! What a jaunce have I!

JULIET I would thou hadst my bones, and I thy news.
            Nay, come, I pray thee speak, good, good Nurse, speak.

NURSE Jesu, what haste! can you not stay a while?
            Do you not see that I am out of breath?   30

JULIET How art thou out of breath, when thou hast breath
            To say to me that thou art out of breath?
            The excuse that thou dost make in this delay
            Is longer than the tale thou dost excuse.
            Is thy news good or bad? Answer to that.   35
            Say either, and I'll stay the circumstance:
            Let me be satisfied, is't good or bad?

NURSE Well, you have made a simple choice, you know not how to
            choose a man: Romeo? no, not he, though his face be better than
            any man's, yet his leg excels all men's, and for a hand and a foot   40
            and a body, though they be not to be talked on, yet they are past
            compare. He is not the flower of courtesy, but I'll warrant him,
            as gentle as a lamb. Go thy ways, wench, serve God. What, have
            you dined at home?

JULIET No, no! But all this did I know before.   45
            What says he of our marriage, what of that?

26 In F and Q2–4, the Nurse here calls for aqua-vitae; Cibber's adaptation contains the stage
      direction, 'Enter Peter with a bottle and cup' (p. 25).

28 A Victorian promptbook, s23, has the note ' 1st time sadly. 2nd time archly'.

29–34 Garrick cut these lines, as well as the earlier 'I would thou hadst my bones, and I thy news'
      (27). Presumably he thought her pertness an offence to decorum, but the effect of the cuts is
      to remove Juliet's sense of humour. Peggy Ashcroft played these lines with great wit and
      youthful vitality; in Gielgud's Oxford production, the scene was 'brilliant in its zest and
      invention, proving that in comedy Miss Ashcroft may well go where she pleases' (*Times*, 11
      February 1932).

37 In Bogdanov 1986, the Nurse was about to take a drink when Juliet stole her little flask of
      brandy on 'Let me be satisfied'; the Nurse waited until it was returned before commencing
      her speech.

NURSE Lord, how my head aches! what a head have I!
    It beats as it would fall in twenty pieces.
    My back a't'other side – ah, my back, my back!
    Beshrew your heart for sending me about   50
    To catch my death with jauncing up and down!
JULIET I'faith, I am sorry that thou art not well.
    Sweet, sweet, sweet Nurse, tell me, what says my love?
NURSE Your love says, like an honest gentleman,
    And a courteous, and a kind, and a handsome,   55
    And I warrant a virtuous – Where is your mother?
JULIET Where is my mother? why, she is within,
    Where should she be? How oddly thou repliest:
    'Your love says, like an honest gentleman,
    "Where is your mother?"'
NURSE   O God's lady dear,   60
    Are you so hot? Marry come up, I trow;
    Is this the poultice for my aching bones?
    Henceforward do your messages yourself.

47 Mrs Stirling and Mary Anderson played the scene in a garden with a fountain; at 'what a head have I', the Nurse dipped her handkerchief in the fountain and wiped her brow with it (s49).

57–60 Ellen Terry gives an interesting comment on the nineteenth-century tradition for playing this scene (a tradition still very much alive throughout the twentieth): 'Tradition said that Juliet must go on coquetting and clicking over the Nurse to get the news of Romeo out of her. Tradition said that Juliet must give imitations of the Nurse on the line "Where's your mother?" in order to get that cheap reward, "a safe laugh". I felt that it was wrong. I felt that Juliet was angry with the Nurse. Each time she delayed in answering I lost my temper, with genuine passion. At "Where's your mother?" I spoke with indignation, tears and rage. We were a long time coaxing Mrs Stirling to let the scene be played on these lines, but this was how it *was* played eventually' (*Story of My Life*, p. 230). In contrast to Terry's own account, Clement Scott described how Terry's 'delicious coaxing of the Nurse, in all the playfulness and enfantillage of Juliet's disposition', had 'girlishness, coquetry, and charm' (*The Theatre*, 1 April 1882). Adelaide Neilson played the scene in a more calculating manner; it 'savoured rather of the arts of a practised intriguer than those of an innocent and affectionate girl' (Marston, *Our Recent Actors*, II, pp. 235–6). William Archer was highly critical of Mrs Patrick Campbell's approach to the scene: 'She showed no intensity and no variety in her expression of eagerness, expectation, disappointment, anger, affection, rapture, but played all on one level of prettiness' (*Theatrical 'World' of 1895*, p. 289).

JULIET Here's such a coil! Come, what says Romeo?
NURSE Have you got leave to go to shrift today?   65
JULIET I have.
NURSE Then hie you hence to Friar Lawrence' cell,
        There stays a husband to make you a wife.
        Now comes the wanton blood up in your cheeks,
        They'll be in scarlet straight at any news.   70
        Hie you to church, I must another way,
        To fetch a ladder, by the which your love
        Must climb a bird's nest soon when it is dark.
        I am the drudge, and toil in your delight;
        But you shall bear the burden soon at night.   75
        Go, I'll to dinner, hie you to the cell.
JULIET Hie to high fortune! Honest Nurse, farewell.

Exeunt

64 The making-up of the quarrel between the Nurse and Juliet was inevitably marked by
    sentimental business in nineteenth-century productions. In Cushman's promptbook, 'Juliet
    kneels . . . looking up tenderly in the Nurse's face – Nurse drops her stick and embraces her
    – Juliet picks up the stick and gives it to her' (s31). Julia Marlowe leaned over the Nurse's
    back and tenderly touched her cheek with a bunch of roses; 'She flings herself over . . . into
    Juliet's waiting arms and the quarrel is ended' (Russell, *Julia Marlowe*, p. 235).

75 In Adrian Noble's nineteenth-century setting (RSC 1995), Susan Brown gave this line without
    the usual leering tone. Folding Lucy Whybrow's delicate Victorian Juliet in her embrace, she
    spoke the line with weary stoicism, as though acknowledging that sexuality really was a
    burden to women in this world. Celia Johnson, as the dignified and genteel Nurse in the
    1978 BBC-TV version, seems slightly embarrassed at her own off-colour joke, and hurries on
    to 'Go, I'll to dinner, hie you to the cell.'

77 SD This exit was one of the highlights of Eliza O'Neill's performance, according to William
    Charles Macready: 'in rushing to her appointment at the Friar's cell, her whole soul was in
    the utterance of the words, "Hie to high fortune! Honest nurse, farewell" ' (Wingate,
    Shakespeare's Heroines, p. 15).

ACT 2   SCENE 6

Enter FRIAR [LAWRENCE] *and* ROMEO.

FRIAR LAWRENCE So smile the heavens upon this holy act,
    That after-hours with sorrow chide us not.
ROMEO Amen, amen! but come what sorrow can,
    It cannot countervail the exchange of joy
    That one short minute gives me in her sight.   5
    Do thou but close our hands with holy words,
    Then love-devouring Death do what he dare,
    It is enough I may but call her mine.
FRIAR LAWRENCE These violent delights have violent ends,
    And in their triumph die like fire and powder,   10
    Which as they kiss consume. The sweetest honey
    Is loathsome in his own deliciousness,
    And in the taste confounds the appetite.
    Therefore love moderately, long love doth so;
    Too swift arrives as tardy as too slow.   15

Enter JULIET.

2.6 The Friar's cell has usually been a retreat of modest proportions and austere properties, often occupying only part of the stage. George Bernard Shaw, writing of the Forbes-Robertson production of 1895, felt that 'though I do not believe a simple friar's cell often ran to the luxury of a couple of frescoes by Giotto, the touch is suggestive and pardonable' (*Our Theatres*, III, p. 209). Usually the cell is marked by at least a crucifix and soft, religious lighting; even Bogdanov's modern-dress production, with its brutalist faux-marble set, made the concession of a stained-glass window projection at the back (RSC 1986).

3 In Michael Attenborough's 1997 RSC production, Ray Fearon looked 'pitifully boyish in his uncomfortably formal suit and slicked down hair', and seemed so ill at ease as to be having second thoughts about the marriage (*Evening Standard*, 13 November 1997). David Tennant also entered nervously combing his hair (Boyd, RSC 2000).

5 After this line, Peter Brook substituted part of the scene from Q1, beginning,

    This morning here she pointed we should meet
    And consummate those never parting bands,
    Witness of our hearts' love, by joining hands,
    And come she will. (S100)

9–14a In the Luhrmann film, these admonitions are addressed to both lovers as they stand at the altar.

15 Robert Demeger's Friar, slightly against the sense of the speech, checked his watch and

>   Here comes the lady. O, so light a foot
>   Will ne'er wear out the everlasting flint;
>   A lover may bestride the gossamers
>   That idles in the wanton summer air,
> And yet not fall, so light is vanity.	20

JULIET Good even to my ghostly confessor.
FRIAR LAWRENCE Romeo shall thank thee, daughter, for us both.

[Romeo kisses Juliet.]

JULIET As much to him, else is his thanks too much.

[Juliet returns his kiss.]

ROMEO Ah, Juliet, if the measure of thy joy
> Be heaped like mine, and that thy skill be more	25
>   To blazon it, then sweeten with thy breath
>   This neighbour air, and let rich music's tongue
>   Unfold the imagined happiness that both
>   Receive in either by this dear encounter.
JULIET Conceit, more rich in matter than in words,	30
>   Brags of his substance, not of ornament;
>   They are but beggars that can count their worth,
>   But my true love is grown to such excess
>   I cannot sum up sum of half my wealth.
FRIAR LAWRENCE
> Come, come with me, and we will make short work,	35

looked round impatiently for Juliet on 'as tardy as too slow'; Juliet's 'somewhat fast' entrance (cf. Q1) was accounted for by her lateness (Bogdanov 1986).

15 SD In Zeffirelli's production, the Friar stepped in between Romeo and Juliet to effect a comic collision; the same business was used at the end of the scene, and repeated in the film (*SS* 15, 1962, p. 151).

16–20 Joseph O'Conor's Friar gave these lines a chilling, premonitory gravity, standing to one side of the rapt and staring lovers (St George's 1976).

20 Robert Demeger, in Bogdanov 1986, had to step into Juliet's line of sight to get her to acknowledge him, so transfixed was she by Romeo.

24 In the Castellani film, the lovers speak to each other from opposite sides of a rather sinister metal grate, while monks chant ominously in the background.

35 Robert Demeger, after an embarrassed pause, interrupted a lingering kiss (Bogdanov, RSC 1986).

> For by your leaves, you shall not stay alone
> Till Holy Church incorporate two in one.

[Exeunt]

37 SD On this exit, Zeffirelli had John Stride's Romeo walk backward so that he continued to face
Juliet, who was supported on the Friar's arm (*SS* 15, 1962, p. 148). Sometimes the lovers
kneel and the Friar actually begins to perform the wedding ceremony. This business seems
first to have been introduced when Fanny Vining played a female Romeo opposite Anna
Cora Mowatt in 1849 (Sprague, *Shakespeare and the Actors*, p. 305). It was repeated in
Beerbohm Tree's elaborate 1913 production and the Zeffirelli film (Crosse, *Diaries*, v, 1913,
p. 159). Many productions take the interval at this point (e.g. Peter Hall, Stratford 1960,
NYSF 1988, Noble 1995). In Victorian times a break was often necessary to change from the
Friar's cell to the elaborate setting of the Verona public square. Suspending the action
allows the audience to enjoy the lovers' happiness for a few minutes longer; a more
disturbing place to break the play is after the deaths of Mercutio and Tybalt in 3.1.

ACT 3 SCENE 1

Enter MERCUTIO [*and his* PAGE], BENVOLIO, *and* MEN.

BENVOLIO I pray thee, good Mercutio, let's retire:
     The day is hot, the Capels are abroad,
     And if we meet we shall not scape a brawl,
     For now, these hot days, is the mad blood stirring.
MERCUTIO Thou art like one of these fellows that, when he enters the   5
     confines of a tavern, claps me his sword upon the table, and says
     'God send me no need of thee!'; and by the operation of the second
     cup draws him on the drawer, when indeed there is no need.
BENVOLIO Am I like such a fellow?
MERCUTIO Come, come, thou art as hot a Jack in thy mood as any in   10
     Italy, and as soon moved to be moody, and as soon moody to be
     moved.

3.1.0 SD In Hands 1989, this scene followed Romeo and Juliet's marriage instantaneously, with
     Benvolio beginning his lines as soon as he and Mercutio entered the stage; an abrupt,
     shocking transition that emphasised the jolting contrasts and sudden mischances of the
     play. Boyd 2000 used similar business, starting this scene instantly just after the final line
     of the preceding scene, without even giving Romeo and Juliet time to leave the stage. By
     contrast, productions that take the interval before this scene often use a good deal of
     business to build up the sultry edginess of 'these hot days'. By having Mercutio and Benvolio
     sitting restlessly at the café tables while the audience was still taking their seats, Adrian
     Noble developed considerable tension (RSC 1995). Similarly, Bogdanov had Benvolio slowly
     and rhythmically tapping his flick-knife against a beer-bottle, until Mercutio leapt up and
     snatched the knife away in irritation (RSC 1986). Zeffirelli's film begins the scene with a
     disturbing image of Mercutio's face draped in a handkerchief which he has sucked into his
     mouth; it creates a macabre, skull-like mask while Mercutio mocks Benvolio's admonitions,
     repeating 'Blah, blah, blah'. Luhrmann has Mercutio standing at the beach, deliberately
     firing his gun into the water (an element associated in the film with the love of Romeo and
     Juliet).
4 In 1947, Peter Brook made this line the keynote of his production; two centuries earlier,
     David Garrick had cut it, perhaps as an offence to decorum.
10 Mercutio usually seems to be talking about himself rather than the pacific Benvolio; in the St
     George's production, however, Philip Voss's Benvolio actually was more quarrelsome than
     David Collings's light-hearted Mercutio. More characteristic was the Benvolio in Hands's 1973
     production, 'a timid and sweet-natured boy who blushes with pleasure to be told his head is
     as full of quarrels as an egg is full of meat' (David, *Shakespeare in the Theatre*, p. 112).

BENVOLIO And what to?

MERCUTIO Nay, and there were two such, we should have none shortly,
for one would kill the other. Thou? why, thou wilt quarrel with   15
a man that hath a hair more or a hair less in his beard than thou
hast; thou wilt quarrel with a man for cracking nuts, having no other
reason but because thou hast hazel eyes. What eye but such an eye
would spy out such a quarrel? Thy head is as full of quarrels as
an egg is full of meat, and yet thy head hath been beaten as addle   20
as an egg for quarrelling. Thou hast quarrelled with a man for
coughing in the street, because he hath wakened thy dog that hath
lain asleep in the sun. Didst thou not fall out with a tailor for
wearing his new doublet before Easter? with another for tying his
new shoes with old riband? and yet thou wilt tutor me from   25
quarrelling?

BENVOLIO And I were so apt to quarrel as thou art, any man should
buy the fee-simple of my life for an hour and a quarter.

MERCUTIO The fee-simple? O simple!

Enter TYBALT, PETRUCHIO, *and others.*

BENVOLIO By my head, here comes the Capulets.   30

MERCUTIO By my heel, I care not.

TYBALT Follow me close, for I will speak to them.
    Gentlemen, good den, a word with one of you.

MERCUTIO And but one word with one of us? couple it with something,
make it a word and a blow.   35

TYBALT You shall find me apt enough to that, sir, and you will give
me occasion.

MERCUTIO Could you not take some occasion without giving?

TYBALT Mercutio, thou consortest with Romeo.

MERCUTIO Consort? what, dost thou make us minstrels? And thou   40

---

29 SD In Bogdanov 1986, Tybalt drove a red convertible sports car onto the stage, causing Michael
Billington, among others, to term the production 'Alfa-Romeo and Juliet' (*Guardian*, 10 April
1986).

31 Ralph Richardson's Mercutio (1935) marked his lack of concern over Tybalt by draping a
yellow silk handkerchief over his face, flicking it off only at 'Could you not take some
occasion without giving?' (595). Charles Kemble (1840), ever the gentleman, was led into the
exchange with Tybalt 'more by the love of excitement than by enmity' (Marston, *Our Recent
Actors*, I, p. 122).

39–40 In Joe Calarco's *R&J*, Mercutio, who nursed a secret love for Romeo, took 'consort' as
implying a homosexual relationship, and overreacted in furious denial.

make minstrels of us, look to hear nothing but discords. Here's my
fiddlestick, here's that shall make you dance. 'Zounds, consort!
BENVOLIO We talk here in the public haunt of men:
        Either withdraw unto some private place,
        Or reason coldly of your grievances,   45
        Or else depart; here all eyes gaze on us.
MERCUTIO Men's eyes were made to look, and let them gaze;
        I will not budge for no man's pleasure, I.

                  Enter ROMEO.

TYBALT Well, peace be with you, sir, here comes my man.
MERCUTIO But I'll be hanged, sir, if he wear your livery.   50
        Marry, go before to field, he'll be your follower;
        Your worship in that sense may call him man.
TYBALT Romeo, the love I bear thee can afford
        No better term than this: thou art a villain.
ROMEO Tybalt, the reason that I have to love thee   55
        Doth much excuse the appertaining rage
        To such a greeting. Villain am I none;
        Therefore farewell, I see thou knowest me not.
TYBALT Boy, this shall not excuse the injuries
        That thou hast done me, therefore turn and draw.   60
ROMEO I do protest I never injuried thee,
        But love thee better than thou canst devise,
        Till thou shalt know the reason of my love;

42 Mercutio generally indicates his rapier, but in Adrian Noble's nineteenth-century
    production, Mark Lockyer's violin-playing Mercutio threatened Tybalt with a real fiddlestick
    (RSC 1995).
46 In the quasi-Elizabethan staging at the St George's in 1976, Benvolio explicitly indicated the
    audience.
54 In response to Tybalt's insult, Maurice Evans's Romeo hesitated a moment, then took off his
    sword and gave it to his page, to the surprise and scorn of the crowd (1935, S95). In Terry
    Hands's 1989 production, some of the Capulets clucked like chickens to mock Romeo's
    submission.
61–5 Irving played this speech, unconventionally, 'with a sort of abject anxiety to avoid a rupture
    . . . which fully justifie[d] the indignation manifested by Mercutio'; Edward Russell praised
    him for showing 'how Romeo's fibre has been weakened . . . by the monopoly which love
    has obtained of his mind' (*Macmillan's Magazine*, XLVI, 1882, p. 332). In the Zeffirelli film,
    Romeo shakes Tybalt's hand; Tybalt (Michael York) then sniffs it with distaste and makes a

And so, good Capulet, which name I tender
As dearly as mine own, be satisfied. 65
MERCUTIO O calm, dishonourable, vile submission!
    'Alla stoccata' carries it away. [*Draws.*]
    Tybalt, you rat-catcher, will you walk?
TYBALT What wouldst thou have with me?
MERCUTIO Good King of Cats, nothing but one of your nine lives that 70
    I mean to make bold withal, and as you shall use me hereafter,
    dry-beat the rest of the eight. Will you pluck your sword out of
    his pilcher by the ears? Make haste, lest mine be about your ears
    ere it be out.
TYBALT I am for you. [*Drawing.*] 75
ROMEO Gentle Mercutio, put thy rapier up.
MERCUTIO Come, sir, your 'passado'.

[They fight.]

        show of washing it in a fountain. In Luhrmann's film, Tybalt's follower 'Abra' makes formal preparations for a pistol duel; Mercutio tries to second Romeo but is rebuffed.

65–6 From the eighteenth well into the twentieth century, it was standard practice to have Romeo leave the stage before Mercutio began to fight on his behalf; apparently audiences, like Mercutio, would have considered Romeo's submission dishonourable. Cibber's 1744 adaptation includes the stage directions 'Romeo walks apart' and 'Romeo returning, interposes' (p. 130). On Romeo's exit, Charles Kemble's Mercutio (1840) made a sudden change from 'the reckless light-hearted aptness for the stimulant of quarrel' to 'the stern, swift scorn, the lightning-like retaliation of one whose heart has been pierced, whose person and cause have been humiliated in his friend' (Marston, *Our Recent Actors*, I, p. 124). Surprisingly, Michael Boyd's 2000 RSC production reintroduced the old business of having Romeo leave the stage before the beginning of the Tybalt/Mercutio fight.

76 Peter Brook had the fight temporarily forestalled by an offstage whistle and the appearance of a group of soldiers; Tybalt and Mercutio crossed to opposite corners of the stage, looking 'innocent', and there was an ' "innocence" reaction' from the crowd (promptbook, s100).

77 SD Zeffirelli, both on stage and in the film, made the fight a high-spirited, mocking game. 'Mercutio, gaining possession of both swords, used one as a whetstone for the other before handing Tybalt's back – stopping to wipe its handle with mocking ostentation' (*SS* 15,1962, p. 149). In the film version it is evident that Tybalt has not intended to kill Mercutio. In Nunn and Kyle's 1976 production, Mercutio's death was likewise accidental: 'the duel over, he fell back into Tybalt's arms and the blade went in' (*Listener*, 8 April 1976). Similarly, Kenneth Branagh made the fight 'a jokey, low-key affair, with Romeo laughingly tugging at his friend throughout' (*Financial Times*, 15 August 1986). In Peter Hall's 1961 production, Mercutio paused during the fight to gargle and spit (s106). For Adrian Noble, Mercutio playfully

ROMEO   Draw, Benvolio, beat down their weapons.
      Gentlemen, for shame forbear this outrage!
      Tybalt, Mercutio, the Prince expressly hath   80
      Forbid this bandying in Verona streets.

                [*Romeo steps between them.*]

      Hold, Tybalt! Good Mercutio!

        [*Tybalt under Romeo's arm thrusts Mercutio in.*]

           Away Tybalt [*with his followers.*]

MERCUTIO   I am hurt.
      A plague a'both houses! I am sped.
      Is he gone and hath nothing?
BENVOLIO   What, art thou hurt?
MERCUTIO   Ay, ay, a scratch, a scratch, marry, 'tis enough.   85
      Where is my page? Go, villain, fetch a surgeon.

                       [*Exit Page*]

ROMEO   Courage, man, the hurt cannot be much.

toasted Tybalt with wine from a café table, and plainly didn't intend any violent outcome (RSC 1995). Ron Daniels marked the escalation of the fight through the weaponry. In his invented postmodern period, the gang members carried heavy sword-sticks, which they used at first as blunt weapons before drawing the blades in the heat of the fight (*SS* 34, 1981, p. 151). Bogdanov (1986) used a similar escalation for his modern-dress fight, beginning with a stick and chain and ending with switchblade knives. Bogdanov also used a lot of comedy in the fight: at one point, menaced by a chain-swinging Tybalt, Mercutio took refuge on the bonnet of Tybalt's prized Alfa-Romeo. In Alby James's Temba production, set in Cuba, Joe Dixon's athletic, dreadlocked Mercutio used scissor-jumps, backflips, and cartwheels in 'a brilliant, vicious, kicking duel' (*Observer*, 10 July 1988). In the elaborate fights B. H. Barry choreographed for the 1988 NYSF production, Courtney B. Vance's gay Mercutio used his sexuality to discomfit Tybalt, at one point swinging him into a dip-kiss. Rupert Wickham used similar business in Judi Dench's 1993 Regent's Park production, forcibly engaging Tybalt in a lingering kiss (*Evening Standard*, 17 June 1993). In Karin Beier's 1994 Düsseldorf production, Bernd Grawert's homosexual Mercutio, distraught at losing Romeo's affections, deliberately impaled himself on Tybalt's knife (*Independent*, 2 November 1994).

82 SD   Jean Cocteau made Mercutio's death a stylised affair in his 1924 production, employing techniques suggestive of Japanese theatre. When Cocteau, playing Mercutio, was wounded, 'Un valet de scène entre mystérieusement et emporte son épée, Mercutio touche sa plaie, regarde ses mains, chancelle et tombe sur les genoux' (Cocteau, *Roméo et Juliette*, p. 130).

87   Zeffirelli's comic treatment of the fight allowed Romeo 'to respond to Mercutio's sour jests

MERCUTIO No, 'tis not so deep as a well, nor so wide as a church-door,
but 'tis enough, 'twill serve. Ask for me tomorrow, and you shall
find me a grave man. I am peppered, I warrant, for this world. A   90
plague a'both your houses! 'Zounds, a dog, a rat, a mouse, a cat,
to scratch a man to death! a braggart, a rogue, a villain, that fights
by the book of arithmetic. Why the dev'l came you between us?
I was hurt under your arm.

ROMEO I thought all for the best.   95

MERCUTIO Help me into some house, Benvolio,
          Or I shall faint. A plague a'both your houses!

       after he is wounded as casually as the text demands – "Courage, man; the hurt cannot be
       much" – without appearing callow' (*SS* 15, 1962, p. 149). In David Leveaux's RSC production,
       revised for London in 1992, Tim McInnery's Mercutio laughed grimly at the recognition that
       his friends didn't actually believe he was dying (*Spectator*, 4 July 1992).

88–90a A key moment for Charles Kemble, according to Marston: 'Here, having achieved this quip,
       there was a bright, though quickly fading smile. He was still the Mercutio of old – the gay,
       rash, loyal, boon-companion. It was a smile to call up tears, it conjured up so much of youth
       and the merry past' (*Our Recent Actors*, I, p. 125). John Barrymore, in the 1936 George Cukor
       film, waves his handkerchief gallantly and smiles to some ladies in an upstairs window as he
       makes his exit.

93–4 Charles Kemble's reproof to Romeo, in 1840, 'was nobly and pathetically redeemed by the
       loving courtesy with which he held out his hand to him, a moment after, in token of full
       forgiveness – a point I believe original with Charles Kemble, and which has since become
       an acting tradition of the character' (Marston, *Our Recent Actors*, I, p. 125). Edwin Booth's
       promptbook similarly has the note 'Mercutio extends his hand. Romeo grasps it
       affectionately' (S37). A much-used Victorian promptbook has 'Mercutio squeezes his hand
       affectionately' (S23). Wilson Barrett, opposite Forbes-Robertson in 1881, had 'a sense of grim
       humour in his extreme agony, and an honest smile upon his dying lips' (Scott, *Yesterday
       and Today*, II, p. 305). By 1935, however, the gentlemanly approach to Mercutio was plainly
       wearing thin; Herbert Farjeon complained that Gielgud, when wounded, showed 'too much
       charm and not enough bitter physical pain. That "plague of both your houses" was surely
       no playful jest' (p. 122). After Olivier and Gielgud switched roles, however, another critic
       argued that 'Mr Gielgud was right in treating his death lightly. Mercutio dies with a string of
       jests on his lips, and "a plague of both your houses" is one of them, not a serious curse'
       (*Evening News*, 29 November 1935). Agate felt that Gielgud's giving the line with 'a smile
       which is all a benison' was 'not good Shakespeare, perhaps, but very beautiful Gielgud'
       (*Sunday Times*, 20 October 1935).

95 These 'suddenly involved and simple words' effectively counterpointed the earlier levity in
       the Zeffirelli version, dramatically changing the tone of the scene and Romeo's character (*SS*
       15, 1962, p. 149). In Hands's 1973 production, 'A gradual dawning awareness of the serious of

They have made worms' meat of me. I have it,
And soundly too. Your houses!

Exit [with Benvolio]

ROMEO This gentleman, the Prince's near ally,   100
        My very friend, hath got this mortal hurt
        In my behalf; my reputation stained
        With Tybalt's slander – Tybalt, that an hour
        Hath been my cousin. O sweet Juliet,
        Thy beauty hath made me effeminate,   105
        And in my temper softened valour's steel!

Enter Benvolio.

BENVOLIO O Romeo, Romeo, brave Mercutio is dead.
        That gallant spirit hath aspired the clouds,
        Which too untimely here did scorn the earth.
ROMEO This day's black fate on moe days doth depend,   110
        This but begins the woe others must end.

[Enter Tybalt.]

BENVOLIO Here comes the furious Tybalt back again.
ROMEO Again, in triumph, and Mercutio slain?
        Away to heaven, respective lenity,
        And fire-eyed fury be my conduct now!   115
        Now, Tybalt, take the 'villain' back again
        That late thou gavest me, for Mercutio's soul

[Mercutio's] wound was expressed first on Mercutio's face, and then spread among his friends to reach its height in Benvolio's anguish' (*SS* 27, 1974, p. 151).

113–20 William Terriss, at the Lyceum in 1884, gave these lines 'with electrical force, and his elocutionary skill, coupled with the grandeur of the subsequent onslaught, was fairly irresistible' according to Arthur Smythe (Mullin, *Victorian Actors*, p. 434). Kyrle Bellew (1890) literally hissed these lines at Tybalt, attacking him with Mercutio's sword. Their short and intense fight ended the act, doing away not only with the Prince's entry but even with Romeo's line 'O, I am fortune's fool' (Brereton, *Romeo*, pp. 31–2). Irving also used Mercutio's sword, as many succeeding Romeos have done (*Macmillan's Magazine*, XLVI, 1882, p. 332). An effective touch in Irving's performance was his shading his eyes 'to ward off the rays of the blinding sun at the beginning of the duel', according to Clement Scott (*The Theatre*, 1 April 1882).

116 Forbes-Robertson flung his cap in Tybalt's face on the word 'villain' (S63).

117–18 Jonathan Hyde, in Ron Daniels's 1980 RSC production, showed uncharacteristic alarm and dismay at learning that he has killed Mercutio (*SQ* 32, 1981, p. 165).

      Is but a little way above our heads,
      Staying for thine to keep him company:
      Either thou or I, or both, must go with him.   120
TYBALT   Thou wretched boy, that didst consort him here,
      Shalt with him hence.
ROMEO   This shall determine that.

          They fight; Tybalt falls.

BENVOLIO   Romeo, away, be gone!
      The citizens are up, and Tybalt slain.
      Stand not amazed, the Prince will doom thee death   125
      If thou art taken. Hence be gone, away!

120   In the Luhrmann film, Romeo repeats this line three times, in a frenzy, while holding Tybalt's gun to his own head; when Tybalt backs away in alarm, Romeo grabs the gun and empties it into Tybalt's body.

122 SD   Cushman made the duel swift and sudden: 'Tybalt is struck dead, as lightning strikes the pine; one blow beats down his guard, and one lunge closes the fray' (Clement, *Charlotte Cushman*, p. 47). Irving was similarly decisive: 'His rapier was a whip. No hope for Tybalt; Romeo was past his guard in a flash' (Pettitt, 'Irving', p. 226). George Bernard Shaw felt that Johnston Forbes-Robertson's gentlemanly demeanour made his fight with Tybalt unconvincing: 'Mr Forbes-Robertson fights with unconcealed repugnance: he makes you feel that to do it in that disorderly way, without seconds, without a doctor, showing temper about it, and actually calling his adversary names, jars unspeakably on him' (Shaw, *Our Theatres*, III, pp. 211–12). Perhaps in order to overcome his aversion at winning such an uncouth combat, Forbes-Robertson had the wounded Tybalt make a final, vicious attempt on Romeo: 'Tybalt snatches Romeo's dagger and tries to stab him – his strength fails him and he falls dead down right' (s63). Some Romeos kill Tybalt in obvious and even accidental self-defence; in the Zeffirelli film Leonard Whiting's Romeo blindly flings his sword out just as Michael York is about to kill him. On the other hand, Romeo's killing of Tybalt may be an act of sudden and overt brutality. Even in 1935, Maurice Evans 'stab[bed] Tybalt viciously again and again in back', while in 1973 Timothy Dalton screamed hysterically and stabbed David Suchet's Tybalt in the groin with a short dagger (s95; *SS* 27, 1974, p. 151). Terry Hands's subsequent production in 1989 also had Romeo stabbing Tybalt repeatedly and dragging his body about the stage. In the Castellani film, St George's 1976, Leveaux RSC 1991, and Noble RSC 1995, Romeo and Tybalt did not even fight – Romeo stabbed Tybalt before he could draw. A Trinidad-set production at the Albany Empire staged Romeo's murder of Tybalt in slow-motion to the accompaniment of an Afro-Caribbean funeral song (*City Limits*, 12 May 1988). In David Leveaux's London RSC production (1992), the dying Tybalt daubed Romeo's face with blood, 'as if marking him for life' (*Guardian*, 26 June 1992).

ROMEO O, I am fortune's fool.
BENVOLIO   Why dost thou stay?

                                        Exit Romeo

        Enter Citizens [as OFFICERS *of the Watch].*

OFFICER Which way ran he that killed Mercutio?
        Tybalt, that murderer, which way ran he?
BENVOLIO There lies that Tybalt.
OFFICER   Up, sir, go with me;   130
        I charge thee in the Prince's name obey.

    Enter PRINCE, *old* MONTAGUE, CAPULET, *their* WIVES, *and all.*

PRINCE Where are the vile beginners of this fray?
BENVOLIO O noble Prince, I can discover all
        The unlucky manage of this fatal brawl;
        There lies the man, slain by young Romeo,   135
        That slew thy kinsman, brave Mercutio.
LADY CAPULET Tybalt, my cousin! O my brother's child!
        O Prince! O husband! O, the blood is spilled
        Of my dear kinsman. Prince, as thou art true,
        For blood of ours, shed blood of Montague.   140
        O cousin, cousin!
PRINCE Benvolio, who began this bloody fray?
BENVOLIO Tybalt, here slain, whom Romeo's hand did slay.
        Romeo, that spoke him fair, bid him bethink
        How nice the quarrel was, and urged withal   145

127a Irving dropped the curtain at this climactic line, cutting the subsequent scene of the Prince
      and the two families. John Gielgud's delivery of the line was 'almost inaudible' in Barry
      Jackson's production, according to Herbert Farjeon (*The Shakespearean Scene*, pp. 120–1).

127 SD In Forbes-Robertson's 1895 Lyceum production, the gallant Benvolio drew his sword to
      prevent anyone from following the fleeing Romeo (s63).

137–41 In Garrick's version it is Capulet, not his wife, who calls for Romeo's blood, in an
      abbreviated version of these lines. In Zeffirelli's film, Lady Capulet's vengeful fury is fuelled
      by an illicit passion for Tybalt. In Declan Donnellan's Regent's Park production, Lady Capulet
      smeared the faces of bystanders with Tybalt's blood (*Observer*, 22 June 1986).

144–65 This lengthy recapitulation is often cut in performance, or at least abbreviated. In the St
      George's production, Philip Voss's Benvolio gave the whole speech, addressing much of
      it to Montague, who was aghast at his son's actions. In David Leveaux's 1991 production,
      Benvolio knelt beseechingly to Lady Capulet for the last two lines. Occasionally, productions

Your high displeasure; all this, utterèd
With gentle breath, calm look, knees humbly bowed,
Could not take truce with the unruly spleen
Of Tybalt deaf to peace, but that he tilts
With piercing steel at bold Mercutio's breast,   150
Who, all as hot, turns deadly point to point,
And with a martial scorn, with one hand beats
Cold death aside, and with the other sends
It back to Tybalt, whose dexterity
Retorts it. Romeo he cries aloud,   155
'Hold, friends! friends, part!' and swifter than his tongue,
His agile arm beats down their fatal points,
And 'twixt them rushes; underneath whose arm
An envious thrust from Tybalt hit the life
Of stout Mercutio, and then Tybalt fled;   160
But by and by comes back to Romeo,
Who had but newly entertained revenge,
And to't they go like lightning, for, ere I
Could draw to part them, was stout Tybalt slain;
And as he fell, did Romeo turn and fly.   165
This is the truth, or let Benvolio die.
LADY CAPULET He is a kinsman to the Montague,
Affection makes him false, he speaks not true:
Some twenty of them fought in this black strife,
And all those twenty could but kill one life.   170
I beg for justice, which thou, Prince, must give:
Romeo slew Tybalt, Romeo must not live.
PRINCE Romeo slew him, he slew Mercutio;
Who now the price of his dear blood doth owe?
MONTAGUE Not Romeo, Prince, he was Mercutio's friend;   175
His fault concludes but what the law should end,
The life of Tybalt.
PRINCE   And for that offence
Immediately we do exile him hence.
I have an interest in your hearts' proceeding:
My blood for your rude brawls doth lie a-bleeding;   180
But I'll amerce you with so strong a fine

emphasise the difference between Benvolio's account and the fight the audience has
witnessed, as at Dartmouth College, 1995, where Benvolio indicated that Romeo 'did . . .
turn and fly' in the opposite direction from where he actually exited.

That you shall all repent the loss of mine.
I will be deaf to pleading and excuses,
Nor tears nor prayers shall purchase out abuses:
Therefore use none. Let Romeo hence in haste,　　　　　　185
Else, when he is found, that hour is his last.
Bear hence this body, and attend our will:
Mercy but murders, pardoning those that kill.

　　　　　　　　　　　　　　　　　　　　　　　Exeunt

185b–6　In the Luhrmann film, 'Captain Prince', the chief of police, speaks these lines over a
　　　　bullhorn, supposing Romeo to be still within earshot.
　187　In Hands 1989, the Prince said 'Bear hence this – body' with bitter disgust and contempt.
　188 SD　Zeffirelli had his second interval here: the bystanders exited mournfully, then the Chorus
　　　　walked the full depth of the stage and slowly lifted his hands to the audience in a gesture of
　　　　despair (*SS* 15, 1962, p. 154). David Leveaux introduced Juliet into the tableau just before the
　　　　lights went down – she stood facing the back wall, her hands raised, then turned and came
　　　　downstage as the front wall of the stage came down, leaving her silhouetted for a moment
　　　　against the darkness to close the act (RSC 1991).

ACT 3 SCENE 2

Enter JULIET *alone.*

JULIET Gallop apace, you fiery-footed steeds,
    Towards Phoebus' lodging; such a waggoner
    As Phaëton would whip you to the west,
    And bring in cloudy night immediately.
    Spread thy close curtain, love-performing Night,   5
    That runaways' eyes may wink, and Romeo
    Leap to these arms, untalked of and unseen:
    Lovers can see to do their amorous rites
    By their own beauties, or if love be blind,
    Ir best agrees with night. Come, civil Night,   10
    Thou sober-suited matron all in black,
    And learn me how to lose a winning match,
    Played for a pair of stainless maidenhoods.
    Hood my unmanned blood, bating in my cheeks,
    With thy black mantle, till strange love grow bold,   15
    Think true love acted simple modesty.
    Come, Night, come, Romeo, come, thou day in night,
    For thou wilt lie upon the wings of night,
    Whiter than new snow upon a raven's back.
    Come, gentle Night, come, loving, black-browed Night,   20

3.2 Surprisingly, given the histrionic opportunities it provides to Juliet, this scene was cut entirely in some Victorian productions; Mary Anderson, Adelaide Neilson, and Maude Adams were among those who sometimes forwent it (Odell, *Shakespeare from Betterton to Irving*, II, p. 402). Even in the twentieth century, Jane Cowl and Eva Le Gallienne did without this scene (Halstead, *Statistical History*, p. 811).

1 ff. The 'Gallop apace' speech was regularly edited for content until the twentieth century; lines 8–16, with their sexual explicitness, were almost always cut (by e.g. Garrick, Phelps, Cushman, Modjeska, Irving, Mary Anderson). Mrs Patrick Campbell, at the Lyceum in 1895, dropped the speech entirely but kept the subsequent scene with the Nurse (Archer, *Theatrical 'World' of 1895*, p. 290). The speech is now usually given entire (eg. RSC 1986, 1989, 1991, 1995, 2000) but was cut completely in the film version of Zeffirelli; Luhrmann includes only lines 20–31a. In Terry Hands's 1973 production, Estelle Kohler was taking washing in from a clothes-line at the beginning of the scene; for Adrian Noble in 1995, Lucy Whybrow's Victorian Juliet delivered the speech from a garden swing.

Give me my Romeo, and when I shall die,
Take him and cut him out in little stars,
And he will make the face of heaven so fine
That all the world will be in love with night,
And pay no worship to the garish sun.   25
O, I have bought the mansion of a love,
But not possessed it, and though I am sold,
Not yet enjoyed. So tedious is this day
As is the night before some festival
To an impatient child that hath new robes   30
And may not wear them. O, here comes my Nurse,

Enter NURSE, *with* [*the ladder of*] *cords* [*in her lap*].

And she brings news, and every tongue that speaks
But Romeo's name speaks heavenly eloquence.
Now, Nurse, what news? What hast thou there? the cords
That Romeo bid thee fetch?

NURSE   Ay, ay, the cords.   35

[*Throws them down.*]

21 The choice between 'I' and Q4's 'he' seems to divide directors about equally. Hands 1989 used 'I', Leveaux 1991 'he'; in Bogdanov 1986, Niamh Cusack used 'he', with many layers of meaning: 'My first reading of the word *die* here is the sexual one: the white of the stars, and his body in white, and the white of him ejaculating inside me, and the cutting up in little white stars, linking, at that pervasively unconscious level of foreboding, with the idea of spiritual death . . .' (Cusack, 'Juliet,' p.129).

22 Stella Colas apparently accompanied this line with 'the upward gesture of snipping with scissors', much to Henry Morley's disgust (*Journal*, p.277).

26 Clare Holman suddenly stretched herself out on her back, arms extended over her head and one knee raised, in a striking and erotic movement (RSC 1991).

26–8a Niamh Cusack gave a slight upward, questioning inflection to these two clauses, as if remarking on the injustice of this state of affairs; her reading suggested a premonition of ill fortune, as well as childish impatience (RSC 1986).

31 Georgia Slowe's very youthful-looking Juliet literally skipped over to the Nurse when she entered in Hands 1989.

35 Ellen Terry recalled of Mrs Stirling that 'She was the only Nurse that I have ever seen who did not play the part like a female pantaloon . . . In the "Cords" scene, where the Nurse tells Juliet of the death of Paris [sic], she did not play for comedy at all, but was very emotional' (*Story of My Life*, p. 230). Though Terry refers to it as the cords scene, the cords and all references to them were cut in Irving's production, as they were in Garrick, Faucit, and

JULIET Ay me, what news? Why dost thou wring thy hands?
NURSE Ah weraday, he's dead, he's dead, he's dead!
        We are undone, lady, we are undone.
        Alack the day, he's gone, he's killed, he's dead!
JULIET Can heaven be so envious?
NURSE   Romeo can,   40
        Though heaven cannot. O Romeo, Romeo!
        Who ever would have thought it? Romeo!
JULIET What devil art thou that dost torment me thus?
        This torture should be roared in dismal hell.
        Hath Romeo slain himself? Say thou but 'ay',   45
        And that bare vowel 'I' shall poison more
        Than the death-darting eye of cockatrice.
        I am not I, if there be such an 'ay',
        Or those eyes shut, that makes thee answer 'ay'.
        If he be slain, say 'ay', or if not, 'no':   50
        Brief sounds determine my weal or woe.
NURSE I saw the wound, I saw it with mine eyes
        (God save the mark!), here on his manly breast:
        A piteous corse, a bloody piteous corse,
        Pale, pale as ashes, all bedaubed in blood,   55
        All in gore blood; I sounded at the sight.
JULIET O break, my heart, poor bankrout, break at once!
        To prison, eyes, ne'er look on liberty!
        Vile earth, to earth resign, end motion here,
        And thou and Romeo press one heavy bier!   60
NURSE O Tybalt, Tybalt, the best friend I had!
        O courteous Tybalt, honest gentleman,
        That ever I should live to see thee dead!
JULIET What storm is this that blows so contrary?
        Is Romeo slaughtered? and is Tybalt dead?   65
        My dearest cousin, and my dearer lord?

      virtually all nineteenth-century productions, with the exception of Cushman, Phelps and
      Mary Anderson. Modern directors (e.g. Hunt, Hands, Noble) tend to include them.

45–51 Few directors have allowed Juliet this extravagant punning. All or part of the speech is cut in
      almost all versions, including Garrick, Faucit, Irving, Brook, and Bogdanov. Samuel Phelps,
      in the amazingly full text he played in 1846 at Sadler's Wells, cut only lines 48–9.

    59 Modjeska made a 'subtle, significant' gesture to her dagger on this line (Winter, *Wallet of
      Time*, I, p. 384).

> Then, dreadful trumpet, sound the general doom,
> For who is living, if those two are gone?
> NURSE Tybalt is gone and Romeo banishèd,
> Romeo that killed him, he is banishèd. 70
> JULIET O God, did Romeo's hand shed Tybalt's blood?
> NURSE It did, it did, alas the day, it did!
> JULIET O serpent heart, hid with a flow'ring face!
> Did ever dragon keep so fair a cave?
> Beautiful tyrant, fiend angelical! 75
> Dove-feathered raven, wolvish-ravening lamb!
> Despisèd substance of divinest show!
> Just opposite to what thou justly seem'st,
> A damnèd saint, an honourable villain!
> O nature, what hadst thou to do in hell 80
> When thou didst bower the spirit of a fiend
> In mortal paradise of such sweet flesh?
> Was ever book containing such vile matter
> So fairly bound? O that deceit should dwell
> In such a gorgeous palace!
> NURSE   There's no trust, 85
> No faith, no honesty in men, all perjured,
> All forsworn, all naught, all dissemblers.
> Ah, where's my man? Give me some aqua-vitae;
> These griefs, these woes, these sorrows make me old.
> Shame come to Romeo!

66–85 The extravagance of Juliet's rhetoric generally results in heavy cuts to this scene (e.g. Garrick, Booth, Irving, Mary Anderson, Forbes-Robertson). Yet William Hazlitt felt Eliza O'Neill was at her best in these speeches, which, along with the later potion speech, 'marked the fine play and undulation of natural sensibility, rising and falling with the gusts of passion, and at last worked up into an agony of despair, in which imagination approaches the brink of frenzy' (*Hazlitt on Theatre*, p. 18).

80–2 Alexandra Gilbreath rubbed her hands sensually over her own body on these lines in Michael Boyd's 2000 RSC production.

88–9 The Nurse's wish for aqua-vitae, though a deft piece of characterisation, has regularly been cut (e.g. by Faucit, Irving). In 1980, Brenda Bruce made 'Ah, where's my man?' a desperate cry for her dead husband, a surprisingly sentimental choice repeated by Susan Brown in 1995 (Noble RSC).

JULIET   Blistered be thy tongue   90
          For such a wish! he was not born to shame:
          Upon his brow shame is ashamed to sit;
          For 'tis a throne where honour may be crowned
          Sole monarch of the universal earth.
          O what a beast was I to chide at him!   95
NURSE Will you speak well of him that killed your cousin?
JULIET Shall I speak ill of him that is my husband?
          Ah, poor my lord, what tongue shall smooth thy name,
          When I, thy three-hours wife, have mangled it?
          But wherefore, villain, didst thou kill my cousin?   100
          That villain cousin would have killed my husband.
          Back, foolish tears, back to your native spring,
          Your tributary drops belong to woe,
          Which you mistaking offer up to joy.
          My husband lives that Tybalt would have slain,   105
          And Tybalt's dead that would have slain my husband:
          All this is comfort, wherefore weep I then?
          Some word there was, worser than Tybalt's death,
          That murdered me; I would forget it fain,
          But O, it presses to my memory,   110
          Like damnèd guilty deeds to sinners' minds:
          'Tybalt is dead, and Romeo banishèd.'

90b–4 Fanny Kemble made a great 'point' with this speech: 'The loftiness of look and gesture with
        which she uttered the last line, cannot be forgotten', according to Anna Jameson (*Sketches*,
        p. 488). Adelaide Neilson similarly found in these lines 'one of those great openings for
        passion which she seldom failed to seize. Her rebuke called forth by the Nurse's malediction
        on Romeo was like a sudden blaze of lightning' (Marston, *Our Recent Actors*, II, p. 234).
        Claire Bloom eschewed 'word-music' and spoke with 'superb harshness', according to
        Tynan (*Curtains*, p. 33).
   97   Eliza O'Neill's 'apologizing tribute of affection' carried 'feminine fondness to a most
        exquisite height' (Jones, *Memoirs*, p. 16).
  101   Lucy Whybrow, shrieking and hysterical before, stopped cold with this line, her sudden
        realisation giving her a new maturity (Noble, RSC 1995).
105–6 Marston praised Neilson for her 'mode of struggling though her perplexity to the comfort
        that, though Tybalt was dead, her husband still lived, and that, however, some half-
        apprehended terror still remained' (*Our Recent Actors*, II, p. 236).
  112   Of Eliza O'Neill: 'Her mode of expressing that *one* word *banishèd*, is an electric shock which
        thrills every vein' (Jones, *Memoirs*, p. 16). Of Fanny Kemble: 'The tone of piercing anguish in

> That 'banishèd', that one word 'banishèd',
> Hath slain ten thousand Tybalts. Tybalt's death
> Was woe enough if it had ended there;   115
> Or if sour woe delights in fellowship,
> And needly will be ranked with other griefs,
> Why followed not, when she said 'Tybalt's dead',
> 'Thy father' or 'thy mother', nay, or both,
> Which modern lamentation might have moved?   120
> But with a rear-ward following Tybalt's death,
> 'Romeo is banishèd': to speak that word,
> Is father, mother, Tybalt, Romeo, Juliet,
> All slain, all dead. 'Romeo is banishèd!'
> There is no end, no limit, measure, bound,   125

which she pronounced the last word, *banishèd*, and then threw herself into the arms of her nurse, in all the helplessness of utter desolation, formed one of the finest passages in her performance' (Jameson, *Sketches*, p. 489). In the 2000 RSC production, Alexandra Gilbreath got a similarly memorable effect, stopping short in the middle of her impassioned speech to make 'banishèd' a breathy whisper (*Mail on Sunday*, 16 July 2000). For Terry Hands in 1973, Estelle Kohler marked the moment by tearing sheets down from the clothes-line where they were hanging (promptbook, SCL).

113–26 Juliet's 'banishèd' speech was evidently an occasion for great physical violence on the part of early-nineteenth-century Juliets. Henry Siddons, son of Sarah Siddons, remonstrated with them: 'I do not know what evil genius persuades so many of our performers, the females in particular, that it is so exquisite a manoeuvre to be perpetually rolling themselves on the ground. A lady acting Juliet . . . will sometimes fall on the boards with such violence, when she hears of the death or banishment of her lover, that we are really alarmed, lest her poor skull should be fractured by the violence of the concussion' (*Illustrations of Gesture and Action*, 1811, quoted in Salgado, *Eyewitnesses*, p. 195).

Mrs Julia Glover (1837, 1845), one of the most celebrated nineteenth-century Nurses, 'wore a look of puzzled indulgence' while listening to Juliet's speech. 'For a while this, with the Nurse, was a whim to be humoured, by no means to be persisted in at the risk of loss or danger' (Marston, *Our Recent Actors*, I, p. 265).

123 Lucy Whybrow's Juliet built to a kind of raging hysteria on these lines, attacking the Nurse, spinning away upstage, then falling onto the ground in a really disturbing moment of madness (Noble, RSC 1995).

125 By this line, Niamh Cusack had expended the violence of her grief; she suddenly looked up from the floor and spoke with a kind of awe, as if only then grasping the extent of her calamity (Bogdanov, RSC 1986).

           In that word's death, no words can that woe sound.
           Where is my father and my mother, Nurse?
NURSE Weeping and wailing over Tybalt's corse.
           Will you go to them? I will bring you thither.
JULIET Wash they his wounds with tears? mine shall be spent,   130
           When theirs are dry, for Romeo's banishment.
           Take up those cords. Poor ropes, you are beguiled,
           Both you and I, for Romeo is exiled.
           He made you for a highway to my bed,
           But I, a maid, die maiden-widowèd.   135
           Come, cords, come, Nurse, I'll to my wedding bed,
           And death, not Romeo, take my maidenhead!
NURSE Hie to your chamber. I'll find Romeo
           To comfort you, I wot well where he is.
           Hark ye, your Romeo will be here at night.   140
           I'll to him, he is hid at Lawrence' cell.
JULIET O find him! Give this ring to my true knight,
           And bid him come to take his last farewell.

                                                   Exeunt

128 Celia Johnson's wise old Nurse, in the 1978 BBC-TV version, speaks this line with a kind of long-suffering good humour, as someone who has seen a lot of weeping and wailing in her time.

134–5 Georgia Slowe spoke these lines with a bitter, conscious irony that was rather shocking in one who had seemed so young and idealistic; evidence of Juliet's sudden, painful growing-up (Hands, RSC 1989).

136 Mary Anderson, when she played this scene, knelt to pick up the ropes the Nurse had dropped, then suddenly buried her face in them (Sprague, *Shakespeare and the Actors*, p. 307). Lucy Whybrow said 'Come cords, come Nurse', with still, toneless misery, as though intending to hang herself with the ropes (RSC 1995). Claire Bloom, on her exit, was 'suddenly gentle and bereaved, cradling Romeo's rope-ladder to her breast' (Tynan, *Curtains*, 33). Alexandra Gilbreath first placed the ropes on her head as a bridal veil, then around her neck as a noose (RSC 2000).

Enter FRIAR [LAWRENCE].

FRIAR LAWRENCE
    Romeo, come forth, come forth, thou fearful man:
    Affliction is enamoured of thy parts,
    And thou art wedded to calamity.

[*Enter*] ROMEO.

ROMEO Father, what news? What is the Prince's doom?
    What sorrow craves acquaintance at my hand,   5
    That I yet know not?
FRIAR LAWRENCE   Too familiar
    Is my dear son with such sour company!
    I bring thee tidings of the Prince's doom.
ROMEO What less than doomsday is the Prince's doom?
FRIAR LAWRENCE A gentler judgement vanished from his lips: 10
    Not body's death, but body's banishment.
ROMEO Ha, banishment? be merciful, say 'death':
    For exile hath more terror in his look,
    Much more than death. Do not say 'banishment'!
FRIAR LAWRENCE Here from Verona art thou banishèd.   15
    Be patient, for the world is broad and wide.
ROMEO There is no world without Verona walls,
    But purgatory, torture, hell itself:
    Hence 'banishèd' is banished from the world,
    And world's exile is death; then 'banishèd'   20

3.3 SD In the Sothern–Marlowe production, the danger to Romeo was established by a series of offstage shouts as the Friar entered hurriedly and bolted the door (570). In Hands's 1973 production, Romeo was concealed below a trap in the floor (promptbook, SCL). In the 1988 NYSF production, Romeo's cry 'Banishèd?' came from offstage as Juliet exited from the previous scene; then Romeo and the Friar entered mid-scene at line 52.

12 Mark Rylance made 'Ha, banishment?' a moment of genuine surprise and confusion. Resigned to death, he was unable to process the unexpected and awful possibility of life without Juliet.

17 ff. Ellen Terry conceded that Irving failed in this scene, partly because he was implausible as a passionate youth: '. . . he came to grief precisely as he had done in *Othello*. He screamed, grew slower and slower, and looked older and older' (*Story of My Life*, p. 232).

Is death mistermed. Calling death 'banishèd',
Thou cut'st my head off with a golden axe,
And smilest upon the stroke that murders me.
FRIAR LAWRENCE O deadly sin! O rude unthankfulness!
Thy fault our law calls death, but the kind Prince,   25
Taking thy part, hath rushed aside the law,
And turned that black word 'death' to 'banishment'.
This is dear mercy, and thou seest it not.
ROMEO 'Tis torture, and not mercy. Heaven is here
Where Juliet lives, and every cat and dog   30
And little mouse, every unworthy thing,
Live here in heaven, and may look on her,
But Romeo may not. More validity,
More honourable state, more courtship lives
In carrion flies than Romeo; they may seize   35
On the white wonder of dear Juliet's hand,
And steal immortal blessing from her lips,
Who even in pure and vestal modesty
Still blush, as thinking their own kisses sin;
But Romeo may not, he is banishèd.   40
Flies may do this, but I from this must fly;
They are free men, but I am banishèd:
And sayest thou yet that exile is not death?
Hadst thou no poison mixed, no sharp-ground knife,
No sudden mean of death, though ne'er so mean,   45
But 'banishèd' to kill me? 'Banishèd'?

24–8 In the Luhrmann film, Pete Postlethwaite, more practical than many Friars, speaks these lines while bandaging Romeo's wounds from the duel.

29–43 Some of Romeo's more homely imagery has usually been cut; Garrick and Cushman removed the cats and dogs, but allowed the flies. Irving allowed the entire speech in his published version, but his promptbook cuts Romeo's 'Flies may do this, but I from this must fly' (S44). This pun has rarely been spoken on the stage; even Bogdanov cut it from his very full text in 1986.

36 This moment was one of Edmund Kean's best, according to Hazlitt; 'in the extravagant and irresistible expression of Romeo's grief, at being banished from the object of his love, his voice suddenly stops and falters, and is choked with sobs of tenderness, when he comes to Juliet's name' (*Hazlitt on Theatre*, p. 33). James Agate complained of Olivier's handling of this line: 'Mr Olivier's Romeo suffered enormously from the fact that the spoken art of poetry eluded him . . . what is the use of Shakespeare writing such an image as: "the white wonder of dear Juliet's hand" if Romeo is not himself blasted with the beauty of it?' (*Sunday Times*, 20 October 1935).

O Friar, the damnèd use that word in hell;
Howling attends it. How hast thou the heart,
Being a divine, a ghostly confessor,
A sin-absolver, and my friend professed,   50
To mangle me with that word 'banishèd'?
FRIAR LAWRENCE Thou fond mad man, hear me a little speak.
ROMEO O thou wilt speak again of banishment.
FRIAR LAWRENCE I'll give thee armour to keep off that word:
Adversity's sweet milk, philosophy,   55
To comfort thee though thou art banishèd.
ROMEO Yet 'banishèd'? Hang up philosophy!
Unless philosophy can make a Juliet,
Displant a town, reverse a prince's doom,
It helps not, it prevails not; talk no more.   60
FRIAR LAWRENCE O then I see that mad men have no ears.
ROMEO How should they when that wise men have no eyes?
FRIAR LAWRENCE Let me dispute with thee of thy estate.
ROMEO Thou canst not speak of that thou dost not feel.
Wert thou as young as I, Juliet thy love,   65
An hour but married, Tybalt murderèd,
Doting like me, and like me banishèd,
Then mightst thou speak, then mightst thou tear thy hair,
And fall upon the ground as I do now,
Taking the measure of an unmade grave.   70

Enter Nurse [within] and knock.

FRIAR LAWRENCE Arise, one knocks. Good Romeo, hide thyself.

54–6 In Zeffirelli's production, the Friar tried to give a Bible to John Stride's Romeo, who angrily
flung it to the floor (*Saturday Review*, 3 March 1962).

64 For Herbert Farjeon, Olivier was 'the only actor I have ever known to succeed in that
diabolically difficult outburst with the Friar. His cry, "Thou canst not speak of that thou dost
not feel!" is living anguish' (*Shakespearean Scene*, p.122). St John Ervine also praised
Olivier's playing of the scene, which he felt courageously confronted audience prejudices:
'There was nothing distasteful to Elizabethans in the sight of Romeo rolling on the floor and
sobbing his heart out, nor anything in them that could cause them to cry, "Look at that wop
blubbing on the floor!" This grief was natural to them as it was to any Veronese, and they
would have been astonished, if not indignant, at any tut-tutting and oh-dear-me-dear-
me-ing from buttoned-up, tight-lipped persons who thought it unmanly to cry or betray the
signs of feeling' (*Observer*, 3 November 1935).

69–70 Romeo's lines plainly indicate an extreme state of emotion physically expressed; yet actors
are regularly criticised for overplaying the scene. To take a recent example, Kenneth

ROMEO Not I, unless the breath of heart-sick groans
        Mist-like infold me from the search of eyes.

                        Knock.

FRIAR LAWRENCE
        Hark how they knock! – Who's there? – Romeo, arise,
        Thou wilt be taken. – Stay a while! – Stand up;   75

                    Loud knock.

        Run to my study. – By and by! – God's will,
        What simpleness is this? – I come, I come!

                        Knock.

        Who knocks so hard? whence come you? what's your will?
NURSE [*Within*] Let me come in, and you shall know my errand:
        I come from Lady Juliet.
FRIAR LAWRENCE   Welcome then. [*Unlocks the door.*]   80

                    Enter NURSE.

NURSE O holy Friar, O tell me, holy Friar,
        Where's my lady's lord? where's Romeo?
FRIAR LAWRENCE
        There on the ground, with his own tears made drunk.
NURSE O he is even in my mistress' case,
        Just in her case. O woeful sympathy!   85

Branagh, according to Martin Hoyle, lay 'flat on the floor, bellowing bitter sobs like a child cheated of a promised treat' (*Financial Times*, 15 August 1986). Charlotte Cushman, playing Romeo in 1845, was able to display a degree of emotion which Victorian actors might have been reluctant to reveal; accordingly, this scene was one of her most famous. 'So high ran her frenzy of grief, and so real was the air of a "mind distraught" with which she repelled the Friar's counsel and reasoning, that when, with unexampled desperation, she dashed herself upon the earth – "taking the measure of an unmade grave", all that is extravagant and unreasonable in Romeo's behaviour was forgotten in the ardour of his love, and the house was roused to the wildest excitement, as if by some tragic event in actual life' (Marston, *Our Recent Actors*, II, p. 76). William Winter praised Forbes-Robertson for 'portraying alternate frenzy and despair in a natural manner, and therefore without extravagance' (*Shakespeare on the Stage*, p. 137).

85–90 The Nurse's remonstrances, with their unconscious obscene double-entendres, have almost always been cut. Even Bogdanov cut 'Why should you fall into so deep an O', presumably not from prudery but because a modern audience wouldn't understand it.

Piteous predicament! even so lies she,
Blubb'ring and weeping, weeping and blubb'ring.
Stand up, stand up, stand, and you be a man;
For Juliet's sake, for her sake, rise and stand;
Why should you fall into so deep an O? 90
ROMEO Nurse! [*He rises.*]
NURSE Ah, sir, ah, sir, death's the end of all.
ROMEO Spakest thou of Juliet? how is it with her?
Doth not she think me an old murderer,
Now I have stained the childhood of our joy 95
With blood removed but little from her own?
Where is she? and how doth she? and what says
My concealed lady to our cancelled love?
NURSE O she says nothing, sir, but weeps and weeps,
And now falls on her bed, and then starts up, 100
And Tybalt calls, and then on Romeo cries,
And then down falls again.
ROMEO   As if that name,
Shot from the deadly level of a gun,
Did murder her, as that name's cursèd hand
Murdered her kinsman. O tell me, Friar, tell me, 105
In what vile part of this anatomy
Doth my name lodge? Tell me, that I may sack
The hateful mansion.

[*He offers to stab himself, and Nurse snatches the dagger away.*]

92 Angela Baddeley, in Byam Shaw's 1958 Stratford production, moved by Romeo's despair, took him in her arms to comfort him, 'as if he were her Juliet' (*SQ* 9, 1958, p. 520).

97–8 Romeo's pun on concealed and cancelled is one few modern directors have tolerated; it was cut by Bogdanov and Noble, for instance. Mark Rylance spoke it (Hands 1989), stressing the first syllable of both words; David Tennant also (Boyd 2000), without emphatic stress.

108 SD From Q1, which also gives the Nurse the line 'Ah!' immediately following. The stage direction probably represents Elizabethan practice, though Gibbons, in the Arden edition, rejects it as interpolated actor's business. Dessen points out that the Nurse's action ironically counterpoints the Friar's questioning of Romeo's manhood in the lines that follow (*Recovering*, p. 92). In practice, the Friar usually grabs the knife (e.g. Zeffirelli film, St George's 1976, BBC-TV 1978, NYSF 1988, Noble 1995), though the Nurse took it in Brook's production (s100) and in Bogdanov 1986. W. Bridges Adams, criticising the tradition of playing the Friar as a weak old man, said, 'He should twist that dagger out of Romeo's hand with the hard sinews begotten of hard living' (Trewin, *Going to Shakespeare*, p. 94).

FRIAR LAWRENCE   Hold thy desperate hand!
Art thou a man? thy form cries out thou art;
Thy tears are womanish, thy wild acts denote   110
The unreasonable fury of a beast.
Unseemly woman in a seeming man,
And ill-beseeming beast in seeming both,
Thou hast amazed me. By my holy order,
I thought thy disposition better tempered.   115
Hast thou slain Tybalt? wilt thou slay thyself,
And slay thy lady that in thy life lives,
By doing damnèd hate upon thyself?
Why rail'st thou on thy birth? the heaven and earth?
Since birth, and heaven, and earth, all three do meet   120
In thee at once, which thou at once wouldst lose.
Fie, fie, thou sham'st thy shape, thy love, thy wit,
Which like a usurer abound'st in all,
And usest none in that true use indeed
Which should bedeck thy shape, thy love, thy wit: 125
Thy noble shape is but a form of wax,
Digressing from the valour of a man;
Thy dear love sworn but hollow perjury,
Killing that love which thou hast vowed to cherish;
Thy wit, that ornament to shape and love,   130
Misshapen in the conduct of them both,
Like powder in a skilless soldier's flask,
Is set afire by thine own ignorance,

108–58 This long speech invariably receives some cuts: Gentleman, writing of Garrick's version, notes that 'there are no less than twenty-seven lines lopped from this speech, which is long and circumstantial enough, as it now stands' (*Bell's Edition*, p. 125). In the St George's production, however, it was given uncut by Joseph O'Conor, who used the length of the speech to show the Friar's changing responses to Romeo – from exasperation through pity, affection, and hope – and his own capacity for thinking on his feet. The speech also gave Peter McEnery's Romeo an opportunity to regain his composure in clearly marked and credible stages.

112–13 Regularly cut, from Garrick onwards.

116a Peter MacNicol interpolated an anguished 'Yes!' from the floor in Les Waters's 1988 NYSF production.

119–34 Regularly cut, from Garrick onwards.

And thou dismembered with thine own defence.
What, rouse thee, man! thy Juliet is alive, 135
For whose dear sake thou wast but lately dead:
There art thou happy. Tybalt would kill thee,
But thou slewest Tybalt: there art thou happy.
The law that threatened death becomes thy friend,
And turns it to exile: there art thou happy. 140
A pack of blessings light upon thy back,
Happiness courts thee in her best array,
But like a mishavèd and sullen wench,
Thou pouts upon thy fortune and thy love:
Take heed, take heed, for such die miserable. 145
Go get thee to thy love as was decreed,
Ascend her chamber, hence and comfort her;
But look thou stay not till the Watch be set,
For then thou canst not pass to Mantua,
Where thou shalt live till we can find a time 150
To blaze your marriage, reconcile your friends,
Beg pardon of the Prince, and call thee back
With twenty hundred thousand times more joy
Than thou went'st forth in lamentation.
Go before, Nurse, commend me to thy lady, 155
And bid her hasten all the house to bed,
Which heavy sorrow makes them apt unto.
Romeo is coming.
NURSE   O Lord, I could have stayed here all the night
To hear good counsel. O, what learning is! 160
My lord, I'll tell my lady you will come.
ROMEO   Do so, and bid my sweet prepare to chide.

[Nurse offers to go in, and turns again.]

135 On this line, Milo O'Shea's Friar strikes Romeo and knocks him to the ground in the Zeffirelli film. By contrast, Joseph O'Conor took a long pause, and, noting that Romeo had begun to pull himself together, took a more hopeful tone (St George's 1976).

142 In Michael Boyd's bleakly pessimistic production, the Friar's upbeat admonition was so ironically out of place that it got a big laugh from the audience (RSC 2000).

145 Julian Glover's angry Scottish Friar gave a big sigh of exasperation at this point, then crossed himself to ward off ill luck before going on with the speech (Noble, RSC 1995).

158 In Hands 1989, Patrick Godfrey's Friar, concluding an intense, nearly uncut speech, made the last word a slight anticlimax, throwing up his hands in exasperation as if questioning whether Romeo were really worth the trouble.

NURSE Here, sir, a ring she bid me give you, sir.
          Hie you, make haste, for it grows very late.
ROMEO How well my comfort is revived by this. 165

                                        [*Exit Nurse*]

FRIAR LAWRENCE
          Go hence, good night, and here stands all your state:
          Either be gone before the Watch be set,
          Or by the break of day disguised from hence.
          Sojourn in Mantua; I'll find out your man,
          And he shall signify from time to time 170
          Every good hap to you that chances here.
          Give me thy hand, 'tis late. Farewell, good night.
ROMEO But that a joy past joy calls out on me,
          It were a grief, so brief to part with thee:
          Farewell. 175

                                        Exeunt

163 The Italian tragedian Ernesto Rossi, who had been extravagantly passionate in depicting
      Romeo's despair, created a moving contrast by 'the quiet joy with which his face lit up as he
      placed on his finger the ring sent by his mistress' (Carlson, *Italian Shakespearians*, p. 166).
171 Mark Rylance's Romeo bolted from the stage, eager to get to Juliet; the Friar, Patrick
      Godfrey, called out 'Give me thy hand' as a desperate question, wanting to stay Romeo's
      sudden haste and to have a further moment of contact with him. Romeo returned after a
      thoughtful pause for an emotional farewell (RSC 1989).
172 The Friar often returns Romeo's dagger on 'Farewell'; in one nineteenth-century
      promptbook, 'Friar returns the dagger, and as Romeo takes it, checks him with his L. hand
      and raises his R. hand to heaven as if to warn him against the impiety of suicide' (s23).
      Joseph O'Conor used similar business, holding the dagger up by the blade, as a cross, and
      giving an admonitory look to Romeo before tipping the handle down into his hand (St
      George's 1976, BBC-TV 1978).
175 At the end of this scene, Robert Demeger's vigorous Friar, worn out by his long ordeal,
      pulled a packet of cigarettes from under his cassock and lit one, to the delighted applause of
      the audience (Bogdanov, RSC 1986).

ACT 3   SCENE 4

Enter old CAPULET, *his* WIFE, *and* PARIS.

CAPULET Things have fall'n out, sir, so unluckily
       That we have had no time to move our daughter.
       Look you, she loved her kinsman Tybalt dearly,
       And so did I. Well, we were born to die.
       'Tis very late, she'll not come down tonight.   5
       I promise you, but for your company,
       I would have been abed an hour ago.
PARIS These times of woe afford no times to woo.
       Madam, good night, commend me to your daughter.
LADY CAPULET I will, and know her mind early tomorrow;   10
       Tonight she's mewed up to her heaviness.

     [Paris offers to go in, and Capulet calls him again.]

CAPULET Sir Paris, I will make a desperate tender
       Of my child's love: I think she will be ruled
       In all respects by me; nay more, I doubt it not.
       Wife, go you to her ere you go to bed,   15
       Acquaint her here of my son Paris' love,
       And bid her – mark you me? – on Wednesday next –
       But soft, what day is this?

3.4 This scene has been cut entirely in some productions, as in Zeffirelli, 1960. Adrian Noble had the characters dressed in black and under umbrellas, as though coming from Tybalt's funeral (RSC 1995). Michael Boyd also put his Capulets in mourning for this scene (RSC 2000). In the 1978 BBC-TV production, by contrast, Michael Hordern's likeable, self-indulgent Capulet is just finishing a healthy dinner, still chewing as he begins his first line.

4a In the Luhrmann film, Diane Venora's Lady Capulet takes the half-line 'And so did I', alluding to her affair with Tybalt; Paul Sorvino's Capulet frowns and knocks back a drink on the end of the line.

11 SD From Q1. In Bogdanov 1986 this stage direction made for a very effective moment, again emphasising the role of small chances in the lovers' doom. Paris had almost left the stage when Capulet called him back, as on a whim. Lady Capulet was startled and displeased by this capricious change of plan, and her silent, unconsenting presence was a powerful part of the scene. After Paris left, Capulet turned to her and spread out his hands to indicate a *fait accompli*; she raised her head and proudly exited in the opposite direction.

17 In NYSF 1988, Capulet said 'mark you me?' angrily to his wife, who had been turned away in apparent displeasure from the time Capulet had recalled Paris.

191

PARIS   Monday, my lord.
CAPULET Monday, ha, ha! Well, Wednesday is too soon,
         A'Thursday let it be – a'Thursday, tell her,   20
         She shall be married to this noble earl.
         Will you be ready? do you like this haste?
         Well, keep no great ado – a friend or two,
         For hark you, Tybalt being slain so late,
         It may be thought we held him carelessly,   25
         Being our kinsman, if we revel much:
         Therefore we'll have some half a dozen friends,
         And there an end. But what say you to Thursday?
PARIS My lord, I would that Thursday were tomorrow.
CAPULET Well, get you gone, a'Thursday be it then. –   30
         Go you to Juliet ere you go to bed,
         Prepare her, wife, against this wedding day.
         Farewell, my lord. Light to my chamber, ho!
         Afore me, it is so very late that we
         May call it early by and by. Good night.   35

                                                    Exeunt

22 Christopher Benjamin's unusually accommodating Capulet addressed 'do you like this haste?' to his wife, making sure the revised arrangements wouldn't upset her (RSC 1995).

29 In the Luhrmann film, Paris looks alarmed by the change in plans, and acquiesces only because he is intimidated by Paul Sorvino's aggressive, drunken Capulet.

34–5 In Leveaux 1991, Jonathan Newth's Capulet made these lines a pointed excuse for not sleeping with Lady Capulet, who was sulking over the proposed change in wedding plans. By contrast, in Boyd 2000, Capulet and Lady Capulet kissed tenderly at the end of the scene, while Romeo and Juliet appeared and kissed on the balcony above them; a poignant juxtaposition of young and old lovers.

ACT 3 SCENE 5

Enter ROMEO *and* JULIET *aloft* [*as at the window*].

JULIET Wilt thou be gone? It is not yet near day:
It was the nightingale, and not the lark,
That pierced the fearful hollow of thine ear;
Nightly she sings on yond pomegranate tree.
Believe me, love, it was the nightingale.   5

3.5 SD This scene creates numerous staging problems in a theatre with realistic scenery, since the
location changes around the actors. The Q1 stage directions indicate that in the Elizabethan
theatre, the scene began at the window or gallery above, from which Romeo descended
(42) to the stage, which then represented the Capulet orchard. Juliet subsequently (67)
descended via a backstage ladder or staircase and entered the main platform, meeting her
mother in what was then understood to be her bedroom. Productions using realistic scenery
have usually placed the whole scene in the bedroom, with Romeo clambering over a
balcony leading backstage. Some Victorian productions avoided the problem (at the
expense of dramatic tension) by dropping the curtain and making the exchange with Lady
Capulet a separate scene (s43). John Gielgud managed to have bedroom, balcony and
orchard onstage through use of a platform and tower, as did Peter Brook with an elaborate
unit set, though in both cases the latter part of the scene (with Capulet) was rather cramped
(production photos, SCL). St George's 1976, NYSF 1988, Hands 1989, and Leveaux 1991 all
began the scene on the balcony with Romeo preparing to descend. The last of these was so
vigorously attacked by critics for its lack of sexiness that Leveaux introduced a bed for the
London revival the following year (*Independent*, 26 June 1992).
    The morning scene has been staged with varying degrees of explicitness as to what
Romeo and Juliet have been doing. It is not now uncommon to have them begin the scene
completely naked and in bed, as in Noble 1995. In Victorian productions they were of course
fully dressed, and Romeo was usually beginning his descent from the window when the
scene began. Modjeska, in her memoirs, decried the salaciousness of 'such naturalistic
details as a disarranged four-poster bed, or the turning of the key of a locked door at the
Nurse's entrance, or Romeo's lacing his jerkin, and a dishevelled Juliet in a *crêpe de chine*
nightgown' (*Memories and Impressions*, p. 138). Katherine Cornell's 1934–5 production
opted for a lukewarm compromise: 'Juliet is lying in bed, Romeo kneeling beside the bed
head, with arms about her' (s95). The Cukor film is resolutely sexless: H. R. Coursen notes,
'The Hays Office must have been pleased to see that, on the dawn of Romeo's departure
from Juliet's chamber, the lovers are clothed as if about to make a dog-sled run for the

ROMEO   It was the lark, the herald of the morn,
        No nightingale. Look, love, what envious streaks
        Do lace the severing clouds in yonder east:
        Night's candles are burnt out, and jocund day
        Stands tiptoe on the misty mountain tops.   10
        I must be gone and live, or stay and die.
JULIET   Yond light is not daylight, I know it, I:
        It is some meteor that the sun exhaled
        To be to thee this night a torch-bearer,
        And light thee on thy way to Mantua.   15
        Therefore stay yet, thou need'st not to be gone.
ROMEO   Let me be tane, let me be put to death,
        I am content, so thou wilt have it so.
        I'll say yon grey is not the morning's eye,
        'Tis but the pale reflex of Cynthia's brow;   20
        Nor that is not the lark whose notes do beat
        The vaulty heaven so high above our heads.
        I have more care to stay than will to go:
        Come, death, and welcome! Juliet wills it so.

South Pole' (p. 49). Zeffirelli had the lovers begin the scene with a sensual embrace on the bed (Old Vic 1960); his film created something of a sensation by showing Romeo's bare buttocks and a glimpse of Juliet's breasts (Holding, *Romeo*, p. 48). In Düsseldorf in 1994, Karin Beier took a deliberately anti-romantic view of the morning scene, having Romeo and Juliet squabble and even slap each other petulantly in their dispute over whether the nightingale or the lark was singing (*Independent*, 2 November 1994). Michael Bogdanov, by contrast, staged the scene very playfully in his 1993 English Shakespeare Company production; Juliet hid one of Romeo's boots under her pillow to prevent him from leaving (*Financial Times*, 1 June 1993). In Ron Daniels's RSC production, Romeo had to make a hasty exit 'as if in a Feydeau farce . . . pulling up his trousers with his fly undone' (*Evening Standard*, 10 October 1981). The Luhrmann film gives a similarly comic tone to Romeo's awkward and hurried dressing.

7b–8   J. C. Trewin recalled that Olivier 'caressed [these] phrases . . . as no other player had done in remembrance' (*Shakespeare on the English Stage*, p. 153). Laurence Olivier was considered daringly sensual with Juliet in this scene, both in Gielgud's 1935 production and in his own 1940 New York version. Gielgud, who played his love scenes with restrained delicacy, felt Olivier 'was inclined to be too athletic in the bedroom scene with Juliet. I have always believed that too much "physical" acting here goes against Shakespeare's intention' (*Acting Shakespeare*, p. 48). In New York Olivier and Vivien Leigh began the scene on her rumpled bed (Wright, *Romeo*, p. 221).

How is't, my soul? Let's talk, it is not day. 25
JULIET It is, it is, hie hence, be gone, away!
It is the lark that sings so out of tune,
Straining harsh discords and unpleasing sharps.
Some say the lark makes sweet division:
This doth not so, for she divideth us. 30
Some say the lark and loathèd toad changed eyes;
O now I would they had changed voices too,
Since arm from arm that voice doth us affray,
Hunting thee hence with hunt's-up to the day.
O now be gone, more light and light it grows. 35
ROMEO More light and light, more dark and dark our woes!

Enter NURSE [*hastily*].

NURSE Madam!
JULIET Nurse?
NURSE Your lady mother is coming to your chamber.
The day is broke, be wary, look about. [*Exit*] 40
JULIET Then, window, let day in, and let life out.
ROMEO Farewell, farewell! one kiss, and I'll descend.

[*He goeth down.*]

JULIET Art thou gone so, love, lord, ay husband, friend?
I must hear from thee every day in the hour,
For in a minute there are many days. 45
O, by this count I shall be much in years
Ere I again behold my Romeo!
ROMEO [*From below*] Farewell!
I will omit no opportunity
That may convey my greetings, love, to thee. 50

24 Of Julia Marlowe: 'At the thought of death, she springs up and runs to the window. There is
still something of the child about her as she goes: it is all woman that turns back into the
room with drawn face, the beginning of suffering and a voice foreboding' (Russell, *Julia
Marlowe*, p. 236).

29–34 These lines are usually cut, from Garrick to the present.

42 SD In Bogdanov 1986 the love scene and the scene with the parents were both played at stage
level, around Juliet's bed; the lovers ran up to the balcony only for the descent. In an
effective and unsentimental touch, Juliet threw Romeo's shoes and coat down after him.
Adrian Noble used similar staging in 1995. At the Swan in 1989, Mark Rylance climbed down
a rope from the highest balcony, creating a moment of real physical danger.

JULIET   O think'st thou we shall ever meet again?
ROMEO   I doubt it not, and all these woes shall serve
       For sweet discourses in our times to come.
JULIET   O God, I have an ill-divining soul!
       Methinks I see thee now, thou art so low,   55
       As one dead in the bottom of a tomb.
       Either my eyesight fails, or thou look'st pale.
ROMEO   And trust me, love, in my eye so do you:
       Dry sorrow drinks our blood. Adieu, adieu!   *Exit*
JULIET   O Fortune, Fortune, all men call thee fickle;   60
       If thou art fickle, what dost thou with him
       That is renowned for faith? Be fickle, Fortune:
       For then I hope thou wilt not keep him long,
       But send him back.

          Enter Mother [LADY CAPULET *below*].

LADY CAPULET   Ho, daughter, are you up?
JULIET   Who is't that calls? It is my lady mother.   65
       Is she not down so late, or up so early?
       What unaccustomed cause procures her hither?

59 Fanny Kemble, 'though half insensible in her nurse's arms, signed a last farewell to her husband' (Jameson, *Sketches*, p. 489). William Archer observed, of Mrs Patrick Campbell, that 'The clinging kiss in which she lets Romeo almost draw her after him through the window was by far the best thing in the scene' (*Theatrical 'World' of 1895*, p. 291). A nineteenth-century promptbook has the note 'Romeo over balcony – Juliet fervently kisses his hand through the rails and falls fainting' (s23). Sean Bean reached up and almost touched Niamh Cusack's fingers before turning to run off (RSC 1986).

60 Westland Marston gives a vivid account of Adelaide Neilson's playing of this moment: 'As Romeo disappeared, her extended arms followed him awhile, with a desperate effort, as if her soul still pursued him; then the arms relaxed and hung supine, she turned mechanically, and lay unconscious; life had fled with him' (*Our Recent Actors*, II, p. 237).

65 Edwin Booth's promptbook indicates that Juliet 'throws over the cords' at this point, hiding Romeo's escape route (s39). Modjeska evidently neglected to untie the ladder, worrying the critic of *The Theatre* (1 October 1880); nonetheless, her 'weary heart-broken desolation' in this scene impressed Westland Marston, while William Winter noted 'the hurried manner in which Juliet was made to throw herself on her couch at the approach of Lady Capulet' (*The Critic*, 4 June 1881; *Wallet of Time*, I, p. 384). Mary Anderson was praised for the 'weary lassitude' and 'indescribable dejection' with which she admitted her mother (Shattuck, *American, Stage* II, p. 106).

[*She goeth down from the window and enters below.*]

LADY CAPULET Why how now, Juliet?

JULIET   Madam, I am not well.

LADY CAPULET Evermore weeping for your cousin's death?
    What, wilt thou wash him from his grave with tears?   70
    And if thou couldst, thou couldst not make him live;
    Therefore have done. Some grief shows much of love,
    But much of grief shows still some want of wit.

JULIET Yet let me weep for such a feeling loss.

LADY CAPULET So shall you feel the loss, but not the friend   75
    Which you weep for.

JULIET   Feeling so the loss,
    I cannot choose but ever weep the friend.

LADY CAPULET Well, girl, thou weep'st not so much for his death
    As that the villain lives which slaughtered him.

JULIET What villain, madam?

LADY CAPULET   That same villain Romeo.   80

JULIET [*Aside*] Villain and he be many miles asunder. –
    God pardon him, I do with all my heart:
    And yet no man like he doth grieve my heart.

LADY CAPULET That is because the traitor murderer lives.

JULIET Ay, madam, from the reach of these my hands.   85
    Would none but I might venge my cousin's death!

LADY CAPULET We will have vengeance for it, fear thou not:
    Then weep no more. I'll send to one in Mantua,
    Where that same banished runagate doth live,
    Shall give him such an unaccustomed dram   90
    That he shall soon keep Tybalt company;
    And then I hope thou wilt be satisfied.

JULIET Indeed I never shall be satisfied
    With Romeo, till I behold him – dead –
    Is my poor heart, so for a kinsman vexed.   95

68a   Anna Nygh's highly-strung Lady Capulet snapped impatiently at Juliet in Bogdanov's 1986
     modern-dress production. In 1989 Linda Spurrier took a long pause before and after her
     short line to allow Juliet time to run down from the balcony to the main stage of the Swan.

75–104 The discussion of poisoning Romeo, with Juliet's cryptic replies, was cut by Garrick and in
     most subsequent productions up to and including Irving. Charlotte Cushman seems to have
     included this whole exchange in her productions, however. Modern productions have
     generally played at least part of the scene.

> Madam, if you could find out but a man
> To bear a poison, I would temper it,
> That Romeo should upon receipt thereof
> Soon sleep in quiet. O how my heart abhors
> To hear him named and cannot come to him,   100
> To wreak the love I bore my cousin
> Upon his body that hath slaughtered him!
> LADY CAPULET Find thou the means, and I'll find such a man.
> But now I'll tell thee joyful tidings, girl.
> JULIET And joy comes well in such a needy time.   105
> What are they, beseech your ladyship?
> LADY CAPULET Well, well, thou hast a careful father, child,
> One who, to put thee from thy heaviness,
> Hath sorted out a sudden day of joy,
> That thou expects not, nor I looked not for.   110
> JULIET Madam, in happy time, what day is that?
> LADY CAPULET Marry, my child, early next Thursday morn,
> The gallant, young, and noble gentleman,
> The County Paris, at Saint Peter's Church,
> Shall happily make thee there a joyful bride.   115
> JULIET Now by Saint Peter's Church and Peter too,
> He shall not make me there a joyful bride.
> I wonder at this haste, that I must wed
> Ere he that should be husband comes to woo.
> I pray you tell my lord and father, madam,   120
> I will not marry yet, and when I do, I swear
> It shall be Romeo, whom you know I hate,
> Rather than Paris. These are news indeed!

116–17 Cut by Garrick, perhaps to prevent making Juliet seem so openly disobedient, or to avoid her Catholic oath. Mrs Patrick Campbell excelled in 'the little outburst of temper after her mother has proposed marriage with Paris', according to William Archer, because 'petulance is the emotion of all others which best comes within her range' (*Theatrical 'World' of 1895*, p. 291). Julia Marlowe was very brash until restrained: 'Nurse unseen by Lady Capulet touches Juliet with gesture of alarm. Juliet's manner changes and becomes less assertive' (570). Eva Le Gallienne played the moment as a grave turning point, taking a long pause before line 116 (Schanke, *Shattered Applause*, p. 83).

118 Julia Marlowe conveyed Juliet's movement into deception 'with tones and not otherwise . . . in the changed feeling and slightly changed tempo' of these lines (Russell, *Julia Marlowe*, p. 236).

LADY CAPULET Here comes your father, tell him so yourself;
     And see how he will take it at your hands.   125

          Enter CAPULET *and Nurse.*

CAPULET When the sun sets, the earth doth drizzle dew,
     But for the sunset of my brother's son
     It rains downright.
     How now, a conduit, girl? What, still in tears?
     Evermore show'ring? In one little body   130
     Thou counterfeits a bark, a sea, a wind:
     For still thy eyes, which I may call the sea,
     Do ebb and flow with tears; the bark thy body is,
     Sailing in this salt flood; the winds, thy sighs,
     Who, raging with thy tears and they with them,   135
     Without a sudden calm, will overset
     Thy tempest-tossèd body. How now, wife,
     Have you delivered to her our decree?
LADY CAPULET Ay, sir, but she will none, she gives you thanks.
     I would the fool were married to her grave.   140
CAPULET Soft, take me with you, take me with you, wife.
     How, will she none? doth she not give us thanks?
     Is she not proud? doth she not count her blest,
     Unworthy as she is, that we have wrought
     So worthy a gentleman to be her bride?   145

126–38 Capulet's laboured metaphors for Juliet's tearfulness have almost always been cut down in performance, from Garrick and throughout the twentieth century. Terry Hands, in 1989, left them in, to good effect. Capulet embraced Juliet and rocked her from side to side, embellishing his ship metaphor as though telling a story to a small child to cheer her up. The moment showed both his genuine concern and his infantilising of her, an effect emphasised by the contrast between Bernard Horsfall's great height and Georgia Slowe's tiny frame. Michael Hordern uses a similarly affectionate, fatherly approach in the 1978 BBC-TV version.

140 After Lady Capulet's line, the Victorian promptbook s23 has the direction, 'Juliet approaches her mother with open arms as if appealing for sympathy.'

143–5 In Noble 1995, Christopher Benjamin, a fawning Victorian daddy, merely teased Lucy Whybrow's Juliet with these lines, leading her to play-act her refusal in a little-girlish manner, utterly misjudging his capacity for violent rage. The scene thus played had more than a little of Lear and Cordelia about it, and Benjamin's outburst at line 152 was truly frightening and totally unexpected by Juliet.

JULIET Not proud you have, but thankful that you have:
             Proud can I never be of what I hate,
             But thankful even for hate that is meant love.
CAPULET How how, how how, chopt-logic? What is this?
             'Proud', and 'I thank you', and 'I thank you not',   150
             And yet 'not proud', mistress minion you?
             Thank me no thankings, nor proud me no prouds,
             But fettle your fine joints 'gainst Thursday next,
             To go with Paris to Saint Peter's Church,
             Or I will drag thee on a hurdle thither.   155
             Out, you green-sickness carrion! out, you baggage!
             You tallow-face!
LADY CAPULET   Fie, fie, what, are you mad?
JULIET Good father, I beseech you on my knees,
             Hear me with patience but to speak a word.

                          [She kneels down.]

CAPULET Hang thee, young baggage, disobedient wretch!   160
             I tell thee what: get thee to church a'Thursday,
             Or never after look me in the face.
             Speak not, reply not, do not answer me!
             My fingers itch. Wife, we scarce thought us blest
             That God had lent us but this only child,   165
             But now I see this one is one too much,
             And that we have a curse in having her.
             Out on her, hilding!
NURSE   God in heaven bless her!
             You are to blame, my lord, to rate her so.

152b Garrick cut the second half of this splendidly characteristic line, perhaps deeming it a
         'quibble'.
156–7 Garrick, Cushman, Phelps, Irving, Mary Anderson, and many others have cut these
         startlingly vivid terms of abuse.
163 Isabella Nossiter's Juliet had a vivid inner life during her father's long harangue: 'You would
         swear it was her cue to speak, till he stops her . . . She turns from him, with a look that speaks,
         "It is in vain to try to move him"; then almost fainting, she leans upon her Nurse' (*Letter*, p. 23).
164a This line is usually a shouted threat to Juliet that Capulet wishes to strike her; Michael
         Hordern's exasperated but non-violent Capulet spoke it to his wife, to excuse his having
         appeared to threaten Juliet (BBC-TV 1978).
169 In the mid-nineteenth century, Mrs Glover's remonstrance 'had a sullen, half-checked
         fierceness in it, like the growl of an angry but wary dog when one attacks his mistress. Her

CAPULET And why, my Lady Wisdom? Hold your tongue, 170
    Good Prudence, smatter with your gossips, go.
NURSE I speak no treason.
CAPULET   O God-i-goden!
NURSE May not one speak?
CAPULET   Peace, you mumbling fool!
    Utter your gravity o'er a gossip's bowl,
    For here we need it not.
LADY CAPULET   You are too hot. 175
CAPULET God's bread, it makes me mad! Day, night, work, play,
    Alone, in company, still my care hath been
    To have her matched; and having now provided
    A gentleman of noble parentage,
    Of fair demesnes, youthful and nobly ligned, 180
    Stuffed, as they say, with honourable parts,
    Proportioned as one's thought would wish a man,
    And then to have a wretched puling fool,
    A whining mammet, in her fortune's tender,
    To answer 'I'll not wed, I cannot love; 185
    I am too young, I pray you pardon me.'
    But and you will not wed, I'll pardon you:
    Graze where you will, you shall not house with me.
    Look to't, think on't, I do not use to jest.
    Thursday is near, lay hand on heart, advise: 190
    And you be mine, I'll give you to my friend;
    And you be not, hang, beg, starve, die in the streets,
    For by my soul, I'll ne'er acknowledge thee,
    Nor what is mine shall never do thee good.
    Trust to't, bethink you, I'll not be forsworn. *Exit* 195

    attachment to Juliet was indeed a sort of animal instinct' (Marston, *Our Recent Actors*, I,
    p. 264).
187 At 'I'll pardon you', Richard Moore's wealthy, self-made Northern Capulet, in shirtsleeves,
    tie and braces, made a lunge of sudden violence and grabbed Juliet by the hair, holding her
    down on her bed while he snarled the rest of the speech in her ear with barely restrained
    brutality (Bogdanov, RSC 1986).
188 Bernard Horsfall picked up Georgia Slowe's tiny, childlike Juliet and actually spanked her on
    this line (Hands, RSC 1989).
192 These terse monosyllables are often the shouted climax of Capulet's rage; in NYSF 1988
    W. B. Brydon hissed them quietly.

JULIET   Is there no pity sitting in the clouds
           That sees into the bottom of my grief?
           O sweet my mother, cast me not away!
           Delay this marriage for a month, a week,
           Or if you do not, make the bridal bed   200
           In that dim monument where Tybalt lies.
LADY CAPULET   Talk not to me, for I'll not speak a word.
           Do as thou wilt, for I have done with thee.   *Exit*
JULIET   O God! – O Nurse, how shall this be prevented?
           My husband is on earth, my faith in heaven;   205
           How shall that faith return again to earth,
           Unless that husband send it me from heaven
           By leaving earth? Comfort me, counsel me.
           Alack, alack, that heaven should practise stratagems
           Upon so soft a subject as myself!   210
           What say'st thou? hast thou not a word of joy?
           Some comfort, Nurse.
NURSE   Faith, here it is:
           Romeo is banished, and all the world to nothing
           That he dares ne'er come back to challenge you;
           Or if he do, it needs must be by stealth.   215

196–7 Mary Anderson 'reached the topmost height of pathos' with these lines, according to William Winter (*Shakespeare on the Stage*, p. 178). Julia Marlowe, who had been kneeling, 'fell together and prone like one crushed with measureless disaster' (Russell, *Julia Marlowe*, p. 236). Judi Dench, in Zeffirelli's production, spoke hurriedly, from the floor, 'as if she needed no strength of mind to frame and speak this question' (*SS* 15, 1962, 151).

202–3 These lines are usually given with shocking coldness, as by Natasha Parry in the Zeffirelli film; in the 1978 BBC-TV version, Jacqueline Hill's sympathetic Lady Capulet speaks them hurriedly and distractedly as she is leaving to calm down her enraged husband.

212b–225 The Nurse's advice used to be given thoughtlessly and sincerely, as in the case of Mrs Glover: 'There was a sort of frank rationality in her mien and manner when she urged Juliet to desert her lover, as of one who spoke from her deepest convictions. Her very conscience seemed to be dishonest' (Marston, *Our Recent Actors*, I, p. 265). While Anne Meara gave similarly forthright advice (NYSF 1988), modern Nurses tend to agonise more, and often speak against their hearts: a more complex but arguably more sentimental reading. In the Zeffirelli film, the camera reveals Pat Heywood's anguish, which is unseen by Juliet. Dilys Laye, in Bogdanov 1986, clearly didn't believe a word of her own advice, and couldn't look Juliet in the face while speaking it. By contrast, Margaret Courtenay's whole-hearted enthusiasm for Paris, in Hands 1989, was so unexpected it drew audience laughter. Brenda Bruce, who played the Nurse for Ron Daniels (RSC 1980), said, 'What I wanted was a

Then since the case so stands as now it doth,
I think it best you married with the County.
O, he's a lovely gentleman!
Romeo's a dishclout to him. An eagle, madam,
Hath not so green, so quick, so fair an eye   220
As Paris hath. Beshrew my very heart,
I think you are happy in this second match,
For it excels your first, or if it did not,
Your first is dead, or 'twere as good he were
As living here and you no use of him.   225
JULIET Speak'st thou from thy heart?
NURSE And from my soul too, else beshrew them both.
JULIET Amen.
NURSE What?
JULIET Well, thou hast comforted me marvellous much.   230
Go in, and tell my lady I am gone,
Having displeased my father, to Lawrence' cell,
To make confession and to be absolved.
NURSE Marry, I will, and this is wisely done.   [*Exit*]

reaction of shock . . . I would like the audience to feel let down by someone whose motives they have trusted' ('Nurse', p. 101). Bruce fussed around making the bed in an attempt to make the advice 'sensible and acceptable'. In the Luhrmann film, Miriam Margolyes gives her advice sincerely, out of genuine fear for Juliet's future if she disobeys her parents.

225 In Luhrmann, Miriam Margolyes says, 'And you no use *to* him', radically changing the import of the line.

226 Estelle Kohler (Hands 1973) took a long pause and spoke her line in 'almost inaudible monotone' in a moment of 'utter devastation' (Holding, *Romeo*, p. 54)

226–30 This brief exchange provides vivid opportunities for both actresses. Juliet's disillusionment with the Nurse has often been a turning point in the role. Fanny Kemble 'raised her head, extended her arm, and with a power that was magical, pronounced "Amen!" ' (Robins, *Twelve Great Actresses* p. 283). Adelaide Neilson revealed 'a depth of irony in her tone, a sense of utter estrangement in her averted looks, as of one who has aspired and believed in vain, and who has no further commerce with the world' (Marston, *Our Recent Actors*, II, p. 237). Julia Marlowe added a second, emphatic 'Amen!' and gave her Nurse a second 'What?' (S70). While the Nurse may fail to hear or understand Juliet's curse (e.g. Anne Meara, NYSF 1988), many respond with visible shock; Pat Heywood in the Zeffirelli film is a clear example.

234 The Nurse's attitude has ranged from upbeat, whole-hearted approval (Margaret Courtenay, RSC 1989), to shame and guilt (Sheila Reid, RSC 1991), to clenched-teeth exasperation (Elvi Hale, St George's 1976).

JULIET [*She looks after Nurse.*]
>   Ancient damnation! O most wicked fiend!   235
>   Is it more sin to wish me thus forsworn,
>   Or to dispraise my lord with that same tongue
>   Which she hath praised him with above compare
>   So many thousand times? Go, counsellor,
>   Thou and my bosom henceforth shall be twain.   240
>   I'll to the Friar to know his remedy;
>   If all else fail, myself have power to die.   *Exit*

242 In Zeffirelli's stage production, Judi Dench spoke this line lightly on the point of running from the stage, a delivery John Russell Brown felt lacking in gravity (*SS* 15, 1962, p. 151).

ACT 4   SCENE 1

Enter FRIAR [LAWRENCE] *and* COUNTY PARIS.

FRIAR LAWRENCE On Thursday, sir? the time is very short.
PARIS My father Capulet will have it so,
　　　And I am nothing slow to slack his haste.
FRIAR LAWRENCE You say you do not know the lady's mind?
　　　Uneven is the course, I like it not.   5
PARIS Immoderately she weeps for Tybalt's death,
　　　And therefore have I little talked of love,
　　　For Venus smiles not in a house of tears.
　　　Now, sir, her father counts it dangerous
　　　That she do give her sorrow so much sway;   10
　　　And in his wisdom hastes our marriage
　　　To stop the inundation of her tears,
　　　Which too much minded by herself alone
　　　May be put from her by society.
　　　Now do you know the reason of this haste.   15
FRIAR LAWRENCE [*Aside*]
　　　I would I knew not why it should be slowed. –
　　　Look, sir, here comes the lady toward my cell.

Enter JULIET.

PARIS Happily met, my lady and my wife!
JULIET That may be, sir, when I may be a wife.
PARIS That 'may be' must be, love, on Thursday next.   20

4.1 Peter Brook cut this entire scene, thus failing to account for the sleeping potion; he later
　　restored it after incurring the wrath of critics (Trewin, *Shakespeare on the English Stage*,
　　pp. 205–6). In Michael Boyd's 2000 RSC production, this scene established Paris as a
　　sinister figure; while he conversed with the Friar, five armed henchmen in black storm-
　　trooper outfits lurked around the cell.

15 In NYSF 1988, Bradley Whitford's Paris sneered this line contemptuously, as though the Friar
　　had no right to question the haste of the marriage.

16 Joseph O'Conor gave this line wincing with guilt and cowardice (St George's 1976, BBC-TV
　　1978).

18 In Hands 1989, Georgia Slowe came running in to see the Friar and found Paris there, to her
　　shock and surprise; there was an effective awkward pause as she stood panting and
　　dumbfounded.

JULIET What must be shall be.
FRIAR LAWRENCE   That's a certain text.
PARIS Come you to make confession to this father?
JULIET To answer that, I should confess to you.
PARIS Do not deny to him that you love me.
JULIET I will confess to you that I love him.   25
PARIS So will ye, I am sure, that you love me.
JULIET If I do so, it will be of more price,
              Being spoke behind your back, than to your face.
PARIS Poor soul, thy face is much abused with tears.
JULIET The tears have got small victory by that,   30
              For it was bad enough before their spite.
PARIS Thou wrong'st it more than tears with that report.
JULIET That is no slander, sir, which is a truth,
              And what I spake, I spake it to my face.
PARIS Thy face is mine, and thou hast slandered it.   35
JULIET It may be so, for it is not mine own.
              Are you at leisure, holy father, now,
              Or shall I come to you at evening mass?
FRIAR LAWRENCE My leisure serves me, pensive daughter, now.
              My lord, we must entreat the time alone.   40
PARIS God shield I should disturb devotion!
              Juliet, on Thursday early will I rouse ye;

24 Garrick cut the rest of the 'quibble' between Juliet and Paris, perhaps thinking Juliet's
    wordplay inappropriate; most nineteenth-century productions followed his lead, including
    Faucit, Irving, Cushman (after line 26), Mary Anderson, Sothern–Marlowe. Bogdanov,
    however, included the whole scene to good effect, with Niamh Cusack's quick and evasive
    replies to Paris demonstrating the wary intelligence of the newly mature Juliet (RSC 1986).
    Hands 1989 likewise included the whole scene, Paris pursuing Juliet in a tight circle, with the
    Friar repeatedly trying to intervene.
29 Phelps, playing a fuller text than most nineteenth-century producers, cut only from here to
    34. Katherine Cornell cut 24–36.
36 Niamh Cusack spoke this line with emphatic bitterness, giving it a contemporary feminist
    edge and providing a sharp climax to the banter with Paris (Bogdanov, RSC 1986).
37 Of Fanny Kemble's reading of these lines: 'The question itself is nothing; but what a volume
    of misery and dread suspense was in that look with which she turned from Paris to the friar,
    and the tone in which she uttered those simple words!' (Jameson, *Sketches*, p. 491). Ellen
    Terry knelt, as though ready to make confession, in order to get Paris to leave (Sprague,
    Shakespeare and the Actors, p. 310).

      Till then adieu, and keep this holy kiss.   *Exit*

JULIET   O shut the door, and when thou hast done so,

      Come weep with me, past hope, past cure, past help!   45

FRIAR LAWRENCE   O Juliet, I already know thy grief.

      It strains me past the compass of my wits.

      I hear thou must, and nothing may prorogue it,

      On Thursday next be married to this County.

JULIET   Tell me not, Friar, that thou hearest of this,   50

      Unless thou tell me how I may prevent it.

      If in thy wisdom thou canst give no help,

      Do thou but call my resolution wise,

      And with this knife I'll help it presently.

      God joined my heart and Romeo's, thou our hands,   55

      And ere this hand, by thee to Romeo's sealed,

      Shall be the label to another deed,

      Or my true heart with treacherous revolt

      Turn to another, this shall slay them both:

      Therefore, out of thy long-experienced time,   60

      Give me some present counsel, or, behold,

      'Twixt my extremes and me this bloody knife

      Shall play the umpire, arbitrating that

      Which the commission of thy years and art

      Could to no issue of true honour bring.   65

      Be not so long to speak, I long to die,

      If what thou speak'st speak not of remedy.

43 In the Sothern–Marlowe promptbook 'Paris reverently kisses Juliet's brow' (570). Niamh Cusack turned so that Paris's kiss missed her mouth and landed on the side of her head (Bogdanov 1986). Hands's Paris, in 1989, kissed Juliet's hand and made no attempt at further intimacy. In Boyd 2000, by contrast, Nicholas Khan's tall, threatening Paris grabbed Juliet and kissed her fiercely, pulling her leg around him in a forcefully sexual embrace.

44 Helena Faucit felt this scene with the Friar was one of Juliet's most important: 'It is for the actress, in this marvellous and most difficult scene, to show, by her look and manner, how everything that is girlish and immature – everything that, under happy circumstances, would have marked the gentle clinging nature of youth, – falls off from Juliet, – how she is transfigured into the heroic woman . . .' (*Shakespeare's Female Characters*, p. 140).

54 Helena Modjeska played Juliet as close to madness, 'unnaturally and icily cold and cunning'; she made much of the dagger, 'which she constantly and uneasily unsheath[ed] with a glittering and deadly determination' (Altemus, *Helena Modjeska*, p. 130).

56 Niamh Cusack stressed 'by thee' harshly, as though warning the Friar that his complicity in the marriage would make him an accessory to her suicide (Bogdanov, RSC 1986).

FRIAR LAWRENCE Hold, daughter, I do spy a kind of hope,
        Which craves as desperate an execution
        As that is desperate which we would prevent.   70
        If, rather than to marry County Paris,
        Thou hast the strength of will to slay thyself,
        Then is it likely thou wilt undertake
        A thing like death to chide away this shame,
        That cop'st with Death himself to scape from it;   75
        And if thou dar'st, I'll give thee remedy.
JULIET O bid me leap, rather than marry Paris,
        From off the battlements of any tower,
        Or walk in thievish ways, or bid me lurk
        Where serpents are; chain me with roaring bears,   80
        Or hide me nightly in a charnel-house,
        O'ercovered quite with dead men's rattling bones,
        With reeky shanks and yellow chapless skulls;
        Or bid me go into a new-made grave,
        And hide me with a dead man in his shroud –   85
        Things that to hear them told have made me tremble –
        And I will do it without fear or doubt,
        To live an unstained wife to my sweet love.
FRIAR LAWRENCE Hold then, go home, be merry, give consent
        To marry Paris. Wednesday is tomorrow;   90
        Tomorrow night look that thou lie alone,
        Let not the Nurse lie with thee in thy chamber.
        Take thou this vial, being then in bed,

77–88 Of Isabella Nossiter, in the Drury Lane production with Barry: 'Her action here is very graceful and great. It is hard to conceive how the height of the tower, and the mountain, could be differently expressed in action; yet she does it so, that we immediately look to where she points, almost thinking they are within our view' (*Letter*, p. 28). Stella Colas paused between each of the imagined horrors, 'as though searching her mind for some image more dreadful than the last' (Brereton, *Romeo*, pp. 26–7).

88 Of Nossiter: 'The last line recalling the idea of Romeo to her mind, she bursts out into tears as she speaks it' (*Letter*, p. 29).

89 In Noble's 1995 production, Julian Glover's Friar prepared the sleeping-drug from scratch during this speech. On a large table covered with chemical equipment he mixed powders and potions, bustling about eagerly and even using Juliet's dagger to chop up some flowers.

93 In Luhrmann's film Pete Postlethwaite's Friar speaks in the foreground while behind him a montage depicts the events he describes, including the discovery of Juliet's body and her funeral.

And this distilling liquor drink thou off,
When presently through all thy veins shall run 95
A cold and drowsy humour; for no pulse
Shall keep his native progress, but surcease;
No warmth, no breath shall testify thou livest;
The roses in thy lips and cheeks shall fade
To wanny ashes, thy eyes' windows fall, 100
Like Death when he shuts up the day of life;
Each part, deprived of supple government,
Shall stiff and stark and cold appear like death,
And in this borrowed likeness of shrunk death
Thou shalt continue two and forty hours, 105
And then awake as from a pleasant sleep.
Now when the bridegroom in the morning comes
To rouse thee from thy bed, there art thou dead.
Then as the manner of our country is,
In thy best robes, uncovered on the bier, 110
Thou shall be borne to that same ancient vault
Where all the kindred of the Capulets lie.
In the mean time, against thou shalt awake,
Shall Romeo by my letters know our drift,
And hither shall he come, and he and I 115
Will watch thy waking, and that very night
Shall Romeo bear thee hence to Mantua.
And this shall free thee from this present shame,
If no inconstant toy, nor womanish fear,
Abate thy valour in the acting it. 120
JULIET   Give me, give me! O tell not me of fear.

108   Julian Glover's Friar laughed with slightly ghoulish enthusiasm at the anticipated result of
his potion (Noble, RSC 1995).

110   Joseph O'Conor stressed 'uncovered', assuaging Juliet's alarm, then rushed ahead to the
discussion of Romeo, using his name to calm Juliet and raise her hopes (St George's, 1976).

112–15   Next to these lines, Ellen Terry wrote 'Yes!!' in her studybook, and at the bottom of the page
admonished herself, 'Do not anticipate . . . the next scene (*Fear*). No. "Tell me *not* of fear" '
(s47).

121   Adelaide Neilson's reaction to the Friar's speech was noteworthy for its quiet intensity:
'There was a momentary shudder, indeed, as she listened to his ghastly description of the
counterfeit death which should follow; but on the whole, her bearing was hushed and stern.
Extremes meet, and the fixed absorption of Juliet in one idea had in its still settled purpose
something that resembled apathy. One thing was to be done, one end, if possible, to be

FRIAR LAWRENCE Hold, get you gone, be strong and prosperous
        In this resolve; I'll send a friar with speed
        To Mantua, with my letters to thy lord.
JULIET Love give me strength, and strength shall help afford.   125
        Farewell, dear father.

                                                              Exeunt

accomplished; violence of emotion or manner would have seemed shallow compared with her inflexible calm' (Marston, *Our Recent Actors*, II, pp. 237–8). By contrast, Olivia Hussey seizes the vial with childish eagerness in the Zeffirelli film.

Enter Father CAPULET, *Mother* [LADY CAPULET], NURSE, *and*
SERVINGMEN, *two or three.*

CAPULET So many guests invite as here are writ.

[*Exit Servingman*]

Sirrah, go hire me twenty cunning cooks.

SERVINGMAN You shall have none ill, sir, for I'll try if they can lick
their fingers.

CAPULET How canst thou try them so?   5

SERVINGMAN Marry, sir, 'tis an ill cook that cannot lick his own
fingers; therefore he that cannot lick his fingers goes not with me.

CAPULET Go, be gone.

[*Exit Servingman*]

We shall be much unfurnished for this time.

What, is my daughter gone to Friar Lawrence?   10

NURSE Ay forsooth.

CAPULET Well, he may chance to do some good on her.

A peevish self-willed harlotry it is.

Enter JULIET.

NURSE See where she comes from shrift with merry look.

CAPULET How now, my headstrong. where have you been gadding?   15

JULIET Where I have learnt me to repent the sin

4.2 This scene was often cut in nineteenth-century productions (Irving, Anderson,
Sothern–Marlowe, etc.), along with 4.4, to speed the play along and to obviate the need for
an additional set. William Poel argued vigorously for the inclusion of both the short Capulet
scenes: 'Until these scenes are restored to the acting version, Shakespeare's tragedy will not
be seen on the stage as he conceived it; and when they are restored, their dramatic power
will electrify the house' (*Stage-Version*, p. 21).

1 In NYSF 1988, Capulet gave this order to Peter, who stupidly repeated it, recalling the earlier
invitation business of 1.2.

9 Garrick and Cushman began the scene here, cutting Capulet's homely banter with the
servants.

16–20 Modjeska was praised for the 'mechanical sweetness' of her submission, 'as of a set tune of
speech played by a wound-up instrument . . . The veiled, tutored voice, the ready yet
precise genuflexion – so different from the vital mood of the late wayward girl' (*The Critic*, 4
June 1881).

Of disobedient opposition
To you and your behests, and am enjoined
By holy Lawrence to fall prostrate here
To beg your pardon.

[She kneels down.]

                       Pardon, I beseech you!   20
Henceforward I am ever ruled by you.
CAPULET Send for the County, go tell him of this.
     I'll have this knot knit up tomorrow morning.
JULIET I met the youthful lord at Lawrence' cell,
     And gave him what becomèd love I might,   25
     Not stepping o'er the bounds of modesty.
CAPULET Why, I am glad on't, this is well, stand up.
     This is as't should be. Let me see the County;
     Ay, marry, go, I say, and fetch him hither.
     Now afore God, this reverend holy Friar,   30
     All our whole city is much bound to him.
JULIET Nurse, will you go with me into my closet,
     To help me sort such needful ornaments
     As you think fit to furnish me tomorrow?
LADY CAPULET No, not till Thursday, there is time enough.   35
CAPULET Go, Nurse, go with her, we'll to church tomorrow.

                           Exeunt [Juliet and Nurse]

LADY CAPULET We shall be short in our provision,
     'Tis now near night.
CAPULET   Tush, I will stir about,
     And all things shall be well, I warrant thee, wife:
     Go thou to Juliet, help to deck up her;   40

20–1 Helena Faucit recalled that 'when I knelt to my father, I had mutely, in kissing his hand, taken leave of him . . .' (*Shakespeare's Female Characters*, p. 143).

23 In Hands 1989, Lady Capulet interjected 'No, not till Thursday' here, repeating it at line 35.

35–46 Bogdanov's Lady Capulet was very upset by her husband's capricious changing of the wedding date, as was the Nurse. The scene provided a telling contrast between the smug, self-satisfied Capulet (Richard Moore), sitting in a dressing gown with whisky and cigar, and the unhappy women who fluttered around him. At the end of the scene, Lady Capulet crumpled up the seating plan she had been making and flung it onto Capulet's desk. Left alone, Capulet called for servants on his desk intercom ('What ho!') but found 'They are all forth' (RSC 1986).

I'll not to bed tonight; let me alone,
I'll play the huswife for this once. What ho!
They are all forth. Well, I will walk myself
To County Paris, to prepare up him
Against tomorrow. My heart is wondrous light,   45
Since this same wayward girl is so reclaimed.

Exeunt

42 Though this line usually is an occasion to show Capulet's return to bustling high spirits, Jonathan Newth (Leveaux 1991) played it with frustration, annoyed at having to busy himself with petty domestic arrangements. Likewise, Newth's line, 'My heart is wondrous light', was not a true statement but an announcement to Lady Capulet, who was lurking upstage, that he had succeeded in imposing his will on the household.

Enter JULIET *and* NURSE.

JULIET Ay, those attires are best, but, gentle Nurse,
I pray thee leave me to myself tonight:
For I have need of many orisons
To move the heavens to smile upon my state,
Which, well thou knowest, is cross and full of sin.   5

Enter Mother [LADY CAPULET].

LADY CAPULET What, are you busy, ho? need you my help?
JULIET No, madam, we have culled such necessaries
As are behoveful for our state tomorrow.
So please you, let me now be left alone,
And let the Nurse this night sit up with you,   10
For I am sure you have your hands full all,
In this so sudden business.
LADY CAPULET   Good night.
Get thee to bed and rest, for thou hast need.
Exeunt [*Lady Capulet and Nurse*]
JULIET Farewell! God knows when we shall meet again.
I have a faint cold fear thrills through my veins   15

4.3 The 'potion scene' was for a long time one of the great set pieces in the standard repertory
of an English actress. 'What a scene this is – so simple, so grand, so terrible!' Helena Faucit
wrote of it. 'What it is to act I need not tell you. What power it demands, and what restraint!'
Faucit claimed to have actually fainted at the end of the speech the first and last times she
played it (*Shakespeare's Female Characters*, p. 145). Critics regularly claimed that it was
always overacted; Poel argued that 'our Juliets do too much "stumping and frumping"
about' (*Stage-Version*, p. 19). While in the nineteenth century it was considered the supreme
test of an actress's Juliet, its importance diminished in the twentieth. Zeffirelli cut it entirely
from his film, partly because he felt Olivia Hussey couldn't make it convincing (Loney,
Staging Shakespeare, p. 260). Luhrmann cut it also.
1 Niamh Cusack began the scene playing a melancholy air (from Debussy's 'Syrinx') on her
flute (Cusack, 'Juliet', p. 133).
14 The parting with Lady Capulet was a key moment for Victorian Juliets. Adelaide Neilson
gave a 'deep, lingering farewell as Lady Capulet retired', which 'contrasted with the forced
lightness which had been assumed in her presence' (Marston, *Our Recent Actors*, II, p. 238).
Eliza O'Neill fell to her knees and gazed after her mother, 'as if this longing, lingering look

That almost freezes up the heat of life:
I'll call them back again to comfort me.
Nurse! – What should she do here?
My dismal scene I needs must act alone.
Come, vial.   20
What if this mixture do not work at all?
Shall I be married then tomorrow morning?
No, no, this shall forbid it; lie thou there.

[*Laying down her dagger.*]

What if it be a poison which the Friar
Subtly hath ministered to have me dead,   25
Lest in this marriage he should be dishonoured,
Because he married me before to Romeo?
I fear it is, and yet methinks it should not,

was to be her last on earth' (Sprague, *Shakespeare and the Actors*, p. 311). Mary Anderson
gave a 'look and gesture of mute appeal when the mother is about to leave the daughter
without kissing her' (*Nineteenth Century*, December 1884). By contrast, Helena Faucit
relaxed suddenly, relieved at no longer having to hide her feelings from her mother (Faucit,
Shakespeare's Female Characters, p. 143). Mrs Patrick Campbell made her poignant
farewell with the Nurse, at first refusing to kiss her and then calling her back for an
emotional embrace (s63).

18 Adelaide Neilson bitterly stressed the 'she' (Marston, *Our Recent Actors*, II, p. 238).
20 Fanny Kemble began the speech seated, with grave determination, and didn't rise until quite
far gone in frenzy; an original and restrained choice, according to Anna Jameson (*Sketches*,
p. 491). Fitzroy Davis gives detailed notes on how Katherine Cornell played the speech:
'Pause. Begins to reflect, then speaks rapidly in low, unmusical voice' (s95).
22–3 Isabella Nossiter answered her own question 'with a melancholy smile' (*Letter*, p. 31). Eliza
O'Neill 'made a fine picture . . . by the determined air with which she drew the dagger, her
eyes glaring with despair' (Brereton, *Romeo*, p. 24).
24 Nossiter marked Juliet's sudden hesitation vividly: 'she moves the vial with slow solemnity
to her head, fixed in her resolution to drink it; but just as it approaches her lips, she starts
and draws it back, her imagination having then formed a new fear, that was before
unthought of' (*Letter*, pp. 31–2).
25–8 Mrs Patrick Campbell 'uncork[ed] the phial and smell[ed] it to reassure herself – a little
touch of exquisitely misplaced realism' (Archer, *Theatrical 'World' of 1895*, p. 292).
29 Ellen Terry, in an audio recording of the speech she made in 1911, speaks this line 'so that
every word is lingeringly delivered and given on a different musical note' (Booth, *Bernhardt*,
p. 100). While some critics felt Terry failed with this speech in the 1882 Lyceum production –
'she simply lacks the *physique* to deliver with sustained force a soliloquy of agonizing terror'

For he hath still been tried a holy man.
How if, when I am laid into the tomb,   30
I wake before the time that Romeo
Come to redeem me? There's a fearful point!
Shall I not then be stifled in the vault,
To whose foul mouth no healthsome air breathes in,
And there die strangled ere my Romeo comes?   35
Or if I live, is it not very like
The horrible conceit of death and night,
Together with the terror of the place
As in a vault, an ancient receptacle,
Where for this many hundred years the bones   40
Of all my buried ancestors are packed,
Where bloody Tybalt, yet but green in earth,
Lies fest'ring in his shroud, where, as they say,
At some hours in the night spirits resort –
Alack, alack, is it not like that I,   45

(G. A. Sala, quoted in Booth, *Bernhardt*, p. 109) – she was aided by atmospheric lighting. According to Edward Russell, 'The faint hues and lines of the room seem to blend with her imaginings in a spectral manner which is notably appropriate and thrilling' (*Macmillan's Magazine*, XLVI, 1882, p. 334).

32 ff. During her recital of the imagined horrors of the tomb, Stella Colas 'turned positively green with fear, and became prematurely old, ugly, and haggard,' according to Clement Scott (*Yesterday and Today*, II, p. 303). Similarly, Adelaide Neilson was praised for her 'look of horror and recoil as her imagination conjures up the thought of what may happen to her in the grim vault', though Joseph Knight felt her reactions were perhaps excessive: 'We can conceive of this scene being enacted with more reserve of force' (Mullin, *Victorian Actors*, pp. 347–8). Julia Marlowe was apparently unusual in giving the speech 'with a stern repression of all declamation, without extravagance', though she made the standard 'point' at the vision of Tybalt's ghost (Russell, *Julia Marlowe*, p. 237). In 1986, Niamh Cusack played the speech 'like a little girl telling herself a story, but a wild and frightening story' (Cusack, 'Juliet,' p. 134).

40 Lucy Whybrow stood up on her bed in revulsion, as though seeing piles of corpses surrounding her on the floor; she remained standing on the bed for the rest of the speech (Noble, RSC 1995).

42–4 Helena Faucit recalled that 'I could never utter these words without an exclamation of shuddering disgust escaping with them' (*Shakespeare's Female Characters*, p. 144). Similarly, Katherine Cornell gave a 'quiver of revulsion' at 'lies fest'ring in his shroud,' and a 'little wail' on 'spirits' (S95).

> So early waking – what with loathsome smells,
> And shrieks like mandrakes' torn out of the earth,
> That living mortals hearing them run mad –
> O, if I wake, shall I not be distraught,
> Environèd with all these hideous fears,   50
> And madly play with my forefathers' joints,
> And pluck the mangled Tybalt from his shroud,
> And in this rage, with some great kinsman's bone,
> As with a club, dash out my desp'rate brains?
> O look! methinks I see my cousin's ghost   55
> Seeking out Romeo that did spit his body
> Upon a rapier's point. Stay, Tybalt, stay!

49–54 Isabella Nossiter made the most of her imagined delirium: 'stamping with rage, she flings her arms about, then strikes her hands with all her force against her forehead, as if to knock her brains out; and resting for some time in a state almost of stupefaction, as overcome with madness, she pants for breath' (*Letter*, pp. 34–5). Stella Colas uttered 'a piercing unearthly shriek' on the word 'dash' (Scott, *Yesterday and Today*, II, p. 303). Katherine Cornell's Juliet 'push[ed] her hands into her temples, leaning taut against the left bedpost' (S95).

55 Actresses in the nineteenth century seized this opportunity for emotional extravagance. Eliza O'Neill seems to have originated the business of emitting a piercing shriek at the sight of Tybalt's ghost; Hazlitt found it excessive and confusing, 'as it preceded the speech which explained its meaning' (*Hazlitt on Theatre*, p. 19). Of Adelaide Neilson, Marston wrote 'No mere report can convey the freezing horror with which she swung round, as on a pivot, with hands screening her eyes, as if recoiling from the sight, which yet fascinated her, of Tybalt's imagined shape behind her' (*Our Recent Actors*, II, p. 238). John Rankin Towse also commented on how Neilson's 'physical vigor enabled her to give thrilling expression to a paroxysm of hysterical horror, with very little suggestion – there was a trace – of rant' (*Sixty Years*, pp. 134–5). In the Castellani film Susan Shentall's Juliet is frightened at the sight of her wedding dress, which stands in the shadows on a large dressmaker's dummy – an effective touch of irony.

57b Fanny Kemble 'used to rush from the back of the stage right down to the footlights, as though she were driving the apparition of Tybalt before her, and then fall on one knee in an attitude which some poetic admirers designated her "Canova" ' (Dutton Cook, *Nights at the Play*, I, pp. 7–8). This sort of business became popular with many actresses, to the despair of critics. Henry Morley was particularly severe on Stella Colas, who 'spends so much force upon the shrieking at and cowering by the bedside from Tybalt's ghost, that she can only add as an insignificant tag to that claptrap stage effect the line in which a greater actress would have found the true climax, "Romeo! I come. This do I drink to thee!" ' (*Journal*, p. 278). Brereton praised Mrs Potter for remembering 'that Romeo, not Tybalt, is uppermost in

Romeo, Romeo, Romeo! Here's drink — I drink to thee.

[*She falls upon her bed, within the curtains.*]

Juliet's mind' (*Romeo*, p. 30). Adelaide Neilson also drew praise for her tenderness in this moment. Westland Marston called it 'the triumph of love over all the dread environments of imagination – the poetry of devotion realized to the eye', though he sadly noted that 'in later years the actress discarded this fine close of her soliloquy in favour of a more stagey ending' (*Our Recent Actors*, II, p. 239). One of the most stagey versions of this moment was that of Helena Modjeska, who flung herself into a great chair 'with her limbs drawn up convulsively, her whole frame quivering, her very teeth chattering, and a cold sweat upon her livid features' (Altemus, *Helena Modjeska*, p. 133).

58 In the 1850s, Anna Cora Mowatt achieved a startling effect with the drinking of the potion, when the prop man accidentally substituted the prompter's ink bottle for the Friar's vial: 'She was astounded; but the spectators, seeing the dark stain on her lips and hands, simply supposed it was a stage trick to simulate the workings of the poison' (Wingate, *Shakespeare's Heroines*, p. 24). The potion business has often caused problems in performance; Charlotte Cushman's promptbook cautions that 'Juliet should be particular to drop the vial well upstage', and specifies that the vial should be 'flat' (s31).

The drinking of the potion was a turning point for the girlish Juliet of Peggy Ashcroft, in Gielgud's 1935 production: 'It is a frightened child who is shaken with fears of what hideous spectres may meet her eyes when she wakens in the tomb: a woman strong on the wings of passion who, mastering her childish fears, cries "Romeo, I come! this do I drink to thee" ' (*New York Times*, 17 November 1935).

58 SD The Q1 stage direction 'She falls upon her bed, within the curtains' implies the use of the Elizabethan playhouse's 'discovery space', and suggests that the action was continuous until the end of 4.5. As Victorian productions sometimes cut 4.5 altogether and ended the act with Juliet's faint, she didn't necessarily need to fall on the bed. Adelaide Neilson collapsed next to the sofa, then staggered over to a table, took up a crucifix, 'and in the act of kissing it falls inanimate' (s22). Margaret Mather, in 1885, rolled down a flight of steps, 'an effective climax to the grandeur of the acting that proceeded it', according to the critic of *Shakespeariana* (Sprague, *Shakespeare and the Actors*, p. 313). Modjeska clutched convulsively at the tablecloth, 'throwing down and extinguishing the lights' and 'winding . . . the cloth around her body as she falls' (Altemus, *Helena Modjeska*, p. 133). Julia Marlowe made an effective 'point' when the sound of the dropped vial 'ringing upon the floor . . . startled her for one instant back to her terrors. She cast one fearful look about her, then conquered herself again, took three steps toward the bed and fell unconscious' (Russell, *Julia Marlowe*, p. 237). Helena Faucit, by contrast, was commended for 'the exhaustion with which Juliet retired to the bed, instead of the ordinary climax when she takes the draught'

(Westland Marston, in Martin, *Helena Faucit*, p. 232). Peter Hall's 1961 production used a similarly quiet finish; Dorothy Tutin sat looking around her, waiting for the potion to take effect, then got into bed and pulled the covers slowly over her (s106). Lucy Whybrow did almost the same thing in 1995.

ACT 4 SCENE 4

Enter lady of the house [LADY CAPULET] *and* NURSE [*with herbs*].

LADY CAPULET Hold, take these keys and fetch more spices, Nurse.
NURSE They call for dates and quinces in the pastry.

Enter old CAPULET.

CAPULET Come, stir, stir, stir! the second cock hath crowed,
      The curfew bell hath rung, 'tis three a'clock.
      Look to the baked meats, good Angelica,   5
      Spare not for cost.
NURSE   Go, you cot-quean, go,
      Get you to bed. Faith, you'll be sick tomorrow
      For this night's watching.
CAPULET No, not a whit. What, I have watched ere now
      All night for lesser cause, and ne'er been sick.   10
LADY CAPULET Ay, you have been a mouse-hunt in your time,
      But I will watch you from such watching now.
                        Exeunt Lady [*Capulet*] *and Nurse*
CAPULET A jealous hood, a jealous hood!

Enter three or four [SERVINGMEN] *with spits and logs and baskets.*

                  Now, fellow,
      What is there?
FIRST SERVINGMAN Things for the cook, sir, but I know not what.   15
CAPULET Make haste, make haste.
                    [Exit First Servingman]
          Sirrah, fetch drier logs.
      Call Peter, he will show thee where they are.

4.4 The Capulet preparations were cut completely by Brook and Zeffirelli, as in many
nineteenth-century productions (*SS* 15, 1962, p. 154). When included, this scene necessarily
requires some kind of staging whereby Juliet's bed can remain in place. Bogdanov used a
revolve, with servants and Capulets bustling in all directions on a darkened stage, while
Juliet remained in the middle. Terry Hands, in both 1973 and 1989, used the balcony, leaving
Juliet's bed in darkness. In Boyd 2000, the servants rushed around Juliet's bed, occasionally
even tossing props to each other over her unconscious body. In the 1978 BBC-TV version,
this scene is set in a busy kitchen where Lady Capulet is supervising the cooking.

11–12 In Hands 1989, Linda Spurrier's unhappily married Lady Capulet was very bitter about her
husband's past mouse-hunting.

SECOND SERVINGMAN I have a head, sir, that will find out logs,
      And never trouble Peter for the matter.
CAPULET Mass, and well said, a merry whoreson, ha!   20
      Thou shalt be loggerhead.

                    [*Exeunt Second Servingman and any others*]
                Good faith, 'tis day.
      The County will be here with music straight,
      For so he said he would.

                (*Play music* [*within*].)

              I hear him near.
      Nurse! Wife! What ho! What, Nurse, I say!

            Enter Nurse.

      Go waken Juliet, go and trim her up,   25
      I'll go and chat with Paris. Hie, make haste,
      Make haste, the bridegroom he is come already,
      Make haste, I say.   [*Exit*]

21 Christopher Benjamin's jolly Capulet, in Noble 1995, was immensely amused by his own rather strained pun.
23 SD In Noble 1995, lively accordion music began at this point and continued until Paris entered in the next scene, creating a macabre and festive atmosphere.

ACT 4   SCENE 5

NURSE Mistress, what mistress! Juliet! Fast, I warrant her, she.
　　　　Why, lamb! why, lady! fie, you slug-a-bed!
　　　　Why, love, I say! madam! sweet heart! why, bride!
　　　　What, not a word? You take your pennyworths now;
　　　　Sleep for a week, for the next night I warrant　　　　　　　　　5
　　　　The County Paris hath set up his rest
　　　　That you shall rest but little. God forgive me!
　　　　Marry and amen! How sound is she asleep!
　　　　I needs must wake her. Madam, madam, madam!
　　　　Ay, let the County take you in your bed,　　　　　　　　　　10
　　　　He'll fright you up, i'faith. Will it not be?

4.5　This scene has often been cut or severely abridged. Mary Anderson cut it altogether for her
　　　Lyceum production, going directly from the potion scene to 'The Pageant of Juliet's funeral'
　　　(s50). Others cutting it included Modjeska, Forbes-Robertson, Maude Adams, Jane Cowl,
　　　Katherine Cornell, and NYSF 1988. At the Lyceum in 1908, an elaborate pantomime was
　　　substituted, described with gleeful venom by Max Beerbohm: 'Down and up goes the
　　　curtain, and enter, with beaming faces, several young ladies attired as bride's-maids, and
　　　carrying white flowers. They approach the bed softly. Suddenly the face of their leader
　　　ceases to beam. Something is wrong. She says nothing . . . but it is evident she thinks the
　　　worst. "O Juliet, Juliet, Juliet, thou art dead", is the language of her eyes. Her companions
　　　are deeply, though noiselessly, affected. But in the midst of their grief a brilliant idea occurs
　　　to them. The flowers that were to have been for the wedding will come in equally well for
　　　the funeral. So, one by one, the ladies deposit their floral offerings on the bed . . .' (*Last
　　　Theatres*, p. 357). In defence of this bit of business, it is an exact illustration of Capulet's line
　　　89. Irving also used a procession of bridesmaids, which Clement Scott found 'singularly
　　　effective and poetical into the bargain' (*The Theatre*, 1 April 1882). Irving's inclusion of this
　　　scene was praised by William Winter: 'the gradual increase of light, the songs of the newly
　　　awakened birds, the music made by serenaders, and the entrance and distraction of the
　　　Nurse combined to cause a thrilling effect' (*Shakespeare on the Stage*, p. 131). Irving
　　　retained some of the mourning speeches, though he cut the Musicians.
　　1　The Victorian promptbook s23 has the evocative stage direction 'Candles nearly burnt out'.
　　5　Francis Gentleman complained, of Garrick's production, that 'the Nurse's remarks before
　　　she attempts to wake Juliet are contemptible, at such a crisis; and commonly make an
　　　audience laugh when they should cry' (*Dramatic Censor*, p. 185). Subsequent managers
　　　heeded his admonition; the bawdiness is cut in Phelps, Faucit, and Irving. Cushman cut line
　　　5 but allowed 'you shall rest but little'.

[*Draws back the curtains.*]

What, dressed, and in your clothes, and down again?
I must needs wake you. Lady, lady, lady!
Alas, alas! Help, help! my lady's dead!
O weraday that ever I was born!   15
Some aqua-vitae, ho! My lord! My lady!

[*Enter Mother*, LADY CAPULET.]

LADY CAPULET What noise is here?
NURSE   O lamentable day!
LADY CAPULET What is the matter?
NURSE   Look, look! O heavy day!
LADY CAPULET O me, O me, my child, my only life!
Revive, look up, or I will die with thee.   20
Help, help! Call help.

Enter Father [CAPULET].

CAPULET For shame, bring Juliet forth, her lord is come.
NURSE She's dead, deceased, she's dead, alack the day!
LADY CAPULET Alack the day, she's dead, she's dead, she's dead!

14 Ellen Terry recalled that Mrs Stirling, as the Nurse, went against tradition by not playing for
any comedy in the scene: 'Her parrot scream when she found me dead was horribly real
and effective' (*Story of My Life*, p. 230). Terry herself played this moment memorably at the
end of her career, in Doris Keane's 1919 production at the Lyric, Shaftesbury Avenue.
Reginald Denham, who played Paris, described 'the gaiety of her laugh – a slightly bawdy
laugh – as she pulls the blinds . . . Then her slight irritation because Juliet is keeping up a
joke too long by pretending to be asleep. Then a slight shadow of apprehension – is she
asleep? – which she brushes aside for a moment. Then the return of that fear, much
stronger this time. Then a frantic shaking of the girl as she attempts to rouse her. Then a
lifting of the eyelids and a great agonised cry . . .' (Denham, *Stars*, p. 90). Edith Evans's
Nurse, in 1935, was a 'massive, lumbering crone', whose 'clumsy totter for help' and 'squawk
of agony' were particularly moving (Trewin, *Shakespeare on the English Stage*, p. 153).
15 In Noble 1995, the Nurse discovered and concealed the potion vial on this line.
23 ff. Leveaux 1991, in spite of having a nearly uncut text to this point, cut most of the mourning
and all of the Friar's speech, as the scene changed almost immediately to 5.1. Juliet's bed
was hoisted up into the flies, where she remained visible, hanging in mid-air, until she was
lowered down again for the tomb scene. Michael Attenborough was also unusual, for a
modern director, in cutting the mourning (*Times*, 7 November 1997).

CAPULET Hah, let me see her. Out alas, she's cold,   25
             Her blood is settled, and her joints are stiff:
             Life and these lips have long been separated;
             Death lies on her like an untimely frost
             Upon the sweetest flower of all the field.
NURSE O lamentable day!
LADY CAPULET   O woeful time!   30
CAPULET Death that hath tane her hence to make me wail
             Ties up my tongue and will not let me speak.

Enter FRIAR [LAWRENCE] *and the* COUNTY [PARIS *with the* MUSICIANS].

FRIAR LAWRENCE Come, is the bride ready to go to church?
CAPULET Ready to go, but never to return. –
             O son, the night before thy wedding day   35
             Hath Death lain with thy wife. There she lies,
             Flower as she was, deflowerèd by him.
             Death is my son-in-law, Death is my heir,
             My daughter he hath wedded. I will die,
             And leave him all; life, living, all is Death's.   40
PARIS Have I thought long to see this morning's face,
             And doth it give me such a sight as this?
LADY CAPULET Accursed, unhappy, wretched, hateful day!

25 In the Nunn–Kyle production of 1976, John Woodvine's brutal Capulet at first assumed his
    daughter was simply refusing to get out of bed; 'he erupted in rage, shaking and flinging her
    frail body to the floor, before collapsing in mute agony at her side' (Holding, *Romeo*, p. 60).
33 In Bogdanov 1986, the Friar entered merrily with the full wedding party and the Musicians
    playing; the pointedly comic staging reflected the multiple ironies of the scene. Similarly, in
    Noble's 1995 production, 'a wedding party full of posy-clutching child bridesmaids erupts
    noisily into Juliet's bedroom' during the mourning scene (*Guardian*, 7 July 1995).
35–40 Capulet's comments about death deflowering Juliet, though thematically important, were
    too explicit for Victorian audiences, and were cut from virtually all productions before the
    twentieth century.
43 ff. In Zeffirelli's production, the mourning was staged formally, and 'anonymous servants were
    introduced mechanically, two at a time, to extend the tableau and so attempt to effect an
    impression of climax' (*SS* 15, 1962, p. 151). Terry Hands, in 1973, overlapped the several
    mourning speeches, treating them 'as a sort of fugue, the first speaker accompanying the
    second with repeated fragments of his theme as a counter-subject' (David, *Shakespeare in*
    the Theatre, p. 113). He used the same business in 1989, setting up a definite rhythm in all
    the mourners' lines which the Friar then picked up for his speech as well, giving the scene

Most miserable hour that e'er time saw
In lasting labour of his pilgrimage!   45
But one, poor one, one poor and loving child,
But one thing to rejoice and solace in,
And cruel Death hath catched it from my sight!

NURSE O woe! O woeful, woeful, woeful day!
Most lamentable day, most woeful day   50
That ever, ever, I did yet behold!
O day, O day, O day, O hateful day!
Never was seen so black a day as this.
O woeful day, O woeful day!

PARIS Beguiled, divorcèd, wrongèd, spited, slain!   55
Most detestable Death, by thee beguiled,
By cruel, cruel thee quite overthrown!
O love! O life! not life, but love in death!

CAPULET Despised, distressèd, hated, martyred, killed!
Uncomfortable time, why cam'st thou now   60
To murder, murder our solemnity?
O child, O child! my soul, and not my child!
Dead art thou. Alack, my child is dead,
And with my child my joys are burièd.

FRIAR LAWRENCE Peace ho, for shame! Confusion's cure lives not   65
In these confusions. Heaven and yourself
Had part in this fair maid, now heaven hath all,
And all the better is it for the maid:
Your part in her you could not keep from death,
But heaven keeps his part in eternal life.   70
The most you sought was her promotion,
For 'twas your heaven she should be advanced,
And weep ye now, seeing she is advanced

surprising energy and pace. Adrian Noble also overlapped the mourning, making it a sort of round, whereby each speaker said the first line loud and at normal speed, then continued in a slower, quiet voice as the others followed (RSC 1995). Michael Boyd rearranged the text to have Paris and Capulet alternate words in their formal lament, suggesting a kind of competitiveness in their mourning (RSC 2000). In the 1978 BBC-TV version, the mourning speeches are played naturalistically, with the close-up camera focusing on the different reactions of each speaker (Paris is cut).

65–83 This speech was central to Bogdanov's anti-capitalist, modern-dress production. Robert Demeger's Friar took the social-climbing Capulets sternly to task, angrily emphasising, 'the most you sought was her *promotion*' (RSC 1986).

Above the clouds, as high as heaven itself?
O, in this love, you love your child so ill 75
That you run mad, seeing that she is well.
She's not well married that lives married long,
But she's best married that dies married young.
Dry up your tears, and stick your rosemary
On this fair corse, and as the custom is, 80
And in her best array, bear her to church;
For though fond nature bids us all lament,
Yet nature's tears are reason's merriment.
CAPULET All things that we ordainèd festival,
Turn from their office to black funeral: 85
Our instruments to melancholy bells,
Our wedding cheer to a sad burial feast;
Our solemn hymns to sullen dirges change;
Our bridal flowers serve for a buried corse;
And all things change them to the contrary. 90
FRIAR LAWRENCE Sir, go you in, and, madam, go with him,
And go, Sir Paris. Every one prepare
To follow this fair corse unto her grave.
The heavens do low'r upon you for some ill;
Move them no more by crossing their high will. 95
[*They all, but the Nurse and the Musicians, go forth, casting rosemary on*
her, and shutting the curtains]
FIRST MUSICIAN Faith, we may put up our pipes and be gone.

84 Bogdanov's businessman Capulet, having conquered his grief, began giving efficient
instructions to his secretary; the wedding baked meats would coldly furnish forth the
funeral tables (RSC 1986).

95 John Gielgud recalled Ellen Terry's performance of the Nurse: 'After the mourners had left
the scene she stood by Juliet's bed, folded the girl's hands, and knelt down beside her body
as the curtain fell. I shall never forget the absolute simplicity with which she did this'
(Trewin, *Shakespeare on the English Stage*, p. 85). In Bogdanov 1986 the Friar stealthily
snatched up the vial while the mourners were leaving. Joseph O'Conor, in the St George's
1976 production, held his hand to Juliet's face to confirm that she was still breathing, thus
raising the question of why no one else had checked.

95 SD A wonderfully specific and homely detail from Q1, seldom realised in performance, though it
was used in the Elizabethan production at St George's 1976.

96 Though virtually always cut before the 1960s, the Musicians have been working their way
back into the play. Poel argued that this scene 'comes as a welcome relief after the intensity
of the previous scenes, and is, besides, a connecting link with the comedy in the earlier part

NURSE Honest good fellows, ah put up, put up,
       For well you know this is a pitiful case.   [*Exit*]
FIRST MUSICIAN Ay, by my troth, the case may be amended.

                        Enter PETER.

PETER Musicians, O musicians, 'Heart's ease', 'Heart's ease'! O,   100
       and you will have me live, play 'Heart's ease'.
FIRST MUSICIAN Why 'Heart's ease'?
PETER O musicians, because my heart itself plays 'My heart is full'.
       O play me some merry dump to comfort me.
MUSICIANS Not a dump we, 'tis no time to play now.   105
PETER You will not then?
FIRST MUSICIAN No.
PETER I will then give it you soundly.
FIRST MUSICIAN What will you give us?
PETER No money, on my faith, but the gleek; I will give you the   110
       minstrel.
FIRST MUSICIAN Then will I give you the serving-creature.
PETER Then will I lay the serving-creature's dagger on your pate. I will
       carry no crotchets, I'll re you, I'll fa you. Do you note me?

of the play' (*Stage-Version*, p. 21). Zeffirelli cut them in 1960, but Peter Hall included them the following year, earning Robert Speaight's praise: 'How wise, how brave of Mr Hall to keep in the musicians! Shakespeare understood his counterpoint, and here was the very dissonance of death' (*SQ* 12, 1961, p. 438). In Hands's 1973 production, the Musicians were grotesquely masked and rather sinister: 'While the keeners dressed Juliet in her wedding gown, they joked and peered at her. Even when the corpse was laid out their jarring comments continued, and they were a disturbing presence in the inset funeral song' (*SS* 27, 1974, p. 151).

98 Peggy Ashcroft recalled that in the Oxford University Dramatic Society production in 1932, while playing the unconscious Juliet, she needed great concentration not to burst into tears when Edith Evans said, 'this is a pitiful case' (*Shakespeare in Perspective*, p. 179). In a sound recording made in 1961, the year of her final appearance as the Nurse at Stratford, Evans's delivery of this line, with a catch in her voice on the word 'case', is still remarkably moving (Shakespeare Recording Society SRS-M 228, 1961).

110 In Bogdanov 'the gleek' was a raspberry; in Edwin Booth's production a snap of the fingers (s39). In Hands 1989 it was Peter's dagger, which he drew angrily in resentment of the Musicians' callousness. Rather against the text, Hands's Peter mourned deeply for Juliet throughout the scene, and put deep emotion into the 'griping griefs' song.

112 In Booth's production (s39) the Musician imitated a fawning bow to characterise 'the serving-creature' (this exchange was transposed to the beginning of the Capulet ball, 1.5).

FIRST MUSICIAN And you re us and fa us, you note us.   115
SECOND MUSICIAN Pray you put up your dagger, and put out your
    wit.
PETER Then have at you with my wit! I will dry-beat you with an iron
    wit, and put up my iron dagger. Answer me like men:
        'When griping griefs the heart doth wound,   120
        And doleful dumps the mind oppress,
        Then music with her silver sound –'
    Why 'silver sound'? why 'music with her silver sound'? What say
    you, Simon Catling?
FIRST MUSICIAN Marry sir, because silver hath a sweet sound.   125
PETER Prates! What say you, Hugh Rebeck?
SECOND MUSICIAN I say 'silver sound' because musicians sound for
    silver.
PETER Prates too! What say you, James Soundpost?
THIRD MUSICIAN Faith, I know not what to say.   130
PETER O, I cry you mercy, you are the singer; I will say for you: It
    is 'music with her silver sound' because musicians have no gold
    for sounding.
        'Then music with her silver sound
        With speedy help doth lend redress.'   *Exit* 135
FIRST MUSICIAN What a pestilent knave is this same!
SECOND MUSICIAN Hang him, Jack! Come, we'll in here, tarry for the
    mourners, and stay dinner.
                                        Exeunt

    132 David Wiles suggests that Will Kemp, as Peter, at this point jingled gold in a purse, but
        withheld the expected payoff from the angry Musicians (*Shakespeare's Clown*, pp. 88–9).
    138 SD At this point in Garrick's version, and in many subsequent productions throughout the
        nineteenth century, came the funeral dirge for Juliet. Writing in 1770, Francis Gentleman was
        bemused: 'Though not absolutely essential, nothing could be better devised than a funeral
        procession, to render this play thoroughly popular; as it is certain that three-fourths of every
        audience are more capable of enjoying sound and show, than solid sense and poetical
        imagination' (*Dramatic Censor*, p. 185).

ACT 5   SCENE 1

Enter ROMEO.

ROMEO If I may trust the flattering truth of sleep,
My dreams presage some joyful news at hand.
My bosom's lord sits lightly in his throne,
And all this day an unaccustomed spirit
Lifts me above the ground with cheerful thoughts.   5
I dreamt my lady came and found me dead
(Strange dream that gives a dead man leave to think!),
And breathed such life with kisses in my lips
That I revived and was an emperor.
Ah me, how sweet is love itself possessed,   10
When but love's shadows are so rich in joy!

Enter Romeo's man [BALTHASAR, *booted*].

News from Verona! How now, Balthasar?
Dost thou not bring me letters from the Friar?
How doth my lady? Is my father well?
How doth my Juliet? That I ask again,   15
For nothing can be ill if she be well.

5.1 The Mantua set may be either ominous and fateful, or ironically pleasant and cheerful. In
Irving's production it was the former, 'a retired poor street approached by a covered entry
. . . squalid, but picturesque', and brooded over by a tree representing fate (*Macmillan's
Magazine*, XLVI, 1882, p. 334). In Sothern–Marlowe it was the latter, with jolly peasants stealing an apple from a fruit vendor, children 'in folly costumes, with folly sticks' engaging
Romeo in a dance, and so forth (s70). In Katherine Cornell's production, Jo Mielziner's set for
this scene featured an eerie, almost expressionist backdrop of a huge, distorted aqueduct
(production photos, NYPL). Michael Bogdanov's 1986 modern-dress production began this
scene with a surreal carnival, including giant, grotesque puppets of Ronald Reagan, Margaret
Thatcher, and Mikhail Gorbachev. In David Leveaux's 1991 RSC production, Juliet was sus-
pended, unconscious, over Romeo's head in the metal cage that served for both her bed and
tomb. After Leveaux revised the production for London in 1992, Juliet drifted across the stage
like a pale ghost, without Romeo being aware of her presence, as he described his dream of
her (*Independent*, 26 June 1992). In Terry Hands's two productions, in the Royal Shakespeare Theatre in 1973 and the Swan in 1989, 5.1 and 5.2 took place on balconies above the
stage, allowing Juliet to remain onstage in her bed, which became her bier.

11 Peter MacNicol made reference to the ring Juliet had given him (NYSF 1988).

BALTHASAR Then she is well and nothing can be ill:
        Her body sleeps in Capels' monument,
        And her immortal part with angels lives.
        I saw her laid low in her kindred's vault,   20
        And presently took post to tell it you.
        O pardon me for bringing these ill news,
        Since you did leave it for my office, sir.
ROMEO Is it e'en so? then I defy you, stars!
        Thou knowest my lodging, get me ink and paper,   25
        And hire post-horses; I will hence tonight.

17–18 According to Ellen Terry, 'It was during the silence after those two lines that Henry Irving as
Romeo had one of those sublime moments which an actor only achieves once or twice in his
life' (*Story of My Life*, p. 234). Presumably the remainder of Balthasar's speech was cut. In
Sothern–Marlowe, at these lines, 'Romeo looks at him and slowly lets his hands fall to his
sides. Balthasar pauses till Romeo's hands fall at side' (s70). Forbes-Robertson's demeanour
at this moment 'was superb in its stony calm' (Winter, *Shakespeare on the Stage*, p. 137). He
had been holding and kissing a rose; during Balthasar's speech, he 'unconsciously plucks
petals from rose, then sees what he has done' (s63). In Alf Sjöberg's 1953 Stockholm
production, Karl Julle's Romeo reacted to the news of Juliet's death with a nervous laugh
(Londré, '*Romeo*', p. 635).

18 Emended to 'Chapel monument' in the Luhrmann film, since the final scene is set in the
church itself. In the Bogdanov production the weird carnival crowd in the background
laughed when Romeo learned of Juliet's death, and gave desultory applause after line 24,
'I defy you, stars' (RSC 1986).

24 Spranger Barry, in 1750, underplayed this line to great effect, according to John Hill: 'This
was too great a grief for noisy exclamation: we read on his gesture, eyes, countenance, and
tone of voice, the most perfect despair, and see him braving even heaven in defiance; yet it
is not bellowed out like the curse of a Sempronius, but strength is given by the very refusing
loudness . . . Struck to death he is above raving about it, and he conveys all that terror to
the audience which he seems to refuse himself' (*The Actor* (1755), pp. 87–8). Many Romeos,
notably Forbes-Robertson and Olivier, have followed Barry's lead in playing the line with
quiet intensity (Wright, *Romeo*, p. 167). Olivier's 'toneless' delivery was 'very moving',
according to James Agate (*Sunday Times*, 20 October 1935). Laurence Harvey showed
'sudden adulthood' (*SQ* 5, 1954, p. 395). Other actors have made Romeo's defiance a cry to
heaven. In this latter group was Ian McKellen (RSC 1976), whose reading was transcribed by
Richard David as 'Then I defy – YOO-HOO STARS!' (*Shakespeare in the Theatre*, p. 117).
Zeffirelli, in his Old Vic production, made an odd, cinematic cut from 4.5 directly to this line;
Tynan found it 'superbly economic', but many critics were bewildered (*Observer*, 9 October
1960).

BALTHASAR I do beseech you, sir, have patience:
          Your looks are pale and wild, and do import
          Some misadventure.
ROMEO   Tush, thou art deceived.
          Leave me, and do the thing I bid thee do.   30
          Hast thou no letters to me from the Friar?
BALTHASAR No, my good lord.
ROMEO   No matter, get thee gone,
          And hire those horses; I'll be with thee straight.
                                      Exit [*Balthasar*]

          Well, Juliet, I will lie with thee tonight.
          Let's see for means. O mischief, thou art swift   35
          To enter in the thoughts of desperate men!
          I do remember an apothecary,
          And hereabouts 'a dwells, which late I noted
          In tattered weeds, with overwhelming brows,
          Culling of simples; meagre were his looks,   40
          Sharp misery had worn him to the bones;
          And in his needy shop a tortoise hung,
          An alligator stuffed, and other skins
          Of ill-shaped fishes, and about his shelves
          A beggarly account of empty boxes,   45
          Green earthen pots, bladders, and musty seeds,
          Remnants of packthread, and old cakes of roses
          Were thinly scattered, to make up a show.
          Noting this penury, to myself I said,
          'And if a man did need a poison now,   50
          Whose sale is present death in Mantua,
          Here lives a caitiff wretch would sell it him.'
          O this same thought did but forerun my need,

35 In the 1911 Thanhouser film, Romeo receives the news of Juliet's death while standing under a large shop sign that reads 'APOTHECARY' – compressing the action but creating an unintentionally comic effect.

42–8 Though the details of the apothecary's shop are often cut, they can have a powerful, hallucinatory effect in performance. Alan Badel recited them 'not as a mere decorative catalogue, but as they would be remembered by a man in a fever' (*Illustrated London News*, 27 September 1952). Mark Rylance, in 1989, dwelled with eerie fascination on the tortoise and the alligator, then paused with a toneless laugh before 'to make up a show'. The rest of the scene had a kind of grim hilarity for Rylance; he laughed, as though drunk, on 'I sell thee poison, line 83.'

And this same needy man must sell it me.
As I remember, this should be the house.   55
Being holiday, the beggar's shop is shut.
What ho, apothecary!

[*Enter* APOTHECARY.]

APOTHECARY   Who calls so loud?
ROMEO Come hither, man. I see that thou art poor.
          Hold, there is forty ducats; let me have
          A dram of poison, such soon-speeding gear   60
          As will disperse itself through all the veins,
          That the life-weary taker may fall dead,
          And that the trunk may be discharged of breath
          As violently as hasty powder fired
          Doth hurry from the fatal cannon's womb.   65
APOTHECARY Such mortal drugs I have, but Mantua's law
          Is death to any he that utters them.
ROMEO Art thou so bare and full of wretchedness,
          And fearest to die? Famine is in thy cheeks,
          Need and oppression starveth in thy eyes,   70

---

56 Sean Bean, for Bogdanov in 1986, made this line a cry of despair and exasperation, another
apparent instance of fate thwarting Romeo. The Apothecary appeared only after the crowd
of the Mantuan carnival had assailed Romeo, knocked him to the ground, and laughed and
mocked at him.

57 SD The Apothecary, as a small but distinctive role, seems to capture the imagination of both
directors and adapters of the play. It was played by the producer of the first American
production, himself a physician, in 1730. It is the role taken by Smike in Dickens's *Nicholas
Nickleby*, memorably expanded in the David Edgar stage version so that 'Who calls so loud?'
become Smike's dying words. It is the role played by the stage-struck producer Fennyman
(Tom Wilkinson) in the film *Shakespeare in Love*. In Terry Hands's 1973 production, the
Apothecary was a sinister figure of fate, who watched over the play's mischances from a
perch high over the stage. For Bogdanov 1986, the Apothecary was a drug pusher; the
Luhrmann film uses the same notion, with M. Emmet Walsh playing a character identified
in the screenplay as 'Crusty', the proprietor of the Globe Theatre pool hall. In Karin Beier's
1994 Düsseldorf production, Romeo was given the poison not by an apothecary, but by the
blood-boltered and resentful ghost of Mercutio (*Independent*, 2 November 1994). Michael
Boyd also had Mercutio provide the poison (RSC 2000).

68–74 Kenneth Branagh's desperate Romeo physically attacked the Apothecary and dragged the
poison away from him (*Financial Times*, 15 August 1986).

        Contempt and beggary hangs upon thy back;
        The world is not thy friend, nor the world's law,
        The world affords no law to make thee rich;
        Then be not poor, but break it and take this.
APOTHECARY My poverty, but not my will, consents. 75
ROMEO I pay thy poverty and not thy will.
APOTHECARY Put this in any liquid thing you will
        And drink it off, and if you had the strength
        Of twenty men, it would dispatch you straight.
ROMEO There is thy gold, worse poison to men's souls, 80
        Doing more murder in this loathsome world,
        Than these poor compounds that thou mayst not sell.
        I sell thee poison, thou hast sold me none.
        Farewell, buy food, and get thyself in flesh.
                                 [Exit Apothecary]
        Come, cordial and not poison, go with me 85
        To Juliet's grave, for there must I use thee.   *Exit*

77 Alan Dessen, considering emblematic stage action on the Elizabethan stage, makes an interesting connection between the Apothecary's producing the vial of poison and the Friar's producing the flower in 2.3 and the sleeping-drug in 4.1. Dessen suggests that the same basket could have been used on all three occasions (*Recovering*, pp. 158–9).

84 A vivid piece of nineteenth-century business from the promptbook s23: 'Apothecary looks at the purse in his hand, kisses the hem of Romeo's cloak, and exits.' In a Drury Lane production of 1827, the actor Meadows made an effective exit: 'His unconsciousness of holding the purse, in his struggle between his horror of poisoning the unknown applicant, and his dread of being starved . . . was very effectively rendered; and so was the manner in which, as he turned away, he noticed the purse, grasped it convulsively, and flung himself, staggering, into his shop' (*The Opera Glass*, 10 February 1827).

ACT 5   SCENE 2

Enter FRIAR JOHN.

FRIAR JOHN Holy Franciscan Friar, brother, ho!

Enter [FRIAR] LAWRENCE.

FRIAR LAWRENCE This same should be the voice of Friar John.
          Welcome from Mantua. What says Romeo?
          Or if his mind be writ, give me his letter.
FRIAR JOHN Going to find a barefoot brother out,   5
          One of our order, to associate me,
          Here in this city visiting the sick,
          And finding him, the searchers of the town,
          Suspecting that we both were in a house
          Where the infectious pestilence did reign,   10
          Sealed up the doors, and would not let us forth,
          So that my speed to Mantua there was stayed.
FRIAR LAWRENCE Who bare my letter then to Romeo?
FRIAR JOHN I could not send it – here it is again –
          Nor get a messenger to bring it thee,   15

5.2 Before this scene, the St George's production staged a brief version of Juliet's funeral: monks brought the bier onto the stage platform, Friar Lawrence blessed it, and the parents knelt while a brief chant was sung. This arrangement violated the sequence of events – Balthasar had reported seeing the funeral in the previous scene – but solved the staging problems neatly. The two Friars played their scene downstage with the bier visible behind them.

1 In Michael Boyd's production, Friar John's lines were given by the ghost of Mercutio, who spoke from the walls above the stage in a creepy effect (RSC 2000).

12 Film versions have found various ways of representing this fatal mishap. In the 1911 Thanhouser silent film, we actually see the letter, which stands in for any other explanation of the plot. In Castellani's film, an elaborate depiction of the plague house and Friar John's incarceration is played over the lines. Zeffirelli shows Balthasar, on horseback, overtaking Friar John's slow donkey and so getting to Mantua first. Similarly, in Luhrmann, Romeo fails to see a delivery slip from the 'Post Haste Dispatch' express mail service; he is later seen driving away from Mantua while the delivery van makes a second attempt to get him the Friar's letter.

17a At 'Unhappy fortune!', Peter Brook's production included the following by-play between the Friars: 'Laugh from John, cut short by Lawrence – mood alters' (s100).

    So fearful were they of infection.
FRIAR LAWRENCE Unhappy fortune! By my brotherhood,
    The letter was not nice but full of charge,
    Of dear import, and the neglecting it
    May do much danger. Friar John, go hence,   20
    Get me an iron crow and bring it straight
    Unto my cell.
FRIAR JOHN Brother, I'll go and bring it thee.   *Exit*
FRIAR LAWRENCE Now must I to the monument alone,
    Within this three hours will fair Juliet wake.   25
    She will beshrew me much that Romeo
    Hath had no notice of these accidents;
    But I will write again to Mantua,
    And keep her at my cell till Romeo come,
    Poor living corse, closed in a dead man's tomb!   *Exit*   30

23 In the 1978 BBC-TV version, John Savident's Friar John is, rather surprisingly, a comic character; already vexed at having been locked in with the plague victims, he is thoroughly exasperated at being sent to fetch a crowbar.

ACT 5 SCENE 3

Enter PARIS *and his* PAGE [*with flowers and sweet water and a torch*].

PARIS Give me thy torch, boy. Hence, and stand aloof.
　　　　Yet put it out, for I would not be seen.
　　　　Under yond yew trees lay thee all along,
　　　　Holding thy ear close to the hollow ground,
　　　　So shall no foot upon the churchyard tread,　　　　　　5
　　　　Being loose, unfirm with digging up of graves,
　　　　But thou shalt hear it. Whistle then to me
　　　　As signal that thou hear'st something approach.
　　　　Give me those flowers. Do as I bid thee, go.
PAGE [*Aside*] I am almost afraid to stand alone　　　　　　10
　　　　Here in the churchyard, yet I will adventure.　　　[*Retires*]

　　　　　　[*Paris strews the tomb with flowers.*]

PARIS Sweet flower, with flowers thy bridal bed I strew –
　　　　O woe, thy canopy is dust and stones! –
　　　　Which with sweet water nightly I will dew,
　　　　Or wanting that, with tears distilled by moans.　　　　15
　　　　The obsequies that I for thee will keep
　　　　Nightly shall be to strew thy grave and weep.

　　　　　　　　Whistle Boy.

　　　　The boy gives warning, something doth approach.
　　　　What cursèd foot wanders this way tonight,
　　　　To cross my obsequies and true love's rite?　　　　　20
　　　　What, with a torch? Muffle me, night, a while.　　　[*Retires*]

5.3 The eighteenth-century tradition of adding an elaborate funeral scene has reemerged in
　　　some modern productions, such as David Leveaux's 1991 RSC version, which used lines of
　　　torch-bearing mourners accompanied by dirge music. In Judi Dench's 1993 Regent's Park
　　　staging, the outdoor theatre allowed for a spectacular torchlit procession that one critic
　　　dubbed 'the best mausoleum scene ever' (*Daily Express*, 22 June 1986).
　　3 Q1 mentions only a single yew-tree; probably, in the original production, it was a stage pillar
　　　rather than a prop (Dessen, *Recovering*, p. 61).
　12 If the bed has remained onstage and become a bier, then Paris is speaking the literal truth
　　　when he says he strews Juliet's bridal-bed with flowers (Holding, *Romeo*, p. 42).

Enter ROMEO *and* [BALTHASAR *with a torch, a mattock,*
and a crow of iron].

ROMEO Give me that mattock and the wrenching iron.
　　　Hold, take this letter; early in the morning
　　　See thou deliver it to my lord and father.
　　　Give me the light. Upon thy life I charge thee,   25
　　　What e'er thou hear'st or seest, stand all aloof,
　　　And do not interrupt me in my course.
　　　Why I descend into this bed of death
　　　Is partly to behold my lady's face,
　　　But chiefly to take thence from her dead finger   30
　　　A precious ring, a ring that I must use
　　　In dear employment; therefore hence, be gone.
　　　But if thou, jealous, dost return to pry
　　　In what I farther shall intend to do,
　　　By heaven, I will tear thee joint by joint,   35
　　　And strew this hungry churchyard with thy limbs.
　　　The time and my intents are savage-wild,
　　　More fierce and more inexorable far
　　　Than empty tigers or the roaring sea.
BALTHASAR I will be gone, sir, and not trouble ye.   40
ROMEO So shalt thou show me friendship. Take thou that,

　　　　　　　[*Gives a purse.*]

　　　Live and be prosperous, and farewell, good fellow.
BALTHASAR [*Aside*] For all this same, I'll hide me hereabout,
　　　His looks I fear, and his intents I doubt.   [*Retires*]
ROMEO Thou detestable maw, thou womb of death,   45
　　　Gorged with the dearest morsel of the earth,
　　　Thus I enforce thy rotten jaws to open,
　　　And in despite I'll cram thee with more food.

　　　　　　[*Romeo begins to open the tomb.*]

21 SD Theophilus Cibber gives a malicious report of David Garrick's playing of Romeo's entrance:
　　　'on the opening of the scene, the actor, with folded arms, advances about three or four
　　　steps, – then jumps, and starts into an attitude of surprise: – at what? – Why, at the sight of
　　　the monument, he went to look for: – and there he stands, till a clap from the audience
　　　relieves him from his post' (*To David Garrick*, p. 69).
41 In NYSF 1988, Peter MacNicol's Romeo took off Juliet's ring and tearfully gave it to Balthasar.
48 SD A notorious problem, based on the Q1 stage direction. As Alan Dessen puts it, 'in the case of

PARIS This is that banished haughty Montague,
              That murdered my love's cousin, with which grief   50
              It is supposèd the fair creature died,
              And here is come to do some villainous shame
              To the dead bodies. I will apprehend him.

                              [*Steps forth.*]

              Stop thy unhallowed toil, vile Montague!
              Can vengeance be pursued further than death?   55
              Condemnèd villain, I do apprehend thee.
              Obey and go with me, for thou must die.
ROMEO I must indeed, and therefore came I hither.
              Good gentle youth, tempt not a desp'rate man,
              Fly hence and leave me. Think upon these gone,   60
              Let them affright thee. I beseech thee, youth,
              Put not another sin upon my head,
              By urging me to fury: O be gone!
              By heaven, I love thee better than myself,

"*Romeo opens the tomb,*" I may understand *Romeo*, but, after much effort, I still have considerable difficulty with both *opens* and *the tomb*' (*Recovering*, p. 176). In Elizabethan times it is most likely that Romeo made some show of breaking into the discovery space at the back of the stage; he may also have opened the stage trap door (Evans, New Cambridge Shakespeare edition, p. 32). Later producers generally had a substantial tomb onstage; the standard business was for Romeo to deliver three blows of the crowbar to the tomb doors, 'which very naturally fly open *outwards*, and there . . . lies Juliet, above ground, ingeniously obvious to the audience' (Boaden, *Memoirs of Mrs Siddons*, II, pp. 282–3). The tomb was generally at the back in productions using the Garrick text; Romeo carried Juliet downstage for their scene together. Samuel Phelps broke with tradition by using Shakespeare's scene and keeping the lovers upstage in the vault the entire time (Allen, *Samuel Phelps*, pp. 231–2). Forbes-Robertson, in turn, took the opposite approach, placing Juliet's bier at the very front of the stage, with the churchyard on a platform at the back (S63). Gielgud had the tomb stage left, with the churchyard stage right (production photographs, TM). The 1976 St George's production neatly solved the tomb problems by having a gated tomb entrance upstage, but using the perimeter of the stage for all scenes outside the tomb; when ready to enter the tomb, all characters went around upstage and came through the gates. Romeo and Paris fought in the tomb, so that Paris's 'Open the tomb' was cut.

62 This line, spoken with grave dignity, was a keynote for Laurence Payne's 'darkling and foredoomed' Romeo in Peter Brook's production (*Manchester Guardian*, 7 April 1947).

> For I come hither armed against myself.   65
> Stay not, be gone; live, and hereafter say,
> A madman's mercy bid thee run away.

PARIS I do defy thy conjuration,
> And apprehend thee for a felon here.

ROMEO Wilt thou provoke me? then have at thee, boy!   70

> *[They fight.]*

PAGE O Lord, they fight! I will go call the Watch.   *[Exit]*
PARIS O, I am slain! *[Falls.]* If thou be merciful,
> Open the tomb, lay me with Juliet. *[Dies.]*
ROMEO In faith, I will. Let me peruse this face.
> Mercutio's kinsman, noble County Paris!   75

---

70 SD The fight with Paris was one of the most famous moments of the play in the eighteenth century. Both Garrick and Barry used the crowbar as a weapon, striking a famous pose as they raised it to attack. Theophilus Cibber mocked Garrick's playing of this moment: 'Romeo is a gentleman, has a sword by his side . . . May we not reasonably suppose that, on his being diverted from his purpose of opening the tomb, when called on by Paris, that he would immediately drop that unwieldy instrument, the iron crow, and have recourse to his sword? – Would not this be the instinctive recourse of the gentleman? But then this *Cyclopedian* attitude would be lost, in which Romeo, now, stands long enough to give Paris time to run him through the body, which would be justifiable, when a man saw such a weapon, raised by an enemy, to dash out his brains' (*To David Garrick*, pp. 69–70). The crowbar has returned to popularity; Zubin Varla used it to kill Paris in the 1995 RSC production.

72 SD The killing of Paris has often troubled directors and actors, since it may turn the audience against Romeo. In the eighteenth century, Francis Gentleman wrote, 'We see no reason of bringing on Paris, nor killing him; there is death enough without this incident' (*Bell's Edition*, p. 145). Edwin Booth took care to establish that Romeo's killing of Paris was self-defence, despite the lines' indication that Romeo is the aggressor; Booth's promptbook reads 'Paris thrusts at Romeo who knocks sword out of his hand and stabs him' (s37). Sothern and Marlowe went even farther, making Romeo unarmed; 'Paris lunges at Romeo . . . Romeo throws his cloak over Paris's sword, taking Paris's dagger stabs him in the breast' (s70). Zeffirelli cut the killing of Paris after filming it. 'You don't want that. I mean, young people wanted us to have the romantic meeting between the dead girl – who was not dead – and Romeo who had threatened to kill himself. If he was a murderer – "Ugly boy, ugly boy!" It wouldn't have worked. And besides, the thing was long enough' (Loney, *Staging Shakespeare*, p. 245). Even the Luhrmann film, which foregrounds the violence of the play, excises this last killing.

What said my man, when my betossèd soul
Did not attend him as we rode? I think
He told me Paris should have married Juliet.
Said he not so? or did I dream it so?
Or am I mad, hearing him talk of Juliet,   80
To think it was so? O give me thy hand,
One writ with me in sour misfortune's book!
I'll bury thee in a triumphant grave.
A grave? O no, a lantern, slaughtered youth;
For here lies Juliet, and her beauty makes   85
This vault a feasting presence full of light.
Death, lie thou there, by a dead man interred.

[Laying Paris in the tomb.]

How oft when men are at the point of death
Have they been merry, which their keepers call

81b In Forbes-Robertson's 1895 Lyceum production, Romeo 'takes Paris's hand and compares it with his own' (s63).

83 Irving's staging of the tomb scene was spectacularly pictorial, even using two different sets. He killed Paris in a moonlit churchyard, and then, after a swift scene change, appeared at the top of a long stone staircase, carrying the body of Paris down into Juliet's tomb. It had been one of his original inspirations for the play, according to Ellen Terry: 'At rehearsals Henry Irving kept on saying, I must go *down* into the vault' (*Story of My Life*, p. 234). Irving's tomb setting 'surpassed in detail and in weird, sepulchral, melancholy beauty', any previous staging, according to William Winter (*Shakespeare on the Stage*, p. 181).

84 Just before 'A grave?', Timothy Dalton's Romeo spoke Q1's line, 'For thou hast prized thy love above thy life', in Terry Hands's 1973 RSC production (promptbook, SCL).

85 In Sothern–Marlowe, 'she holds rose petals in her folded hands and is covered from head to foot with a light gauze shroud' (s70). In the Gielgud production, Peggy Ashcroft lay uncovered in a pale, blue-green gown on a simple, sloping bier, which Olivier's Romeo touched 'lovingly', according to James Agate: 'his smaller gestures were infinitely touching' (*Sunday Times*, 20 October 1935).

87 According to G. B. Shaw, Johnston Forbes-Robertson's Romeo, in 1895, 'was a gentleman to the last. He laid out Paris after killing him as carefully as if he were folding up his best suit of clothes' (*Our Theatres*, III, p. 212). The promptbook s63 records that Forbes-Robertson 'covers Paris with his own cloak and crosses himself reverently'.

88–120 Though he included the entire scene with Paris, Jean Cocteau cut almost all of Romeo's speech in the tomb, replacing it with the note, 'Il prononce un grand nombre de fois le nom

A light'ning before death! O how may I   90
Call this a light'ning? O my love, my wife,
Death, that hath sucked the honey of thy breath,
Hath had no power yet upon thy beauty:
Thou art not conquered, beauty's ensign yet
Is crimson in thy lips and in thy cheeks,   95
And Death's pale flag is not advancèd there.
Tybalt, liest thou there in thy bloody sheet?
O, what more favour can I do to thee
Than with that hand that cut thy youth in twain
To sunder his that was thine enemy?   100
Forgive me, cousin. Ah, dear Juliet,
Why art thou yet so fair? Shall I believe
That unsubstantial Death is amorous,
And that the lean abhorrèd monster keeps
Thee here in dark to be his paramour?   105
For fear of that, I still will stay with thee,
And never from this palace of dim night
Depart again. Here, here will I remain
With worms that are thy chambermaids; O here
Will I set up my everlasting rest,   110

de Juliette' (*Roméo et Juliette*, p. 193). In the few lines he included, Cocteau stressed the irony of Romeo's fascination with Juliet's lifelike appearance: 'Elle n'a pas l'air mort. Elle est belle . . . elle n'est pas blanche comme les mortes . . . elle n'est pas mort . . . Tu n'es pas morte, n'est-ce pas, Juliette? N'est-ce pas, Juliette?'

97–100 These lines are often cut if producers find it too awkward to put Tybalt onstage, but Mark Rylance merely called them out into the darkness of the vault, an effective choice (Hands, RSC 1989).

101 In the nineteenth century, particularly when the Garrick text was in use, it was traditional for Romeo to carry Juliet from the tomb up to the front of the stage for the dying scene. This practice inevitably resulted in awkward mishaps. When the wealthy eccentric Robert Coates performed at Bath in 1808, 'The dying scene was irresistibly comic . . . for Romeo dragged the unfortunate Juliet from the tomb, much in the same manner as a washerwoman thrusts into her cart the bag of foul linen' (R. H. Gronow, *Reminiscences and Recollections*, 1862, quoted in Salgado, *Eyewitnesses*, p. 198). When Fanny Kemble played opposite Ellen Tree's Romeo in 1829, the dead Juliet hissed to her companion, 'If you attempt to lift or carry me down the stage, I will kick and scream till you set me down' (Kemble, *Records of a Girlhood*, p. 201).

102–5 Most nineteenth-century texts cut the references to Death as Juliet's paramour; Sothern included it, though he did cut the 'worms that are thy chambermaids' (570).

And shake the yoke of inauspicious stars
From this world-wearied flesh. Eyes, look your last!
Arms, take your last embrace! and, lips, O you
The doors of breath, seal with a righteous kiss
A dateless bargain to engrossing Death! 115
Come, bitter conduct, come, unsavoury guide!
Thou desperate pilot, now at once run on
The dashing rocks thy seasick weary bark!
Here's to my love! [*Drinks.*] O true apothecary!
Thy drugs are quick. Thus with a kiss I die. [*Dies.*] 120

111 Mark Rylance made this line the climax of the speech, shouting resentfully at his 'inauspicious stars' (Hands, RSC 1989).

115 It has become common, in recent decades, to reintroduce the Garrick notion of Juliet waking early, before Romeo dies and in some cases before he even drinks the poison. In Trevor Nunn and Barry Kyle's 1976 production, Juliet's fingers moved just behind Romeo's head while he was taking his last embrace. In Adrian Noble's 1995 production, Romeo held Juliet in his arms for a long kiss – Juliet slowly, half consciously raised one arm up to touch his face, but just before she touched him Romeo released her and let her body subside onto the bier, her arm falling back as well. In the Luhrmann film, Juliet reaches up to touch Romeo's face just as he drinks the poison, and the lovers share a few anguished moments of horrified realisation before Romeo dies.

119–20 As E. H. Sothern swallowed the poison, Julia Marlowe extended her right hand over the side of the bier and dropped some of the rose petals she had been holding (s70). Peter McEnery took a long pause after drinking the poison, and then looked dubiously at the bottle before suddenly feeling its effects (St George's, 1976). Mark Rylance gasped and fell to the floor instantly, giving an appreciative laugh before 'O true apothecary! / Thy drugs are quick' (Hands 1989). In Karin Beier's 1994 Düsseldorf production, Matthias Leja's Romeo changed his mind after taking the poison, and stuck his finger down his throat in a desperate attempt to vomit it up (*Evening Standard*, 3 November 1994). In dying, Romeo generally slumps onto the bier with Juliet, though in a Broadway production of 1847, James Anderson rolled down a flight of fourteen steps (Sprague, *Shakespeare and the Actors*, p. 317). Olivier, in his 1940 New York production, stretched out his hand toward Vivien Leigh's Juliet, unable to reach her; stirring in her sleep, she nearly touched his hand, but just missed (Sprague, *Shakespeare and the Actors*, p. 319).

120 In all versions of the play produced between the late seventeenth and mid-nineteenth centuries, Romeo did not die immediately after taking the poison, but had a substantial dialogue with Juliet in the tomb. David Garrick's version, which held the stage unrivalled from 1748 to 1845, is reproduced in the Appendix. Eliza O'Neill achieved a powerful effect when Romeo finally collapsed from the poison, 'in her closely clinging to the body, and

Enter FRIAR [LAWRENCE] *with lantern, crow, and spade.*

FRIAR LAWRENCE Saint Francis be my speed! how oft tonight
   Have my old feet stumbled at graves! Who's there?
BALTHASAR Here's one, a friend, and one that knows you well.
FRIAR LAWRENCE Bliss be upon you! Tell me, good my friend,
   What torch is yond that vainly lends his light   125
   To grubs and eyeless skulls? As I discern,
   It burneth in the Capels' monument.
BALTHASAR It doth so, holy sir, and there's my master,
   One that you love.
FRIAR LAWRENCE   Who is it?
BALTHASAR   Romeo.
FRIAR LAWRENCE How long hath he been there?
BALTHASAR   Full half an hour.   130
FRIAR LAWRENCE Go with me to the vault.
BALTHASAR   I dare not, sir.
   My master knows not but I am gone hence,
   And fearfully did menace me with death
   If I did stay to look on his intents.
FRIAR LAWRENCE Stay then, I'll go alone. Fear comes upon me. 135
   O, much I fear some ill unthrifty thing.
BALTHASAR As I did sleep under this yew tree here,
   I dreamt my master and another fought,
   And that my master slew him.   *[Retires]*
FRIAR LAWRENCE   Romeo!

[Friar stoops and looks on the blood and weapons.]

   Alack, alack, what blood is this which stains   140
   The stony entrance of this sepulchre?

falling with it to the ground, as if her delicate form were overpowered by the weight which
she was never tired of supporting' (Jones, *Memoirs*, p. 19).

120 SD The Italian tragedian Ernesto Rossi kept the Friar offstage to allow a striking piece of
business. Juliet awoke after Romeo had given his last line and fallen unconscious, but before
he was dead. Not noticing him in the dim vault, she wandered out into the churchyard.
Romeo awoke to find her gone, then suddenly saw her in the distance 'like a spectre',
according to Henry James: 'his eyes fall upon her as he slowly rises. His movement of
solemn terror as he slowly throws up his arms and continues to rise and rise, until, with his
whole being dilated, he stands staring and appalled, on tiptoe, is, although it is grotesque in
description, very well worth seeing' (Carlson, *Italian Shakespearians*, p. 168).

What mean these masterless and gory swords
To lie discoloured by this place of peace?

[*Enters the tomb.*]

Romeo! O, pale! Who else? What, Paris too?
And steeped in blood? Ah, what an unkind hour   145
Is guilty of this lamentable chance!

[*Juliet rises.*]

The lady stirs.
JULIET O comfortable Friar, where is my lord?
I do remember well where I should be;
And there I am. Where is my Romeo?   150

[*Noise within.*]

FRIAR LAWRENCE I hear some noise, lady. Come from that nest
Of death, contagion, and unnatural sleep.
A greater power than we can contradict
Hath thwarted our intents. Come, come away.
Thy husband in thy bosom there lies dead;   155
And Paris too. Come, I'll dispose of thee
Among a sisterhood of holy nuns.
Stay not to question, for the Watch is coming.
Come go, good Juliet, I dare no longer stay.   *Exit*
JULIET Go get thee hence, for I will not away.   160
What's here? a cup closed in my true love's hand?

146 SD Helena Faucit was commended for 'the stiffened movement of the limbs' as she attempted
to rise after waking (Martin, *Helena Faucit*, p. 279).

155 In Frank Benson's 1905 Stratford production, which cut the Friar John scene (5.2), Friar
Lawrence had the additional explanatory lines, 'My messenger was stayed in Mantua / And
could not bear my letters to thy lord' (s79).

159 Some modern productions have done much to accentuate the Friar's cowardice. Milo
O'Shea repeats 'I dare no longer stay' three times in the Zeffirelli film as he stumbles out in
terror. In Noble 1995, Julian Glover left Juliet still barely conscious on her bier, shouting his
lines about sheltering her in a nunnery even as he was already heading out of the door. It
was a shocking moment, noted by many critics, and gave his final speech a dimension of
tragic guilt (*Observer*, 9 April 1995).

160 Of Julia Marlowe: 'Into that one line, uttered with no raised voice, uttered so slowly and
lethally, into every syllable and sound of it, she put a finality more appalling than any
vehemence could have been' (Russell, *Julia Marlowe*, p. 238).

Poison I see hath been his timeless end.
O churl, drunk all, and left no friendly drop
To help me after? I will kiss thy lips,
Haply some poison yet doth hang on them,   165
To make me die with a restorative.
Thy lips are warm.
CAPTAIN OF THE WATCH [*Within*] Lead, boy, which way?
JULIET Yea, noise? Then I'll be brief. O happy dagger,

[*Taking Romeo's dagger.*]

This is thy sheath;

[*Stabs herself.*]

there rust, and let me die.   170

[*Falls on Romeo's body and dies.*]

Enter [*Paris's*] *Boy and* WATCH.

PAGE This is the place, there where the torch doth burn.
CAPTAIN OF THE WATCH
The ground is bloody, search about the churchyard.
Go, some of you, whoe'er you find attach.

[*Exeunt some of the Watch*]

[*The Captain enters the tomb and returns.*]

169–70 Both Helena Modjeska and Mrs Patrick Campbell made an unusual choice in propping Romeo's dagger against the wall of the tomb and flinging themselves onto it (Shattuck, *American Stage*, II, p. 127; Winter, *Shakespeare on the Stage*, p. 138). Helena Faucit lay on Romeo's breast and 'raised his nerveless arms and folded them above her head' (Sprague, *Shakespeare and the Actors*, p. 317). Fitzroy Davis gives a very full account of Katherine Cornell's death. On 'This is thy sheath', she brought the dagger slowly down to her chest, 'meanwhile smiling very palely and translucently'; she said 'there rust' in 'a low, gentle voice', then spoke 'and let me die' joyfully, 'but with peaceful rather than hectic joy – she presses the dagger against her heart, and jerks it downward left, under her left breast . . . her body contorts slightly and she slips slowly down around Romeo, her head on the pillow, above his' (s95). In the 1988 NYSF production, Cynthia Nixon placed the dagger between her body and Romeo's; her suicide became a kind of sexual embrace with her dead husband.

170 SD Many productions, particularly in the nineteenth and early twentieth centuries, ended with Juliet's death (e.g. Edwin Booth s37, Mary Anderson s50, Sothern/Marlowe); many others fast-forwarded to the Prince addressing the families at line 291 (e.g. Helena Faucit s21, s23, Zeffirelli). Peter Brook, in 1947, cut from Juliet's death to the last lines of the play, spoken by the Chorus (s100).

Pitiful sight! here lies the County slain,
And Juliet bleeding, warm, and newly dead, 175
Who here hath lain this two days burièd.
Go tell the Prince, run to the Capulets,
Raise up the Montagues; some others search.
> *[Exeunt others of the Watch]*
We see the ground whereon these woes do lie,
But the true ground of all these piteous woes 180
We cannot without circumstance descry.

> *Enter [one of the Watch with] Romeo's man [Balthasar].*

SECOND WATCHMAN
Here's Romeo's man, we found him in the churchyard.
CAPTAIN OF THE WATCH
Hold him in safety till the Prince come hither.

> *Enter Friar [Lawrence] and another Watchman.*

THIRD WATCHMAN Here is a friar that trembles, sighs, and weeps.
We took this mattock and this spade from him, 185
As he was coming from this churchyard's side.
CAPTAIN OF THE WATCH A great suspicion. Stay the Friar too.

> *Enter the* PRINCE *[with others].*

PRINCE What misadventure is so early up,
That calls our person from our morning rest?

> *Enter Capels* [CAPULET, LADY CAPULET].

CAPULET What should it be that is so shrieked abroad? 190

---

175 Terry Hands's 1973 RSC production 'glaringly displayed' Juliet's corpse with 'gory redness seeping from her abdomen' (*Evening Standard*, 29 March 1973).

188 SD This assembly of the two families, presided over by the Prince, recalls the similar groupings in 1.1 and 3.1. The 1976 St George's production, attempting to reproduce Elizabethan stagecraft, staged the final tomb scene very formally; the Prince was in the centre on the upper stage, with the families arrayed on opposite sides in symmetrical arrangements, Benvolio mirroring the Nurse, etc. In the 1978 BBC-TV version, the interrogation of the Watch takes place in a public setting on the steps of the tomb, but only the Prince and the parents go inside with the bodies.

190–3 In Michael Bogdanov's 1993 English Shakespeare Company production, the members of the two families entered the tomb flashing electric torches around the darkened auditorium and whispering the lovers' names (*Financial Times*, 1 June 1993).

LADY CAPULET O, the people in the street cry 'Romeo',
    Some 'Juliet', and some 'Paris', and all run
    With open outcry toward our monument.
PRINCE What fear is this which startles in your ears?
CAPTAIN OF THE WATCH
    Sovereign, here lies the County Paris slain,   195
    And Romeo dead, and Juliet, dead before,
    Warm and new killed.
PRINCE Search, seek, and know how this foul murder comes.
CAPTAIN OF THE WATCH
    Here is a friar, and slaughtered Romeo's man,
    With instruments upon them, fit to open   200
    These dead men's tombs.

[Capulet and Lady Capulet enter the tomb.]

CAPULET O heavens! O wife, look how our daughter bleeds!
    This dagger hath mistane, for lo his house
    Is empty on the back of Montague,
    And it mis-sheathèd in my daughter's bosom!   205
LADY CAPULET O me, this sight of death is as a bell
    That warns my old age to a sepulchre.

[They return from the tomb.]

Enter MONTAGUE.

PRINCE Come, Montague, for thou art early up
    To see thy son and heir now early down.
MONTAGUE Alas, my liege, my wife is dead tonight;   210

202–5 John Woodvine's ferocious Capulet, in Nunn's 1976 production, kicked Romeo's corpse and brandished a dagger at the bumbling Friar. 'The reconciliation that followed was hard-won, but perhaps for that reason more real', according to Anthony Dawson (*Watching Shakespeare*, pp. 130–1).

206 Shirley Anne Field's Lady Capulet, in Hull Truck's modern-dress production, laid Juliet's teddy bear between the dead lovers, a gesture of uncomprehending, misplaced sentiment (*Independent*, 11 June 1990).

210 The report of the death of Lady Montague has often been cut (by Garrick, Cushman, Phelps, etc.). Terry Hands cut it in 1973 but included it to good effect in 1989: it helped 'to build the larger pattern of the ending in which the audience is made increasingly aware of the full social context of the private tragedy' (Holding, *Romeo*, p. 73). Montague's loss of his wife was also included in Les Waters's 1988 NYSF production; Neil Vipond's solitary, desolated

           Grief of my son's exile hath stopped her breath.
           What further woe conspires against mine age?
PRINCE Look and thou shalt see.

        [*Montague enters the tomb and returns.*]

MONTAGUE O thou untaught! what manners is in this,
           To press before thy father to a grave?   215
PRINCE Seal up the mouth of outrage for a while,
           Till we can clear these ambiguities,
           And know their spring, their head, their true descent,
           And then will I be general of your woes,
           And lead you even to death. Mean time forbear,   220
           And let mischance be slave to patience.
           Bring forth the parties of suspicion.
FRIAR LAWRENCE I am the greatest, able to do least,
           Yet most suspected, as the time and place
           Doth make against me, of this direful murder;   225
           And here I stand both to impeach and purge
           Myself condemnèd and myself excused.
PRINCE Then say at once what thou dost know in this.
FRIAR LAWRENCE I will be brief, for my short date of breath
           Is not so long as is a tedious tale.   230
           Romeo, there dead, was husband to that Juliet,
           And she, there dead, that Romeo's faithful wife:
           I married them, and their stol'n marriage day
           Was Tybalt's doomsday, whose untimely death

      figure was an affecting presence in the scene, and his final offer to build Juliet a statue
      seemed noble rather than crass.

215 In Hands's 1989 production Capulet pulled a dagger and sprang with a roar of anger at
      Montague, and the servants on both sides drew their swords. The text was cut so that the
      Friar launched almost immediately into his story at line 231, using it to try to prevent a
      further outbreak of the feud. This gave the long recapitulation of events an immediacy and
      urgency it sometimes lacks.

229 ff. The Friar's final recapitulation has often been trimmed (Garrick), or cut entirely (Cushman,
      Modjeska, Irving). Some recent productions have included a fairly full text, often
      emphasising the Friar's guilt and shame. Julian Glover struck himself angrily on the chest
      when he said 'I married them' (Noble, RSC 1995). Joseph O'Conor broke down while
      recounting his ill-fated plan, and was barely able to continue (St George's 1976). Patrick
      Godfrey's Friar collapsed with shame and self-loathing while recounting his own cowardice
      in fleeing the tomb (Hands 1989).

        Banished the new-made bridegroom from this city,   235
        For whom, and not for Tybalt, Juliet pined.
        You, to remove that siege of grief from her,
        Betrothed and would have married her perforce
        To County Paris. Then comes she to me,
        And with wild looks bid me devise some mean   240
        To rid her from this second marriage,
        Or in my cell there would she kill herself.
        Then gave I her (so tutored by my art)
        A sleeping potion, which so took effect
        As I intended, for it wrought on her   245
        The form of death. Mean time I writ to Romeo
        That he should hither come as this dire night
        To help to take her from her borrowed grave,
        Being the time the potion's force should cease.
        But he which bore my letter, Friar John,   250
        Was stayed by accident, and yesternight
        Returned my letter back. Then all alone,
        At the prefixèd hour of her waking,
        Came I to take her from her kindred's vault,
        Meaning to keep her closely at my cell,   255
        Till I conveniently could send to Romeo.
        But when I came, some minute ere the time
        Of her awakening, here untimely lay
        The noble Paris and true Romeo dead.
        She wakes, and I entreated her come forth   260
        And bear this work of heaven with patience.
        But then a noise did scare me from the tomb,
        And she too desperate would not go with me,
        But as it seems, did violence on herself.
        All this I know, and to the marriage   265
        Her nurse is privy; and if ought in this
        Miscarried by my fault, let my old life
        Be sacrificed, some hour before his time,
        Unto the rigour of severest law.
PRINCE We still have known thee for a holy man.   270
        Where's Romeo's man? what can he say to this?
BALTHASAR I brought my master news of Juliet's death,
        And then in post he came from Mantua
        To this same place, to this same monument.
        This letter he early bid me give his father,   275

          And threatened me with death, going in the vault,

          If I departed not and left him there.

PRINCE Give me the letter, I will look on it.

          Where is the County's page that raised the Watch?

          Sirrah, what made your master in this place?   280

PAGE He came with flowers to strew his lady's grave,

          And bid me stand aloof, and so I did.

          Anon comes one with light to ope the tomb,

          And by and by my master drew on him,

          And then I ran away to call the Watch.   285

PRINCE This letter doth make good the Friar's words,

          Their course of love, the tidings of her death;

          And here he writes that he did buy a poison

          Of a poor pothecary, and therewithal

          Came to this vault to die, and lie with Juliet.   290

          Where be these enemies? Capulet, Montague?

          See what a scourge is laid upon your hate,

          That heaven finds means to kill your joys with love!

          And I for winking at your discords too

          Have lost a brace of kinsmen. All are punished.   295

CAPULET O brother Montague, give me thy hand.

          This is my daughter's jointure, for no more

          Can I demand.

MONTAGUE   But I can give thee more,

          For I will raise her statue in pure gold,

          That whiles Verona by that name is known,   300

          There shall no figure at such rate be set

          As that of true and faithful Juliet.

CAPULET As rich shall Romeo's by his lady's lie,

          Poor sacrifices of our enmity!

PRINCE A glooming peace this morning with it brings,   305

          The sun for sorrow will not show his head.

          Go hence to have more talk of these sad things;

296–8 In the Nunn–Kyle production of 1975, John Woodvine's formerly violent Capulet delivered these lines 'in a hollow monotone, which brought to life the full impact of his daughter's death upon a proud and energetic man' (Holding, *Romeo*, p. 62).

305 Irving had dropped the curtain after Juliet's death, and raised it again on a final image of reconciliation for the last few lines. The Prince, the families, and the citizens of Verona were arranged on the steps of the vault, 'every one on the stage holding a torch', according to Ellen Terry (*Story of My Life*, p. 227).

Some shall be pardoned, and some punishèd:
For never was a story of more woe
Than this of Juliet and her Romeo.   310

[Exeunt omnes]

310 SD Zeffirelli's production concluded with an elaborate dumbshow: 'anonymous servants embraced in pairs, symmetrically placed as a statuesque expression of general grief; mechanically, without being ordered to do so, they moved the bodies of Romeo and Juliet to the catafalque; in a slow procession, accompanied by singing offstage, the supposedly reconciled families departed with composed neatness at opposite sides of the tomb, without a look at the dead bodies and without recognition of each other; Benvolio and the Nurse were then reintroduced to take silent farewells of the bodies; and, finally, to swelling music, the lights faded with impressive slowness until the curtain fell' (*SS* 15, 1962, p. 152). Not all recent productions have stressed reconciliation: in George Malvius's 1983 Swedish production, as a crowd gathered to view the bodies of the lovers in the tomb, a Montague and a Capulet boy recommenced the fighting (Londré, '*Romeo*,' p. 630). In Stratford, Ontario in 1961, the two families rushed jealously forward to reclaim their dead children, only to find that the bodies still clung together in death; only then did the impulse toward reconciliation emerge (Londré, '*Romeo*', p. 639). In the Luhrmann film, the families stand in shock as the shrouded bodies of their children are loaded into an ambulance; all lines referring to reconciliation are cut. Michael Boyd's production had the dead lovers get up and walk out of the tomb, noticed only by the Friar, while the families were busy feeling sorry for themselves and making empty gestures of reconciliation (RSC 2000). Perhaps the most cynical of modern conclusions was that of Michael Bogdanov's 1986 RSC production. Bogdanov staged the final moments of the play as a media event, with the two fathers shaking hands for photographers in front of the golden statues of their dead children, while the Prince, a Mafia Don, read part of the Prologue (in past tense) from cue cards for the television cameras.

APPENDIX

FROM ACT 5, SCENE 4 AS ADAPTED BY DAVID GARRICK (1748)

ROMEO . . . Come, bitter conduct, come, unsavoury guide,
 Thou desperate pilot, now at once run on
 The dashing rocks my sea-sick weary bark!
 No more! Here's to my love! Eyes look your last;
 Arms take your last embrace; and lips do you
 The doors of breath seal with a righteous kiss.
 Soft! Soft! She breathes and stirs!

Juliet wakes.

JULIET Where am I? Defend me, powers!
ROMEO She speaks, she lives, and we shall still be blessed!
 My kind propitious stars o'erpay me now
 For all my sorrows past. Rise, rise, my Juliet,
 And from this cave of death, this house of horror,
 Quick let me snatch thee to thy Romeo's arms,
 There breathe a vital spirit in thy lips
 And call thee back to life and love! (*Takes her hand.*)
JULIET Bless me! How cold it is! Who's there?
ROMEO Thy husband.
 It is thy Romeo, love; raised from despair
 To joys unutterable! Quit, quit this place,
 And let us fly together. (*Brings her from the tomb.*)
JULIET Why do you force me so? I'll ne'er consent.
 My strength may fail me, but my will's unmoved.
 I'll not wed Paris: Romeo is my husband.
ROMEO Her senses are unsettled. Restore 'em heaven!
 Romeo is thy husband; I am that Romeo,
 Nor all th'opposing powers of earth or man
 Can break our bonds or tear thee from my heart.
JULIET I know that voice. Its magic sweetness wakes
 My trancèd soul. I now remember well
 Each circumstance. O! my lord, my Romeo!
 Had'st thou not come, sure I had slept forever;
 But there's a sovereign charm in thy embraces
 That can revive the dead. O honest friar!
 Dost thou avoid me, Romeo? Let me touch
 Thy hand, and taste the cordial of thy lips.

You fright me – speak! O let me hear some voice
Besides my own in this drear vault of death
Or I shall faint. Support me!
ROMEO O! I cannot;
I have no strength, but want thy feeble aid,
Cruel poison!
JULIET Poison! what means my lord, thy trembling voice?
Pale lips! and swimming eyes! Death's in thy face!
ROMEO It is indeed. I struggle with him now.
The transports that I felt, to hear thee speak
And see thy op'ning eyes, stopt for a moment
His impetuous course, and all my mind
Was happiness and thee; but now the poison
Rushes through my veins. I've not time to tell –
Fate brought me to this place to take a last,
Last farewell of my love and with thee die.
JULIET Die! Was the friar false?
ROMEO I know not that.
I thought thee dead. Distracted at the sight,
Fatal speed! drank poison, kissed thy cold lips,
And found within thy arms a precious grave.
But in that moment – O –
JULIET And did I wake for this?
ROMEO My powers are blasted,
'Twixt death and love I'm torn, I am distracted!
But death's strongest – and must I leave thee, Juliet?
O, cruel, cursed fate! in sight of heaven –
JULIET Thou ravest; lean on my breast.
ROMEO Fathers have flinty hearts, no tears can melt 'em.
Nature pleads in vain – children must be wretched.
JULIET O! my breaking heart!
ROMEO She is my wife; our hearts are twined together.
Capulet forbear! Paris loose your hold!
Pull not our heart-strings thus; they crack, they break.
O! Juliet! Juliet! (*Dies.*)
JULIET Stay, stay for me, Romeo.
A moment stay. Fate marries us in death,
And we are one; no power shall part us. (*Faints on Romeo's body.*)

Enter Friar Lawrence, with lantern, crow, and spade.

FRIAR LAWRENCE Saint Francis be my speed! how oft tonight
Have my old feet stumbled at graves! Who's there?
Alack, alack! what blood is this which stains
The stony entrance of this sepulchre?
Ah, Juliet awake and Romeo dead!
And Paris too! O, what an unkind hour
Is guilty of this lamentable chance.

JULIET Here he is still, and I will hold him fast.
    They shall not tear him from me.
FRIAR LAWRENCE Patience, lady.
JULIET Who is that? O, thou cursed friar! Patience!
    Talk'st thou of patience to a wretch like me?
FRIAR LAWRENCE O fatal error! Rise, thou fair distressed
    And fly this scene of death.
JULIET Come not thou near me,
    Or this dagger shall quit my Romeo's death. (*Draws a dagger.*)
FRIAR LAWRENCE I wonder not thy griefs have made thee desperate.
    What noise without? Sweet Juliet, let us fly;
    A greater power than we can contradict
    Hath thwarted our intents. Come, haste away!
    I will dispose thee, most unhappy lady,
    Amongst a sisterhood of holy nuns.
    Stay not to question, for the watch is coming.
    Come, go, good Juliet. I dare no longer stay.

                                                           Exit.

JULIET Go, get thee hence, for I will not away.
    What's here? a vial? Romeo's timeless end.
    O churl! drink all, and leave no friendly drop
    To help me after. I will kiss thy lips;
    Haply, some poison yet doth hang on them. (*Kisses him.*)

                Watch and Page within.

WATCH Lead, boy; which way?
JULIET Noise again!
    Then I'll be brief. O happy dagger! (*Kills herself.*)

BIBLIOGRAPHY

Periodical sources of reviews are not listed in the bibliography.

PROMPTBOOKS AND RELATED MATERIAL

Promptbooks listed in Shattuck, *The Shakespeare Promptbooks*, are coded s, followed by Shattuck's catalogue number.

Anderson, Mary. Lyceum, 1884. NYPL. s49.
  Lyceum, 1884. FSL. s50.
Anglin, Margaret. New York, c. 1900. NYPL. s61.
Benson, Frank. c. 1905, SCL. s79.
  1908, SCL. s80.
Bogdanov, Michael. Stratford, RST, 1986. SCL.
Booth, Edwin. 1868. FSL. s39.
  New York, Booth's Theatre, 1869. FSL. s37.
Brook, Peter. Stratford, SMT, 1947. SCL. s100.
Byam Shaw, Glen. Stratford, SMT, 1954. SCL. s101.
  Stratford, SMT, 1958. SCL. s102.
Cornell, Katherine. New York, Martin Beck, 1935 (with notes by Fitzroy
    Davis). NYPL. s95.
Cowl, Jane. New York, Henry Miller, 1923. HTC. s91.
Cushman, Charlotte. Acting Edition. London: Lacy, 1855.
  US, 1852. HTC. s31.
Faucit, Helena. Covent Garden, 1836. FSL. s14.
  et al., 1844–77. FSL. s22.
  c. 1845. FSL. s21.
Forbes-Robertson, Johnston. Lyceum, 1895 (Owen Chambers transcription).
    SCL. s63.
Hall, Peter. Stratford, RST, 1961. SCL. s106.
Hands, Terry. Stratford, RST, 1973. SCL.
Hunt, Hugh. Old Vic, 1952. TM.
Irving, Henry. Lyceum, 1882. FSL. s44.
  Acting Edition. London: Chiswick, 1882.
Kean, Charles. Haymarket, 1841. FSL. s16.
Marlowe, Julia, and E. H. Sothern. FSL. s70.
Neilson, Adelaide. 1876. FSL. s43.
Nunn, Trevor, and Barry Kyle. Stratford, RST, 1976. SCL.

Phelps, Samuel. Sadler's Wells, 1846. FSL. s26.
    Sadler's Wells, c. 1846–7. FSL. s27.
Roberts, J. B. 1847. FSL. s28.
Terriss, William. Lyceum, 1884. Studybook. NYPL.
Terry, Ellen. Lyceum, 1882. Studybook. HTC. s47.
Zeffirelli, Franco. Old Vic, 1960. TM.
Multiple users. 1818–71. FSL. s23.

OTHER WORKS

*A Letter to Miss Nossiter: Occasioned by her first appearance on the stage: in which
    is contained remarks upon her manner of playing the character of Juliet;
    interspersed with some other theatrical observations.* London: 1753.
    Attributed to MacNamara Morgan.
Allen, Percy. *The Stage Life of Mrs Stirling.* London: Fisher Unwin, 1922.
Allen, Shirley S. *Samuel Phelps and Sadler's Wells Theatre.* Middletown, CT:
    Wesleyan University Press, 1971.
Altemus, Jameson Torr. *Helena Modjeska.* New York: Blom, 1883 (reissued
    1969).
Anderson, Mary. *A Few Memories.* New York: Harper and Brothers, 1896.
Andrews, Joseph A., ed. *'Romeo and Juliet': Critical Essays.* New York: Garland,
    1993.
Archer, William. *The Theatrical 'World' of 1895.* London: Walter Scott, 1896.
    The Theatrical 'World' of 1896. London: Walter Scott, 1897.
Armstrong, Cecil F. *A Century of Great Actors: 1750–1850.* London: Mills and
    Boon, 1912.
Ashcroft, Peggy. 'From *Shakespeare in Perspective*' (London: Ariel Books,
    1982), reprinted in *'Romeo and Juliet': Critical Essays,* ed. Joseph A.
    Andrews. New York: Garland, 1993.
Atkinson, Brooks. *Broadway.* New York: Macmillan, 1970.
Auerbach, Nina. *Ellen Terry: Player in Her Time.* London: J. M. Dent, 1987.
Babula, William. *Shakespeare in Production, 1935–1978: A Selective Catalogue.*
    New York: Garland, 1981.
Baker, Michael. *The Rise of the Victorian Actor.* London: Croom Helm, 1978.
Ball, Robert Hamilton. *Shakespeare on Silent Film.* London: George Allen and
    Unwin, 1968.
Baldwin, Thomas Whitfield. *The Organization and Personnel of the
    Shakespearean Company.* Princeton University Press, 1927.
Bate, Jonathan. *The Genius of Shakespeare.* London: Picador, 1997.
Beerbohm, Max. *Last Theatres, 1904–1910.* London: Rupert Hart-Davis, 1970.
*Bell's Edition of Shakespeare's plays as they are now performed at the Theatres
    Royal in London, regulated from the prompt-books at each house.* With notes
    by Francis Gentleman. 11 vols. London: 1774. Vol. II.

Bingham, Madeleine. *Henry Irving and the Victorian Theatre*. London: George Allen and Unwin, 1978.

Bly, Mary. 'Bawdy Puns and Lustful Virgins: the Legacy of Juliet's Desire in Comedies of the Early 1600s'. *SS* 49 (1996), 97–109.

Boaden, James. *Memoirs of the Life of John Philip Kemble, Esq*. 2 vols. London: Longman, 1825.

Memoirs of Mrs Siddons. 2 vols. London: Colburn, 1827.

Booth, Michael, and John Stokes and Linda Bassnet. *Bernhardt, Terry, Duse: The Actress in her Time*. Cambridge University Press, 1988.

Bradbrook, Muriel. '*Romeo and Juliet* in Performance'. *Shakespeare in his Context: The Constellated Globe*. Totowa, NJ: Barnes and Noble, 1989.

Brady, Frank. *Citizen Welles*. New York: Scribner's, 1989.

Brereton, Austin. '*Romeo and Juliet*' on the Stage (1662–1890). Sydney: Marcus and Andrew, 1890.

Brook, Peter. *The Shifting Point*. New York: Harper and Row, 1987.

Brown, David. *Tchaikovsky: The Early Years 1840–1874*. New York: Norton, 1978.

Brown, Ivor. *Shakespeare Memorial Theatre 1954–56: A Photographic Record*. London: Max Reinhardt, 1956.

Brown, John Mason. *Dramatis Personae*. New York: Viking, 1963.

Brown, John Russell. 'Franco Zeffirelli's *Romeo and Juliet*'. *SS* 15 (1962), 147–55.

Bruce, Brenda. 'Nurse in *Romeo and Juliet*'. *Players of Shakespeare*, ed. Philip Brockbank. Cambridge University Press, 1985.

Burke, Kenneth. *The Philosophy of Literary Form*. Rev. edn. New York: Vintage, 1957.

Campbell, Thomas. *Life of Mrs Siddons*. 2 vols. London, 1834.

Carlson, Marvin. *The Italian Shakespearians*. Washington: Folger Books, 1985.

Cibber, Theophilus. *To David Garrick, Esq; with Dissertations on Theatrical Subjects*. London: W. Reeves and J. Phipps, 1759.

Romeo and Juliet, a tragedy, revised, and altered from Shakespeare, by Mr Theophilus Cibber. London: C. Corbett and G. Woodfall [n.d.: dedication 25 Nov 1748].

Clarke, Mary Cowden. *The Girlhood of Shakespeare's Heroines*. London: J. M. Dent, 1906.

Clarke, Mary, and Clement Crisp. *The Ballet Goer's Guide*. New York: Alfred A. Knopf, 1981.

Clement, Clara Erskine. *Charlotte Cushman*. Boston: James R. Osgood, 1882.

Cocteau, Jean. *Oedipe-Roi. Roméo et Juliette*. Paris: Librairie-Plon, 1928.

Coe, Robert. 'Verona, Mississippi'. *American Theatre*. 6:2 (May 1989).

Cohn, Albert. *Shakespeare in Germany in the Sixteenth and Seventeenth Centuries: An Account of English Actors in Germany and the Netherlands and of the Plays Performed by them During the Same Period*. London: Asher, 1865.

Cole, John William. *The Life and Theatrical Times of Charles Kean*. 2 vols. London: Rich and Bentley, 1859.

Coleman, John. *Fifty Years of an Actor's Life*. 2 vols. London: Hutchinson, 1904.

Collison-Morley, Lacy. *Shakespeare in Italy*. Stratford-upon-Avon: Shakespeare Head Press, 1916.

Conrad, Peter. *To Be Continued: Four Stories and Their Survival*. Oxford University Press, 1995.

Cook, Dutton. *Nights at the Play*. 2 vols. London: Chatto and Windus, 1883.

Cooke, William. *Memoirs of Charles Macklin, Comedian*. 2 vols. London: James Asperne, 1804.

Coursen, H. R. *Shakespeare in Production: Whose History?* Athens: Ohio University Press, 1996.

Crosse, Gordon. *Diaries*. 19 vols. (Unpublished: originals in the Shakespeare Collection, Birmingham Central Library.)

Crowl, Samuel. *Shakespeare Observed*. Athens: Ohio University Press, 1992.

Cusack, Niamh. 'Juliet'. *Players of Shakespeare 2: Further Essays in Shakespearean Performance*, ed. Russell Jackson and Robert Smallwood. Cambridge University Press, 1988, pp. 121–35.

David, Richard. *Shakespeare in the Theatre*. Cambridge University Press, 1978.

Davies, Thomas. *Memoirs of the Life of David Garrick, Esq*. 2 vols. London: Longman, Hurst, Rees, and Orme, 1808.

Davis, Philip. 'Nineteenth-Century Juliet'. *SS* 49 (1996), 131–40.

Davis, Tracy C. *Actresses as Working Women: Their Social Identity in Victorian Culture*. London: Routledge, 1991.

Dawson, Anthony B. *Watching Shakespeare: A Playgoer's Guide*. New York: St Martin's Press, 1988.

Dench, Judi. 'A Career in Shakespeare'. *Shakespeare: An Illustrated Stage History*, ed. Jonathan Bate and Russell Jackson. Oxford University Press, 1996.

Denham, Reginald. *Stars in My Hair*. London: T. Werner Laurie, 1958.

Denson, Alan. *Franco Zeffirelli's Production of William Shakespeare's 'Romeo and Juliet'*. Kendal, Westmorland: Alan Denson, 1968.

Dent, Alan. *Nocturnes and Rhapsodies*. London: Hamish Hamilton, 1950.

Dessen, Alan C. *Recovering Shakespeare's Theatrical Vocabulary*. Cambridge University Press, 1995.

Downes, John. *Roscius Anglicanus* (1708 facs.), ed. Montague Summers. London: Fortune Press, n.d.

Edgar, David. *The Life and Adventures of Nicholas Nickleby*. Garden City, NY: Nelson Doubleday, 1982.

Edinborough, Arnold. 'Artistic Success in Canada'. *SQ* 11:4 (1960), 455–9.

Evans, G. Blakemore, ed. *Romeo and Juliet* (New Cambridge Shakespeare).
   Cambridge University Press, 1984.

Farjeon, Herbert. *The Shakespearean Scene*. London: Hutchinson, 1949.

Farley-Hills, David, 'The "Bad" Quarto of *Romeo and Juliet*'. *SS* 49 (1996),
   27–44.

Faucit, Helena, Lady Martin. *On Some of Shakespeare's Female Characters*.
   Edinburgh: William Blackwood, 1891.

Fenwick, Henry. 'The Production'. *Romeo and Juliet: The BBC-TV
   Shakespeare*. London: BBC, 1978.

Fiske, Roger. 'Shakespeare in the Concert Hall'. *Shakespeare in Music*, ed.
   Phyllis Hartnoll. London: Macmillan, 1966.

Fitzgerald, Percy. *Lives of the Kembles*. 2 vols. London: Tinsley Brothers, 1871.
   Sir Henry Irving, a Record of Over Twenty Years at the Lyceum. London:
   Chatto and Windus, 1895.

Fletcher, George. *Studies of Shakespeare*. London: Longman, 1847.

Foster, Donald W. 'The Webbing of *Romeo and Juliet*'. *Critical Essays on
   Shakespeare's 'Romeo and Juliet'*, ed. Joseph A. Porter. New York:
   G. K. Hall, 1997, pp. 131–49.

Gentleman, Francis. *The Dramatic Censor*. 2 vols. London: Bell, 1770. Vol. I.

Gielgud, John. *Early Stages*. New York: Macmillan, 1939.
   Stage Directions. London: Heinemann, 1963.

Gielgud, John, with John Miller. *Acting Shakespeare*. New York: Scribner's,
   1992.

Gourlay, Logan, ed. *Olivier*. New York: Stein and Day, 1974.

Granville-Barker, Harley. *Prefaces to Shakespeare*. With illustrations and notes
   by Muriel St Clare Byrne. Princeton University Press, 1963. Vol. IV.

Grebanier, Bernard. *Then Came Each Actor*. New York: David McKay,
   1975.

Gruen, John. *The World's Great Ballets*. New York: Henry J. Abrams, 1981.

Gurr, Andrew. 'The Date and the Expected Venue of *Romeo and Juliet*'. *SS* 49
   (1996), 15–25.

Halio, Jay L. *'Romeo and Juliet': A Guide to the Play*. Westport, CT: Greenwood
   Press, 1998.
   'Handy-Dandy: Q1/Q2 *Romeo and Juliet*'. *Shakespeare's 'Romeo and Juliet':
   Texts, Contexts, and Interpretation*, ed. Jay L. Halio. Newark: University of
   Delaware Press, 1995, pp. 125–50.

Halstead, William P. *Statistical History of Acting Editions of Shakespeare*. Vol.
   XIV of *Shakespeare as Spoken*. Washington, DC: University Press of
   America, 1983.

Harrison, Clifford. *Stray Records, or Personal and Professional Notes*. London:
   Richard Bentley, 1893.

Hayman, Ronald. *Gielgud*. London: Heinemann, 1971.

Hazlitt, William. *Hazlitt on Theatre*, selected and ed. William Archer and Robert Lowe. New York: Hill and Wang, 1957.

Hiatt, Charles. *Ellen Terry and Her Impersonations: An Appreciation*. London: George Bell, 1898.

Highfill, Phillip A., Jr, Kalman A. Burman, and Edward A. Langhams. *A Biographical Dictionary of Actors, Actresses, Musicians, Dancers, Managers, and Other Stage Personnel in London, 1660–1800*. 16 vols. Carbondale: Southern Illinois University Press, 1973.

Hill, Errol. *Shakespeare in Sable*. Amherst: University of Massachusetts Press, 1984.

Hill, John. *The Actor: A Treatise on the Art of Playing*. London: 1750.
The Actor: A Treatise on the Art of Playing. London: 1755.

Hillebrand, Harold Newcomb. *Edmund Kean*. New York: Columbia University Press, 1933.

Hobson, Harold. *Theatre*. London: Longmans, Green, 1948.

Hogan, Charles B. *Shakespeare in the Theatre, 1701–1800*. 2 vols. Oxford University Press, 1952.

Holden, Anthony. *Olivier*. London: Weidenfeld and Nicolson, 1988.

Holderness, Graham. *William Shakespeare: 'Romeo and Juliet'* (Penguin Critical Studies). London: Penguin, 1990.

Holding, Peter. *'Romeo and Juliet': Text and Performance*. London: Macmillan, 1992.

Hoppe, Harry R. *The Bad Quarto of 'Romeo and Juliet': A Bibliographical and Textual Study* (Cornell Studies in English, 36). Ithaca, NY: Cornell University Press, 1948.

Irace, Kathleen O. *Reforming the 'Bad' Quartos: Performance and Provenance of Six Shakespearean First Editions*. Newark: University of Delaware Press, 1994.

Irving, Laurence. *Henry Irving: The Actor and His World*. London: Faber and Faber, 1951.

Jameson, Anna. *Sketches of Art, Literature and Character*. Boston: Houghton Mifflin, 1983.
Shakespeare's Heroines. London: J. M. Dent, 1901.

Jones, Charles Inigo. *Memoirs of Miss O'Neill; containing her public character, private life, and dramatic progress, from her entrance upon the stage*. London: Printed for D. Cox, 1816.

Jusserand, J. J. *Shakespeare in France Under the Ancien Regime*. New York: Putnam, 1899.

Kemble, Frances Ann. *Records of a Girlhood*. New York: Holt, 1879.

Kendall, Alan. *David Garrick: A Biography*. London: Harrap, 1985.

Kennedy, Dennis. *Looking at Shakespeare: A Visual History of Twentieth-Century Performance*. Cambridge University Press, 1993.

Kennedy, Dennis, ed. *Foreign Shakespeare: Contemporary Performance.* Cambridge University Press, 1993.

Kilbourne, Frederick W. *Alterations and Adaptations of Shakespeare.* Boston: The Poet Lore Company, 1906.

King, T. J. *Casting Shakespeare's Plays: London Actors and Their Roles, 1590–1642.* Cambridge University Press, 1992.

Knight, G. Wilson. *Principles of Shakespearean Production.* London: Faber and Faber, 1936.

Leach, Joseph. *Bright Particular Star: The Life and Times of Charlotte Cushman.* New Haven: Yale University Press, 1970.

Levenson, Jill L. *Romeo and Juliet* (Shakespeare in Performance Series). Manchester University Press, 1987.

'"*Alla Stoccado* Carries it Away": Codes of Violence in *Romeo and Juliet*'. *Shakespeare's 'Romeo and Juliet': Texts, Contexts, and Interpretation,* ed. Jay L. Halio. Newark: University of Delaware Press, 1995, pp. 83–96.

Levenson, Jill L., ed. *Romeo and Juliet* (The Oxford Shakespeare). Oxford University Press, 2000.

Levith, Murray J. *Shakespeare's Italian Settings and Plays.* New York: St Martin's Press, 1989.

Londré, Felicia Harrison. '*Romeo and Juliet*'. *Shakespeare Around the Globe: A Guide to Notable Postwar Revivals,* ed. Samuel Leiter. New York: Greenwood Press, 1986, pp. 625–59.

Loney, Glenn, ed. *Staging Shakespeare: Seminars on Production Problems.* New York: Garland, 1990.

Macready, William Charles. *Reminiscences,* ed. Frederick Pollock. 2 vols. London: Macmillan, 1875.

Manvell, Roger. *Shakespeare and the Film.* New York: Praeger, 1971.

Marshall, Gail. *Actresses on the Victorian Stage: Feminine Performance and the Galatea Myth.* Cambridge University Press, 1998.

Marston, Westland. *Our Recent Actors.* 2 vols. London: Sampson Low, 1888.

Martin, Theodore. *Helena Faucit, Lady Martin.* Edinburgh: Blackwood, 1900.

Martinez, John. *The Swords of Shakespeare: An Illustrated Guide to Stage Combat Choreography in the Plays of Shakespeare.* Jefferson, NC: McFarland, 1996.

Merill, Lisa. *When Romeo Was a Woman: Charlotte Cushman and her Circle of Female Spectators.* Ann Arbor: University of Michigan Press, 1999.

Monaco, Marion. *Shakespeare on the French Stage in the Eighteenth Century.* Paris: Didier, 1974.

Montrose, Louis. *The Purpose of Playing: Shakespeare and the Cultural Politics of the Elizabethan Theatre.* University of Chicago Press, 1996.

Morley, Henry. *Journal of a London Playgoer*. Leicester University Press, 1974 (first published 1866).

Mullin, Donald. *Victorian Plays: A Record of Significant Productions on the London Stage, 1837–1901. Bibliographies and Indexes in the Performing Arts*, no. 4. New York: Greenwood Press, 1987.

ed. *Victorian Actors and Actresses in Review*. Westport, CT: Greenwood Press, 1983.

Munro, John, ed. *The Shakspere Allusion-Book: A Collection of Allusions to Shakspere from 1591 to 1700*. 3 vols. London: Chatto and Windus, 1909.

Novy, Marianne. 'Violence, Love, and Gender in Romeo and Juliet'. *'Romeo and Juliet': Critical Essays*, ed. Joseph A. Andrews. New York: Garland, 1993, pp. 359–70.

O'Connor, Garry. *Ralph Richardson: An Actor's Life*. London: Hodder and Stoughton, 1982.

Odell, George C. D. *Shakespeare from Betterton to Irving*. 2 vols. New York: Scribner's, 1920.

Annals of the New York Stage. 15 vols. New York: Columbia University Press, 1927–49.

Otway, Thomas. *Works*, ed. J. C. Ghosh. 2 vols. Oxford: Clarendon Press, 1932.

Oxenhandler, Neal. 'The Theatre of Jean Cocteau'. *Jean Cocteau and the French Scene*. New York: Abbeville, 1984, pp. 125–52.

Pascoe, Charles Eyre. *The Dramatic List: A Record of the Principal Performances of Living Actors and Actresses of the British Stage*. London: Hardwicke and Bogue, 1879.

Pedicord, Henry William, and Fredrick Louis Bergmann, eds. *Garrick's Adaptations of Shakespeare, 1744–1756*, vol. III of *The Plays of David Garrick*. Carbondale: Southern Illinois University Press, 1981.

Pepys, Samuel. *The Diary of Samuel Pepys*, ed. Robert Latham and William Mathews. 11 vols. Berkeley: University of California Press, 1970.

Pettitt, Henry R. 'Irving as Romeo'. *We Saw Him Act: A Symposium on the Art of Sir Henry Irving*, ed. H. A. Saintsbury and Cecil Palmer. London: Hurst and Blackett, 1939.

Poel, William. *The Stage-Version of 'Romeo and Juliet'*. London: London Shakespeare League, 1915.

Porter, Joseph A., ed. *Critical Essays on Shakespeare's 'Romeo and Juliet'*, New York: G. K. Hall, 1997.

Powell, Kerry. *Women and the Victorian Theatre*. Cambridge University Press, 1998.

Poznansky, Alexander. *Tchaikovsky: The Quest for the Inner Man*. New York: Schirmer, 1991.

Raby, Peter. *The Stratford Scene, 1958–1968*. Compiled and ed. Peter Raby, with an introduction by Michael Langham. Toronto, Vancouver: Clarke, Irwin, 1968.

Rankin, Hugh F. *The Theater in Colonial America*. Chapel Hill: University of North Carolina Press, 1960.

Richards, Sandra. *The Rise of the English Actress*. London: Macmillan, 1993.

Robins, Edward. *Twelve Great Actresses*. New York: G. P. Putnam's Sons, 1900.

Rothwell, Kenneth S. *A History of Shakespeare on Screen: A Century of Film and Television*. Cambridge University Press, 1999.

Rowell, George. *Queen Victoria Goes to the Theatre*. London: Paul Elek, 1978.

Rubin, Leon. *The Nicholas Nickleby Story: The Making of the Historic Royal Shakespeare Company Production*. London: Heinemann, 1981.

Ruggles, Eleanor. *Prince of Players*. New York: Norton, 1953.

Russell, Charles Edward. *Julia Marlowe, Her Life and Art*. New York: Appleton, 1926.

Sadie, Stanley, ed. *The New Grove Book of Operas*. London: Macmillan, 1996.

Salgado, Gamini. *Eyewitnesses of Shakespeare*. London: Sussex University Press, 1975.

Schanke, Robert A. *Shattered Applause: The Lives of Eva Le Gallienne*. Carbondale: Southern Illinois University Press, 1992.

Scott, Clement. *The Drama of Yesterday and Today*. 2 vols. London: Macmillan, 1899.

Shattuck, Charles. *The Shakespeare Promptbooks*. Urbana: University of Illinois Press, 1965.

  John Philip Kemble Promptbooks. 11 vols. Vol. VIII. Charlottesville: Published for the Folger Shakespeare Library by the University Press of Virginia, 1974.

  Shakespeare on the American Stage. 2 vols. London: Associated University Presses, 1987.

Shaw, George Bernard. *Our Theatres in the Nineties*. 3 vols. London: Constable, 1931.

Sheldon, Esther K. *Thomas Sheridan of Smock-Alley*. Princeton University Press, 1967.

Simpson, Harold, and Mrs Charles Braun. *A Century of Famous Actresses: 1750–1850*. London: Mills and Boon, 1913.

Speaight, Robert. *William Poel and the Elizabethan Revival*. London: Heinemann, 1954.

  'The Old Vic and Stratford-upon-Avon, 1960–61'. *SQ* 12:4 (Autumn 1961), 425–41.

  Shakespeare on the Stage. Boston: Little, Brown, 1973.

Spencer, Hazelton. *Shakespeare Improved*. New York: Frederick Ungar, 1927 (republished 1963).

Sprague, Arthur Colby. *Shakespeare and the Actors: The Stage Business in His Plays (1660–1905)*. Cambridge, MA: Harvard University Press, 1944.

Stebbins, Emma. *Charlotte Cushman: Her Letters and Memories of Her Life*. Boston: Houghton, Osgood, 1878.

Stoker, Bram. *Personal Reminiscences of Henry Irving*. 2 vols. London: Macmillan, 1906.

Stone, George Winchester, Jr. '*Romeo and Juliet*: the Source of its Modern Stage Career'. *Shakespeare 400; Essays by American Scholars on the Anniversary of the Poet's Birth*, ed. James McManaway. New York: Holt, Rinehart and Winston, 1964.

Stone, Lawrence. *The Family, Sex and Marriage in England, 1500–1800*. London: Weidenfeld and Nicolson, 1977.

Styan, J. L. *The Shakespeare Revolution: Criticism and Performance in the Twentieth Century*. Cambridge University Press, 1976.

Sussman, Herbert. *Victorian Masculinities: Manhood and Masculine Poetics in Early Victorian Literature and Art*. Cambridge University Press, 1995.

Terry, Ellen. *The Story of My Life: Recollections and Reflections*. New York: McClure, 1908.

  Four Lectures on Shakespeare, ed. Christopher St John, London: Hopkinson, 1932.

The London Stage, ed. W. Van Lennep et al., 5 parts in 11 vols. Carbondale: Southern Illinois University Press, 1960–8.

Thompson, Peter. 'Shakespeare Straight and Crooked: a Review of the 1973 Season at Stratford'. *SS* 27 (1974), 143–54.

Towse, John Rankin. *Sixty Years of the Theatre*. New York: Funk and Wagnalls, 1916.

Trewin, J. C. *Mr Macready: A Nineteenth-Century Tragedian and his Theatre*. London: Harrap, 1955.

  Shakespeare on the English Stage. London: Barrie and Rockliff, 1964.

  Going to Shakespeare. London: George Allen and Unwin, 1978.

Tynan, Kenneth. *Curtains: Selections from the Drama Criticism and Related Writings*. London: Longmans, 1961.

  Tynan Right and Left. London: Longmans, 1967.

Vardac, A. Nicholas. *Stage to Screen: Theatrical Method from Garrick to Griffith*. Cambridge, MA: Harvard University Press, 1949.

Warner, Kerstin P. *Thomas Otway*. Boston: Twayne, 1982.

Warren, Roger. 'Shakespeare in Performance, 1980'. *SS* 34 (1981), 149–60.

Weaver, William. *Duse*. New York: Harcourt Brace Jovanovich, 1984.

Wells, Stanley, ed. *Nineteenth-Century Shakespeare Burlesques*. 5 vols. London: Diploma Press, 1977.

Wiles, David. *Shakespeare's Clown*. Cambridge University Press, 1987.

Williams, Simon. *Shakespeare on the German Stage*. Vol. I: 1586–1914.
Cambridge University Press, 1990.
Williamson, Jane. *Charles Kemble, Man of the Theatre*. Lincoln: University of
Nebraska Press, 1964.
Wingate, Charles. *Shakespeare's Heroines on the Stage*. New York: Thomas Y.
Crowell, 1895.
Winter, William. *Other Days, Being Chronicles and Memories of the Stage*. New
York: Moffat, Yard, 1908.
The Wallet of Time. 2 vols. New York: Moffat, Yard, 1913.
Shakespeare on the Stage. Second series. New York: Moffat, Yard, 1915.
Wright, Katherine L. *Shakespeare's 'Romeo and Juliet' in Performance:
Traditions and Departures*. Lewiston, NY: Edwin Mellen Press, 1997.
Young, Susan. *Shakespeare Manipulated: The Use of the Dramatic Works of
Shakespeare in 'teatro di figura' in Italy*. London: Associated University
Presses, 1996.
Zeffirelli, Franco. *Zeffirelli: The Autobiography of Franco Zeffirelli*. London:
Weidenfeld and Nicolson, 1986.

INDEX

York, Michael *77*, 78, 92, 167

Zeffirelli, Franco, Old Vic (1960) 2, 60–3,
    89, 93, 96, 137, 139, 140, 142, 144, 146,
    163, 164, 168, 170, 175, 185, 194, 204,

224, 230, 251; *Romeo and Juliet* (1968
film) 77–8, *77*, 87, 89, 92, 93, 101, 113,
121, 123, 127, 132, 135, 144, 148, 152,
156, 164, 165, 167, 168, 172, 194, 202,
210, 214, 234, 239